TRUE CRIME

TRUE CRIME

BY
ALLAN HALL

ABBEYDALE
PRESS

ISBN: 978-1-86147-189-5

3 5 7 9 10 8 6 4 2

Published by Abbeydale Press
An imprint of Bookmart Limited
Registered Number 2372865
Trading as Bookmart Limited
Blaby Road, Wigston
Leicestershire, LE18 4SE

Originally incorporated in *The Encyclopedia of True Crime*
and
Crimes & Victims published by Bookmart Limited.

Production by Omnipress Ltd, Eastbourne

Printed in Great Britian

Contents

Murderous Men

Organized Crime

War Crimes

Murder Most Foul

Evil Women

Partners in Crime

Crimes of Terror

MURDEROUS MEN

JOE DOHERTY
IRA HITMAN

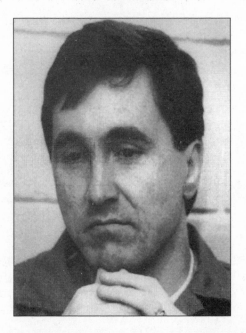

He grew up in bitterness and with a strong sense that he was a victim. Joe Doherty took his revenge with evil acts of killing and maiming the innocent – all in the name of patriotism.

The murder of a Special Air Services officer in a grubby Belfast street in 1980 would, on the surface, have little connection with the 1986 bombing of Libya's deranged dictator Colonel Gaddafi in Tripoli. One was carried out by a psychopathic Irish Republican Army terrorist called Joe Doherty who dressed up his murderous outrage in the guise of freedom fighter. The other was carried out by trained pilots on the orders of Ronald Reagan, US president, as a warning to Gaddafi to desist from his global sponsorship of terrorist causes.

Not until 1992, when the fugitive gunman Doherty was finally brought back in chains from America to serve a life sentence for his killing of Captain Herbert Richard Westmacott did the correlation between his murder and the Tripoli bombing raid become clear. For it was Mrs Thatcher, as much as any police officer, intelligence operative and FBI agent, whose long arm stretched across the Atlantic to bring Doherty home from America – where he sought political sanctuary – to face justice. Doherty was 'payback' for Tripoli because Mrs Thatcher had allowed US war planes to take off from British bases on their mission. She weathered a great deal of criticism at the time over the decision and made it plain to her American opposite numbers that, one day, a favour might have to be returned. That favour came in the form of 37-year-old Joseph Patrick Doherty, the killer that Mrs Thatcher would not let get away.

The story of Joseph Doherty – street-thug, rioter, ambusher, political assassin and propaganda pawn – is an odyssey from the breeding ground of hatred through to the highest levels of international intrigue and diplomacy. If he had chosen another path as a youngster, one away from the gun and the hard men who ruled his ghetto area of West Belfast, he might now be a father with a secure job and a bright future. Instead, he will be almost a pensioner when he is finally released. The only value he has to the IRA now is to embellish the memories of 'the cause' when the stories are told around pub fires and in meeting halls where the Republican ethos is worshipped like a religion.

Before he became infamous, Joe Doherty was born into a system that preached and prasticed unfairness towards the Catholic minority in Northern Ireland. Artificial electoral boundaries, discrimination towards Catholics in schools, housing, jobs and civil rights, and terror in the form of the police 'B Specials', combined to fuel the resurgence of the Republican movement that was dormant, if not dying, by the time Doherty was born in 1955, to a family who celebrated Irish rebel heroes in the uprising with Britain in the early part of the century, which won the south its independence. Doherty says that when he was five he felt the first stirrings of a grave injustice being committed in his country. He said: 'I remember going to school and being taught English instead of our national language. You take the history classes we went to. It was mostly on the Tudors and royal heads, kings and queens of England. We were told nothing about our own country. When we took geography we were given the map of England, Scotland and Wales, Europe, the United States, but we were never given a map of our own country. So it was resented by a young person at my age that I couldn't learn where the hell I am living. I knew more about Birmingham and Manchester than I knew about my own city and the beautiful countryside that was around it.' Bitter words from one of the oppressed.

The glamour of the gun soon lured Doherty into the clutches of the IRA, the illegal but best guerrilla operation in the world. Involved with petty crime from the age of 14 – offences like housebreaking and theft – he joined the organization Na Fianna Eireann, the junior wing of the Provisional IRA. In these early days, with the burning resentment against British troops in his land growing inside him, he was a willing recruit. In the far-flung, remote regions of County Donegal and on the west coast of Ireland, he attended the indoctrination and training sessions that would give him both the spirit and the practical tools to become an effective IRA operative. In this role he became an intelligence scout for the IRA killers on the streets of Belfast; warning of the approach of a police or army patrol, luring soldiers into ambushes and assisting in diversions when terrorists or arms had to be removed from an area rapidly.

He also became a member of the notorious knee-capping squads. These vigilantes were an important factor in IRA rule in the early days of the troubles – patrolling dances and drinking halls, dispensing rough and ready justice to those who they deemed were either drunkards, drug pushers or potential enemies of the IRA. Doherty would later claim that he was little more than a concerned citizen when he carried out these vigilante duties, but he had shown himself, to his IRA superiors, ruthless and efficient – two qualities they prized very highly indeed.

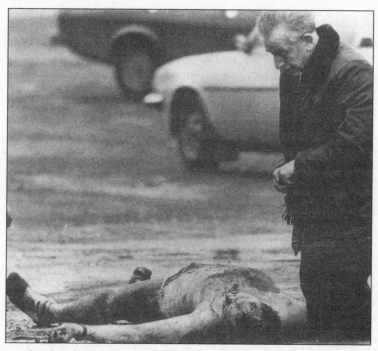

A priest kneels by the body of David Howe, killed when he inadvertently blundered into an IRA funeral procession.

PRISON LESSONS IN TERRORISM

Doherty's pathological loathing of the British continued to rise as army attempts to root out and contain terrorism spilled over into his own neighbourhood. He witnessed his family being pulled from their beds at midnight by soldiers and was continually quizzed by intelligence officers about his membership of the junior IRA. On 22 January 1972, a day after his seventeenth birthday, he found himself interned without trial at one of the several British camps. He claimed he was tortured in Girdwood camp. While human rights investigators have determined that some terrorists were subjected to cruel and inhuman treatment while in internment camps, not a shred of evidence exists to say that Doherty was mistreated, and certainly he never suffered the use of electric shock apparatus which he claimed was in common use in the camp.

Later he was interned on the prison ship *Maidstone* and in Long Kesh, where IRA cell leaders marked him down as a zealot who would soon be ready for active service in the field – namely, killing people. Inside the camps was a well-organized IRA network that kept prisoners indoctrinated with lectures on the Republican movement and the weapons they would be using on their release. Doherty joined the adult arm of the IRA upon his release, swearing his allegiance to the terrorists in the traditional way: placing his hand upon a Bible, a .45 revolver and the Irish tricolour, he thus became a volunteer in C Company, 3rd Battalion of the Irish Republican Army. During the early seventies, outfits like Doherty's caused tremendous civilian loss of life with indiscriminate bombings, sectarian murders and numerous shootings of security and police personnel, but he was never charged with any specific murders, although security personnel had plenty of suspicion. The only charge they nailed him on, came in 1973 when he served three months for being caught in possession of a starting pistol; a tool he used to intimidate neighbourhood youths.

Upon his release, shortly before Christmas of that year, he was told to report for active duty to the 3rd Battalion. He was ordered to stay 'on the run', avoiding the homes of friends and family in favour of unknown IRA sympathizers, because the IRA had plans for him. In February 1974 he removed 80 pounds of gelignite from one of the organization's dumps and moved it by car to another unit across town. Unfortunately for him an army spot check found him and his portable, unprimed bomb, and both were taken into custody. He was given a three-year sentence, compounded shortly afterwards with another 18 months after a futile prison escape attempt ended in abject failure. In jail he rose in the IRA ranks and was an officer in charge of other men. His masters on the other side of the wire bided their time for Joe Doherty, because they were nurturing big plans.

He was released shortly before Christmas 1979 – the last Christmas he would know as a free man: he was neither a fugitive on the run, nor a man held behind bars.

MASTERING A LETHAL WEAPON

After he walked free again Joe Doherty was singled out for special training with the M60 heavy machine gun, a fearsome weapon capable of cutting a man in two with a split-second burst. He later denied ever being trained in the handling of these, but an IRA informer told his Special Branch handlers in Ulster that Doherty was so familiar with every nut and rivet of the weapon, that he could break it down and then re-assemble it wearing a blindfold. This gun, one of a batch stolen from an armoury in America, was to play a major part in his designated IRA 'mission' the following year.

His unit was assigned to kill policemen and soldiers by using the high-powered weaponry acquired from America. Again, Doherty and his cohorts were not charged in this period with any offences and, naturally, he has been at pains to play down any of his activities. The incident that would land him with a life sentence for murder came towards the middle of 1980. His IRA masters chose to mount an attack on a British army patrol – any patrol, it did not matter which – that passed by a house that his unit would take over

The horrific reality of the IRA's actions was seen in London when nine soldiers and seven cavalry horses were blown apart by terrorist bombs in Hyde Park in 1982.

on the Antrim Road. Doherty knew that military vehicles from the Girdwood base passed by all the time; there was bound to be a rich target. Almost certainly 'blooded' in IRA actions by this time, Doherty and his gang were chosen for the operation on the direct instructions of the leader of the Belfast Brigade of the terror organization.

Doherty personally planned the operation, ordering that the M60 heavy machine gun was to be fired from one window while the rifles and revolvers used by the gang were positioned at another. He ordered his gang to hijack a vehicle the evening before the ambush in order to transport themselves and their weapons to the scene. He gave orders for the family in a house overlooking the spot where they intended to spring the trap to be held hostage. Both were standard IRA procedures for this kind of assassination. But unknown to Doherty and his allies, the eyes of army intelligence were already upon them. Members of the 14th Intelligence Company had, through an IRA informer, learned of the operation planned for 2 May 1980. A unit of the Special Air Services was given careful instruction to tackle them on the day.

The night before the ambush, a blue Ford Transit van was hijacked by volunteers, handed over to Doherty's team and driven to the rear of house number 371 in the Antrim Road – designated for the takeover the next day and the base for the ambush. The following morning 19-year-old Rosemary Comerford and her two-year-old son Gerard were alone in the house. She recalled: 'At 10.30 a.m. a knock came on the door and I opened it. Two men were standing there and one of them said they were Irish Republican Army. The man who spoke had a handgun pointing at me. This man said they were going to take over the house and they were going to hold me and my son as hostages. He then took us into the bedroom at the rear of the house. The other man who did not speak remained in the bedroom with us. I could hear the other man moving about. I think the man who stayed in the bedroom with us brought the handgun with him. At about 12.30 p.m. my sister Theresa called and the man who was in the bedroom with me told me to go and see who it was. He told me to let her in and said she'd have to stay in the bedroom with us. My husband Gerard came home and the same thing happened.'

At 2 p.m. that day, as Doherty and his 'freedom fighters' took up positions in the occupied house that gave them the best view on to the anticipated killing zone, Captain Herbert Westmacott, 34, and his men were on their way to the scene. The SAS career veteran and his men were trained precisely for this kind of urban assault. SAS headquarters in England was equipped with houses such as these which Westmacott and his men had neutralized time and time again in their training missions. But a terrible blunder in trying to determine what was the exact entrance to the house gave the gunmen inside vital seconds. The entrance to the house was actually through 369 and not through the door marked 371. Captain Westmacott fell in a pool of blood outside the entrance to 371 after the hitmen inside opened up first. The British government would later charge Doherty with being the triggerman. As he was led away from the scene of the murder Doherty said of the M60 that killed Captain Westmacott said: 'that's my baby'.

Trapped inside like rats Doherty and his men believed they would endure first smoke, then stun grenades before the SAS mounted a charge on their positions that would leave no prisoners. But, as if to disappoint the IRA propaganda machine about such atrocities, they gave the killers inside the kind of chance never afforded to Captain Westmacott. A priest was brought in at Doherty's request to oversee their surrender after the SAS had surrounded them for several hours. Forensic tests taken later on his clothing showed that, of the four-man gang, he had the most ballistic residue on him, indicating that it was probably Doherty who fired the M60 which killed Captain Westmacott.

British interrogators were intent on breaking down Doherty when he was in custody: they knew he was a valued IRA operative who had probably killed before. But he was well versed in the cat-and-mouse games that his handlers had taught him. Every question that was not answered with a refusal was answered with a question. Doherty was a misty-eyed Republican who fondly remembered his grandfather's medals from his time spent fighting the British earlier in the century. He wavered between bravado and mute silence to arrogance and foul language during his interrogation sessions, but he finally cracked when his mother's name was mentioned. He admitted he had tried to get out of the movement but had failed and only wanted a better Ireland to live in. He did not admit to killing Westmacott specifically, only that he had fired a gun.

BACK IN THE BOSOM OF THE IRA

Doherty soon found himself back in the cold familiarity of the Crumlin Road jail after his inquisitors had finished with him. Here he was among familiar faces and old IRA comrades, and the bravado that led him to kill easily returned. He was back under the discipline of the IRA where top-level decisions were taken by his masters to turn him into a cross between a martyr and Robin Hood. At the time of the beginning of his trial in April 1987 things were going badly for the IRA leadership; the hunger strike at the Maze prison was claiming lives, with five volunteers dead and no sign of the Thatcher government backing down. The leadership of the terror gang badly needed a propaganda break and they saw their opportunity in gaining it with Doherty. He had already refused to recognize the court sitting in justice on him and the fact that he had killed a member of Her Majesty's most elite force ensured that his name was already high up in the newspapers. His leaders instructed him to work on escape plans for himself and seven of his fellow inmates.

Doherty handed his commanders their much-needed propaganda victory on 10 June 1981, when he and seven others made a successful break out from the jail. Using guns smuggled in by IRA sympathizers they overpowered guards – clubbing one brutally – and dressed in prison uniforms to pass a series of checkpoints leading to the staff entrance to the jail. Finally out in the street, a gun battle ensued in a car park between the security forces and the IRA units sent to pick up the escapees. Doherty fled through the warren of streets in the Shankhill area of town – a fiercely loyalist enclave, but nothing happened to him and he was able to reach his own turf unscathed. Once there he was kept away from his family and friends – the first target of searches by the army – and sheltered at the homes of sympathizers who had no record of IRA membership or of terrorist offences. Within days he was moved south of the border into the Irish Republic where he was hidden in an even more remote region. As he bided his time for several months he heard the news from Belfast that Lord Justice Hutton had found him guilty of murder

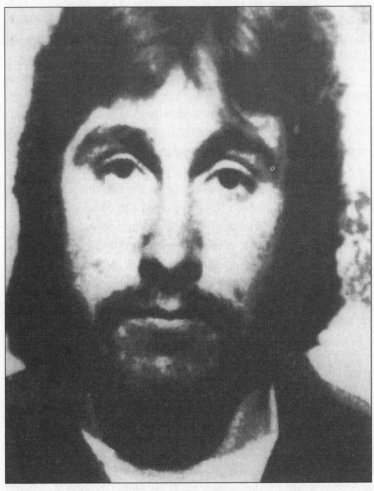

Joe Doherty hid behind a beard and long hair
when he fled to the USA.

in absentia, sentencing him to life imprisonment with a recommendation to the Home Secretary that he should serve a minimum of 30 years inside. It did much to take the edge from his fame as 'The Great Escaper' as he was now known among Republican sympathizers. His masters in Belfast knew that his pursuers would leave no stone unturned in their hunt for him and so took the decision to give him a new identity and send him off to America, where a massive Irish community – which gave literally millions of dollars each year to the war chests of their fighting units – would ensure his safety as a fugitive. He left Ireland under the name of Henry J. O'Reilly in February 1982... ready to bury himself in anonymity until his overlords called him to service once again, when the heat was off.

Margaret Thatcher was not prepared to let the killer of a British officer escape so easily. In his authoritative book on Doherty entitled *Killer in Downtown*, author Martin Dillon wrote: 'Doherty was a prestige target and, little did he know then, to the British prime minister at the time, Margaret Thatcher. The killing of Westmacott and the escape of his killers angered her. Doherty was the only one unaccounted for and eventually became so important that she would demand to be personally briefed about him. Thatcher believed that his recapture would enhance relations between Britain and Ireland and repair damage to security in Northern Ireland resulting from the "Great Escape." Neither the IRA nor Doherty needed to be convinced of her intentions or her determination to see them fulfilled. But they were unaware then of her growing personal interest in him.'

DOHERTY'S NEW LIFE IN NEW YORK

In New York, Doherty got a job with a construction company while lodging with a family sympathetic to the Republican cause in Ulster. He also worked as a shoe-shine boy, a bell-hop in a hotel and, with a fake social security number, managed to get a job as a barman at Clancy's Bar in Manhattan. Here he earned upwards of $120 per day with tips and thought the going was good. He had a girlfriend, a comfortable apartment in New Jersey and had adapted to life outside the strict discipline of the IRA with ease. He thought he had it made.

On the right, the then Mayor of New York, David Dinkins, his political antennae keenly aware of the massive Irish-American vote in his city, woos the Irish murderer, Joe Doherty. Dinkins was not heard to give sympathy to Irish – or other – victims of Doherty's killing habits.

But the heat was on in Ireland to get him back. Thatcher, receiving almost weekly intelligence briefings on his suspected whereabouts, gave her Royal Ulster Constabulary chiefs and army intelligence officers but one brief: find him. The Federal Bureau of Investigation in America was contacted in 1983 and a full file sent over to officers in New York listing every physical trait of the wanted man together with a profile of his habits and psychological breakdown. Soon questions were being asked around town among a network of IRA informers and it came to the notice of FBI agent Frank Schulte that there was a young man working at Clancy's Bar who fitted the bill. On 18 June 1983, he was seized at work. Margaret Thatcher was informed later that same day and she thought that he would be home in a matter of days to begin his 30-year sentence. But it would be many years of tortured manoeuvrings and murky intrigue before Doherty heard the slam of a British cell door clang behind him.

The scene of horror at Enniskillen, Northern Ireland, when the IRA slaughtered worshippers at a Remembrance Day service in 1987. Eleven people were killed.

Joe Doherty found himself in the enviable position of being a hero to a large part of the Irish-American population in New York. To these citizens of the Big Apple he was not the common murderer as depicted by Mrs Thatcher and the British establishment; rather he was a freedom fighter, a hero in the armed struggle to rid Ireland of the English 'oppressor'. He soon found himself with the kind of fame usually reserved for a showbusiness celebrity. Everyone wanted to press Doherty's flesh – the American senator Jesse Jackson was among 100 politicians who petitioned for him to be granted political asylum in America. Eventually Mayor David Dinkins of New York would come to name the block outside the Manhattan Correctional Centre where he was held 'Joe Doherty Corner'. To Mrs Thatcher and all the victims of IRA terrorism it was the equivalent of renaming a London street after the Boston strangler, for Doherty is also a crude killer.

Initially Doherty was charged with illegal entry into the USA – he had, after all, committed no crimes in America. Time after time after time courts ordered his release on bail and a full immigration hearing, only to have the legal process blocked from on high. Clearly, the hand of something or someone much bigger than the usual legal process was being brought into play repeatedly. Ronald Reagan, who enjoyed an unusually cozy relationship with Mrs Thatcher, was, like her, dedicated to the opposition of terrorism. She expected him to deliver Doherty up to her, but he was thwarted at every turn by the procedures of the US judicial system. In 1986 came the Libyan bombing when Reagan took his own stand against world terrorism by attempting to kill Colonel Gaddafi. Mrs Thatcher stood alone among Western leaders by allowing the American war planes to take off from British bases on their mission. When Britain continued to be frustrated by the American courts Mrs Thatcher's emissaries diplomatically reminded America that they 'owed' Britain a favour. The favour was Doherty for Tripoli and it was said so by Sherard Cowper Coles, a senior British diplomat, to Otto Obermaier, US attorney assigned to prosecuting him. He told Obermaier: 'The prime minister believes you owe us this one. She allowed your government to use our territory for your F1-11s when they were on their way to bomb Tripoli.'

But the legal process ground on and on in Doherty's favour. The American court system, examining the statues of the constitution of the United States and every similar case that had gone before, could not find sufficient arguments to warrant the deportation of Doherty. At one bail hearing in September 1990, after he had won over a dozen court cases that kept being referred to higher and higher authorities, Doherty gave a classic terrorist's 'doublespeak' account for his killing of Westmacott. He said: 'It was to bring

Mrs Thatcher was guarded by a young marine as she went to show her respects to the dead bandsmen in Deal, Kent. She called the terrorists 'monsters' and was relentless in her fight against them.

pressure on the British government, to force them to negotiations. That was the reason I was involved in the operation, to bring to the British government that their presence in the North of Ireland is unworkable, politically and militarily, and that they cannot suppress the IRA, that the IRA can survive and strike back.' This from a man who lied to the American courts that he had left the organization in 1982.

THE SUPREME COURT REJECTED ANY
FURTHER HEARINGS

By 1992 he was the longest-held political prisoner, held without a charge other than that he had come into the country illegally, in America. There was still intense pressure on the White House – now under the occupancy of the Bush administration – from No. 10 Downing Street, whose keys had passed to John Major. By February 1992 Joe Doherty's case reached the highest court in the land, the Supreme Court. He prayed for an immigration hearing, a separate tribunal that might allow him the political sanctuary he craved. But, almost nine years after he had first been arrested and locked up, it ended for him. The Supreme Court rejected any and all further hearings. On 19 February they came for him – as he rightly predicted they would – to, in his own words, 'complete my sentence in the hell of a British prison'. Doherty was taken from a new lock-up in Kentucky and flown to Northern Ireland where IRA men in Belfast's Crumlin Road jail, scene of his great escape, welcomed him with cake and tea. The saga of Joe Doherty ended in complete victory for Mrs Thatcher and the opponents of terrorism everywhere. Doherty's supporters, and particularly his lawyer in America, Mary Pike, argued that the American judicial system had been bent, perverted to the cause of Britain and not the interests of the Stars and Stripes. However, one senior British diplomat, who wishes to remain anonymous, said: 'He was a top operative before he got caught and he tried to con the people of America that he had seen the senselessness of violence, that he had reformed. He cannot complain of dirty tricks because he formerly employed every one in the book. Yes, America did owe Britain one for Tripoli – and now the debt has been repaid in full.'

JEFFREY DAHMER

THE CANNIBAL KILLER

He seemed to be just another quiet worker at the chocolate factory but there have been few monsters to equal Jeffrey Dahmer sadist, sodomite, killer and cannibal.

It was a balmy Milwaukee night in July 1991 when horrified police uncovered the secret life of America's most twisted serial killer, Jeffrey Dahmer. His one-bedroomed flat had been turned into a slaughterhouse for his hapless victims and, as the case unfolded, revelations of cannibalism, perverted sex, brutal murder and other unspeakable horrors shocked the whole world.

Photos of police forensic experts carting out vats of acid filled with bones and decomposing body parts, filled television screens around the world and ensured that Milwaukee would forever be known for something other than its beer.

Even though 31 year-old Dahmer pleaded guilty to the murders of 15 young men he still had to go to trial because he claimed that he was insane - and only a jury could decide whether his acts were the work of a twisted madman or of a cold, calculating, killing machine. The trial itself was one of the most disturbing America had ever witnessed, and a national audience of millions of television viewers were to hear tales of human carnage, bizarre sex, sick killings and grisly fantasies that would have ensured a XXX rating, had it been a movie.

The strange case of Jeffrey Dahmer ended with a verdict of Guilty and sane. The judge was forced to sentence Dahmer to mandatory, consecutive life terms in prison with no chance of parole for 930 years. The jury disregarded the testimony of psychiatric experts who said that Dahmer was 'psychotic' and suffered from unstoppable sexual urges caused by the mental disease of necrophilia. Dahmer himself appeared to undergo a physical change when he was in prison for the six months before the trial. Expressing remorse and asking to be put to death, the Milwaukee Monster had lost the mad, staring eyes that he had when he was first arrested. But experts still could not agree about his thought processes.

Like the capture of many serial killers, the arrest of Jeffrey Dahmer happened almost by accident. It had been a routine night for Milwaukee police patrolmen Robert Rauth and Rolf Mueller on 22 July 1991 when they spotted a black man running towards their car with a pair of handcuffs dangling from his wrist.

HE HAD FLED FOR HIS LIFE

The man with the handcuffs was Tracy Edwards and he told them a wild story about a man in the Oxford Apartments who had threatened to cut out Tracy's heart and eat it. He had fled for his life. It would turn out that Edwards had narrowly avoided becoming victim number 18 for America's most bizarre and warped serial killer, Jeffrey Dahmer.

Carolyn Smith weeps as court testimony describes the horrible death that her son, Eddie, suffered in the hands of Dahmer.

The two veteran policemen, used to responding to trouble in the rundown section of Milwaukee that had become their beat, took Edwards back to the ordinary–looking block of flats and rang the buzzer of one of Dahmer's neighbours. 'Open up, this is the police,' they told John Batchelor through the intercom. He let them in and looked at his watch–it was 11.25 p.m.

Nothing had prepared the two cops for what they would find after they rapped on the door of apartment number 213 as Tracy Edwards stayed a safe distance away down the corridor. A slight man with dirty-blonde hair and wearing a blue T-shirt and jeans opened the door. As they entered the dingy flat the policemen smelled a foul stench. A hi-tech electronic lock on Dahmer's front door further heightened their suspicions and they started to ask what had been going on. Mueller spotted some pots on top of the stove, some of them filled with a gooey substance, and lots of dirty dishes.

Edwards had told the policemen that he had met Dahmer at a downtown shopping mall and agreed to come back to his flat to drink some beer. When he said he wanted to leave Dahmer threatened him with a knife and put the handcuffs on one of his wrists, holding the other end in his hand. When Edwards later recounted his incredibly lucky escape from the Milwaukee Monster to a packed courtroom, he was too frightened to even look across at the defendant. We must assume that Jeffrey Dahmer had wielded a similar dread power over most of his victims.

After several hours inside the Dahmer lair, during which time Dahmer lay on top of Edwards' chest and listened to his heart, the killer began to get restless. Edwards testified that Dahmer began going in and out of a trance, chanting and swaying back and forth. This gave Edwards the opportunity to escape. Officer Mueller radioed back to police headquarters to 'run a make' on Dahmer. When they replied that the man was still on probation for a second degree sexual assault charge against a 13-old boy, the officers instructed Dahmer to lie face down on the floor so they could handcuff him and take him in. It was then that Officer Mueller wandered over to the refrigerator and opened it. 'Oh my God! There's a goddam head in there. He's one sick son of a bitch.'

Jeffrey Dahmer had been found out and his killing spree had been brought to an abrupt end, but as the gory details of his murderous orgy began to emerge it became clear that for more than a year, he had been killing people and chopping them up.

A COLLECTION OF POLAROIDS SHOWING DAHMER'S VICTIMS

As forensic specialists began to pour into the apartment building to catalogue the series of horrors, neighbours, awakened by all the commotion, started filing out into the streets. Police found a barrel drum filled with acid and the remains of three human torsos. Decomposed hands and genitals were kept in a lobster pot in one of his cupboards along with human skulls, hands and fingers. A collection of Polaroids was found showing each of Dahmer's fifteen victims in various states of undress and then, according to the forensic report, 'in different degrees of surgical excision'. They had been slaughtered, butchered and then dissolved.

Photographs from gay magazines hung on Dahmer's bedroom walls and a collection of pornographic videos, heavy metal records and a tape of *The Exorcist II* littered the living room. The only normal foodstuffs police found in Dahmer's flat were packets of crisps, a jar of mustard, and some beer. Not only had he been murdering and butchering his prey, he had been eating their flesh as well. He would later tell police how he fried one of his victim's biceps in oil and had it for dinner. In his freezer, police found human hamburgers made up of strips of muscle and flesh. Horrified neighbours watched as police in protective anti-toxic suits carried the evidence out of the building.

Dahmer grew up in a normal American family. His father Lionel worked as a research chemist in Bath, Ohio where he married Joyce Flint in 1959. Jeffrey was born exactly nine months after his parents got married, and doesn't seem to have had a terribly traumatic childhood. His parents divorced when he was 18 and he was left to fend for himself. He was just about to graduate from the Revere High School and he moved into a motel to be by himself while his mother and father sorted out custody of his 11-year-old brother. By this time, however, Dahmer was beginning to show signs of being 'a little odd'. He had trouble having relationships with girls, he was considered 'weird' by many of his classmates, and his favourite pastime was imitating mentally retarded people. 'He was a class clown but not in a wholesome sense,' recalled Dave Borsvold. 'He was only amused by the bizarre. He used to trace outlines of bodies out on the floor with chalk. He was definitely a little bit different.' But he did not seem dangerous.

His high school guidance counsellor George Kungle said:'Jeff was never a discipline problem—he was a quiet but not necessarily introverted guy. He never let anyone get to know him well. I would try and talk to him, like you would any kid, hoping to get some insights. He just never said a whole lot about himself.

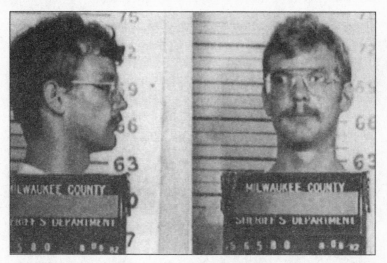

In 1982, he was photographed by police when he was arrested for disorderly conduct

A FATHER'S SENSE OF SHAME

During a bitter divorce Jeffrey's father accused his wife of 'extreme cruelty and gross neglect' and he made references to her 'mental illness' and the medical treatment she was receiving. Even the experts do not know what causes a serial killer to develop, but in Dahmer's case a hereditary mental illness might not be too far from the mark. 'In retrospect I wish I had done more in terms of keeping in touch of what he was doing and visiting him more often' said Dahmer's father when he discovered what his son had been doing.

'I don't know about feeling guilty for what he did, but I feel guilty that I didn't do more. I feel a deep sense of shame. I think any father who has some sense of responsiblity feels the transfer of shame or the responsibility somehow for this. When I first heard about it I could not associate him with what I was hearing was done. Absolutely not. I didn't think in my wildest dreams he was capable of something like that,' added Dahmer Sr, who paid for an expensive criminal defence lawyer, Gerald Boyle, to act for his son. 'I didn't look at him and see a monster. He acts—under most conditions—polite, kind, courteous. I can only imagine in my mind those occasions when he attacked the victims that was the monster who was out of control.' In Revere High School's yearbook Dahmer is described as a 'very valuable' member of the tennis team. He also played in the school band. In the space reserved for what he would like to do with his life, he said he wanted to attend Ohio State University and then pursue a career in business. It would later emerge that Dahmer had already committed his first murder the year he left school. He often killed and mutilated animals in the woods behind his home, before he killed a young male hitch-hiker, Stephen Hicks, who was on his way to a rock concert. Dahmer did indeed go to Ohio State in September of 1978 but he dropped out in January the next year to join the army. Friends who remember him say he was set on the idea of becoming a military policeman.

Instead, Dahmer ended up becoming a medical orderly and was sent to Germany to the Baumholder base in Rhineland-Palatinate state. The army has not revealed why he was discharged before his commission was up, but members of Dahmer's family say it was because of alcoholism. His time in the forces equipped him with a rudimentary knowledge of anatomy. When Dahmer returned to America he started drifting into casual, blue-collar jobs that paid little and afforded little respect from anyone. After six months in Miami he moved to Bath, Ohio, where he received a disorderly conduct charge for having an open container of alcohol on the street. In January 1982 he moved to Milwaukee to live with his grandmother, where he displayed a pattern of bizarre sexual activity by exposing himself to young children until he was charged with sexual abuse of a 13-year-old boy. The young boy's brother was to be a murder victim.

Shortly before he was due to be sentenced for the abuse of the boy, Dahmer wrote a lucid letter to the judge in the case asking for leniency and promising never to do it again. 'The world has enough misery in it without my adding more to it,' he wrote. 'That is why I am requesting a sentence modification. So that I may be allowed to continue my life as a productive member of our society.' The year was 1988 and, unknown to the law, he had already killed four times.

Regardless of his letter Dahmer was sentenced to eight years in jail, though he was released after serving just ten months because he proved to be a model prisoner and was told to report regularly to a probation officer.

For almost two years probation officer Donna Chester sat across a table from Dahmer for 15 minutes every first Tuesday of each month. Never in a million years did she dream that he could be capable of the brutal butchery of the 11 young men. Thirty-five-year-old Chester, who still works for the Wisconsin State Probation Service, was assigned to Dahmer's case in March 1990 after he was released from prison. To Chester, Jeffrey Dahmer was no different from most of the one hundred and twenty-one criminals who were part of her caseload. He was trying to make his way back into society with the help of counselling and supervision after a bout in jail, time that he said he regretted.

As he sat in her room in the district office he would tell Donna how his counselling sessions were going, he would talk about his hobbies, his personal life and the things he did in his spare time. What she did not realize was that this was no ordinary sex offender working his way diligently through rehabilitation. Jeffrey Dahmer held a dark secret close to him. And he was so good at it that Donna even cancelled a home visit to his apartment. A spokesman for the Department of Corrections, Joe Scislowicz, said it was unfair to blame Donna Chester for what happened. He remembered Dahmer as polite, punctual and reliable. 'He was only unable to report on two occasions in two years, otherwise he was here at the same time every month,' said Scislowicz. 'Both times he called ahead and said he wouldn't be able to make it and gave a good reason. He was excused from appearing both times. He was very meticulous about reporting to his probation officer once a month. I'm told he was like that in his work, too.'

NAKED AND BLEEDING, HE RAN FROM DAHMER

Scislowicz would not elaborate on the kind of rehabilitation treatment Dahmer was going through–saying it was a breach of privacy. He said his case file shows that Dahmer felt he was making some progress at working towards his goal of becoming a 'useful contributor to society'. Chester's inability to see through Dahmer's tissue of lies brought criticism from Milwaukee police chief Philip Arreola, who spoke out about how the system failed its people and its policemen. 'We try to put these people away for a long time and they get let back out on to the streets,' he said. 'Now we can see the tragic results of a system that has simply ceased to function.'

It was a hard pill for the probation department, and Chester, to swallow. They felt they had done all they needed to keep tabs on Dahmer. As Scislowicz said: 'There was a lot of evidence he was doing alright. Most people who have a residence and a good paying job tend to stay out of trouble. This is such an exception, it's not fair to blame it on any individual.'

A Milwaukee policeman is obliged to photograph human bones found in the alley behind Dahmer's apartment

Arreola got a taste of his own medicine just a few days later when it emerged that a tragic, careless act by three bigoted policemen allowed Dahmer to continue with his killing spree unabated. Choking back tears of embarrassment the police chief had to admit that he was bringing in the Internal Affairs Division to investigate reports that three officers actually came face to face with Dahmer on the night of 27 May. One even went inside his flat –and not one of them thought anything was wrong.

The incident involved Konerak Sinthasomphone, a 14-year-old Laotian refugee who was seen running out of Dahmer's apartment apparently bleeding. Neighbours, mostly black people, called in the police but were more or less told to 'stop bothering the white guy' according to witnesses. Not only was Sinthasomphone naked and bleeding, but he had been drugged with a heavy dose of sleeping pills–Dahmer's favourite form of rendering his victims unconscious before strangling them–and there were tiny drill marks in his head. Dahmer had fantasized about creating zombie-like lovers who could be his sex slaves and he began to experiment on some of them by doing crude lobotomies with an electric drill and some acid. One poor victim stayed awake for an entire day before finally dying. As soon as the police left the building Dahmer, who told them the boy was his lover, strangled Sinthasomphone, and dismembered his body–all the while taking Polaroid pictures. The three policemen responsible have been fired.

Within hours of his arrest Dahmer admitted to killing 17 people, 12 of them inside his Milwaukee flat and two in a different state. He identified photographs of missing persons for detectives. Forensic psychologists and other experts all testified at his trial, which drew large crowds for three weeks at the Milwaukee County Safety Building. But they could not agree on whether he was able to stop his urge to kill, a crucial aspect of his insanity defence. Dahmer sat emotionless, occasionally stifling yawns, as he listened to detectives and psychiatrists recount hundreds of hours of interviews they had conducted with him to try to understand his vile and terrible acts.

Relatives of his victims, who were almost all black, listened intently to the gruesome testimony. They hugged each other and cried as they heard for the first time what really happened to their loved ones. At the end of the trial, after a jury found that Dahmer was sane, the relatives gave voice to their horror and grief.

For one young woman, seeing Dahmer face to face was too much. Rita Isbell stared into the eyes of the Milwaukee Monster as Judge Laurence Gram invited her to make a statement before sentence was to be imposed. Rita became hysterical when he started talking about her dead brother, Errol Lindsey, who was just 19 when he was butchered and dismembered by Dahmer in his Milwaukee apartment in 1991. Dahmer had satisfied his twisted fantasies by having sex with the corpse. 'I never want to see my mother go through what she went through because of you,' said Isbell. 'Do you understand Jeffrey? Jeffrey, I hate you,' she shouted. Isbell, wearing a sweatshirt that read '100 per cent black', then ran around the outside of the witness box and towards the table where Dahmer was sitting with his lawyers. 'You Mother ****er, I'll kill you Jeffrey,' she screamed hysterically as five court officers held her back.

After other families called him 'a devil' and asked the judge to ensure that he never saw daylight again, Dahmer surprised and stunned everyone by asking to make his own statement–an articulate and far-reaching apology he had composed himself in his prison cell. Asking for 'no consideration' in his sentencing and declaring that he would have rather had the death penalty–something the state of Wisconsin does not have–Dahmer said: 'It is over now. This has never been a case of trying to get free. I really wanted death for myself. I hope God can forgive me. I know society and the families can never forgive me. I promise to pray every day for their forgiveness. I have seen their tears. If I could give my life right now to bring their loved ones back I would. This was not about hate. I never hated anyone. I knew I was sick or evil or both. Now I have some peace. I know the harm I have caused. I can't undo the terrible harm I have caused but I cooperated as best I could. I am very sorry.

'I understand their rightful hate,' he said of the victims' families, some of whom said they wished he would go to hell. 'I know I will be in prison for the rest of my life. I will turn back to God. I should have stayed with God. I tried and failed and created a holocaust. Only the Lord Jesus Christ can save me from my sins.' Dahmer promised to devote his time behind bars as a study for doctors and psychologists. He said he would turn himself into a human guinea pig so that they could further examine his bizarre mind to try and find what would make a human being turn into such a monster. The killer vowed to help psychiatrists to understand what made him do the ghastly things that he did on his killing, mutilation and cannibalistic spree.

'I pledge to talk to the doctors to help find some answers,' Dahmer said in a prepared statement. 'I know my time in jail will be terrible but I deserve whatever I get because of what I did.' Dahmer–who admitted to detectives that he studied the Satanic scripts–read a passage from the Bible and declared: 'Jesus Christ came to the world to save the sinners, of whom I am the worst, Dahmer apologized to the victims' families, his probation officer, and even the policemen who were fired. He also apologised to his father Lionel and stepmother Shari, who both sat quietly and listened intently every day of the court proceedings.

'I regret that the policemen lost their jobs,' said Dahmer. 'I know they did their best. I have hurt my mother, father, stepmother and family. I love them all so much. I only hope they find the same peace I have. I take all the blame for what I did. I hurt many people. I decided to go through with this trial for a number of reasons. I wanted to show these were not hate crimes. I wanted the world to know the truth. I didn't want any unanswered questions. I wanted to find out what it was that caused me to be bad or evil. Perhaps if there are others out there, this all might have helped them.'

ROUND-THE-CLOCK SURVEILLANCE IN ISOLATION

Dahmer was sentenced to a total of 1070 years in prison on 15 consecutive counts of murder plus extra sentences for habitual criminality with no possibility of parole for 930 years. Just one day after the sentence he was taken to Wisconsin's toughest jail – the maximum security Columbia Correctional Institution – where he is held in a segregated cell. The Portage prison houses 575 of the worst criminals in the state – sex offenders, murderers, drug dealers and now Jeffrey Dahmer. There is a chance that he could be absorbed into the main prison population but for now he will be under round-the-clock surveillance in isolation. 'At the beginning we will be observing him twenty-four hours a day to ensure that he is not a danger to himself,' said Columbia's warden Jeffrey Endicott. 'The best way for us to do that is to have him in that section of the prison. It is safest for all concerned.'

Endicott added that many inmates are moved out of the isolation block after a few days, but that Dahmer may be kept there longer than others. Many of the 150 sex offenders in the prison never leave their single cells or mingle with other prisoners. Fellow serial killer Henry Lee Lucas, who is on death row in a Texas prison, said that life in jail for him was 'pure hell'. Lucas, who was convicted of 11 murders and suspected of committing 140 more, says Dahmer will have a rough time of it. 'He'll be lucky to stay alive in prison. There's a thing in prison about kids, you know,' he said. 'If somebody kills a kid like that he'll have a hard way to go.' Dahmer will have no contact with other prisoners at first and even though he says he no longer wants to kill, guards have been told to take every precaution when dealing with him. All of his food is passed to him through a drawer in a wall to avoid contact and he will be kept under constant surveillance 24 hours a day by guards who sit inside a protected 'control bubble'. Columbia Correctional Institution is a large complex, with five watchtowers, razor wire – topped high security fences and electronic surveillance of its 19-acre perimeter. There is no chance that Dahmer could escape. He is allowed to exercise once a day but is always accompanied by several guards. And he must wear the bright orange jumpsuit uniform he was given when he walked in the front door of the prison.

Dahmer will not be allowed any more than six books, four magazines, ten pictures and fifteen letters. Each week he receives more than two dozen letters – some from women who want to meet him and fall in love. Dahmer came from a middle-class family, but was affected in early life by a trauma or rejection which sent him over the edge.

He is similar to many of America's worst mass murderers, in that he can be perfectly normal while he is not in his 'killing mode', and that may work to his advantage in jail. Ed Gein was working as a babysitter while he was spending his nights digging up graves; Ted Bundy worked at a Samaritans' hotline in Seattle in between killings; John Wayne Gacy performed as a clown at children's parties; and David Berkowitz now spends much of his time counselling other inmates at a New York state high security prison. He helps them with their problems, reads their mail to them and cleans floors. He is considered a model prisoner and will be elligible for parole in ten years. 'Many of these killers are frequently glib and superficially charming, helpful, sweet and kind,' said Helen Morrison, a Chicago psychiatrist and serial killer expert. 'I'm sure Dahmer falls into that same category.' Judith Becker, who testified at the Dahmer trial for the defence, says it is too soon to tell how the prison term will affect Dahmer's personality or his mind. 'He did indicate to me that he hated what he had been doing when he talked about a "nuclear explosion" that had happened within him since he had been caught,' she said. 'He's talked about killing himself, but obviously he won't be able to do that in prison. He says he is sorry for what he did and that he feels pain for the relatives of the victims. He has already had a lot of time on his own to think about that, and he seems to be coping with it now. The fantasies have stopped, he says. But there is no way of really knowing if they will start up again.'

THE CHANCES ARE THAT HE COULD BECOME A MODEL PRISONER

'The prosecution made a strong case by identifying that Dahmer was able to make definite decisions not to do things at certain times,' said David Barlow, an assistant professor of criminal justice at the University of Wisconsin. Richard Kling, who defended serial killer John Wayne Gacy, added: 'I don't think there is a person in the world who would come in and say Dahmer isn't abnormal. The problem is that abnormal doesn't add up to insanity.' How he deals with being in prison is something that will fascinate psychiatric experts for years to come. The chances are that he could become a model prisoner, with the ability to be outwardly friendly to both fellow inmates and guards.

During the trial McCann pointed out Dahmer's ability to manipulate doctors and psychiatrists for his own ends. His supply of prescription sleeping pills – which he used for drugging his victims before he strangled them – came from doctors who thought he was having trouble sleeping.

Dahmer also deliberately misled court-appointed therapists who were trying to help him after he was convicted of sexual assault. 'He rejected the hand that could have helped him,' said McCann. 'He knew what he was doing.' No matter what happens, the files on Jeffrey Dahmer will provide endless hours of research material for the FBI's academy in Quantico, Virginia – where special agents are trained to produce profiles of serial killers. Although the project is temporarily dormant after the departure of its director, Robert Ressler, Dahmer's court files will be entered into the FBI's extensive databanks on serial killers.

'SILENCE OF THE LAMBS'

Ressler, who has interviewed such killers as Charles Manson, Sirhan Sirhan, Ted Bundy, John Wayne Gacy, and 'Son of Sam' killer David Berkowitz, will attempt to see Dahmer so that he can include his files in his rogue's gallery. 'How can a person be sane and do these horrendous acts?' He would be a fascinating study for me,' said Ressler, who now runs his own investigating company. 'Any information we can collect on individuals like Dahmer is like gold dust in tracking down others out there who might be doing the same thing.'

In the film *Silence of the Lambs* Jodie Foster played a young FBI agent who had to befriend the demented Hopkins character – Hannibal the Cannibal – so that she could help catch another serial killer, a murderer based on Wisconsin's other famous maniac, Ed Gein. Gein killed women and then skinned them to satisfy his twisted transvestite fantasies. He also dug up freshly buried bodies so that he could use their skin to build himself a body. He was

The Milwaukee Monster is wheeled into court. His hands and legs were shackled in irons, as befits a dangerous beast.

found mentally incompetent to stand trial in 1957 and so never had the opportunity to plead guilty. He died at the Mendota Mental Health Institute in Madison in 1984. Other psychiatric experts have pointed out that a thorough investigation of Dahmer would be invaluable as research material into sexual perversion.

Judith Becker said: 'We could learn a tremendous amount from studying Dahmer because necrophiliacs are extremely rare. I have not seen anywhere in the literature the successful treatment of this disorder.' Even the most highly qualified experts cannot agree on what kind of demons live inside the mind of Jeffrey Dahmer. He showed early on in his life a twisted fascination with the macabre and the bizarre. Some psychiatrists claim that the emotional distance between him and his parents might have contributed to his feelings of abandonment. Those feelings fuelled his ghastly killing spree – he told doctors that he killed his victims because he didn't want them to leave him. Some experts say being locked up for life with other criminals who won't be leaving might actually appeal to the perverse needs of Jeffrey Dahmer.

'One great myth about serial killers is that they secretly want to get caught,' said James Fox, a professor of criminal justice at Boston's Northeastern University and author of *Mass Murder: The Growing Menace*. 'That's just not true, these guys enjoy what they do. They might get a little guilty afterwards for a while, but the fantasies that drive them are so powerful that they have to do it again soon. Dahmer will not be able to do it again now that he's in jail and I'm sure he won't be happy about that. He doesn't even have any of his souvenirs – the photos or even the body parts - to look at anymore. That may be why he has asked for the death penalty, he has nothing else to live for. Souvenirs are very important to the disorganized serial killers because they remind them of the best times they had. Dahmer's murders were driven by his fantasies of destruction, tied up with a sexual desire.'

Prosecutor E. Michael McCann said that Dahmer has always managed to control his violent tendencies when he has been in closely controlled situations and some feel that prison life will do him a lot of good.

DAHMER LONGS FOR DEATH

Worst of all for Dahmer will be the long hours of contemplation he will have to spend alone. He told detectives after his arrest that he wished Wisconsin or Ohio had the death penalty. Now he will have to spend the next 40 years thinking about what he did. 'It will probably tear him apart,' said one expert. 'If the court didn't think he was insane when he killed, just wait a few years and see what the torture of his acts does to his mind.'

Dahmer may have to go through the trial process all over again in Ohio where he killed his first victim in 1978. But Ohio, like Wisconsin, has no death penalty – the one thing that Dahmer has wished for.

The world will be a safer place without Jeffrey Dahmer. But the world might never know what it was that drove him to commit some of the worst crimes in American history. One thing is certain, inmates at Columbia will not be jumping over each other for a chance to share a cell with him.

VICTIMS AS NAMED BY PROSECUTOR'S OFFICE:

1 January 1988 – James Doxtator
Killed at age 15 at Dahmer's grandmother's house. Strangled after drinking sleeping potion. Dismembered, bones smashed with a sledgehammer.

2 March 1988 – Richard Guerrero
Killed at age 23 at grandmother's house. Drugged him and then dismembered the body.

3 March 1989 – Anthony Sears
Killed at age 24 at grandmother's house. Strangled and dismembered. Dahmer kept his skull. boiled off the skin and then painted the skull as a souvenir.

4 May 1990 – Raymond Smith, aka Ricky Beeks
Killed at age 30 in Apartment 213. Strangled after being drugged. Dahmer had sex with the dead body. Dismembered him but kept the skull and painted it.

5 July 1990 – Edward Smith
Killed at age 28. Dismembered and disposed of in rubbish bags.

6 September 1990 – Ernest Miller
Killed at age 23. Dahmer slit his throat, dismembered him and kept his biceps in the freezer to eat later. Also kept the skull and skeleton which he bleached.

7 October 1990 – David Thomas
Killed at age 23. Killed even though he was not Dahmer's 'type' for fear that he would tell police he had been drugged. Body disposed of.

8 February 1991 – Curtis Straughter
Killed at age 17. Strangled with a strap after being drugged. Dismembered him but kept the skull.

9 April 1991 – Errol Lindsey
Killed at age 19. Strangled him and then had sex. Dismembered the body and kept the skull.

10 May 1991 – Anthony Hughes
Killed at age 32. Strangled and dismembered him but kept the skull.

11 May 1991 – Konerak Sinthasomphone
Killed at age 15. Murdered after police left Dahmer's apartment following telephone call from neighbours. Strangled, dismembered but kept the skull.

12 June 1991 – Matt Tamer aka Donald Montrell
Killed at age 21. Strangled with a strap. Kept his head in the freezer and put his body in the acid-filled barrel.

13 July 1991 – Jeremiah Weinberger
Killed at age 24. Strangled with his hands. Put his head in the freezer and his body in the barrel.

14 July 1991 – Oliver Lacy (above)
Killed at age 25. Strangled him and then had sex. Placed head in the bottom of the fridge and kept his heart in the freezer to eat later. Also kept his body in the freezer.

15 July 1991 – Joseph Bradehoft
Killed at age 25. Strangled with a strap while he slept. Dismembered, head put in the freezer and body in the barrel.

Two additional victims Dahmer has admitted killing were not in the Milwaukee charges. They were:

Stephen Hicks, killed in Dahmer's parents home in Bath, Ohio. Dahmer killed him with a barbell, then disposed of the body in the woods.

Stephen Tuomi, killed in Milwaukee hotel room in September 1987. Dahmer says he doesn't remember how he killed the man, but he took his body back to his grandmother's house in a trunk and dismembered him.

PETER SUTCLIFFE

THE YORKSHIRE RIPPER

In the 1970s Yorkshire women were terrorized by a serial killer who, like the notorious Jack the Ripper, inflicted hideous mutilations on his victims. Was Peter Sutcliffe a paranoid schizophrenic, or just 'a wilfully evil bastard'?

Late on the afternoon of 22 May 1981, a dark-haired, bearded, scruffy little man rose to his feet in the dock beneath the dome of Number One Court at the Old Bailey to hear judgment passed upon him. Found guilty of murdering 13 women, and attempting to murder seven others, 35-year-old Peter William Sutcliffe, 'The Yorkshire Ripper', was sentenced to life imprisonment with a recommendation that he should serve at least 30 years.

AN ORDINARY MURDER

The Ripper murders began in 1975 in the rundown Chapeltown area of Leeds. A milkman spotted a frosted bundle of what appeared to be rags on the white rimed grass. He went and peered at it. It was a woman's body.

She lay on her back, her dyed blonde hair dark and spiky with dried blood. Her jacket and blouse had been torn open and her bra pulled up, revealing breasts and abdomen, and her trousers were round her knees, though her pants were still in position. Her torso had been stabbed and slashed 14 times, after her death from two crushing hammer blows to the back of the skull.

The dead woman's name was Wilma McCann. She was 28 years old, and what the police classed as a 'good-time girl'. Because Mrs McCann's purse was missing, West Yorkshire Metropolitan Police treated the case as murder in the pursuance of robbery. Despite the brutality of the attack there seemed no other motive. Yet, when another murder was committed just over two and a half months later, the similarities convinced the police that they were dealing with a double murderer.

ANOTHER GOOD-TIME GIRL

Emily Jackson, like Wilma McCann, came to Chapeltown only once or twice a week to sell herself on a casual basis.

Her body was discovered in the early morning of 21 January 1976. She had also been killed from behind by two blows from a heavy hammer. Her breasts were exposed and her trousers pulled down, though again her pants were in place. On her right thigh was stamped the impression of a heavily ribbed wellington boot. The only solid clue the police had so far was that the perpetrator took size seven in shoes.

Assistant Chief Constable George Oldfield and Superintendent Richard Holland at a 'Ripper' press conference.

SERIAL KILLER ON THE LOOSE

No progress was made on either case and a year passed by. Then, on 5 February 1977, the killer struck again. Another 'good-time girl', 28-year-old Irene Richardson, was discovered by a jogger on Soldiers' Field, not far from Chapeltown. She was lying on her face and had died from three hammer blows to the back of her skull. Her killer had stripped her from the waist downwards. Her neck and chest had been subjected to a frenzied knife attack. The pattern of wounds now left no doubt that the police were dealing with a serial killer.

This alarmed the street-girl population, and their numbers in Chapeltown declined. Not so, however, in the red-light district of Bradford, some ten miles away, where 'Tina' Atkinson lived and worked. On Sunday, 24 April, Tina's friends called for her at her flat, but got no answer. She had been out boozing the night before and the door was ajar so they went in. Tina lay naked on her bed, the back of her head crushed by four hammer blows. Seven knife wounds had lacerated her stomach, and her side had been slashed open.

Any doubts about the killer's identity were dispelled by a clue found imprinted on the bottom bedsheet. It was the mark of a size seven wellington boot, identical with the imprint found on Emily Jackson's thigh.

The police believed that the killer was specifically targeting prostitutes and so began touring the red-light districts, questioning street girls about any regulars who might have acted suspiciously. But it soon became clear that the Yorkshire Ripper regarded any woman out alone at night as fair game.

THE RIPPER SPREADS HIS NET

On Sunday, 26 June 1977, a 16-year-old girl named Jayne MacDonald was found slumped and dead in a street on the fringes of Chapeltown. She had sustained at least three hammer blows to the head. She had been stabbed once in the back and several times through the chest. But she was no prostitute or good-time girl. A fortnight later, a Bradford housewife, Maureen Long, was struck down near her home but miraculously survived.

The police stepped up their enquiries. Three hundred and four officers were assigned to the case. And to head them, veteran detective George Oldfield, Assistant Chief Constable (Crime), came out from behind his desk at administrative HQ in Wakefield.

The next time the Ripper struck he changed his location and killing pattern, but left a vital clue.

On 1 October 1977, Jean Bernadette Jordan, was picked up near her home in Moss Side, Manchester and driven by her murderer to the Southern Cemetery two miles away. She demanded £5 in advance and was paid with a crisp new note, which she stored in her purse.

As she climbed from the Ripper's car on to allotment land adjoining the large cemetery, Mrs Jordan was knocked to the ground with a hammer blow and beaten 11 times more. Then she was pulled into a clump of bushes. Disturbed by a car, the killer then fled.

The £5 note had been given to Sutcliffe in his wage packet two days before the attack. He realized that it might be a valuable clue, so eight days later returned to the scene. He searched in vain for the handbag, then attacked the decaying body with a shard of glass. Two days after the second attack, Mrs Jordan's remains were discovered, along with the missing handbag which had fallen among the bushes. The £5 note, serial number AW51 121565, was traced to the wage packets of the road haulage firm T. and W. H. Clark. One of their drivers was Peter Sutcliffe, who had worked there since October 1976.

LIVING VICTIMS

Detectives visited Sutcliffe at his home. He seemed a steady, quiet man and the officers left, satisfied that he was not the Ripper.

But had they had time and reason to do so, they would have discovered from old Bradford City Police files that Peter Sutcliffe had once been questioned by police regarding an attack back in August 1969. This first attack was not quite motiveless. Earlier that summer he had suspected his girlfriend Sonia of seeing another man. To 'get even', he had approached a Bradford prostitute, but had been unable to maintain an erection. The woman had laughed at him, taken his £10 and got her pimp to chase him away.

In August he had seen her in the St Paul's red-light district, crept after her, and hit her violently on the back of the head with a stone in a sock. The woman had noted the number of his van and Sutcliffe had been traced. But because he had no record, he had been let off with a caution.

Since then he had left five women damaged but alive. Each of these living victims had tried to describe their attacker. One described him as thirtyish, about 5 ft 10 ins tall, and bearded. Another had described him accurately as having a black, crinkly beard.

Police search for clues in their hunt for the Yorkshire Ripper.

On the evening of 21 January 1978, a 22-year-old 'career' prostitute named Yvonne Pearson was seen in Bradford, climbing into a car driven by a man described as having a dark beard and black, piercing eyes – it was Sutcliffe. He took her to waste ground in Arthington Street, killed her with a club hammer and jumped on her chest until her ribs cracked. He then piled an old abandoned horsehair sofa on top of her. About a month later, when the body remained undiscovered, Sutcliffe returned and placed a current copy of the *Daily Mirror* under one of her mouldering arms. Between this killing and the newspaper incident he had also paid a visit to Huddersfield.

On the snowy night of Tuesday, 31 January 1978, Sutcliffe picked up Helen Rytka. They went into a timber yard under railway arches near the centre of the town and, uncharacteristically, Sutcliffe managed to have intercourse with her before killing her in his usual fashion.

Immediately after this murder, the police were optimistic. Helen's abduction had taken place in the early evening on a busy street. But despite tracing 100 passers-by, and with all but three cars and one man eliminated, there was no real result.

The bus stop at Leeds' Arndale Shopping Centre, where Jacqueline Hill was accosted and murdered by the Yorkshire Ripper.

The police were convinced that the Ripper lived in the locality of Leeds or Bradford, but they little realized that, by the end of 1978, they had interviewed him no fewer than four times. Apart from two visits concerning the £5 note clue, they had called at his home because routine checks had turned up Sutcliffe's car registration in red-light areas. They also called to check on tyre tracks to compare them with some found near the scene of Irene Richardson's murder.

But they did not check two vital clues they knew about the Ripper against Sutcliffe. The Ripper was a B secretor – a rare blood type. And he took size seven boots – very small for a man.

On the night of 16 May 1978, two months after Yvonne Pearson's body was found, Sutcliffe killed Vera Millward, a 41-year-old prostitute. He then waited eleven months before he killed again. His next victim was 19-year-old Josephine Whittaker, a clerk in the Halifax Building Society headquarters. She was attacked and killed with sickeningly familiar ferocity.

TAUNTS AND HOAXES

Between Josephine's death and September of the same year there was another lull. This time it was filled by a brutal hoax which almost certainly cost three women their lives.

Since March 1978 George Oldfield had received two letters supposedly from the Ripper. Shortly before the Whittaker murder a third letter came, mentioning Vera Millward's death. All three letters were postmarked from Sunderland. On the third, traces of engineering oil, similar to those found on Josephine Whittaker's body, were discovered. This seemed to confirm that the letters were written by the Ripper.

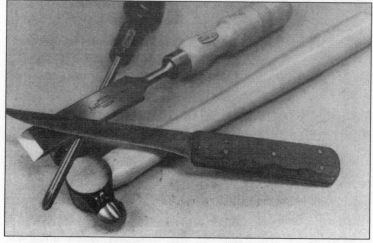

Peter Sucliffe's murder weapons could have been bought at any local hardware store.

Peter and Sonia Sutcliffe's house in
Garden Lane, Heston, Bradford

When, on 18 June 1979, a tape recording addressed in the same handwriting as the letters was received, West Yorkshire police were convinced that this was their man. The tape, a taunting message to Oldfield, was in a broad Geordie accent. Therefore, the West Yorkshire police became convinced that anyone without a Geordie accent could be eliminated from their enquiry. This, of course, put Sutcliffe temporarily in the clear.

In July Sutcliffe was visited by Detective Constable Laptew, who had noticed that his car had been spotted in one red-light area on 36 separate occasions. Laptew was deeply suspicious of Sutcliffe but he went unheeded by his superiors who were convinced their killer was a Geordie. As a result, Sutcliffe went on to kill three more times.

On 1 September 1979 Sutcliffe ambushed and killed a social sciences student named Barbara Leach.

On 18 August 1980 his victim was 47-year-old civil servant Margaret Walls. Because she had been bludgeoned and strangled, but not mutilated further, the Ripper Squad were reluctant to add her to their list of victims. But there was no question of the authenticity of his thirteenth and final slaying.

There was tight security as a crowd assembled to watch the arrival of Peter Sutcliffe at Dewsbury Magistrates' Court.

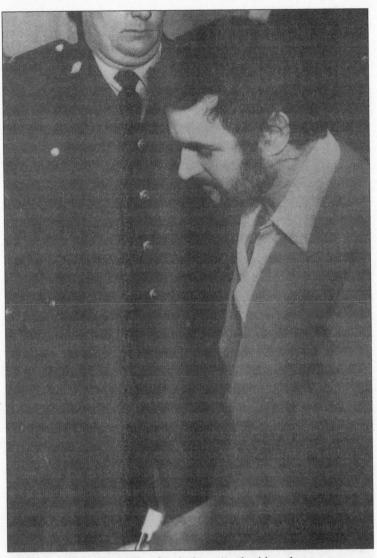
Peter Sutcliffe after being attacked in prison.

Twenty-year-old Jacqueline Hill, a language student at Leeds University, was walking home when she was dragged by Sutcliffe on to waste land and savaged with a hammer, a knife and a screwdriver. This brutal death caused a backlash of frustration among the public and police.

The Home Office set up a 'super squad' of four outside detectives and a forensic scientist. The idea was that this team should review the evidence. They did make some progress but, eventually, it was by chance that Peter Sutcliffe was caught. On 2 January 1981, two police officers were cruising along Melbourne Avenue, Sheffield – a haunt of prostitutes – when they saw a girl getting into a Rover V8 3500. They stopped the driver, a short, bearded man, who gave his name as Peter Williams. It was discovered that his number plates were false and had been stolen from that town.

The bushes in Melbourne Avenue were searched, and officers found a ball-pen hammer and a knife, which eventually were to be matched to the Ripper's crimes. Then Sutcliffe finally confessed to the Dewsbury police. 'I'm glad it's all over. I would have killed that girl if I hadn't been caught.'

What made him do it? Some experts argued that he was a paranoid schizophrenic who had little control over the delusions and impulses that haunted him, while one of the Home Office pathologists who worked on the case echoed the thoughts of the general public: 'He was quite simply a wilfully evil bastard.'

While awaiting trial in Arrnley gaol, Leeds, Sutcliffe was overheard by a warder planning with his wife Sonia that he would fake 'madness' and 'be out in ten years'. As it was, his plot failed. He was sent to Parkhurst maximum security prison on the Isle of Wight. Peter Sutcliffe's mental condition did begin to deteriorate, and in March 1984 he was moved to Ward One of Somerset House, Broadmoor Institution for the Criminally Insane, where he remains.

HAROLD SHIPMAN
DOCTOR DEATH

Until recently Britain's worst serial killer was Victorian serial poisoner, Mary Ann Cotton, who murdered an estimated 21 people in the 1870s. Now that dubious distinction is claimed by Dr Harold Shipman.

Dr Shipman ran a one-man practice in Hyde in the north of England. Most of Harold Shipman's patients were elderly women, living alone and vulnerable. They adored their doctor, Harold 'Fred' Shipman, and even when their contemporaries began dying in unusually high numbers, patients remained loyal to the murderous MD. It seemed that as long as he spared them, his victims loved their doctor – to death.

A KILLER'S CHILDHOOD

Harold Frederick Shipman was born into a working-class family on 14 June 1946 and was known as Fred or Freddy. His childhood, however, was far from normal. He always kept a distance between himself and his contemporaries – mainly due to the influence of his mother, Vera. The reason for this distance was to become clear in later years.

It was Vera who decided who Harold could play with, and when. For some reason she wanted to distinguish him from the other boys – he was the one who always wore a tie when the others were allowed to dress more casually. His sister Pauline was seven years older, his brother Clive four years his junior, but in his mother's eyes, Harold was the one she held the most hope for.

Shipman was comparatively bright in his early school years, but rather mediocre when he reached upper school level. Nonetheless, he was a plodder determined to succeed, even down to re-sitting his entrance examinations for medical school.

Funnily enough, he had every opportunity to be part of the group – he was an accomplished athlete on the football field and the running track. In spite of this, his belief in his superiority appears to have prevented him from forming any meaningful friendships.

There was something else that isolated him from the group – his beloved mother had terminal lung cancer. As her condition deteriorated, Harold willingly played a major supportive role.

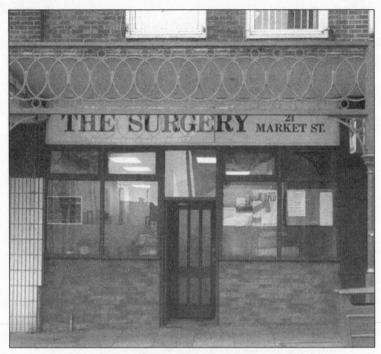

Dr Shipman's surgery in Hyde, Greater Manchester.

WATCHING VERA DIE

Shipman's behaviour in his mother's final months closely paralleled that of Shipman the serial killer. Every day after classes, he would hurry home, make Vera a cup of tea and chat with her. She found great solace in his company and always eagerly awaited his return. This is probably where Shipman learned the endearing bedside manner he would later adopt in his practice as a family physician. Towards the end, Vera experienced severe pain, but, because pumps to self-administer painkillers did not exist at that time, Vera's sole relief from the agony of cancer came with the family physician.

No doubt young Harold watched in fascination as his mother's distress miraculously subsided whenever the family doctor injected her with morphine. Ms Shipman grew thinner and frailer day by day, until on 21 June 1963 the cancer claimed her life. Harold felt a tremendous sense of loss following his mother's death. After all, she was the one who made him feel special, different from the rest. Her passing also left him with an indelible image – the patient with a cup of tea nearby, finding sweet relief in morphine.

This must have made a great impact on the 17-year-old, as it was a scene he would recreate hundreds of times in the future once he became a doctor – with no regard for human life or feeling.

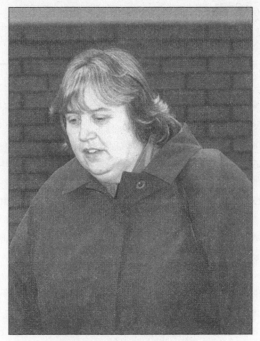

Primrose, Shipman's wife.

HAROLD THE STUDENT

Two years after his mother died, Harold Shipman was finally admitted to Leeds University medical school. Getting in had been a struggle – he'd had to rewrite the exams he'd failed first time around. His grades, however, were sufficient enough for him to collect a degree and serve his mandatory hospital internship.

It is surprising to learn that so many of his teachers and fellow students can barely remember Shipman. Those who do remember claim that he looked down on them and seemed bemused by the way most young men behaved. 'It was as if he tolerated us. If someone told a joke he would smile patiently, but Fred never wanted to join in. It seems funny, because I later heard he'd been a good athlete, so you'd have thought he'd be more of a team player.' He was simply remembered as a loner. The one place his personality changed, however, was on the football field. Here, he unleashed his aggression and his dedication to win was intense.

Shipman finally found companionship in a girl, Primrose, who was three years his junior. He married her when he was only 19 years old.

Primrose's background was similar to Fred's, whereby her mother restricted her friendships and controlled her activities. Being rather a plain girl, Primrose was delighted to have finally found a boyfriend. Shipman married her when she was only 17 and five months pregnant. By 1974 he was a father of two and had joined a medical practice in the Yorkshire town of Todmorden. At this stage in his life Fred seemed to undergo a transformation. He became an outgoing, respected member of the community in the eyes of his fellow medics and patients.

But the staff in the medical offices where he worked saw a different side of the young practitioner. He had a way of getting things done his way – even with the more experienced doctors in the practice.

ADDICTION

His career in Todmorden came to a sudden halt when he started having blackouts. His partners were devastated when he gave them the reason – epilepsy. He used this faulty diagnosis as a cover-up. The truth soon came to the surface, when the practice receptionist Marjorie Walker came across some disturbing entries in a druggist's controlled narcotics ledger. These records showed how Shipman had been prescribing large and frequent amounts of pethidine in the names of several of his patients, when in fact the pethidine had found its way into the doctor's very own veins.

Not only that, he'd also written numerous prescriptions for the drug on behalf of the practice. Although this was not unusual because drugs were kept for emergencies, the prescribed amounts were excessive.

Following the discovery of Shipman's over-prescribing, an investigation by the practice uncovered the fact that many patients on the prescription list had neither required nor received the drug.

When confronted in a staff meeting, Shipman's way of dealing with the problem was to provide an insight into his true personality. Realizing his career was on the line, he first begged for a second chance.

When this request was denied, he became furious and stormed out, threw his medical bag to the ground and threatened to resign. The partners were dumbfounded by this violent – and seemingly uncharacteristic – behaviour.

Soon afterwards, his wife Primrose stormed into the room where his peers were discussing the best way to dismiss him. Rudely, she informed the people at the meeting that her husband would never resign, proclaiming, 'You'll have to force him out!'

And this was exactly what they had to do. They forced him out of the practice and into a drug rehabilitation centre in 1975.

Two years later, his many convictions for drug offences, prescription fraud and forgery cost him a surprisingly low fine – just over £600. Shipman's conviction for forgery is worth noting, because he was to use this skill later when faking signatures on a patently counterfeit will – that of his last victim, Katherine Grundy.

BACK TO WORK

Today, it is unlikely Harold Shipman would be allowed to handle drugs unsupervised, given his previous track record. However, within two years, he was back in business as a general practitioner in the Donneybrook Medical Centre in Hyde in the north of England. How readily he was accepted demonstrates his absolute self-confidence – and his ability to convince his peers of his sincerity. Again, he played the role of a dedicated, hardworking and community-minded doctor. He gained his patients' absolute trust and earned his colleagues' respect, but perhaps he was not watched carefully enough. In Hyde, Harold Shipman was home free – and free to kill!

A DIARY OF DEATH

Because of the nature of the Shipman case, it may never be possible to document every murder he committed, but it is estimated that he is responsible for the deaths of at least 236 patients over a 24-year period.

JEAN LILLEY, 58

Mrs Lilley was visited by Dr Shipman on the morning of her death on 25 April 1997. A neighbour became increasingly concerned about the length of time that the GP had been with Mrs Lilley, who was suffering from a cold. She found her friend's body within moments of the doctor leaving her home. An ambulance crew later said Mrs Lilley had been dead for some time, killed by a lethal dose of morphine. She was the only one of the 15 victims to have been married at the time of her death. Shipman contacted her husband by mobile phone to tell him his wife had died.

MARIE WEST, 81

On 6 March 1995, Harold Shipman injected Mrs West, his first victim, with a fatal dose of diamorphine (the medical term for heroin), unaware that her friend was in the next room. Shipman first told Mrs West's son that she had died of a massive stroke, then said it was a heart attack. Mrs West ran a clothes shop in Hyde, a suburb of Manchester, where all the victims came from.

KATHLEEN GRUNDY, 81

A former mayoress of Hyde and the last victim, Mrs Grundy (above) died on 24 June 1998. She was found fully clothed on a settee at home. Dr Shipman killed her with a heroin overdose on a visit to take a blood sample. He has also been found guilty forging her will and two letters to secure her £386,000 estate, as well as altering his medical records to suggest that the widow was addicted to morphine.

IRENE TURNER, 67

Mrs Turner was found dead fully clothed on her bed by her neighbour, after Dr Shipman had called at Mrs Turner's house on 11 July 1996. Earlier, he had asked the neighbour if she could help pack Mrs Turner's belongings for hospital, but told her to wait for a few minutes before going over. Morphine was later found in Mrs Turner's body.

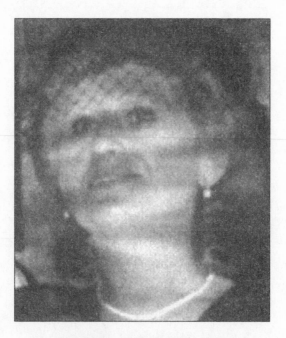

BIANKA POMFRET, 49

Mrs Pomfret, a German divorcee, was found dead at her home by her son William on the same day she had been visited by Shipman, on 10 December 1997. Excessive morphine levels were found in her body, but the GP claimed Mrs Pomfret had complained to him of chest pains on the day of her death. He fabricated a false medical history to cover his tracks after killing her.

KATHLEEN WAGSTAFF, 81

Shipman confused Mrs Wagstaff with another patient, Anne Royal, whose daughter was married to Kathleen's son Peter, and called on the wrong person on 9 December 1997 to announce she had died. Harold Shipman visited Angela Wagstaff at her workplace to tell her her mother had died, but the dead woman was in fact her mother-in-law Kathleen. After injecting Mrs Wagstaff with, morphine, Shipman put her death down to heart disease.

LIZZIE ADAMS, 77

Mrs Adams, a retired sewing machinist, died at home on 28 February 1997. Dr Shipman stated that she had died of pneumonia and pretended to call for an ambulance, although no such call was made.

NORAH NUTTALL, 65

Mrs Nuttall, a widow, died on 26 January 1998 after visiting Shipman's surgery for cough medicine. The GP later visited Mrs Nuttall at her home, where her son Anthony found his mother slumped in a chair.

MAUREEN WARD, 57

Mrs Ward, a former college lecturer, died on 18 February 1998. Although she had been suffering from cancer, she was not ill at the time of her death. Dr Shipman claimed she died of a brain tumour.

WINIFRED MELLOR, 73

Mrs Mellor, a widow who had been Dr Shipman's patient for 18 years, was found dead on 11 May 1998 in a chair at home, with her left sleeve rolled up to suggest a heroin habit, following an earlier visit by Dr Shipman. He killed her with a fatal injection of morphine, and then returned to his surgery to create a false medical history to support a cause of death from coronary thrombosis.

JOAN MELIA, 73

Shipman murdered the divorcee on a visit to her home in Hyde on 12 June 1998. She was found dead by a neighbour in her living room, having earlier visited Dr Shipman at his surgery about a chest infection. Shipman issued a death certificate stating she had died from pneumonia and emphysema. Her body, later exhumed, was found to contain morphine. The GP also claimed to have phoned for an ambulance, but didn't.

IVY LOMAS, 63

Dr Shipman killed Mrs Lomas at his surgery on 29 May 1997 in Market Street, Hyde. He then saw three more patients before telling his receptionist that he had failed to resuscitate her. Morphine was later found in her body. She was such a regular there that Shipman told a police sergeant who was called after her death he thought her a nuisance. He joked that part of the seating area should be reserved for her and a plaque be put up.

MURIEL GRIMSHAW, 76

Mrs Grimshaw was found dead at her home on 14 July 1997. Shipman, who was called to examine her, said there was no need for a postmortem. Morphine was later found in her body.

MARIE QUINN, 67

Dr Shipman injected Mrs Quinn with morphine at her home on 24 November 1997. Shipman claimed she had contacted him complaining of feeling unwell before her death, but her telephone bills showed no such call was made.

PAMELA HILLIER, 68

Shipman gave Mrs Hillier's family a confusing account of how she had died, on 9 Feb 1998, saying she had high blood pressure, but that it wasn't high enough to give him major concern, although she had died from high blood pressure. He had in fact given her a lethal dose of morphine.

ANGELA WOODRUFF

In this macabre and still unfinished story, Shipman's former patients are grateful indeed he was finally stopped. The feeling that they could have been next will always haunt them, and there is little doubt that some owe their lives to a determined and intelligent woman named Angela Woodruff.

This lady's dogged determination to solve a mystery helped ensure that, on Monday, 31 January 2000, the jury at Preston Crown Court found Shipman guilty of murdering 15 of his patients and forging the will of Angela's beloved mother, Katherine Grundy.

Following her mother's burial Ms Woodruff returned to her home, where she received a troubling phone call from solicitors. They claimed to have a copy of Ms Grundy's will. A solicitor herself, Angela's own firm had always handled her mother's affairs, in fact her firm held the original document lodged in 1986. The moment she saw the badly typed, poorly worded paper, Angela Woodruff knew it was a fake. It left £386,000 to Dr Shipman.

It was at this time that Angela went to her local police. Her investigation results ultimately reached Detective Superintendent Bernard Postles. His own investigation convinced him Angela Woodruff's conclusions were accurate.

THE TRIAL BEGINS

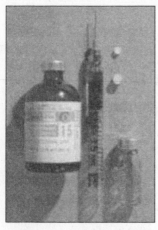

Shipman used morphine to overdose his victims.

To get solid proof of Kathleen Grundy's murder, a post-mortem was required which, in turn, required an exhumation order from the coroner. By the time the trial had begun, Det. Supt. Postles' team would be uncomfortably familiar with the process. Of the 15 killed, nine were buried and six cremated. Katherine Grundy's was the first grave opened. Her body was the first of the ongoing post-mortems. Her tissue and hair samples were sent to different labs for analysis, and the wait for results began.

At the same time, police raided the doctor's home and offices. It was timed so that Shipman had no chance of learning a body had been exhumed for a post mortem. Police had to be certain no evidence could be destroyed or concealed before their search. When the police arrived, Shipman showed no surprise; his approach was one of arrogance and contempt as the search warrant was read out.

One item crucial to police investigations was the typewriter used to type the bogus will. Shipman produced an old Brother manual portable, telling an improbable tale of how Ms Grundy sometimes borrowed it. This unbelievable story was to go against Shipman – especially when forensic scientists confirmed it was the machine used to type the counterfeit will and other such fraudulent documents.

The search of his house also yielded medical records, some mysterious jewellery and a surprise. The Shipman home was littered with filthy clothes, old newspapers and, for a doctor's home, it was nothing short of unsanitary. But an even bigger surprise was due.

When toxicologist Julie Evans filed her report on the cause of Ms Grundy's death, Det. Supt. Postles was astounded. It was discovered that the morphine level in the dead woman's body would undoubtedly have been the cause of death. Not only that, her death would have occurred within three hours of having received the fatal overdose.

Shipman would claim later that the stylish and conservative old lady was a junkie. Even today psychologists speculate on the possibility that he wanted to be caught. Otherwise, why would he hand them the typewriter and use a drug so easily traced back to him? Others believe he saw himself as invincible, believing that, as a doctor, his word would never be questioned.

The detective realized the case went far beyond one death and the scope of the investigation was broadened immediately.

THE VERDICT AND SENTENCE

The outcome of all the tests carried out was consistent. In case after case, it was proved that the victims had not died from old age or natural disease. Typically, morphine toxicity was the cause of death.

It took the judge, Mr Justice Forbes, two weeks to meticulously dissect the evidence heard by the jury. He urged caution, noting

Judge Justice Forbes presided in Shipman's trial.

that no witness had actually seen Shipman kill, and he also urged the jurors to use common sense in arriving at their verdict.

At 4.43 p.m. on Monday 31 January 2000, the foreman declared all the jury members' verdicts were unanimous – they found Shipman guilty on 15 counts of murder and one of forgery.

The disgraced doctor stood motionless, showing no sign of emotion as he heard the jurors' verdicts read. Wearing black, Shipman's wife, Primrose, also remained impassive. Her boys – one beside her and the other seated behind – looked down and seemed to visibly shrink on hearing the results.

In the public gallery, some gasped as Shipman's previous forgeries were described. The defence counsel asked that sentence be passed immediately.

The judge passed 15 life sentences for the murders and a four-year sentence for forgery.

Then the judge broke with the tradition that usually involves writing to the Home Secretary about his recommendations on length of the sentence:

'In the ordinary way, I would not do this in open court, but in your case I am satisfied justice demands that I make my views known at the conclusion of this trial . . . My recommendation will be that you spend the remainder of your days in prison.'

Fifteen murders, a mere fraction of the suspected death toll, had been dealt with and the 57 day trial was over. But there was one last life for Shipman to take.

At 6.20 a.m. on Tuesday, 13 January 2004, Harold Shipman was found hanging from the window bars in his cell in Wakefield Prison by a ligature made of bed sheets. Staff at the prison tried to revive him but he was pronounced dead at 8.10 a.m. As Shipman died before his 60th birthday, his widow, Primrose, will receive a pension of £10,000 per year, and a tax-free lump sum reported to be in excess of £100,000. Had he died after 60, the pension would have been halved, with no additional sum. This, it is believed, is the reason for his suicide.

Within hours of his suicide, the word "justice" had been graffitied 12 times across his former Hyde surgery.

IAN HUNTLEY
CHILD KILLER

The mother of Holly Wells could not have known that when she took the picture of her ten-year-old daughter with best friend Jessica Chapman at just after 5 p.m. on Sunday, 4 August 2002, in their beloved Manchester United football shirts, it would be a photo that would dominate front pages of both national and international newspapers for weeks to come – used first in the search for the two missing girls and then in the hunt for their murderer.

The truth of exactly what horror befell Jessica Chapman and Holly Wells after leaving Holly's house on that fateful day may never be completely revealed.

'TEENAGERS SCREAMING'

There were just two confirmed sightings of the girls before they simply vanished. The first, at 6.17 p.m., was on CCTV footage, which showed them walking happily together across the car park of the Ross Peers sports centre in Soham. The second, and last, sighting was at 6.30p.m. when they were seen walking along Sand Street by somebody who knew them. A jogger claims to have heard what he believed to be 'teenagers screaming' between 10 and 11 p.m. in the Warren Hill area near to Newmarket, but did not report it to the police until two days later.

The alarm was raised at 7.30 p.m. by Holly's parents when they realized that the girls were not upstairs playing, as they had originally thought. Consequently, at the break of dawn the following morning, police and volunteers began the search for the girls in Soham, and by midday, following the broadcast of a national appeal, the search was on, not only in Soham but across the country. By the end of the day, the girls' parents had attended a press conference in which they appealed for information regarding their daughters' safety and whereabouts. The police search continued into the night.

NATIONWIDE SEARCH

The girls' disappearance triggered one of the biggest police searches British history. Hundreds of local people, friends and neighbours had joined the police in the search for the girls, and amongst the volunteers was 29-year-old Ian Huntley, the caretaker at Soham Village College, which occupied the same site as the primary school that the girls attended. He not only helped in the search, but also informed the police that he too had seen the girls on the day

The last ever photograph of Holly Wells and Jessica Chapman alive. After the photograph was taken, they changed into trousers and set off on a walk, from which they were never to return.

they went missing. He told them how the girls had come to his door, 'happy' and 'giggly', and he had watched them walk away and continue down the road. He spoke to the media and even sought out Holly Wells's father, 'Kev' as he called him, to offer his condolences.

On Tuesday 6 August, the football star David Beckham joined the parents and families of the girls in appealing for Holly and Jessica to come home, and a reconstruction of the girls' last confirmed movements was filmed on Saturday 10 August.

The news that everyone had been dreading came a week later, on 17 August. Two naked and decomposing bodies had been found in a ditch in Lakenheath, Suffolk, approximately ten miles from the village of Soham where the girls lived. The nation's worst fears were confirmed when the police announced that these were indeed the bodies of Holly and Jessica. The following week, the burnt remains of the clothing that the girls had been wearing when they disappeared was discovered by police in a bin in the Soham Village College.

Reward Posters for Holly Wells and Jessica Chapman are shown outside St. Andrew's Church in Soham, Cambridgeshire.

THE CARING CARETAKER

It had very quickly become clear to the police that Ian Huntley, the Soham caretaker who had been so helpful with their enquiries and who had been happy to talk to the media, was one of the last people to see the girls alive. They arrested him on the day the bodies of the two girls were found, and three days later he was charged with both of their murders. His girlfriend, Maxine Carr, a temporary teaching assistant in Holly and Jessica's class, was also arrested, although charged not in connection with the murder of the girls, but for lying to the police and perverting the course of justice in providing a false alibi for Huntley's whereabouts on the day of the murder. Both denied the charges against them.

Parents of murdered Soham schoolgirls Holly Wells and Jessica Chapman, Kevin and Nicola Wells and Leslie and Sharon Chapman hold a press conference

'PANICKED AND FROZE'

The courtcase, which lasted over a year, made headline news nationally and worldwide, and in it, Huntley did finally admit that the girls had died in his house. However, he denied murder. Rather, he claimed that the deaths of both girls were the result of a tragic sequence of events. He claims to have been outside his house washing his dog when the girls passed by, and he noticed that Holly was suffering with a nose bleed. He therefore invited the girls into his house and took them up to his bathroom, where he intended to curb the flow of blood from Holly's nose. Holly sat on the edge of the bath while he dampened a tissue to hold to her face. However, as he approached her with the tissue, he stumbled and bumped into her, causing her to fall backwards into the bath, already filled with approximately 45cm of water. She banged her head as she fell, which caused Jessica to begin screaming at Huntley, accusing him of pushing her friend. To stop Jessica screaming, Huntley placed his hand over her mouth, where it remained until he realized that instead of simply calming the second little girl, her body was now limp and no longer supporting itself. As he let go of Jessica, her body slumped to the floor. He turned to the bath, where Holly's lifeless body lay. He checked her pulse, no longer beating, and then put his face close to Jessica's, where there was no longer breath. He said he 'panicked and froze' when he realized what had happened, unable even to attempt to revive them. His next memory of the events was being sat on the carpet in his bathroom, next to a pile of his own vomit. He knew he should call the police, he said, but also knew that they would never believe that such a tragedy had occurred when he failed to believe it himself.

He pleaded guilty to manslaughter only, but went on to concede all the other given facts of the case – that he had bundled the bodies of Holly and Jessica into his car, bending their legs to make them fit, cut the clothing from them – their red Manchester United shirts, trousers, underwear, the bra which Holly's mother had bought for her only the day before – and left the corpses to bum in a remote ditch where the nettles grew thickly. He had then taken the girls' clothing and deposited it in a bin at Soham Village College.

Prosecutor Richard Latham supported this with forensic evidence that hairs, proven to be Huntley's, were found amongst the charred remains of the clothes in the bin, and that his fingerprints were present on the bin liner. He also presented evidence regarding Huntley's car. All four tyres on the car had been replaced the day following Jessica and Holly's disappearance. Latham claimed that this was to prevent his car being traced in any way to the girls' bodies.

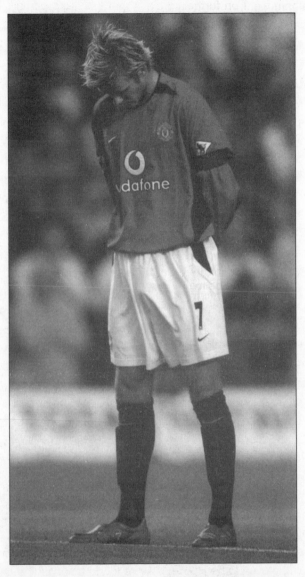

Holly and Jessica's football hero, David Beckham, looks to the ground during the minute silence during the Barclaycard Premiership match between Chelsea and Manchester United in London on August 23, 2002, a tribute to the two murdered school children.

Latham went on further to claim that Huntley's primary motive had been sexual. He asserts that the girls were lured into Huntley's house, possibly in the belief that Maxine Carr was inside, and that when his advances towards one or the other had been rejected, both girls had had to die. 'They had to die in his own selfish self-interest. Each were potential witnesses – he was quite merciless.'

Huntley's version of events, that the death of the two girls had simply been the result of a tragic accident, was believed neither by the public, nor the jury who found him guilty on two counts of murder, the most serious of all the charges he could have faced, and when trial judge Justice Moses sentenced him to two life imprisonments a hushed 'yes' echoed around the courtroom. Moses told Huntley that he was 'the only person who knows how you murdered them', and said that he displayed 'no regret' after the murders, even increasing the pain of the families by continuing to lie and deceive the police and investigators.

The burnt remains of one of the red Manchester United shirts belonging to the two murdered ten year old girls, which were found along with traces of Huntley's hair in the school grounds where he worked.

CATALOGUE OF OFFENCES

Information regarding Huntley's past had to be kept private during the trial in order not to influence the court, but on the conclusion of his case, a dark and disturbing catalogue of offences against children and teenagers was made public. It emerged that between the years of 1995 and 1999, Huntley was investigated by police no less than ten times following accusations of rape, under-age sex, assault on children and adults, and burglary.

Current regulations state that anybody applying to work with or around children has to undergo local police checks to ensure their suitability. Huntley's past went undetected by two police forces, Cambridgeshire and Humberside. Humberside, where the alleged offences had been reported, defended themselves by saying that the Data Protection Act declares it unlawful to hold data concerning allegations which did not lead to a conviction. They have faced criticism from other police forces who believe this to be too strict an enforcement of the Act. Perhaps aware of these regulations anyway, Huntley had changed his name when applying for the job in Soham to Ian Nixon – his mother's maiden name.

Much is still not known about what actually happened inside Huntley's house. It is reported that Huntley and Carr had cleaned the house of every DNA trace of the girls. There were no hairs, blood or saliva and not a single fingerprint. The clean-up operation had centred around the dining room, although what happened to the girls in that room has never emerged.

'LOVELY GIRLS'

Maxine Carr, although not present on the day of the girls' deaths, was living with Huntley in the house where the girls died. On that fateful Sunday, she was in fact visiting her parents in Grimsby, although told police that she had been at home with Huntley all day in order to protect him. On 20 August, she was charged with lying

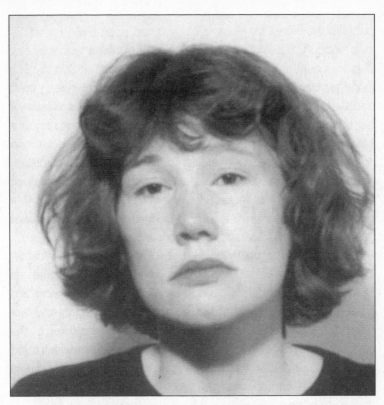

Police photograph of Maxine Carr following her arrest in August 2002. She was found guilty of conspiring to pervert the course of justice, but cleared of helping an offender.

to the police. She appeared in court on charges of assisting an offender and perverting the course of justice. In response to the first charge, she claimed that she had no knowledge of what had actually transpired in the house, and had only lied to protect Huntley, believing him to be innocent. She was found not guilty. She was therefore found guilty of the second, less serious, charge of perverting the course of justice and received a sentence of three and a half years' imprisonment. By the time the trial had concluded though, she had already served 16 months in prison, almost half of her sentence, and was later released on probation on 10 May 2004. During the trial she spoke of Holly and Jessica as 'lovely girls', and referred to Huntley as 'that thing', saying that she would not take the blame for his actions, and had been feeling guilty for long enough, believing that she could have prevented Holly and Jessica's deaths if she had been in the house on that Sunday. The judge proclaimed her imminent release to be a sentence in itself, and that she would lead a terrible existence, forever looking over her shoulder. For her involvement with Ian Huntley, Carr is now a hate figure and considered to be at such a risk from the public that she has been issued with a new identity. Threats have already been made on her life, some claiming that she would be dead within a week of her release from prison. Consequently, on her release from Foxton Hall Prison in Derbyshire, Maxine Carr was moved to a secret location pending her official release.

As a result of speculation by British newspapers on whether Carr would be given plastic surgery, or sent to live abroad, an injunction was granted by London's High Court preventing any photographs of Carr, or details of her whereabouts, treatment or new life, being published. Her movements may be protected by the courts for the rest of her life. This was granted for reasons of her health and safety, and also to enable the Probation Service to supervise her and ensure that she settles back into society and doesn't re-offend.

However, documents containing full details of her release and new identity were stolen from the car of a Home Office official parked in Hampstead Heath just days before her release date. In spite of this, the Home Office confirmed that her release had not been compromised and would go ahead as planned. They stated that there was nothing in the stolen documents that could give away her new location and identity.

Ian Huntley is no safer in prison than Maxine Carr is out of it. Knocked unconscious by another inmate who is now considered a 'hero' by fellow prisoners, Huntley has reportedly become the target of a deadly 'race' between two prison gangs to murder him. Bets have been placed on which will succeed, and prison guards are on 'extra high alert' for his safety. Rumours have leaked to the prison authorities that plans are first to disfigure Huntley by throwing boiling water on him, and then to kill him. An unnamed source described Huntley as a 'scared rabbit' in prison. He had previously been rushed to hospital in a 'life-threatening condition' having taken an overdose in an attempt to take his own life.

Candles are lit in remembrance of Holly Wells and Jessica Chapman inside St Andrew's Church on August 18, 2002 in Soham, Cambridgeshire.

HUNTLEY'S HOUSE OF HORROR

The house, 5 College Close, owned by the local education authority, has been pulled down, along with the hangar at the Soham Village College in which the burned clothing was discovered. Until recently, for legal reasons, the house could not be touched, but lawyers for Huntley gave their consent to demolition, stating that no further evidence from the house would need to be used in any appeal. Plans for the sites are to be discussed with the relatives of Jessica and Holly.

GRAHAM YOUNG

THE BROADMOOR POISONER

*Is it possible for a child to be born evil? Graham Young was
a prodigy in poison, experimenting with deadly potions even
before he was 16. He killed his family and friends as if they
were laboratory rats.*

Even as a small child, Graham Young was entranced by poisons.
Other people may regard such substances with alarm and
caution but Graham played with them, learnt their various deadly
properties and longed to use them.

Like Ian Brady, the infamous Moors Murderer, Graham Young
had a lonely childhood, and in his sullen resentment of the world,
turned to other outsiders in his search for role models. Dr
Crippen, the wife murderer, was an idol, as was the Victorian

poisoner, William Palmer. In contemplating their lives and dreadful acts, Graham Young found a kind of solace which he never got from his family.

He was born in September 1947, and his mother died when he was just three months old. He was cared for by his father's sister, Auntie Winifred, and her husband, Uncle Jack, and theirs was an affectionate household. But at the age of two his life changed when he was sent to live with his father, who had married a 26-year-old woman called Molly. Psychologists would later say that 'the terrible coldness' that characterized Young was formed by the trauma of separation from his first home. He never trusted any affection after that, believing only that it would end in pain and rejection.

Relations with his stepmother were cordial but she never lavished on him the brand of intense loving he craved. Perhaps she found it difficult, for Graham was rummaging through the chemist's rubbish bins in his search for poisons, and was reading books on Satanism by the time he was nine years old. He began wearing a swastika badge that he found at a jumble sale and refused to take it off, even for his teachers at school. Yet Graham was an exceptionally intelligent child, with a strong scientific ability. To celebrate his achievement in passing the 11-plus examination, his father gave the boy his first chemistry set.

This gift was the key to the wonderful world of poisons that Graham longed to master. The phials and bunsen burners, the laboratory pipettes and crucibles became his toys at an age when most boys have their pockets stuffed with conkers and fudge. His private games were also more sinister than those of the normal child. Graham liked to witness the death throes of the mice that he fed with the poisons he brewed from his chemistry set. When his stepmother angrily removed a live mouse and demanded that he stop bringing them into the house, he drew a picture of a craggy tombstone toppling over a mound, inscribed with the words: 'In Hateful Memory of Molly Young, R.I.P.' Graham made sure that the poor woman saw this nasty little drawing.

The youngster took to stealing chemicals from his school and he took to carrying a bottle of ether from which he would frequently take sniffs; he raided his stepmother's cosmetics cabinet to get at nail polish remover, which he used to kill a frog in one of his experiments in the effects of poison. By the time he was 12, his teachers at the John Kelly Secondary School in Willesden knew that Graham had an unusual expertise, not only in poisons, but in his general pharmaceutical knowledge. The child knew the ingredients of most household medicines and was able to diagnose minor illnesses.

But medicine and its life-saving properties were not of real interest to the child boffin. He preferred poisons and their deadly effects. When he was 13, Graham found a book that would forever change his life. It was the story of the nineteenth-century poisoner Dr Edward Pritchard, who killed his wife and his mother with the poison antimony. Antimony, a slow-working toxin, causes cramps, nausea and swellings in the victim. These symptoms have often led to an incorrect diagnosis from doctors, and this fact has, naturally, made the poison a favourite among murderers.

Chemist Geoffrey Reis in the High Street, Neasden, sold Graham Young the poison antimony. The boy lied about his age and claimed he was 17. Reis explained to the police that the boy's knowledge of poisons was so vast, and he outlined in such detail the chemical experiments in which he intended to use the restricted merchandise, that the chemist naturally assumed him to be older than a mere 13-year-old. And neither was Graham Young strictly truthful in describing his experiments to the chemist.

Chris Williams was one of Graham's few schoolboy friends who shared his love of chemistry. He had even invited Chris to his bedroom laboratory to share the pleasure of watching mice die in agony. But Chris Williams began hanging around with another boy, and Graham interpreted this as a personal rejection. Chris had to be punished. Graham began to lace his friend's sandwiches with antimony and watched the results with satisfaction. After Chris had suffered two violent vomiting attacks, his family sent him to a specialist who was unable to diagnose the problem. Throughout the early part of 1961, Graham continued to administer doses of poison to his school chum.

David Tilson, a victim who survived the poisons.

EPIDEMIC OF POISONING

Young took to carrying a phial of antimony around with him all the time, calling it 'my little friend'. But his stepmother found the bottle, marked with a skull and crossbones, and put a stop to her stepson's shopping trips when she herself informed the chemist, Mr Reis, of Graham's age. Thwarted but by no means defeated, Graham switched to a new supplier, and a new target. Molly Young would be punished for this.

In October and November 1961, Mrs Young suffered severe vomiting attacks. Then Graham's father experienced similar symptoms, as did his Auntie Winifred. On one occasion, Graham spiked his own food in error and he, too, was violently ill, but this did not deter the young poisoner. Using antimony tartrate which he bought from Edgar Davies – another chemist similarly fooled by his advanced knowledge of poisons – he moved on to his stepsister. The girl tasted something odd and spat out her tea, accusing her mother of leaving some washing-up liquid in the cup.

Graham Young was incarcerated in hospitals and prisons, but he still managed to experiment with his poisons.

Winifred was the first to be diagnosed as a poison victim when she had to be helped from a London Underground train on her way to work one morning, in the summer of 1962. Dizzy, her eyes blinded with pain and feeling very ill, she was rushed by ambulance to the Middlesex Hospital where a doctor said she was suffering from belladonna poisoning, the toxin released from the berries of the deadly nightshade weed. Winifred believed that her nephew was to blame, but a search of his room failed to give evidence to her fears. Molly Young's health continued to decline as Graham fed her increasing doses of the antimony tartrate. Early in 1962 she died. At the age of 14, Graham Young had committed the perfect murder. He was arrested on suspicion of causing his stepmother's death, but he was released without charge. Molly was cremated and the evidence, the poison in her bloodstream, went with her.

The sweet face of a boy, but the Young family were not entirley fooled. They knew something was wrong with the child, Graham.

Graham Young was now assured of his powers to punish those who annoyed or rejected him. Besides, he still had some unfinished business. Dad was to be fed further doses of antimony, as was his unfortunate schoolfriend, who continued to suffer violent attacks of nausea, but was still alive. Fred Young collapsed and was rushed to Willesden Hospital where doctors diagnosed arsenic poisoning. 'How ridiculous!' sneered Graham when he visited his father in hospital. 'Fancy not knowing how to tell the difference between antimony and arsenic poisoning!' He explained to the doctors that his father showed all the symptoms of antimony poisoning, but offered no explanation as to how the poison had entered his father's system. His father was informed that he was lucky to be alive, but that his liver was permanently damaged. He was allowed home, but was back in hospital within a couple of days because Graham could not resist giving his father another dose in his morning tea.

The Young family were, by now, thoroughly alarmed by their suspicions that their own Graham might be causing their various illnesses. They did not like the way Graham seemed to brighten up and become keenly interested whenever he was discussing the finer points of poison with hospital staff. His father told Aunt Winifred to keep an eye on him, but it was to be his chemistry master at school who spotted the boy's toxic ways. The teacher went through Graham's desk at school, discovering notebooks with lurid pictures of men in their death throes, empty bottles of poison by their sides. He discovered phials of antimony tartrate alongside the drawings, plus detailed notes of what dosages of particular poisons are needed to kill an adult human being. After voicing his concerns to the school headmaster, the two teachers decided to inform the police. The police, in turn, decided to get a psychiatrist to help them trap Graham.

Posing as a careers guidance officer, the psychiatrist interviewed the boy, asking him what he would like to do when he left school. The doctor was both astounded and horrified at the detailed knowledge the boy had about poisons and their effects. One by one Graham reeled them off, leaving no doubt whatsoever in the psychiatrist's mind that this boy was a psychopath. His report prompted the police to search Young's room. This revealed seven different types of poison stashed in various hiding places and included a copious amount of antimony tartrate.

Graham Young encountered the police when he came home from school. He reeked of the ether he habitually sniffed, and vehemently denied any involvement in the poisoning of his family. But Young's vanity overcame him. As he liked to brag to the doctors and the psychiatrist, showing off his knowledge of poison, so he could not resist telling the police that he was a successful poisoner.

He confessed all, listing the dosages, the times and the methods he used to dispense the poison.

At Ashford Remand Centre he was subjected to a battery of psychiatric and psychological testing. The doctors who examined him recognized that his was a rare problem, for Young was incapable of comprehending his guilt. 'He has a distinct lack of moral sense, an idea that he is neither bound to nor governed by the rules which apply to other members in society,' was the official verdict. Indeed, Young relished telling the doctors, who were probing his warped emotional state, about his potions and how he loved his father, but that he came to view his parent as a guinea pig for experiments in poison. He told them: 'I chose my family because they were close at hand, where I could observe and note the results of my experiments.' There was no remorse, however. 'I love my antimony,' he explained. 'I love the power it gives me.'

The case of the schoolboy poisoner captured the public imagination when he came before the stern judge Mr Justice Melford Stevenson on 6 July, 1962, at the Old Bailey. This is Britain's highest court where, half a century before, Graham's hero Dr Crippen had been condemned to death.

Graham Young was charged with poisoning his father, his aunt and his school chum. He spoke only once at his trial, to plead guilty to the charges, but a statement that he made while in custody was read out. Graham told the police: 'I knew that the doses I was giving were not fatal, but I knew I was doing wrong. It grew on me like a drug habit, except it was not me who was taking the drugs. I realized how stupid I have been with these poisons. I knew this all along but I could not stop it.'

A psychiatrist, after testifying that Young was suffering from a psychopathic disorder, recommended the accused be incarcerated in Broadmoor, Britain's top security mental hospital. The judge asked whether a grim, forbidding place such as Broadmoor was the right institution for such a young boy, but after further testimony from Dr Donald Blair, a psychiatrist who had also examined Young, he – the judge – was left with little choice. Blair told the court: 'There is no doubt in my mind that this youth is, at present, a very serious danger to other people. His intense obsession and almost exclusive interest in drugs and their poisoning effect is not likely to change, and he could well repeat his cool, calm, calculating administration of these poisons at any time.'

Young was sent to Broadmoor with an instruction that he should not be released without the permission of the Home Secretary. It was not, however, the last that the world would hear of Graham Young and his potions.

John Williams who told the court of Young's attempts to kill him with poison.

POISONER BEHIND BARS

Far from being an unsuitable place for Graham, Broadmoor was actually a home from home for him. The institute is a hospital, after all, and the young poisoner was surrounded by all the medicines and drugs and poisons that he could wish for. He enjoyed lecturing the staff on toxins, and often gave advice to nurses on drugs when no doctors were on hand. Suspicion, however, fell upon him when a fellow inmate, 23-year-old double murderer John Berridge, died of cyanide poisoning. But Graham was never charged with his murder, although he spent many hours explaining to other inmates how the poison could be extracted from the leaves of the laurel bushes that grew in the hospital grounds.

Young's room in Broadmoor became a shrine to Nazism, heavily decorated with swastikas. He even grew a toothbrush moustache and combed his hair in a fashion that imitated that of Adolf Hitler. He managed to secure a 'green card' – the special pass allowing him to freely roam the hospital wards and gardens. The pass was issued by the psychiatric staff in contradiction to the wishes and advice of the day-to-day nursing staff. The card gave Young the opportunity to collect leaves and plants that contained poisonous materials, and to steal chemicals. The nursing staff often found jars of poison, not on the shelves where they were supposed to be, but in odd places. Young owned up to hiding some of these, but not all. Inexplicable outbreaks of stomach aches and cramps were endured by both staff and patients; hindsight dictates that Young had been busy dispensing his potions freely round the large prison hospital.

With the support of two senior doctors who did not want to see him institutionalized for the rest of his life, Graham was able to convince the parole board to free him for Christmas in 1970. He spent it with his Auntie Win, but his return to Broadmoor after the holidays made him more resentful than ever. He wrote a note that nursing staff found, saying: 'When I get out of here I intend to kill one person for every year I have spent inside.'

Nursing staff say they heard him boasting, when he thought no staff were listening, how he wanted to be the most infamous poisoner since Crippen. The note he wrote remained on their files, yet Graham Young was released after nine years. At the age of 23 he returned to his forgiving Auntie Winifred at her home in Hemel Hempstead, Hertfordshire, before moving on to a hostel in Chippenham where he began his new life.

Fredrick Young, Graham's father and the long-suffering Aunt Winnie. Graham tried to poison both of them.

ANOTHER FRIEND POISONED

Within weeks he was up to his old tricks again. A keen amateur footballer called Trevor Sparkes, who was with Young at a training centre, suffered cramps and pain over a six-month period, and was so debilitated by the mysterious 'illness' that he would never play football again. Sparkes would testify that he and Young enjoyed a friendship, and it never occurred to the footballer that he was being systematically poisoned by his friend.

In April 1971, Graham saw an advertisement offering employment for a storeman with the John Hadland Company of Bovingdon in Hertfordshire. Hadland's was a well-established family firm that manufactured high-grade optical and photographic equipment. Graham impressed Managing Director Godfrey Foster at the interview, and explained that his long break from regular employment was due to a nervous breakdown. Foster checked up with the training centre and also Broadmoor, and he received such glowing references as to the young man's abilities and recovery that he offered him the job without hesitation.

On Monday, 10 May 1971, Graham Young arrived at Hadland's. The company thought they were getting a storeman. In reality, they had hired an angel of death. Young rented a bedsit, and the cupboards and shelves were soon filled with a collection of poisons. At work he was regarded as a quiet, remote young man unless the conversation turned to politics or chemistry when he became belligerent and articulate. His best friend at work was 41-year-old Ron Hewitt whose job he was taking. Ron stayed on to show the new man the ropes and introduced him to the other hands at the plant. Many showed great kindness to Young, lending him money and giving him cigarettes when he had none. Young repaid their warmth by rushing to serve them from the morning tea trolley.

On Thursday, 3 June, less than a month after Graham started work, Bob Egle, 59, who worked as storeroom boss, was taken ill with diarrhoea, cramps and nausea. Next, Ron Hewitt fell violently ill, suffering the same symptoms but with burning sensations at the back of his throat. Workers at Hadland's called the mystery pains 'the bug'. In fact, the symptoms were caused by doses of thallium, an extremely toxic poison. Young bought the poison from chemists in London, and then laced his workmates' tea with the deadly but tasteless and odourless chemical. On Wednesday, 7 July, Bob Egle died. His was a horrible, painful death, yet there was no inquest on his body because doctors diagnosed his illness as bronchial-pneumonia linked to polyneuritis.

In September, after a relatively pain-free summer for the staff at Hadland's because Young was often absent from work, Fred Biggs, a part-time worker, died after suffering agonizing cramps and pains over a 20-day period. Young feigned sympathy for him, as he had

97

for his other victims. 'Poor old Fred,' he said to colleague, Diana Smart 'It's terrible. I wonder what went wrong with him. I was very fond of Fred.' Four other workers fell victim to awful illnesses, two of them losing all their hair, followed by severe cases of depression.

The company became so concerned by the poor health of their workforce, that they called in a local doctor, Iain Anderson, to check the employees, but he was unable to determine the source of the 'bug'. But then Anderson talked to Graham Young who, unable to suppress his vanity, reeled off mind-numbing statistics about poisons and their effects and Anderson's amazement turned to suspicion. He consulted the company management, who called Scotland Yard. The police ran a background check on all company employees, while forensic scientists from the government research station at Aldermaston were asked to analyse samples taken from the poorly members of staff. The scientists proved that thallium had caused the deaths and the illnesses among the staff at Hadland's. Graham Young was arrested at his father's house, and as he was led away, asked the police: 'Which ones are they doing me for, then?'

However, in custody Young claimed that he was innocent, despite the fact that a phial of thallium was found in his jacket pocket and a list of six names of Hadland's employees was found in his bedsit. The list was significant: it included the two men who had died and the four stricken with horrible illnesses. But Young could not resist for long his need to boast.

He detailed his first murder, that of his stepmother, and explained why he decided to poison his workmates. Graham Young said: 'I suppose I had ceased to see them as people – or, more correctly, a part of me had. They became guinea pigs.' Detective Chief Superintendent Harvey Young, in charge of the case, warned Graham that this confession could put him in jail for life. But the prisoner said: 'You have to prove that I did it.' He intended to withdraw his statement in court, which in due course he did.

On 3 December, Graham Young was charged with murdering Egle after the analysis of the ashes of his cremated corpse revealed traces of thallium in them. He pleaded not guilty. He was also charged with the murder of Fred Biggs and the attempted murders of two others and of further administering poison to two others.

In prison, Young enquired of his guards whether Madame Tussaud's waxworks in London were planning to put his effigy next to those of his heroes, Hitler and the poisoner Palmer. He threatened to kill himself in the dock of the court if he were found guilty. But there were no theatricals from the prisoner when he was convicted on all charges by a jury that took less than an hour to deliberate on the evidence. After a brief chat with his family, he was taken away to begin a life sentence in July 1972.

Graham Young taken into court by law officers. He was given a long sentence, but died in prison – not of self-administered poison but a heart attack.

A DEADLY FUNGUS

Young was not sent back to Broadmoor but, initially, was sent to Wormwood Scrubs, then to the top security Park Lane Mental Hospital near Liverpool. He was in this institution for two years before officials realized he had lost none of his madness. In 1990, they discovered that Graham had grown, in the prison grounds, a deadly fungus that he mixed with his own excrement to concoct a deadly toxin.

He was transferred to the top security prison of Parkhurst on the Isle of Wight where he was found dead in his cell on 2 August 1990. At first, officials thought that he had killed himself with one of his own poisons, but a post-mortem revealed that a heart attack had been the cause of death.

There were few people to weep for him. His sister, also called Winifred, felt sad for him. She said that he craved publicity and infamy, and he certainly achieved these ambitions. But she also said that he was depressive and lonely. When she suggested he ease his loneliness by going to social clubs or dances, he replied: 'Nothing like that can help me, I'm afraid. You see, there is this terrible coldness inside of me . . .'

Broadmoor, the mental hospital where Young was confined.

ORGANIZED CRIME

THE KRAY TWINS
A LETHAL DOUBLE ACT

From playground bullies via the boxing ring, East End twins Reggie and Ronnie Kray went on to build a gangland empire, the like of which London had never seen before. 'The Firm' allowed no liberties to be taken, and was feared by all.

On 24 October 1933 twin boys were born to Mrs Violet Kray of 178 Vallance Road, Bethnal Green. She named them Reginald and Ronald.

The twins grew up in London's East End, surrounded by street traders, boxers and petty criminals. Fighting was a way of life for children in Bethnal Green. But Reggie and Ronnie seemed to derive enormous pleasure out of terrifying and hurting other human beings.

BOXERS

At 14 they found another, more acceptable outlet for their violent tendencies – boxing.

Both lads showed real promise as amateurs, but demonstrated a completely different approach to the sport, a difference which was reflected in their personalities as men. Reggie was a skilful and resourceful boxer, whereas Ronnie was a slugger, totally fearless and vicious. The net result of these contrasting styles, however, was the same. They both won every fight.

At 16 the twins turned professional and maintained their unbeaten record, until their careers were brought to an abrupt halt. They both got into a street fight, during which they beat up a police constable. They were let off with a probationary sentence. But fight managers dislike boxers with a reputation for violence outside the ring, since any serious conviction usually costs a fighter his licence.

The next watershed in the Krays' young lives came in March 1952, when they were called up to do their National Service. They had no intention of spending two years in the Royal Fusiliers and made that immediately and absolutely clear. The boys absconded and were back at Vallance Road for tea after a mere six hours of army service.

They were arrested, escaped, arrested again and escaped again. They continued their running battle with the army for more than a year before the Royal Fusiliers gave up on them. After spending nine months in a military prison at Shepton Mallet they were given a dishonourable discharge.

MANAGEMENT PROSPECTS

When they were released in 1953, the twins went straight back to the East End.

While they considered their career prospects, the twins established semi-residence in the Regal Billiard Hall in the Mile End Road. It was a seedy, down-at-heel place which had become a popular hang-out for small-time criminals.

Around the time the Krays arrived at the Regal, there was a sudden outbreak of violence and vandalism. The twins never seemed to be directly involved, but there were fights every night and there were anonymous threats to burn the place down.

The manager eventually left and the twins approached the owners with an offer. They would pay the owners £5 a week to take the hall over. The owners accepted, the Krays became managers, and the violence and vandalism stopped as abruptly as it had

The twins were adored by their mother Vi, for whom they could do no wrong. But their career in boxing soon came to an end when they were put on probation for beating up a police constable.

started.

Reggie, who proved an astute businessman, set about renovating and redecorating the Regal and before long it was becoming a successful commercial concern.

It also continued to serve as a meeting point for local criminals, but now the Krays offered them a genuine service. There were lock-up cubicles under the seats for thieves' tools, and stolen goods could be stashed round the back. The Krays received a cut of every job planned or executed from their premises.

The billiard hall was now making good money, and the Krays were supplementing this with extortion. Clubs, billiard halls, unlicensed gambling dens and illicit bookmakers from Bethnal Green and Mile End were soon paying a 'pension' to 'the Firm', as the Kray gang was now known.

Despite their growing reputation, however, the Krays still had no real power. Each section of the East End had its own 'guv'nor', and the twins hadn't yet achieved 'guv'nor' status.

However, their activities were causing some displeasure with these established gang bosses. There were a number of bloody showdowns and, despite being outnumbered and outgunned by their rivals, the twins always seemed to come out on top.

ASPIRATION 'UP WEST'

By 1955, the Firm was the established power through Hackney and Mile End to Walthamstow. And they were starting to make real money.

But the twins had their sights set on bigger things. Reggie wanted the 'good ife', the wealth that West End crime offered and Ronnie craved the kudos that came with being a big-time gangland boss.

Ronnie spent most of his time planning elaborate deals and alliances which would establish the Firm 'up West', but none of them ever quite worked out. The Krays were too wild and too dangerous for the established West End gangs to deal with. They closed ranks and shut the twins out.

This frustrated Ronnie, and the more frustrated he became, the more violent his thinking became. He grew increasingly paranoid and psychotic, toting his guns in public and threatening to 'do' people all the time.

Ronnie finally had his chance to use his gun for real when a young docker tried to cheat one of the Firm's associates. The docker gave Ronnie some lip and Ronnie promptly shot him in the leg.

Everyone in the East End, including the police, knew that the Firm was responsible for the shooting, and after a few hours they picked up a man they believed to be Ronnie Kray and put him into an identification parade.

'Yes, but I'm not Ronald Kray,' said the man in the line-up. 'I'm Reggie Kray. I can prove it – and, what's more, I can prove I wasn't anywhere near where this bloke says he was shot.' The police, angry and embarrassed, had no option but to free Reggie with an apology.

From the Regal Billiard Hall in London's Mile End Road, the Kray twins soon moved on to bigger and better enterprises. At a charity evening in the Kentucky Club, they line up for a phoograph with brother Charles (behind Ronnie, right).

OUT FOR REVENGE

The police, who do not like to be bested, now had it in for the Krays. Their chance to nail one of them came the following year, in 1956.

Terry Martin, a street trader from Stepney, had been taking 'extreme liberties', and Ronnie decided that he needed 'teaching a lesson'. He dragged Martin out of the Britannia pub in Watney Street, slashed him twice on the head with a bayonet, stabbed him in the shoulder and then kicked him unconscious.

Ronnie was being driven home in his new black Buick when police picked him up. They found a crowbar and a bayonet in the car and when they asked how he got blood on his shirt, Ronnie shrugged 'I 'ad a nose bleed, di'n' I?'

Ronnie was found guilty of grievous bodily harm and sentenced to three years' imprisonment.

It was the first time since they were born that the twins had been separated for more than a few days at a time, and most East End pundits said it would be the end of the Firm.

They were wrong. Reggie, freed from his brother's manic influence, not only continued to run the gang's illegal activities but also embarked on several legitimate enterprises. He rented an empty shop in Bow Road with his older brother Charles and converted it into a drinking club, the Double R – in honour of himself and his absent brother.

The club was a huge success, not only with local villains but also with certain members of the entertainment and sporting fraternities who considered it was chic to rub shoulders with the criminal element.

INSANITY

In prison, Ronnie Kray soon showed signs of severe mental illness. He became paranoid and depressed and complained of 'hearing voices'. He couldn't sleep, and wouldn't eat because he was convinced that he was being poisoned.

He was transferred to the psychiatric wing of Winchester Prison for observation. There he was put on sedatives and showed some signs of improvement until the morning he received news that his favourite auntie, Rose, had died of cancer.

By that evening Ronnie was totally incoherent and had to be strapped into a straitjacket for his own protection. The following day, doctors at Winchester certified Ronald Kray as legally insane. Ronnie was transferred to Long Grove Hospital near Epsom where he received the very best psychiatric treatment. He was diagnosed as a paranoid schizophrenic.

Doctors treated his illness with a new wonder drug called Stematol. Within days Ronnie was stabilized and was showing marked signs of improvement. But he was still technically insane which meant that, despite the fact that he had only a year of his sentence to serve, the authorities could detain him indefinitely.

Bride and Groom and best man pose for the camera at the wedding reception.

108

Alarmed by this prospect, Reggie Kray decided something had to be done to rectify the situation. He drove up to Long Grove, switched clothes with his brother and took his place in the hospital while Ronnie walked to freedom.

On the run, Ronnie was taken to see a top Harley Street psychiatrist who, not knowing his patient's true identity, pronounced him sane.

But Ronald Kray was most certainly not sane. Without close medical supervision, his condition deteriorated rapidly. Even Reggie was eventually forced to face the fact that his brother needed professional help. So he did the unthinkable. He called the police.

Ronnie was returned not to hospital, but to jail to complete his sentence. He was no longer technically insane so the ploy had worked. He was released in the spring of 1959.

CLEVER BUSINESS MOVES

During Ronnie's absence, Reggie and Charles Kray had proved extremely shrewd. They had moved away from street violence and consolidated their section of the East End by negotiation, albeit with underlying menace. They had also formed a loose partnership with one of the big-time West End bosses, Billy Hill. Hill had recently gone into semi-retirement but retained extensive interests in the West End, particularly illicit gambling, and he had needed someone to look after the show.

In the mid-fifties, gambling fever had hit London. Illegal casinos had become a major industry which was almost completely controlled by the underworld. Even high-society *chemin de fer* parties at their secret Belgravia and Mayfair addresses were paying a 'fee' to the Mob to ensure that their sport continued uninterrupted.

Hill had introduced Reggie and Charles Kray to several of these parties where they acted as minders. It was a good source of income and, more important, it gave them contacts and a presence in the West End.

Parliament was on the verge of legalizing gambling, a move which was intended to legitimize the industry and to remove the criminal element from it. Reggie Kray, however, reckoned it would be just like Las Vegas – a licence to print money.

The casinos would have to be run by someone, and who better than the men who already knew the ropes, men like Reggie Kray? All he had to do was keep his nose clean and grab the opportunity when it came along. The only problem was Ronnie. He was now back on the scene, paranoid and hostile, toting guns and talking about 'doing' people.

Ironically, it was Ronnie's thuggery that eventually got the Krays their first solid stake in the West End. He had been putting pressure on racketeer landlord Peter Rachman to pay protection.

Rachman was too clever to let himself get on that particular treadmill, but knew he would have to do something to get Ronnie off his back. So he negotiated a deal which gave the Krays an interest in Esmerelda's Barn, a newly licensed casino in Belgravia's Wilton Place.

In addition to this, the Krays established themselves as 'security consultants' to other casinos in Mayfair, Chelsea and Knightsbridge, some 30 in all, each paying £150 a week for the benefit of the Firm's expertise.

By 1962, the American Mafia had started to buy stakes in some of the smarter casinos and the Krays established themselves as the Mob's London minders.

Despite Ronnie's ongoing lunacy, Reggie continued with his efforts to smarten up the Krays' image. He opened a new, plusher club in the East End, and became actively involved in a whole range of charitable works – old folks' homes, cancer appeals and boys' clubs.

By this time a certain policeman, Detective Inspector Leonard 'Nipper' Read was starting to take an unhealthy interest in the Kray twins and their Firm.

As the twins' influence grew 'up West', so did their ambition to rub shoulders with showbiz personalities.

LAUNDRYMEN TO THE MOB

By 1965, business was booming for the twins. They had their casinos and clubs and their protection racket, and they were involved in large-scale fraud.

Then, in April, they were approached by one of their American Mafia contacts, Angelo Bruno, to launder $55,000 worth of stolen bearer bonds. They were part of a $2 million consignment of bonds that the Mafia was holding in New York. If the Krays did well, they could act as the exclusive Mafia fence in London.

The whole idea appealed to the Firm – particularly to Ronnie, whose dream of being a big-time Mob boss seemed finally to be becoming a reality. The Firm bought the first shipment of bonds at a quarter of their face value and found, with the help of a crooked merchant banker, Alan Cooper, no trouble in disposing of them. Things had never looked better.

ORGY OF VIOLENCE

But soon people started 'taking liberties' again and Ronnie couldn't stand for that. The target of his displeasure on this occasion was one George Cornell, an enforcer for the rival Richardson gang.

On 9 March 1966, Ronnie slipped his 9mm Mauser automatic into his shoulder holster, collected henchman Ian Barrie, and told 'Scotch' Jack Dickson to drive them down to one of Cornell's hang-outs, a pub called the Blind Begger.

When they arrived, Cornell was sitting perched on a stool at the far end of the bar, drinking a beer with a couple of friends.

'Well, look who's here!' said Cornell, smiling. But his smile soon evaporated as Barrie fired two warning shots into the ceiling. Ronnie Kray never spoke. He raised his Mauser and shot Cornell through the head. The massive 9mm shell exploded his skull and he died instantly.

When the police arrived at the Blind Begger, nobody had seen anything. The identity of George Cornell's killer, however, was the worst-kept secret in the East End. And among those who were fully aware of his identity was Detective Inspector 'Nipper' Read.

Rather than lying low after the murder of Cornell, Ronnie seemed to have his taste for violence heightened and he embarked on an orgy of maiming and killing.

All reason seemed to leave the twins at this point in time. Perhaps their most bizarre escapade involved Frank 'Mad Axe Man' Mitchell. Mitchell, an old friend of Ronnie's, was serving a 32-year sentence in Dartmoor for robbery with violence.

On 12 December 1966 they had him snatched from a working party on the moor. A massive manhunt ensued and the Krays hid Mitchell in a friend's flat in Barking. But it wasn't long before the twins regretted taking Mitchell on. His incessant, childlike demands on them became intolerable. He, too, would have to be taught a lesson.

On Christmas Eve, Reggie Kray told Mitchell that he was going to be moved down to a safe house for the holiday. At 8.30 p.m., he was bundled into the back of a van which sped off down Barking Road. Frank Mitchell was never seen again.

THE KILLING OF JACK 'THE HAT'

The Firm was falling apart at the seams, but desertion from the ranks was rare. Deemed a 'diabolical liberty', it was dealt with appropriately.

One exception was Jack 'The Hat' McVitie, a strong-arm man who had worked with the Krays at various times over the years. He was definitely a liberty-taker. He had taken money from Reggie for a contract killing and then bungled it. He had threatened the twins behind their back. And, worst of all, he had described Ronnie as a 'fat poof'.

The twins agreed that McVitie must be punished. At Ronnie's insistence, Reggie would be the one to mete out that punishment.

McVitie was lured to a basement flat in Stoke Newington with the promise of a lively party. Arriving at the flat just before midnight, he demanded: 'Where's all the birds and all the booze?'

As Ronnie Kray got up to greet him from the sofa, Reggie stepped out from behind the door, aimed a .32 automatic at McVitie's head and pulled the trigger.

The gun jammed and Reggie threw himself at his hapless victim. Ronnie watched the ensuing struggle, egging his brother on with hysterical screams. McVitie broke free and dived through a window, but Reggie caught his legs and dragged him back into the room and plunged a carving knife into his face, chest and stomach. He slid on to the floor and died in an ocean of his own blood.

Like Mitchell and the others, McVitie's body was spirited away and never found. But again the East End underworld and the police, notably Detective Inspector 'Nipper' Read, were well aware of what had happened and who was responsible.

GUNNING FOR THE TWINS

'Nipper' Read was a textbook detective. Hard-working, methodical and totally dedicated, he was a 5ft 7in terrier who had his teeth into the Krays and wasn't about to let go.

After the McVitie murder Read was assigned a team of 14 detectives and set up an undercover operation in an anonymous block of government offices south of the Thames. Their sole task was to build a case against the Kray twins.

Read knew that any attempt to convict the Krays of a specific crime was doomed to failure. They were too powerful and too well organized. They could intimidate witnesses and threaten jurors. They had the money to retain top lawyers and pay others to take the blame or provide them with an alibi.

No – if Read was to get them, he would have to persuade one or more of their past victims to testify against them.

Read made a list of 30 people whom the Krays had maimed or robbed over the past decade. Then he and his team went about the laborious process of questioning them all.

As well as making countless enquiries in London, detectives travelled to Scotland, Canada, Belgium, Spain and the United States.

They were met with a wall of silence. The reason for people's reticence was not hard to understand. In the words of one potential witness whom the Krays had maimed and ruined, but who was reluctant to talk: 'I hate the sight of blood, particularly my own.'

Evidence might have been slow in materializing, but 'Nipper' Read and his team did start to accumulate information, first from Leslie Payne, the Krays' erstwhile business manager, and later from Alan Cooper, the merchant banker who had fenced the Mafia's bearer bonds.

The police were gradually building up a complete picture of the Firm's activities. But they still didn't have any hard evidence which they could take in front of a jury.

Six months passed and the investigation had stalled. Read,

however, felt confident that, if the Krays and their associates were all safely behind bars, reluctant witnesses would summon up the courage to come forward.

He would have to arrest and charge the Krays before he had finished preparing his case. It was a massive gamble, but Read was rapidly running out of options.

At 6 a.m. on 9 May 1968, 60 police officers descended on 24 separate addresses across London. 'Nipper' Read had his revolver drawn as his men broke down the door of Braithwaite House where the twins each had a flat.

He needn't have worried. Both men were sound asleep, Reggie with a girl from Walthamstow, Ronnie with a fair-haired teenage boy from Bethnal Green.

An unlikely pairing. The homosexual Ronnie in conversation with Christine Keeler, central character in the sex-and-security scandal involving War Minister John Profumo and Russian spy Ivanov, in 1963

FIGHT TO THE FINISH

The twins were charged with murder, extortion and sundry other offences, and were remanded in Brixton Jail.

Read had only a few weeks before the preliminary hearings in which to persuade witnesses to talk and thereby clinch his case. His job wasn't made any easier by the fact that two of the Firm, Ronnie Hart and Ian Barrie, were still on the loose.

Because the twins were still on remand and technically innocent, they were allowed as many visitors as they wanted. It was therefore easy for them to pass messages to their fugitive henchmen, who in turn could continue to intimidate witnesses.

So Read went all out to get the two men. Hart was the first to be caught. The police found him hiding in a caravan with his girlfriend. He gave them no trouble and confessed to everything.

Three days later they picked up Barrie in Mile End. He was drunk, broke and frightened. He, too, told the police everything they wanted to know.

With the threat of a Kray reprisal force removed, the whole situation changed. Conmen, club owners and racketeers suddenly got their memories back. When the trial opened on 6 July, long-forgotten victims, accomplices saving their own skins, and eye-witnesses all trooped through the witness box.

The death blow for the Krays came, however, with the appearance of the barmaid from the Blind Beggar. Previously she had been too frightened to identify Ronnie after the shooting of George Cornell. Now she said she was absolutely certain that it had been Ronnie Kray who had fired the fatal shot.

The defence made a brave attempt at discrediting the witnesses, but the barmaid's story stuck and the Krays were effectively finished.

The twins were arrogant and defiant throughout the long trial, but even they must have realized that the verdict was a foregone conclusion. They were found guilty of the murders of Cornell and McVitie and sentenced to life imprisonment, '...which', Mr Justice

Melford Stevenson said, 'I recommend should not be less than 30 years.' If his wishes were respected, the Kray twins would be 64 before they were released.

It would be easy to write off Reggie and Ronnie Kray as a couple of vicious East End thugs. They certainly were that, but they were much more besides. They were professionals of violence who operated on a scale previously unknown in Britain.

The odds against their rise to power were enormous. They were both mentally unstable and had no education or finesse. Yet they came closer to building a crime empire on the lines of Al Capone than any other criminal organization that London has ever known. They were truly dangerous men on the grand scale.

After the murder of George Cornell the Kray twins were held for questioning by the police for 36 hours, before returning to Vallance Road to give an informal press conference.

AL CAPONE

PUBLIC ENEMY NO. ONE

*Neither a Mafioso nor even a Sicilian, by the age of 26 Al
Capone had connived and murdered his way to become the
biggest gangland boss in the most lawless city in America.
But what was the truth and how much was legend?*

For most people the very mention of organized crime conjures up a whole range of vivid images – the roaring twenties, Chicago, bootleg whiskey, speakeasies and, of course, Al Capone.

It is not that Chicago, or even America, ever had a monopoly on organized crime, it is merely the very public nature of its criminals that is so evocative. Gangsters with colourful nicknames like 'Pretty Boy' Floyd, 'Legs' Diamond, 'Machine Gun' Jack McGurn and Al 'Scarface' Capone, captured the public imagination and became a part of criminal folklore.

THE YOUNG BROOKLYN IMMIGRANT

Contrary to popular myth, Al Capone was never a member of the Mafia. He wasn't even a Sicilian. He hated Sicilians and spent most of his active years at loggerheads with various branches of the Mob. Capone was a gangster pure and simple, a racketeer whose only loyalty was to himself and his immediate family.

Born in Brooklyn in 1899, Alphonse was the fourth son of Gabriele and Teresa Capone, a Neapolitan couple who had emigrated from Italy some six years earlier. As a teenager, Al ran with the murderous Five Points gang which was led by fellow-Italian and partner-to-be John Torrio.

He had his first brush with the Mafia when he was 15. The Black Hand, a Mafia murder squad, had been extorting money from his father. Capone hunted down the two men responsible and shot them dead. Torrio was impressed by the young man's nerve and ruthless efficiency. Six years later, in 1919, when Torrio was in the process of building his bootlegging empire in Chicago, he remembered the name of Al Capone.

Torrio had been in Chicago for about five years when the Volsted Act was passed and America went dry. The country developed an immediate and insatiable thirst which organized crime was ready and willing to slake. In Chicago, drinkers were supplied by one of a dozen big gangs, each with its own clearly defined territory.

Torrio's gang controlled the South Side of the city and soon teamed up with the Irish Druggan-Lake gang who supplied the inner West Side. The North Side of Chicago was the territory of Dion O'Banion, a florist and failed safe-cracker, who had a flower shop opposite the Holy Name Cathedral.

Capone's career as a big-time mobster lasted a mere six years, but in that time he acquired all the trappings and habits of a rich man.

O'Banion could have made a legitimate income by supplying floral tributes to the victims of gangland slayings. Instead he teamed up with two Polish Catholics, George 'Bugs' Moran and Hymie Weiss. Together, these three were the biggest challenge to Torrio's pre-eminence in the city.

The other important gang were the Gennas who controlled the West Side. These six brothers from Marsala in Sicily were the most ruthless of all the Chicago gangsters; they didn't only kill for gain and self-protection – they killed for fun.

In the first year of Prohibition, there was comparatively little trouble between the rival gangs. There was more than enough business for everyone, and most of the gangsters' energy was devoted to maintaining supply to meet the enormous demand.

By 1920, however, things were getting better organized and some of the smaller gangs were looking to expand their territories. The O'Donnell gang from the South Side started hijacking Torrio's beer trucks and smashing up his speakeasies. Torrio retaliated by killing several of O'Donnell's drivers. Elsewhere in the city, other gangs were at each other's throats.

Chicago was no place to bring up his children, said Capone, and in 1928, after an unsuccessful attempt to settle in Callifornia, he purchased a house on Palm Island, Miami.

Torrio could see the way things were going and decided that, if he was to fulfil his ambition and have overall control of Chicago, he would need to import some extra muscle. So he called up Al Capone, now 21 and a lieutenant in the Five Points gang, and made him an offer he couldn't refuse: 25 per cent of existing turnover and 50 per cent of all new business.

In the early days of the partnership Capone did the killing for both himself and Torrio. One of his first victims was a small-time crook called Joe Howard. Howard had ideas above his station and one night hijacked two of Torrio's booze trucks. The following evening, Joe was having a drink in his neighbourhood bar. Capone walked in with a broad grin on his face. It was happy hour.

'Hi, Al,' Joe said, sticking out his hand. Capone fired six shots into his body at point-blank range, and Howard fell to the bar-room floor with a smile of welcome still on his face. The police immediately put out an arrest warrant on Capone, but had to release him when all the eye-witnesses developed amnesia.

By the end of 1923, Capone had gained control of the middle-class Chicago suburb of Cicero and made it his personal headquarters. By a combination of bribery and intimidation, he had the entire administration in his pocket – mayor, town clerk and town attorney. So backed, he was free to do whatever he liked. His illegal casinos and brothels and bars were open day and night.

14 February 1929. At 10.30 a.m., while Al established an alibi in Miami, six members of Bugs Moran's gang were shot down in a garage by Capone's men disguised as policemen.

By this time Torrio and Capone were each making in excess of $100,000 a week, but they were still a long way from gaining absolute control of the city. The O'Banion gang and the Gennas still controlled the North and West sides. Capone was in favour of all-out war to eliminate the competition; Torrio preferred to sit back and pick his moment.

In late October 1924, the O'Banion gang hijacked a large shipment of the Gennas' Canadian whiskey. They swore revenge. 'To hell with them Sicilians,' O'Banion said to reporters. A war was in the offing and this was just the situation Torrio and Capone had been waiting for.

WAR BREAKS OUT IN CHICAGO

On 4 November O'Banion was in the back room of his florist's when he heard someone come into the shop. He went out to welcome three customers.

Six shots rang out, the last of which exploded into O'Banion's left cheek. He sprawled back into his flower display as his assassins made good their escape. When the police arrived at the shop, Dion O'Banion was dead.

Torrio, Capone and the Genna brothers were all questioned by the police, but all had satisfactory explanations as to their whereabouts at the time of the killing. The street outside O'Banion's shop had been crowded, yet no one had seen anything. Faced with the customary wall of silence, the coroner was forced to bring in a finding of 'unlawful killing at the hands of a person or persons unknown'.

The tradition of lavish funerals for American gangsters started with O'Banion. His body lay 'in state' at the undertaker's for three days. A contemporary report describes the scene: 'Silver angels stood at the head and feet with their heads bowed in the light of ten candles that burned in solid golden candlesticks they held in their hands. Beneath the casket, on a marble slab that supports its glory, is the inscription: "Suffer the little children to come unto me." And over it all the perfume of flowers.'

At the funeral, mounted police kept order as the cortege of gangsters rolled slowly through the streets of Chicago, followed by 26 trucks of flowers, valued at more than $50,000. Among the floral tributes was a basket of red roses with a card which read, 'From Al'. Both Capone and Torrio solemnly attended the funeral, but no one was fooled – least of all Hymie Weiss, O'Banion's most trusted lieutenant and the new boss of his organization. Weiss was a cold-blooded killer who had devised a method of assassination in which the victim was seated in the front passenger seat of the car with his killer directly behind him. He was then shot in the back of the head. After such a murder, Weiss would calmly say that his victim had been 'taken for a ride'. And so the expression became part of modern parlance.

Weiss, who was genuinely heartbroken by O'Banion's death – observers described him as crying like a baby – swore to get his revenge. Days later Capone's car was machine-gunned. Al escaped unhurt, but two weeks later John Torrio was gunned down in front of his wife by another O'Banion man, Bugs Moran.

Torrio recovered from his wounds, but only weeks later he was jailed for nine months for operating a brewery. Badly shaken by Moran's attack, he had steel screens fitted to the windows of his cell and hired three extra deputy sheriffs to stand sentry.

On his release in October 1925, he announced that he was leaving Chicago, which he described as being 'too violent'. The fact is, at the age of 48, Johnnie Torrio had lost his nerve. This was a game for young men, and the young man on the spot was Al Capone.

THE KING IS DEAD – LONG LIVE THE KING!

So, at the age of 26, Al Capone inherited the entire Torrio empire. His promotion to unrivalled boss of Chicago was helped by the demise of the six Genna brothers. Angelo, Mike and Antonio were killed in separate gun battles within the space of six weeks. The three surviving brothers fled to their home town of Marsala in Sicily.

While there is no evidence to connect Capone with the killings, he made no secret of his pleasure at the Gennas' departure.

The Sicilians might have been out of the way, but Hymie Weiss wasn't finished yet. His second attempt on Capone's life was anything but subtle, and highlighted the level of lawlessness that existed in Chicago in 1925. In broad daylight, eight carloads of gunmen made an assault on Capone's Cicero headquarters, the Hawthorne Inn, firing more than 1,000 rounds into the building in a matter of seconds.

Again Capone escaped unscathed and, with customary largesse, paid $10,000 out of his own pocket to save the sight of a woman who had been injured in the crossfire. Capone had overlooked the first attempt on his life by the North Side gang, considering it legitimate revenge for the killing of their boss Dion O'Banion. Now he had had enough.

When Herbert Hoover was elected President of the United States in 1929, he named Capone as his prime target in an attack on lawlessness. The mobster was finally indicted on a chage of income tax evasion. Here seated with his lawyers, he looks confident of a successful outcome to the hearing.

On 11 October 1926, Weiss was machine-gunned to death on the steps of Holy Name Cathedral.

Now only Bugs Moran was left alive to challenge Capone's absolute control of Chicago. And Moran could wait. Ten days after the execution of Weiss, Capone chaired a meeting of Chicago gang bosses to negotiate a peaceful division of Cook County: 'We're a bunch of saps to be killing each other,' he postulated.

For a while after that the peace held and there were no gangland slayings. Everyone was making a fortune, and none more than Al Capone. His turnover was truly astonishing. In Cook County he controlled 10,000 speakeasies, each purchasing an average of six barrels of beer a week costing a total of $3.5 million. In addition they were each buying two cases of liquor at $90, making another $1.8 million. (Beer was costing Capone about $5 a barrel to make, and liquor about $20 a case.) Added to all this, Capone had his other rackets – gambling and vice – which contributed to a grand total of about $6.5 million per week.

He had huge overheads, of course, not least of which was his illicit payroll. Everyone was on the take in Chicago, from humble patrolmen to the city's mayor 'Big Bill' Thompson, whose 1927 re-election campaign Capone financed to the tune of $260.000. It is estimated that his annual graft bill to the police, judges and politicians came to more than $30 million.

Capone was no longer the flashy, loud-mouthed thug that arrived in Chicago in 1919. He was now an immaculately tailored, even conservative figure, sporting hand-made silk shirts and solitaire diamond tie-pins. Despite the fact that he was still only 26, he gave the impression of being a successful, middle-aged businessman.

Capone's public image was important to him and he was given to ostentatious displays of generosity. He paid for church roofs to be restored; he gave $10,000 to Pennsylvania's striking miners and, during the Depression, he opened a string of soup kitchens and contributed more than $2 million of his own money to help down-and-outs.

Everyone in Chicago knew that Al Capone was a bootlegger, and most of them didn't care. To the vast majority of ordinary people Prohibition was a nonsense anyway, so bootlegging wasn't a real crime. He had become a success story, a working-class hero.

THE ST VALENTINE'S DAY MASSACRE

By 1928 Al Capone felt secure enough about his hold on Chicago to spend time away from the city. He was a devoted family man, who wanted his dependants to benefit from his vast wealth. Chicago was no place to bring up children, he said, and so he set about looking for a suitable second home away from the turmoil of the big city.

He quite liked the look of California, but California didn't like the look of him and summarily booted him out. Next he tried Florida and, despite the violent objections of honest citizens, managed to procure a magnificent house on Palm Island, Miami.

Capone spent Christmas and the New Year of 1929 in his new home. He had a lot to be thankful for. He was not yet 30, had amassed a vast fortune and was the undisputed boss of America's second city. Unfortunately for Capone, one man didn't quite see it like that.

The style of elaborate gangster funerals in Chicago was set by that of Dion O'Banion.

Bugs Moran had neither forgotten nor forgiven the murder of his two associates Dion O'Banion and Hymie Weiss. He decided to take advantage of Capone's absence to make him pay. With his North Side gang, Moran regularly hijacked Capone's liquor shipments and then started to move in on some of his other legitimate businesses, notably dog racing and dry cleaning.

Capone may have been in Florida, but his finger was very much on the pulse. He heard all about Moran's activities and decided that they had to stop. Over the telephone he instructed Jake Guzik, his most trusted aide in Chicago, to 'take care' of Moran. The time and method of execution were discussed in minute detail, and on 14 February 1929 Capone made a point of keeping an appointment in Miami with a city official. He wanted a watertight alibi for that particular Valentine's Day.

At 10.30 a.m., as Al Capone was trying to explain to the Miami official where he had got the money to buy his Palm Island home, six of Moran's men were waiting for a truckload of hijacked whiskey in a garage on Chicago's North Clark Street. They were Frank and Peter Gusenberg, Moran's top executioners; James Clark, a Sioux Indian and Moran's brother-in-law; Al Weinshank, his accountant; Adam Heyer, his business manager; and Johnny May, a burglar and safe-cracker. There was also a seventh man, whose presence has never been satisfactorily explained – an optician called Dr Richard Schwimmer. Moran himself should have been there, but had been delayed.

Shortly after 10.30 Mrs Max Landesman of 2124 North Clark Street heard shots from the garage next door. She looked out of the window and saw a man leaving the garage and getting into a large touring car. From the flat below, Miss Josephine Morin saw two men, apparently under arrest, come out of the garage with their hands up. They were followed by two uniformed police officers. All four of them got into a black Cadillac and drove off.

Mrs Landesman hurried over to the garage, pushed open the door and saw seven men sprawled on the floor, blood streaming from their bodies. Minutes later Sergeant Tom Loftus arrived on the scene with a dozen other officers. Only one of the victims, Frank

Gusenberg, was conscious, and Loftus tried to persuade him to say who had done the shootings. Gusenberg declined to comment and was shipped to hospital along with the other six victims, all of whom were pronounced dead on arrival.

Loftus maintained a vigil at Gusenberg's bedside but, true to the gangster's code of honour, he died three hours later without revealing anything.

Moran had arrived on Clark Street 15 minutes late, and, seeing the police cars outside the garage, assumed that there had been a raid and promptly left. Later, when he heard about the massacre, he said: 'Only Capone kills like that!'

The police were of the same opinion. So they picked up Capone's top killer, 'Machine Gun' Jack McGurn. McGurn claimed to have been with his girlfriend at the time of the killings. He was indicted for perjury, but married his girl so that the police could not force her to testify against him. Other Capone men were questioned but soon released for lack of evidence.

In the end, no one was ever charged in connection with the St Valentine's Day massacre. But no one was in any doubt that it was carried out on the direct orders of Al Capone from the safety of his Florida retreat.

Even though Moran had survived, Capone returned to Chicago confident that he had finally crushed any opposition to his authority. Instead he found that two of his own lieutenants, John Scalise and Albert Anselmi, had been conspiring to take over the outfit. Al invited them, along with other gang members, to a meeting at a restaurant in Hammond, Indiana. Capone was his usual jovial self until halfway through the meal, at which point he rounded on the two conspirators: 'I understand you want my job,' he said. 'Well, here it is!' and promptly clubbed them both to death with a baseball bat. It was a salutary lesson to the assembled diners.

Early in his career, Capone was known for his surgical use of violence. It was never used gratuitously – only as a tool to protect himself and to promote his business interests. This was no longer the case. Anyone who incurred his displeasure – policemen, politicians, journalists – could expect to be summarily dispatched.

'GET CAPONE!'

In March 1929, Herbert Hoover was inaugurated President of the United States. He came to office primed with a promise to tackle lawlessness in America and he named Al Capone as his primary target.

By May of that year, Capone was feeling the heat. There were rumours of a massive contract out on his life. Some said it had been taken out by Bugs Moran, others that it was the families of Scalise and Anselmi. Whatever the truth, Capone decided it would be wise to get out of circulation for a while and, rather than going to Florida, he contrived to have himself arrested for a minor firearms offence in Philadelphia. He was expecting to get a jail sentence of 30 days, but in the event he was sent to prison for a year. Capone was initially horrified but he soon adapted to the situation. His status was such that he was able to continue running his Chicago empire from his prison cell with the minimum of inconvenience.

While Capone was in prison, the new administration in Washington was devising ways to keep him there for ever. President Hoover discussed a variety of approaches with his various agencies – the Prohibition Bureau, the Justice Department's Federal Bureau of Investigation (FBI) and the Treasury Department. Their brief was simple. Get Al Capone any way you can.

The Justice Department set about destroying Capone's booze empire by brute force. In the space of six months they raided and wrecked 30 of his breweries and seized 50 of his heavy trucks. But this was no more than an annoyance for Capone.

In Washington it was the Treasury that really took the Capone challenge on board. Their Special Intelligence Unit sent top investigator Frank Wilson to Chicago to look at Al Capone's books.

Wilson had already enjoyed spectacular success jailing gangsters who had escaped conviction for years. Among his victims were Frank Nitti, Capone's deputy; Jack Guzik, his

The trial concluded, Capone is led away from Chicargo
Federal Court on 24 October 1931 to begin
his eleven-year sentence.

accountant; and Capone's brother, Ralph. They had received prison terms of between 18 months and five years. But Al Capone himself would prove tougher for Wilson than his associates.

Capone had never filed a tax return in his life. This was not a crime, so long as he did not earn more than $5,000 in any given year. It was Frank Wilson's job to prove that he had. Considering Capone's lavish lifestyle, this might appear to have been a simple matter. It wasn't. Capone had no bank accounts in his own name and all his assets were listed to third parties.

Wilson and his team started a detailed probe into Capone's personal spending. They found that in the three-year period 1926-29 he had purchased more than $25,000 worth of furniture for his homes in Chicago and Florida. He had spent $7,000 on suits and $40,000 on telephone calls. In all, the Treasury men unearthed $165,000 worth of taxable spending. They could have gone to court with that and they would probably have secured a conviction, which would have jailed Capone for about three years. But that

Guarded by a US Marshall, Al Capone puts a brave face on his defeat as he is taken by train to Atlanta Federal Penitentiary.

wasn't good enough. Wilson had been told to go for broke.

After months sniffing around Chicago, Wilson managed to persuade some of Capone's casino employees to turn state's evidence. Now he had Al where they wanted him. He was charged with failing to pay tax on $1 million in the years from 1925 to 1929 and, while this was a fraction of Capone's true income, it could still mean 30 years in a federal prison.

Capone's attorneys initially struck a deal with the prosecution – if Capone pleaded guilty, he would receive a sentence of not more than two and a half years. Judge Wilkerson, however, was outraged by this and threw it out. Capone withdrew his plea and elected to go to trial.

His associates immediately set about bribing or threatening members of the jury, but this was discovered and, at the very last minute, a new jury was sworn in. They heard stories of Capone's extravagant lifestyle – a lifestyle he could not possibly have supported on the $450 a month he claimed to earn – and on 24 October they returned a verdict of guilty on all charges. He was sentenced to 11 years and fined $50,000, the most severe sentence ever imposed for a tax offence.

Capone was sent to Cook County jail pending an appeal and when that failed, in May 1932, he was shipped to Atlanta Federal Penitentiary. A year later he became one of the first convicts to take up residence at Alcatraz in San Francisco Bay. He emerged from there in 1939 a physical and mental wreck. He was still only 38 years old.

Capone had been diagnosed as suffering from syphilis shortly after his imprisonment in 1931. The disease had now reached its tertiary stage and his brain was being eaten up. After his release he returned to his home on Palm Island, Florida where he lived for another seven years, increasingly mad, surrounded by his adoring family.

In 1947 he suffered a fatal brain haemorrhage. He was 48 years old. His body was shipped back to Chicago and buried in an elaborate mausoleum in Mount Olivet cemetery.

CARELESS THIEVES
GREAT TRAIN ROBBERY

It was called the 'robbery of the century', yet when thieves audaciously robbed a mail train of £2.5 million they were unbelievably careless in concealing the evidence. The law was draconian, but the public secretly admired them.

Shortly after 2 a.m. on Thursday, 8 August 1963, the Glasgow to London mail train was nearing the end of its journey. As it passed through Leighton Buzzard in Bedfordshire, half an hour should have seen it safely into Euston. It wasn't to be, however.

A few miles further down the line, the driver, 48-year-old Jack Mills, spotted an amber signal. He slowed the big diesel and prepared to stop. A mile on, at Sears Crossing, he was faced with a red light and pulled to a halt. Mills sent his fireman, David Whitby, down the line to phone ahead for information. Within a matter of seconds, however, Mills found himself confronted by a gang of masked men clambering into his cab.

He tried to fight them off but was coshed into submission, as the biggest and most audacious robbery in history began. Half an hour later the train had been divided, moved and relieved of 128 mail sacks containing more than £2.5 million in used banknotes.

FEW CLUES TO START WITH

By the time Detective Superintendent Malcolm Fewtrell, head of the Buckinghamshire CID, arrived the robbers and their spoils were long gone. Fewtrell, a seasoned professional, started routine investigative procedures, gathering physical evidence and interviewing the eighty-odd people who had been on the train.

But no one, not even Mills, Whitby or the post office sorters from whose HVP (high-value packages) coach the mail sacks had been taken, could give Fewtrell anything to go on.

It was soon obvious to Fewtrell that he was not dealing with any ordinary crime. This robbery was the work of a highly organized team, and the investigation would be on a scale far beyond the meagre resouces of his force. After consulting with his Chief Constable, he elected to 'call the Yard' – to ask for the assistance of the Metropolitan CID.

Later that day, Fewtrell attended a meeting at the headquarters of the Post Office. Present were Post Office officials including their own senior investigator, Frank Cook, and George Hatherill, deputy

Post Office workers lean out from the robbed train as the police start their search for clues.

chief of the CID at Scotland Yard, together with a team of detectives.

Cook told the police that, in his estimation, the haul from the robbery might well be in excess of £3 million. The police for their part could give little comfort to the Post Office. All they could say for certain was that approximately 15 men had been involved in the robbery and that the fireman, David Whitby, had noticed an army lorry parked on the Bridego Bridge where the robbery took place.

Hatherill agreed to send two of his most able detectives - Gerald McArthur and Jack Prichard – down to Buckinghamshire to assist the local police with their enquiries. The two men returned to Aylesbury with Fewtrell that night.

The three detectives had to try and put themselves in the robbers' shoes. What would they do immediately after the robbery? A total of 128 mail sacks would not be easy to hide or transport for long distances without attracting attention.

The police decided that the robbers would hole up somewhere near the scene of the crime and distribute the money at their leisure, partly because one of the robbers had ordered the men in the HVP coach not to move for 'half an hour'. This suggested that the gang had a safe haven within half an hour's drive from the scene of the crime.

It was a guess, but they decided to back it with all their resources. Every policeman from Buckinghamshire and neighbouring forces was mobilized in a search of barges, houses and barns in a 30-mile radius of Bridego Bridge.

So far the police were spot on. The perpetrators of the Great Train Robbery were holed up some 20 miles from Bridego Bridge at Leatherslade Farm. They had purchased it through a nominee some weeks earlier, specifically for this purpose.

The robbery itself had gone like clockwork. The only minor hitch had been Mills, the train driver, who had offered token resistance. The haul, something over £2.5 million, had been less than they had expected. But even after they had paid their German backers a million for financing the robbery, each member of the 17-strong gang had received £90,000, a huge sum of money in 1963. All in all, no one was complaining.

TWO GANGS WITH COMBINED TALENTS

The robbery, which had been almost a year in the planning, was the work of not one but two London-based gangs or 'firms'. The first firm, the men who conceived the idea and did most of the groundwork, consisted of Buster Edwards, Gordon Goody, Charlie Wilson, Bruce Reynolds, John Daly, Jimmy White, Ronnie Biggs and Jimmy Hussey.

They were a loose-knit team of thieves who had worked together over the years on numerous occasions with a varying degree of success.

In January 1963, Buster Edwards and Gordon Goody were approached by a friend, Brian Field, a crooked solicitor's clerk who had worked for them in the past. He claimed to have information for them about a huge shipment of cash which was theirs for the taking.

Roy James, known as 'the Weasel', was arrested in December after a chase over the roof of this house in a mews in St John's Wood, north London.

Field introduced them to an Irishman (whose name is still unknown) who told them about the high-value-package coach which made up part of the overnight mail train from Glasgow to London. It was on this coach that the banks sent all their surplus cash down to London.

Normally the coach would carry about 60 bags, the Irishman told them, but if they timed their raid to follow a bank holiday they might find upwards of 200, each holding about £25,000 – a total haul in excess of £5 million.

Edwards and Goody were incredulous. But they assured the Irishman that if such a robbery were possible, they had the team to pull it off. They arranged a meeting with Bruce Reynolds and Charlie Wilson.

All four of them were torn between euphoria and scepticism. Before they went any further, they had to check that their informant was himself well informed.

So they staked out Euston station and saw for themselves HVP sacks being offloaded from the night mail train. There was no doubt that the prize was there. The only way the job could be done, they decided, was to stop the train on the track, separate the engine and the HVP coach from the main body of the train, and ransack it at their leisure. The trouble was, how do you stop a train at a predetermined spot?

Buster Edwards had a solution to the problem of stopping the train. He had heard of a south London firm, headed by one Thomas Wisbey, which had been robbing trains on the London to Brighton line for a couple of years. They had an expert who knew how to tamper with the signalling system.

Buster approached the rival gang boss and, after a period of intense haggling, terms were agreed. Wisbey would let them have his man, Roger Cordrey, as long as Wisbey himself and his partner Bob Welsh were included in the robbery as full partners.

And so the team to rob the mail train started to take shape, and the preparation began: researching a suitable location for the ambush, buying a hide-out, instructing various members of the gang in their specific tasks, and rehearsing the ambush in the most minute detail.

And now it had all paid off. The Great Train Robbers were sitting in Leatherslade Farm with more than £2.5 million in used notes.

That team of faces, already known to the police, would soon be known to the world at large. The first piece of bad news for the robbers came over the radio in the form of a public appeal by the police. They were asking for information on strange goings-on in remote dwellings, and they wanted to know about movements of army vehicles.

In the summer of 1965, after serving little more than a year of his sentence, Ronald Biggs escaped from Wandsworth prison. More than 150 armed police surrounded Winterfold House in Surrey when told he was hiding out there, but a six-hour search revealed no trace of him.

This presented the robbers with two problems. They had originally planned to stay at Leatherslade Farm until the Sunday night and then disperse the money using army Land Rovers. This was now clearly out of the question.

For the first time they were in a state of disarray and, from this point on, it was effectively every man for himself. They cleared up the farm as best they could, burning clothes and mailsacks, but in their haste to get away they were forced to leave the job half done. The various members of the gang returned to their homes and jobs in London, unaware they had left a plethora of clues for their pursuers.

THE INVESTIGATION TAKES OFF

Once the scale of the robbery was appreciated, Scotland Yard decided to beef up its support for the investigation. They brought in Chief Superintendent Tommy Butler to head up the London end. Butler would prove the downfall of many of the Train Robbers.

The first mention of Leatherslade Farm came from a cowman called John Mans on Monday, 12 August. In outbuildings the police found an army lorry and the two Land Rovers. Once inside the farm proper, half-burnt mailsacks and money wrappers left them in no doubt that they had found the hide-out.

Fewtrell and McArthur dashed to the farm. After a cursory glance they ordered that the whole area be cordoned off in readiness for the forensic team.

In London, Butler and his team had compiled a list of possible suspects to be pulled in for questioning. The bulk of the gang's names appeared on that list.

Charlie Wilson escaped from Winson Green prison in August 1964. I January 1967 he was recaptured in Montreal, Canada, and was brought back to Britain by Dectective Chief Superintendent Butler.

For more than five years Bruce Reynolds was a wanted man. Eventually, in November 1968, police found him in this rented house in Torquay.

Roger Cordrey, the signals expert, was the first to be picked up. The local police found him in Bournemouth along with £141,000 in used notes, money which he found extremely difficult to explain.

The next break for the police came on Friday, 16 August. A man called John Ahern was taking a stroll in the woods near Dorking in Surrey when he came upon a briefcase, a holdall and a camelskin bag containing no less than £100,900 More important, a receipt was found made out by a German restaurant in the name of Herr and Frau Field.

Fewtrell and McArthur knew that one Brian Field, a solicitor's clerk, had acted for several of their suspects, including Buster Edwards and Gordon Goody. They also knew that the company for which Field worked had acted in the purchase of Leatherslade Farm. They went to his home and questioned him but did not arrest him yet.

The following day, more money – £30,440 – was found in an old caravan in the Dorking Woods by Surrey Police. Fingerprints in the caravan matched those on file for Jimmy White. At Leatherslade Farm fingerprint experts were also doing well. They had identified the prints of Charlie Wilson and Bruce Reynolds. Wilson was picked up within a few hours, but Reynolds had gone to ground.

On Thursday, 22 August local police arrested Gordon Goody in Leicester where he was having dinner with a girlfriend. They questioned him and then released him for lack of evidence.

Ronnie Biggs was next. He was pulled in on 4 September, and three days later they brought in Jim Hussey for questioning. Thomas Wisbey was questioned, released and then rearrested.

PLAYING A WAITING GAME

By the middle of September the police were fairly certain they had a complete picture of who had robbed the mail train, but Tommy Butler was in no particular hurry to find them. He reckoned that, by playing the waiting game, he stood a better chance of catching them with some of the money.

However, Butler did decide it was time to pull in Brian Field. He charged him with conspiring to rob a mail train and for being an accessory after the fact.

Police efforts were now on two fronts. The Flying Squad were trying to track down Buster Edwards, Bruce Reynolds, John Daly, Roy James and Jimmy White. The forensic team, for their part, were building up a case against them and the men already in custody, trying to tie them to the scene of the crime. It was thanks to this work that they felt confident enough to rearrest Gordon Goody on 3 October.

Over the next few weeks, Butler and his men arrested Bob Welsh and John Daly. They ran Roy James to ground in the St John's Wood area of London and, after a spectacular rooftop chase, took him into custody and charged him.

By the end of the year, nine of the 16 men who had been at Bridego Bridge were in jail awaiting trial. Bruce Reynolds, Buster Edwards and Jimmy White were still on the run, while the other four had been overlooked or released for lack of evidence.

With no prospect of an early arrest of the three fugitives, the authorities decided to press ahead with the trial of the others.

SHOW TRIAL

The trial began on 20 January 1964. All the accused pleaded not guilty to all charges except for Roger Cordrey. He pleaded guilty to robbery and was removed from the dock to await sentence, while the trial of the others continued.

Only Mr W. Raeburn QC, counsel for John Daly, was successful in persuading Mr Justice Davies that his client had no case to answer. Daly walked from the court a free man. The jury returned with a verdict of guilty on all the accused.

On Wednesday, 15 April the convicted prisoners were brought to court to be sentenced. Mr Justice Edmund Davies called first for Roger John Cordrey. The judge told him that he would take into consideration Cordrey's plea of guilty and the fact that his share of the stolen money had been recovered, and would reduce his sentence accordingly. 'In respect of the four counts you must go to prison for concurrent terms of twenty years.' There was a moment's stunned silence from the court, and then a gasp. Journalists and barristers alike were astounded by the severity of the sentence. If this was Mr Justice Davies' idea of leniency, what would the others get?

One by one the guilty men faced the bench: Ronnie Biggs, 30 years, Thomas Wisbey, 30 years; Bob Welsh, Jim Hussey and Roy James, 30 years, Brian Field, 25 years. The convicted men were whisked off to various prisons around the country where the true horror of their situation sank in. Even with full remission, most of them would not be released for at least 20 years.

Ronald Biggs hid out in Australia, where he worked as a carpenter, until a new spate of publicity forced him to flee to Brazil. Here police search his baggage, left behind in a Melbourne motel.

EXPATRIATES

To the gang members still on the loose, news of the sentences was no less shattering. Any idea they may have had about turning themselves in, hoping to make a deal, evaporated. Bruce Reynolds sneaked out of the country in August 1964, Buster Edwards spent a short time in Germany having plastic surgery before leaving for Mexico City in March 1965.

In the same month that Reynolds fled to France, Charlie Wilson was sprung from Winson Green prison in Birmingham. He too was smuggled out of the country and headed for the South of France. Less than a year later Ronnie Biggs escaped from Wandsworth and flew to Australia via Paris. By 1967 Edwards, Wilson and Reynolds had all been rearrested.

Ronnie Biggs was now the only member of the gang still at large. In 1969 he fled from Australia to Brazil, which had no extradition treaty with the United Kingdom, and went about making himself into an international superstar. He hosted parties, made film appearances and even recorded a track with the Sex Pistols. Ronnie eventually returned to Britain on Monday 7 May 2001, ending an amazing 35 years on the run. He was met by police, immediately arrested and transported to Belmarsh Prison, where, despite rapidly failing health, he remains to this day.

BRINK'S-MAT

ROBBERS STRIKE GOLD

It was almost by chance that the trio of vicious armed robbers realized they had struck gold. Their getaway van drove off groaning under the weight of three tons of bullion. Yet the biggest haul in criminal history proved harder to track down than a needle in a haystack.

At 6.25 on the morning of Saturday, 26 November 1983, a group of men were gathered outside Unit 7, a warehouse on the Heathrow International Trading Estate in Hounslow, London.

Despite its unprepossessing appearance, Unit 7 is one of the world's biggest safes. It is used by Brink's-Mat, Britain's leading security company, to store hugely valuable cargoes of precious metals, currency, bonds, jewels, fine art and other high-risk consignments en route for Heathrow International Airport.

The ground floor of the building is a huge vault containing three safes. Above this are the manager's office, a radio room, a common room and a locker room for the 30 or so guards who usually work from the building.

At precisely 6.30 Michael Scouse, the senior duty guard and 'keyman', unlocked the unit, leaving the rest of the crew outside. He switched off the alarm system, then returned to the main door. He allowed the other men to enter and locked the door again from the inside.

Scouse reset the alarms and went up to the office. He was joined by Robin Risley, the crew leader for the day. Risley knew the men had been brought in specially for a bullion run. Scouse looked through his bills of lading. 'It's gold. Three tons. Gatwick airport for the Far East via Cathay Pacific Airways. It's got to be there by 8 a.m.'

Risley walked over to the common room, where the rest of the crew were warming themselves up with cups of tea. They were discussing the run when the doorbell rang. It had to be Tony Black, late as usual. The guards heard Scouse go down the stairs to let him in. Seconds later, Black walked into the common room. The 31 year–old guard looked pale and drawn as he glanced around the room. He muttered that he needed to go to the toilet, and then went back downstairs.

A couple of minutes later, the guards heard footsteps returning. They paid no attention until a voice bellowed out, 'Get on the floor or you're fucking dead!'

A figure appeared in the doorway of the common room. He was about 5ft 8in, dressed in a black blazer and black trousers. His face was covered with a canary-yellow balaclava and he brandished a 9mm Browning automatic.

The guards, immobilized by fear, failed to react quickly enough for the intruder's satisfaction. Without a word, he pistol-whipped one of them, sending him crashing to the floor. The other guards quickly dropped to the floor.

'Lie still and keep quiet,' the intruder said in a Cockney accent. As he spoke, two other masked men rushed into the room. Soon the gang had handcuffed all four guards. They also taped their legs together and placed cotton bags, secured with drawstrings, over their heads.

In the radio room, Michael Scouse was suffering a similar ordeal. After letting in the late arrival, Tony Black, Scouse had returned to the radio room. Seconds later he had found himself confronted by two masked men brandishing handguns.

'Are you Scouse?' a voice asked. Scouse nodded and a knife sliced through the front of his jeans. Petrol was poured down his front and over his genitals.

'You'd better do as I say, or I'll put a match to the petrol and a bullet through your head. You have two numbers . . . What are they?'

With a gun pressed under his chin, Scouse was in no mood for heroics. He shouted the numbers: '94-45-57-85'.

That combination opened the vault door. But there were several other lines of defence that needed to be neutralized before the intruders could reach their treasure.

They were fully conversant with the sophisticated arrangement of silent alarms, combinations and time locks. And they knew exactly what authority Scouse had as shift supervisor. There was no way to bluff them, so Scouse had no option but to lead them through the maze of defences.

As the robbers stepped into the vault, their attention was immediately focused on the three safes at the far end of the room. They totally ignored the stacks of small boxes, bound with metal straps, which littered the floor. They didn't know, and Scouse wasn't about to tell them, that these were the real treasure. Each of these

The Police arrive at Unit 7 of the Brink's - Mat warehouse on the morning of November 26, 1983.

inconspicuous little boxes contained a gold ingot. Together they were worth more than £25 million.

Scouse explained to the gang leader that he couldn't open the safes alone. He had the keys, but only Robin Risley knew that day's combination. Risley was dragged down to the vault and was told to enter the relevant numbers.

Risley was in a panic. The safe numbers had just been changed and he had barely committed them to memory. As he fumbled with the dials, the intruders became increasingly impatient. As Risley continued to struggle with the locks and pleaded with the Cockney, another member of the gang asked Scouse what was in the boxes. Scouse, realizing that it was the only chance to save Risley and probably himself, told him that they contained bullion.

The man ripped open one of the boxes and saw that Scouse was telling the truth. Immediately the gang lost interest in Risley and the safes, and turned their attention to shifting the three tons of gold into the loading bay.

The gang leader asked Scouse how the shutter doors to the loading bay opened. Scouse replied that that was Tony Black's job. The leader went back upstairs. 'Which one of you is Black?' he asked. Black, who was lying in a pool of petrol on the office floor, identified himself and was frogmarched into the radio room at knifepoint. He opened the shutter doors by remote control and a van drove into the warehouse.

Fifteen minutes later the same van drove out again, suspension groaning under the weight of £25 million worth of gold, the biggest haul in criminal history.

Within minutes of Michael Scouse freeing himself and raising the alarm, the Flying Squad were at the scene of the robbery. The investigation was headed by Commander Frank Cater.

From the outset, Cater had no doubt that this was an inside job. The most obvious suspects were the guards. They had all been taken to the casualty department of Ashford Hospital. The pistol-whipped Peter Bentley was treated for head wounds, and Scouse and Risley were suffering from petrol bums. The other men were unhurt.

By 10 a.m., all six men were being grilled by Cater and his team at Hounslow police station.

PRIME SUSPECT

The most obvious suspects, because of their special knowledge and responsibilities, were Scouse and Risley. But, as the morning wore on and more information about the six men came into the incident room, another name caught Cater's eye.

Anthony John Black stuck out like a sore thumb. He did not have a criminal record himself, but his common-law brother-in-law, Brian Robinson, was well known to the police.

Despite the fact that he was sure that Black was the man he was after, Commander Cater elected to send him home along with the other guards. At 8 a.m. on Sunday, 4 December, more than a week after the raid, detectives arrived simultaneously at the homes of all six guards and invited them down to Hounslow police station for further questioning. Five of the guards were asked to go over their statements again. It was all routine.

Tony Black, however, was given the full treatment. His interrogation, led by Detective Inspector Tony Brightwell, lasted more than six hours as they went over his statement again and again in minute detail.

Then Detective Sergeant Alan Branch dropped his bombshell. He looked Black straight in the eye and asked, 'What does your brother-in-law think about the robbery?'

The fact that the police knew about his connection with Brian Robinson obviously shook Black, but he was not ready to fold yet. The game of cat and mouse lasted until 3 p.m. the following day. The police piled more and more pressure on the prisoner and he was obviously getting ready to crack.

When Detective Constable John Fordham was stabbed to death by Kenneth Noye in January 1985, dozens of plain clothes police combed the house and grounds in search for the missing gold.

'Can I have a cup of tea?' Black asked. Detective Sergeant Nicholas Benwell left the interview room and returned with a plastic cup from the vending machine. Black took a sip and looked up. 'Where do I start?' he asked.

Even when the thieves were in prison, the police still had to track down the loot, like these bars of bullion found in Kenneth Noye's garage.

MOLE TURNS GRASS

When Tony Black decided to talk, he talked with a vengeance. It took Sergeant Benwell more than eight hours to take down his statement. He explained how he had been approached by his sister's common-law husband, Brian Robinson, to provide inside information about shipments, security arrangements, the layout of the warehouse and details of personnel and procedures. Black admitted that on the day of the robbery, he had let the gang into the warehouse.

According to Black, Robinson had two accomplices. One was a man in his early thirties called Mick. The other was a giant of a man who went by the name of Tony.

Shortly after Black finished his statement, Detective Sergeant Branch came into the interview room with two files containing mugshots of known associates of Brian Robinson. Black leafed through the photographs and did not hesitate in identifying two of them – Tony White and Mick McAvoy.

Having broken every rule in the criminal code book, Tony Black was taken back to his cell.

At 6.30 the following morning, Tuesday 6 December, the Flying Squad picked up Robinson, McAvoy and White. The three men were taken to separate police stations well away from Hounslow. Robinson was polite but firm in his denial of any wrongdoing, and provided the police with a detailed alibi for the day of the robbery. White was aggressive and blunt. McAvoy would say nothing without his lawyer being present.

Under normal circumstances, Frank Cater knew that breaking the three men down would take time. He decided to take a short cut. He showed them Tony Black's statement. White was the first to capitulate. He admitted being a party to the robbery and wanted to explore the possibility of doing a deal. At the end of the interview, however, White refused to sign his statement and he would later withdraw his admission of guilt at his trial.

Brian Robinson realized that, in the light of Black's testimony, his position was hopeless. He admitted that he had helped set up the robbery but denied being involved in the execution of the crime itself.

McAvoy stuck to his tactic of silence until he too had read Black's statement, at which point he folded completely.

There would be no deal for McAvoy or White, but there certainly was for Tony Black. On 17 February 1984, Black – the 'Golden Mole' – stood trial at the Old Bailey. In less than an hour he was arraigned, tried and sentenced to six years' imprisonment. This meant that, with full remission and parole, he would serve no more than two years.

Black's next appearance in court was at the Old Bailey in October 1984 – not as the accused but as the chief prosecution witness in the trials of Brian Robinson, Mick McAvoy and Tony White. Black's testimony lasted almost three days and was frequently interrupted by catcalls and abuse from the public gallery. Nobody, it seems, likes a grass.

Since identity parades and forensic evidence had proved inconclusive, the prosecution's case rested almost totally on Black's evidence. In the cases of Brian Robinson and Mick McAvoy, this proved sufficient to convince the jury of their guilt. But Tony White, who claimed the police had tricked and coerced him into his confession, was found not guilty.

The judge warned Robinson and McAvoy that he had no choice but to impose a heavy sentence of 25 years' imprisonment.

ONGOING INVESTIGATION

For the police, the matter did not end with the conviction of Black, Robinson and McAvoy. There was still the small matter of £26 million in gold bullion to be accounted for.

The police used their vast network of criminal intelligence to narrow down the field in their hunt for the Brink's-Mat haul. They came up with a list of names, known associates of Robinson and

White. This list included Kenneth Noye, a Kent businessman and property dealer with a considerable criminal pedigree.

After months of investigation, Cater became convinced that Noye was the main link in an elaborate chain through which the Brink's-Mat bullion was being channelled. It went from Noye to his friend Brian Reader and on to Garth Chappell, John Palmer and Scadlynn Ltd, a bullion dealer in Bristol.

The police's main problem was that if they moved in on any member of that chain, the others would be alerted and go to ground. In the short term it was decided to keep the key players under surveillance. Detective Chief Superintendent Brian Boyce, who had taken over the Brink's-Mat case, was sure that at least part of the bullion was being stored at Hollywood Cottage, Noye's Kent mansion.

John Palmer's house outside Bath. Armed police raided the house on the morning after the death of DC Fordham, but found Palmer and his wife had left for a holiday in the Canary Islands.

THE WAITING GAME GOES TRAGICALLY WRONG

By January 1985 Boyce was getting ready to move in. The round-the-clock observation on Hollywood Cottage was intensified. On the evening of Thursday 10 January, Detective Constables John Fordham and Neil Murphy of the elite C11 surveillance team were sent into the grounds of the house for close observation. Seconds later, three Rottweilers leapt out of the dark.

Murphy made a dash for the perimeter fence. Once safely in the road, he waited for his partner. Detective Constable Fordham never materialized.

Almost half an hour elapsed before Detective Constables David Manning and John Childs went into the grounds of Hollywood Cottage to look for their missing colleague. Almost immediately they saw Fordham lying on his back, with the Rottweilers pulling at his clothes. Standing over the fallen policeman was Kenneth Noye, pointing a shotgun at him.

Manning whipped out his warrant card and shouted, 'I am a police officer.' He walked over to where Fordham was lying and immediately saw blood oozing from his chest and stomach. 'He's done me,' Fordham gasped. 'He's stabbed me.'

Noye was dragged off and charged with malicious wounding, a charge which had to be changed to murder a few hours later. With the tragic loss of Detective Constable Fordham, the nature of the police operation became public and Boyce had to move quickly.

Within an hour of the stabbing, police raided the home of Brian Reader and discovered almost £70,000 in new £50 notes along with several lumps of yellow-coloured metal. They took these away, together with notebooks, diaries and address books – anything that would help establish Reader's connection with other members of the bullion chain.

The search of Hollywood Cottage and its grounds did provide ample evidence that Kenneth Noye was involved in the Brink's-Mat robbery. In a shallow gully beside the garage wall, they found 11 gold bars, weighing some 13kg and worth something in excess of £100,000.

The makeshift smelting shack found in the grounds of John Palmer's house. Inside, police discovered a foundry crucible and lifting gear, and in the house itself they came across two ingots of gold, still warm.

Nearly 50 officers sealed off the village of Litton, home of Garth Chappell. Inside Chappell's home they discovered a briefcase containing £12,500 in £50 notes. Armed police raided John Palmer's house. Palmer was not there. Three guests at the house informed police that Mr and Mrs Palmer had left the day before with their children for a three-week holiday in the Canary Islands. In the grounds of the house, police found a makeshift smelter. In the house itself they discovered two gold ingots, still warm, along with a selection of firearms and a large quantity of cash.

It took months for the detectives to piece everything together. As they had suspected, the gold had been passed from Noye to Reader and from him to Chappell. Chappell had paid Reader for each shipment in £50 notes, and Reader had paid Noye.

Once in possession of the gold, Chappell would resmelt it, mixing it with copper to hide its purity. Scadlynn would then sell it on the open market as scrap. In the space of six months, Chappell had managed to dispose of about half of the Brink's-Mat haul – some £13 million worth of gold.

Noye was jailed for 13 years and fined £250,000. Chappell received ten years and a £200,000 fine. Reader was sentenced to ten years, and John Palmer, who returned from Spain voluntarily, was found not guilty.

WAR CRIMES

POL POT
THE MURDER MACHINE

A gentle nation, ancient in its culture, pious in its faith, was cruelly dismembered by a Marxist fanatic. Pol Pot turned Cambodia into a killing field while the world turned its back on this lost nation.

Imagine a government that comes to power, then declares that money is banned. Not only money, but the forces that provide money – commerce, industry, banking – are also proscribed. The new government decrees that society will become agrarian again, just like it had been in the Middle Ages. Great cities and towns will be depopulated and the people will be moved to the countryside, where they will live and work raising crops and cattle. But families will not be allowed to stay together. The government, in its infinite wisdom, realizes that children must not be influenced by outdated and archaic bourgeois thoughts passed down by their parents, So they are taken away and brought up as the vanguard of the regime, imbued with and steeped in the philosophy of the new order. No messing about with books until they are in their late teens – there is no need for books anymore, so they are burned – and children from the age of seven will begin working for the state.

For the new agrarian class, there are 18-hour days, back-breaking work, followed by 're-education' in Marxist–Leninist thought from their new masters. Anyone who dissents, or who shows signs of 'regression' to the old ways, is not allowed to live –

Leading a column of his faithful followers, Pol Pot treks through the Cambodian jungle.

nor are intellectuals, teachers and college professors; nor those people who are literate because they might read thoughts which are not Marxist- Leninist, and spread a poisonous philosophy among the re-educated workers in the fields. Priests, with their outmoded theology, politicians of any hue other than that of the ruling party and those who made fortunes under previous governments are no longer needed: they too are eliminated. There is no trade, there are no telephones, there are no churches or temples, there are no bicycles, birthday parties, marriages, anniversaries, love or kindness. At best, there is work for the state – torture, degradation and, at worst, death.

This nightmare scenario was not a figment of some science fiction writer's imagination. It became a terrible reality in Cambodia, where leader Pol Pot turned the clock back and pushed civilisation out, hoping to find his own warped vision of a classless society. His 'killing fields' were littered with the corpses of those who did not fit into the new world that his brutal subordinates were shaping. As many as three million people may have perished during Pol Pot's regime in Cambodia – the same number of unfortunates killed in the gas chambers of the Auschwitz death factory run by the Nazis in the Second World War. Life under Pol Pot was intolerable and

Refugees flee from the city of Phnom Penh.

Cambodians were forced to tragically re-christen their south-east Asian country. They gave it the macabre name of the Land of the Walking Dead.

The Cambodian tragedy was a legacy of the Vietnam War that first marked the end of French colonialism before escalating into the conflict against the Americans. Fifty-three thousand Cambodians were slain on the fields of battle. Between 1969 and 1973 American B-52 aircraft carpet-bombed huge tracts of Cambodia, dropping as many tons of highexplosive on the tiny land as had fallen on Germany in the last two years of the Second World War. The Viet Cong fighters in Vietnam used their neighbour's lush jungles as encampments and staging posts for operations against the Americans, and these hideouts were the targets of the war planes.

Prince Norodom Sihanouk, ruler of Cambodia and heir to its great religious and cultural traditions, renounced his royal title ten years before the onset of the Vietnam War, but remained the head of his country. He tried to guide his country along a path of neutrality, a delicate balancing act for a country surrounded by warring states and conflicting ideologies. He had been crowned King of Cambodia, a French protectorate, in 1941, but abdicated in 1955. However, he returned, after free and fair elections, as head of state.

Between 1966 and 1969, as the Vietnam War escalated in intensity, he upset policymakers in Washington by ignoring the arms smuggling and the Vietnamese guerilla camps in the jungles of Cambodia. At the same time, he was only mildly critical of the punishing air raids being launched by America. On 18 March 1970, while he was in Moscow, his prime minister, General Lon Nol, with the backing of the White House, staged a coup, after which he changed the name of Cambodia back to its ancient title, Khmer. The Khmer Republic was recognized by the United States, which, however, one month later, chose to launch an invasion against the newly named land. Sihanouk went into exile in Peking… and here the ex-king chose to form an alliance with the devil himself.

Not much is known about Pol Pot, the man with the fat face and sparkling eyes, the man with the face of an avuncular old grandfather and the heart of a murderous tyrant. He was the monster with whom Sihanouk threw in his lot, swearing with this Communist guerilla chief that they would mould their forces into a single entity with the aim of destroying American forces. Pot, brought up by a peasant family in the Kampong Thom province of the country, had been educated at a Buddhist monastery where, for two years, he lived as a monk. In the 1950s he won a scholarship to study electronics in Paris where, like so many other students of the time, he became involved in left-wing causes. Here he heard about – although it is unclear whether they actually met – another Cambodian student, Khieu Samphan, a political science student whose controversial but exhilarating plans for an 'agrarian revolution' were to inspire the ambitions of the peasant, Pol Pot.

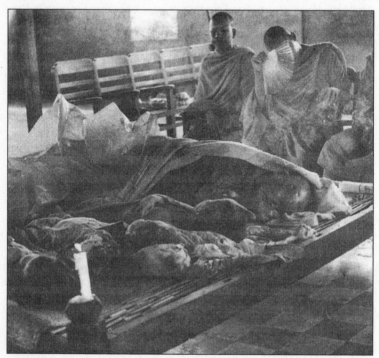

Buddhist monks mourn the dead killed by the Khmer Rouge.

A TERRIBLE REALITY

Samphan's theory was that, in order to progress, Cambodia must regress; it must turn its back on capitalist exploitation, fat-cat bosses created by the former French colonial overlords, and reject corrupted bourgeois values and ideals. Samphan's twisted theory decreed that people must live in the fields and that all the trappings of modern life must be annihilated. If Pol Pot himself had remained an obscure figure, this theory may have remained a coffee bar philosophy rattling around the boulevards and parks of Paris. Instead it became a terrible reality.

Between 1970 and 1975 the Khmer Rouge – the Red Army led by Pol Pot – became a formidable force in Cambodia, controlling huge tracts of the countryside. On 17 April, 1975, Pol Pot's dream of power became a reality when his armies marching under the red flag, entered the capital, Phnom Penh. Within hours of the coup, Pol Pot called a special meeting of his new cabinet members and told them the country was now called Kampuchea. He outlined the plans for his brave new world which would begin taking shape within days. He ordered the evacuation of all cities and towns, a process to be overseen by newly created regional and zonal chiefs.

He ordered the abolition of all markets, the destruction of churches and the persecution of all religious orders. Although privileged himself, in having been educated abroad, he harboured a loathing for the educated classes, and so all teachers, professors and even kindergarten teachers were ordered to be executed. The educated peasant, Pol Pot, feared the educated classes.

The first to die were the senior cabinet members and functionaries of Lon Nol's regime, followed by the officer corps of the old army. All were buried in mass graves. Then came the evacuation of the cities, towns and villages. Pol Pot's twisted dream was to put the clock back and make his people the dwellers of an agrarian, Marxist society. Pol Pot was aided by his evil deputy, Ieng Sary. Doctors were murdered because they, too, were 'educated'. All religious groups were exterminated because they

A weary soldier is welcomed by hysterical refugees fleeing the guerilla onslaught.

were 'reactionary'. The term Pol Pot used for his extermination policy was *'Khchatkhchay os roling'* – it translates as 'scatter them out of sight'. The sinister reality meant the death of thousands.

Buddhist temples were desecrated or turned into whorehouses for the troops or even became abbatoirs. Before the terror, there were some 60,000 monks in Cambodia: after it was over, just 3,000 returned to their shattered shrines and their holy places of worship.

Pol Pot also decreed that ethnic minorities did not, in fact, exist. Vietnamese, Thai and Chinese festivals, languages and cultures were ruled illegal, to be practised under punishment of death. His was to be a pure Khmer society. The deliberate and forceful eradication of ethnic groups fell most heavily on the 'Cham' people. Their ancestors had formed the Kingdom of Champa, once a country in what is now Vietnam.

The Cham migrated to Cambodia during the eighteenth century to live as fishermen along Cambodia's rivers and the Tonle Sap lake. They were an Islamic people and were, perhaps, the most distinctive ethnic group in modern Cambodia, for they never adandoned or diluted their language, cuisine, costume, hairstyles, burial customs or religion. The Cham were obvious targets for the young fanatics of the Khmer Rouge who fell upon them like a plague of locusts. The villages were torched, the people marched into the swampy, mosquito-plagued hinterland, fed pork – strictly against their religion – and the religious leaders executed. When villagers resisted whole communities were murdered, their bodies flung into huge pits and covered over with lime. Of 200,000 Cham people alive before the new order, barely 100,000 survive today. Those who survived the initial terror found that life under the new regime was infinitely harder than a quick death – hence the phrase 'Land of the Living Dead', coined by those forced to live under these conditions.

BOURGEOIS CRIMINALS

Pol Pot believed that all adults were tainted by feudal, bourgeois attitudes, with 'sympathies' for foreign regimes which Pol Pot had decreed were alien to the national way of life. Urbanites, in particular, were rooted out and placed in work camps where hundreds of thousands were literally worked to death or murdered if they spoke French – a major crime in Khmer Rouge eyes because it showed a bourgeois attitude, with a link to, and sympathy with, the colonial reign of the past.

In vast encampments, devoid of any comforts save a straw mat to sleep on and a bowl of rice at the end of every day, the tradesmen, dockers, clerks, bankers – many alive only because they managed to hide their professions – and numerous other citizens, toiled in conditions that would have shamed Japanese prison-of-war camps in the Second World War. The camps were organized, much like the concentration camps of the Nazis, to ensure that 'natural selection' took its toll of the aged and the ill, the very young, and pregnant women. Given a poor diet, deprived of strength, hundreds and thousands succumbed to disease, starvation and the clubbings of their brutal overseers. With no medical men to treat them, save for the attention of a few

Coils of barbed wire marked the Cambodian border with Thailand.

'traditional' herbalists whom the new government tolerated, the life span of a prisoner in the camps was pathetically low. They were frog-marched out at dawn into malaria-ridden swamps where they worked 12 hours a day, planting rice and clearing jungles in futile attempts to reclaim more farmland. Then they were frog-marched back at night, under gunpoint and often under the blows and bayonet-thrusts of their guards, to a bowl of rice, gruel and a morsel of dried fish. Then, exhausted though they were, they had to endure Marxist indoctrination sessions, when irredeemable bourgeois elements were rooted out to be taken away for punishment while the others chanted, parrot-fashion, the benefits and joys of the new state. There was one day off in every ten, when people could look forward to 12 hours of indoctrination. Wives were separated from their husbands, their children were either put to work at the age of seven or given away to the barren wives of party functionaries, so as to be brought up in the mould of fanatical warriors of the revolution. Pol Pot was a thorough man.

Bonfires were made of the books from universities and schools, as wretched, maltreated citizens were forced to chant as the works of civilization perished in the flames. There were 'hate-ins', when people were whipped before pictures of members of the old regime. It was a nightmare world, sinister and hopeless, for the Cambodian people were literally isolated from the world. There was no postal service, no diplomatic ties with any country, no telephones and no travel; it was truly a nation lost to the world.

To reinforce his battle against enemies real and imagined, Pol Pot set up a system of interrogations, tortures and executions in his prison camps. Much like the Spanish Inquisition of old, Pol Pot and his henchmen knew that all who came through the portals of these grim places were guilty – all they had to do was to confess that guilt. To convince its followers that cruelty was necessary and good for the nation, the regime taught its young bureaucrats that torture had a special, political significance.

Taught by the Chinese, the Khmer security officers were enmeshed in a hard and cruel ideology, revealed in documents captured after the overthrow of Pol Pot. These dossiers show that torture attained a high level in his nation. One document, the 'S-21 Interrogator's Manual', later handed over to United Nations' investigators, reads: 'The purpose of doing torture is to get their responses. It's not something we do for the fun of it. Thus, we must make them hurt so they will respond quickly. Another purpose is to break them psychologically and make them lose their will. It's not something that is done out of individual anger or for self-satisfaction. Thus we beat them to make them afraid but absolutely not to kill them. When torturing them it is necessary to examine their state of health first and necessary to examine the whip. Don't greedily want to kill them. Politics is very important whereas torture is secondary. Thus the question of doing politics takes the lead at all times. Even when questioning it is always necessary to do constant propaganda.'

TORTURE WITHOUT REASON

'At the same time it is necessary to avoid any question of hesitancy or half-heartedness, of not daring to do torture, which makes it impossible to get answers to our questions from our enemies, which slows down and delays our work. In sum, whether doing propaganda or torturing or bringing up questions to ask them or accusing them of something, it is necessary to hold steadfastly to a stance of not being half-hearted or hesitant. We must be absolute. Only thus can we work to good effect. We torture them but forget to give the reason first. Only then do they become totally helpless.' The notorious Chinese water torture, crucifixions and suffocations with a plastic bag were three among numerous torture methods practised by the evil men of the Khmer Rouge.

The S21 facility, from which the document took its name, was the most infamous institution in the whole of Cambodia. Based in the north-east of the country, at least 3,000 victims of the regime died there. Only seven prisoners are known to have survived – prisoners kept alive because they had administrative skills necessary to their overlords in the running of the dreadful place.

Torture was only one instrument of fear brandished over the heads of the cowed populace. The frequency with which people were executed was another. Many times, inmates in the new country camps were caught eating the flesh of their dead comrades in their desperation for food. The penalty for this was a horrible death of being buried up to the neck in mud and left to starve and thirst while ants and other creatures gnawed at the victim. Then the heads were cut off and stuck on pikes around the settlement with the words painted on a sign hanging from the neck: 'I am a traitor of the revolution!'

Dith Pran, a Cambodian interpreter for American journalist Sydney Schanberg, emerged from the years of slaughter as a witness to the horrors of Pol Pot's reign. His own experiences, including his threatened execution, were chronicled in the film *The Killing Fields*, in which the torment of the Cambodian people was, for the first time, starkly revealed to the world. Pran's journey from his civilized childhood to a prison camp, where he pretended to be illiterate in order to survive, was a harrowing tale that reduced audiences to tears of pity. 'Many times,' said Pran, 'I prayed that I was dead rather than having to endure the life that I was forced to live. But some of my family had gotten away to America and it was for them that I carried on living. It was a nightmare time.'

A Khmer Rouge soldier menaces civilians with his gun. The population of Phnom Penh were quickly subdued by the the thugs of Pol Pot's army.

STACKS OF SKULLS

Pran was one of the lucky ones who survived the Asian holocaust to be reunited with his family in 1979 in San Francisco. Even now, the mass graves of the unknown, unnamed dead continue to be unearthed in remote corners of the sad country, the skulls stacked against the graves like so many footballs.

It was military muscle and not moral right that, in the end, halted the bloodbath and allowed for some semblance of sanity to return to the blighted land. Britain had, it must be acknowledged, spoken out in 1978 against alleged human rights abuses, after receiving reports, through intermediaries in Thailand, about the reign of terror in Cambodia, but the protest was ignored. Britain reported to the United Nations Commission on Human Rights, but the hysterical Khmer Rouge representative responded: 'The British Imperialists have no right to speak of the rights of man. The world knows well their barbarous and abject nature. Britain's leaders are living in opulence atop a pile of rotting corpses while the proletariat have only the right to be unemployed, to steal and prostitute.' Regrets were sent from Pol Pot flunkies who said that they were too busy to attend UN enquiries on the allegations to the Commission hearings in New York.

In December 1978, Vietnamese forces, who had been skirmishing for years with the Khmer Rouge over a disputed border region, launched a major offensive with mechanized infantry divisions and full armoured support. The infrastructure of Cambodia had disintegrated so badly by this time, that battlefield reports had to be biked great distances to Khmer Rouge command posts because there were no telephones left in operation.

The Vietnamese, early in 1979, found themselves masters of a blighted land. Pol Pot had fled in his white armoured Mercedes from Phnom Penh, just hours before the Vietnamese troops arrived to liberate the ghostly city. He went scurrying back to his masters in China, glad of the sanctuary, but bitter that they had not come to his aid in resisting the well-armed and determined North Vietnamese onslaught.

Massive amounts of aid flooded into Cambodia as the world realized the full horror of the Khmer Rouge regime and the devastation of the country. The Khmer Rouge were, like the Nazis, particularly methodical when it came to detailing their crimes; investigators found daily logs of shootings, torture, hundreds of photo albums of those to be executed – including those of wives and children of 'intellectuals' liquidated in the earliest days of the terror – and the detailed loggings of the infamous killing fields. These fields, intended to be the basis of the worker's Utopia, a land without money or want, became, instead, the burial pits of a people crushed under the yoke of a cruel tyranny.

Pol Pot seemed to fade into the background but has emerged in recent years to become a major political force vying for power in this embittered region. Like all tyrants, he said that mistakes were made by those under him, that he had faced rebellions on all fronts and that those who died were 'enemies of the state'. In 1981 back in Cambodia, he told a meeting of old friends at a secret location near the Thai border that he was 'too trusting. My policies were sound. Over-zealous regional commanders and sub-district personnel may have misinterpreted orders. To talk about systematic murder is odious. If we had really killed at that rate, we would have had no one left to fight the Vietnamese. I have been seriously misinterpreted.'

The fall of Phnom Penh is celebrated by young guerillas of the Khmer Rouge.

ANGEL OF DEATH

Misinterpretation on the scale of three million dead – almost 25 per cent of the population of the nation – seems too small a word to describe what was done in his name and under his orders. But following Hitler's code, that the bigger the lie, the more people will believe it, Pol Pot has, once again, become a power-player in the region and is able to rally forces in the countryside that continue to believe in him and are still loyal to him. Now he is a major force once again, only waiting to ride into the country, like some avenging angel of death, to finish off what he started before: his great agrarian revolution.

For Dith Pran and other survivors, the prospect of Pol Pot's return to power, the possibility that he will plunge his tortured land into new depths of depravity, fills them with horror. When the United Nations first announced that the Khmer Rouge would be part of the power-sharing peace process in Cambodia, Pran said: 'I am still shocked when I see the Khmer Rouge flag flying on UN territory. How would you feel if you were Jewish and you saw Hitler's flag flying at the United Nations? Some people went on a fast for three days to protest this, but I did not. I have starved for four years and that is enough for any man.'

There is international lobbying for world governments to have the Cambodian massacres recognized as war crimes in the same way as the Hitlerian genocide of the Jews has been recognized. Yang Sam, of the Cambodian Documentation Commission in New York, is the Cambodian equivalent of Simon Wiesenthal (1908-2005), the Nazi death camp survivor who, from his office in Vienna, devoted his life to tracing and collating evidence against Nazi war criminals. Sam, a survivor of the terror, collects information against the butchers of his own land. He said: 'Those most responsible for the Cambodian genocide – the cabinet members of Pol Pot's regime, the central committee of his Communist party, the Khmer Rouge military commanders whose troops committed so much of the killing, those officials who oversaw, directed and ran the nationwide network of torture chambers, prison execution centres and extermination facilities – continue to remain active in Cambodia and international political life. Based in enclaves along the Thai–Cambodian border, they conduct guerilla war seeking to return to power in Phnom Penh. They have not been held accountable for their crime under international law and that is a tragedy of monumental proportions.

'Us survivors remember our families being taken away, many of them, and our friends brutally murdered. We witnessed members of our families and others die of exhaustion from forced marches and slave labour and from the brutal conditions of life to which the Cambodian people were subjected by the Khmer Rouge.

'We also saw Pol Pot's soldiers destroy our Buddhist temples, end schooling for our children, suppress our culture and eradicate our ethnic minorities. It is difficult for us to understand why the free and democratic nations of the world do not take action against the guilty. Surely this cries out for justice?' But there is no justice here.

The legacy of the Pol Pot years. The skulls of the anonymous dead serve to remind the world of the man's dreadful regime.

STALIN
CRIME AT KATYN WOOD

In the secret heart of the forest, the proud officers of the Polish army were brutally executed. Even their murderers were so shamed by the killings that they denied the facts. But the dreadful truth of Katyn Wood has not remained hidden.

Adolf Hitler, leader of the German Nazi party, sent his emissary Joachim von Ribbentrop to Moscow in August 1939. He wanted a pact with Josef Stalin, bloodthirsty leader of the Soviet peoples. Yet Stalin represented the Slavic races that Hitler had threatened time and time again, in his manic outpourings, to destroy for ever. And Hitler, in Stalin's eyes, was a fascist running dog who persecuted the Communists without mercy. The former champagne salesman, von Ribbentrop, emerged after several days of diplomatic niceties with his Soviet counterpart, foreign minister Vyacheslav Molotov, to proclaim to a stunned world that a new non-aggression pact had been signed between the two former adversaries. This was Realpolitik at its most cynical – the conclusion of distasteful business for the mutual benefit of mutual enemies.

The West viewed the Molotov–Ribbentrop Pact as the precursor to an aggressive war of conquest in Western Europe. With the Soviets promising no action if Germany made 'territorial claims' upon her neighbours, strategists saw that Hitler had effectively silenced his biggest, and a potentially lethal, foe without a shot being fired in anger.

But what the West did not know – and would not find out until a month later, when the armies of Hitler launched their attack on Poland which was to start the Second World War – was that 'the pact' contained a secret clause that divided Poland between Hitler and Stalin. Between them, the two great dictators, who despised each other and the systems each represented, had forged a compact to ensure that this independent nation should cease to exist.

Betwixt the two, Poland became a vassal state. Polish Jews were soon earmarked for destruction by the Nazis, while under the Soviets, the intelligentsia and anti-Communist elements were rooted out for 'special treatment' by the NKVD, the forerunner of the KGB but that concentrated less on espionage and more on mass murder and political suppression.

One other segment of polish national life was hated by both sides – the officer corps of the army who were proud, disciplined, fiercely independent men.

It was precisely because they were troublesome to both dictators, that one of the most heinous cimes in wartime history went unsolved for over 40 years. In 1940, 4,000 Polish officers, from generals to lieutenants, were bound, shot in the back of the head and buried in massive lime pits, surrounded by thick fir trees that made up the forest of Katyn, near Smolensk in western Russia. All the victims had their hands tied to nooses around their necks which tightened when they struggled; all bore the same single-entry head wound testifying to methodical execution by shooting.

Polish women weep over their loved ones after the bodies were disinterred.

For close on five decades the crime at Katyn Wood was not acknowledged or admitted by the perpetrators. The Germans claimed the Russians did it; the Russians that the Germans were the perpetrators. It was not until the demise of the Soviet Union and the release of KGB files that the truth came out – that the

Poles were executed because they were the 'class enemy' of the Soviet people. On 13 April 1990 Mikhail Gorbachev acknowledged his nation's culpability… 47 years after the day that Germany claimed her soldiers in the east had stumbled across the mass graves in the forest.

The events in the clearings of the Katyn Forest during those days of April 1940 make for grim reading. Even now the scars left by the liquidation of these proud warriors remain deep. This is the story of Stalin's massacre of the army allied to Britain – the nation for whom Britain went to war in the first place.

The tale, from being part of the first national army to stand up to Hitler to that degrading execution in the vast mass grave of the Katyn Forest, was a short one for these Polish officers.

First, Hitler's Stuka dive-bombers and armoured columns brought terror to the civilian population as Operation Case White – the conquest of Poland – began on 1 September. Hitler used a transparently lame excuse for sending his troops across the border; namely, that German soldiers in a frontier post had been killed by marauding Poles. Sixteen days later, with their cities in flames and their armies all but routed, the desperate Poles then had to endure an attack from their eastern neighbour, Russia. Again, it was a flimsy excuse that brought the Red Army pouring over the frontier. In reality, it was the fulfillment of the secret clause in the contemptible Molotov–Ribbentrop Pact.

Stalin camouflaged his military intervention by claiming his soldiers were being sent merely to protect the rights of Belorussians and Ukrainians, living in Polish territory near the border with the Soviet Union. At 3 a.m. on 17 December, hours after Soviet troops, backed up by the death squads of the NKVD, were pouring across the border, Waclaw Grzybowski, the Polish ambassador to Moscow, was summoned to the foreign ministry where he was confronted by Molotov who, shedding all diplomatic niceties, informed him: 'The Polish state ceases to exist. We are aiding you to extricate your people from an unfortunate war in which they have been dragged by unwise leaders and to enable them to live a peaceful life.'

By 5 October, the day the last Polish units ceased fighting, Germany had two-thirds and the Soviet Union one-third of Polish territory. Germany took close to 600,000 prisoners-of-war; the Red Army captured another 230,000 men. In the wake of the fighting troops came the SS battalions on the German side, and the NKVD secret police units of Stalin. Both groups were remarkably similar in their initial actions. Round-ups began of intellectuals, university professors, nobles, known radicals, truculent churchmen; anyone who was deemed to pose the smallest threat.

Hitler had used the state as his instrument of repression and murder since achieving power in 1933, but he was a mere apprentice in the art of massacre compared to Stalin. On his hands was the blood of tens of millions of people, murdered across the vast steppes, shot in the cellars of the NKVD prisons, worked to death in the great Gulag archipelago that stretched over the frozen Siberian wastes. Stalin, in his Kremlin office, decreed that the vanquished Poles in the territory he now ruled would, indeed, receive no treatment that had not already been meted out in large measure to his own suffering masses. None could accuse the Man of Steel of inconsistency in his harshness.

Early in November, after a secret edict from Stalin, NKVD units began separating and moving out from a vast string of POW camps the 15,000 Polish officers whom they had captured. They were taken to camps set up in old monasteries that had perished under Bolshevism, all of them within Russian territory. In these camps was the best of the best of Polish national life: educated, cultured, passionate men, many of them reservists who had simply abandoned their comfortable lives to put on a uniform and fight for the land they loved.

Only a handful would ever see it again.

The NKVD were preparing for mokrara rabota – the agency's slang for bloodletting. For months the NKVD superiors at the prison camps that held the Poles, had been sending reports back to their Lubyanka masters, suggesting that some of the Polish officers might be transported to Moscow, where they could be assimilated and indoctrinated into the Soviet system. But Josef Stalin had already made up his mind about their fate.

The liquidations at the Katyn Forest began on 3 April and did not end until 13 May, five weeks later. In the previous week the prisoners were rounded up in their camps at Kozelsk, Starobelsk and Ostashkov and taken in batches to railheads to board cattlewagons for unknown destinations. However, the 4,400 Poles from Kozelsk camp were bound for the forest at Katyn.

The Russian admission of responsibility for the massacre at Katyn Wood made headlines all over the world.

HOPE OF REPATRIATION

Since their capture, these men had existed on meagre rations and were given few facilities to communicate with their families. During the days that they were herded into trains, they were given a better diet, kindling hope among them that they were indeed being repatriated to a new life. Each man received three dried herrings, half a pound of bread and some sugar. For some lucky few there was even an issue of Russian cigarettes to treasure.

The NKVD wanted the officers lulled into a state of well-being. Had there been any inkling of what lay in store for them, there would have been bloody mutinies from the brave prisoners in the camps.

But once at the railheads, away from the camps and their comrades, the treatment changed immediately. New NKVD men were waiting to board them on the trains, men armed with clubs and dogs and with the vicious, four-sided bayonets issued to the NKVD. Many prisoners were severely, gratuitously beaten as they clambered aboard the trains. Waclaw Kruk, a lieutenant, was one of the officers never to return from Katyn.

A diary was later found near his body in which he wrote down his feelings, feelings that must have been those of all the Poles as they moved out of the camps into the unknown: 'Yesterday a convoy of senior officers left: three generals, twenty to twenty-five colonels and the same number of majors. We were in the best of spirits because of the manner of their departure. Today, my turn came. But at the station we were loaded into prison cars under strict guard. Now we are waiting to depart. Optimistic as I was before, I am now coming to the conclusion that this journey does not bode well.' His diary was found in 1943, near a body tagged 'number 424'.

Another corpse, that of Major Adam Solski, also had a journal near it. Experts who examined it concur that the condemned man wrote the final words less than 20 minutes before he was murdered. It makes sad reading. 'Few minutes before five in the morning: reveille in the prison train. Preparing to get off. We are to go somewhere by car. What next? Five o'clock: ever since dawn the day has run an exceptional course. Departure in prison van with tiny cell-like compartments; horrible. Driven somewhere in the woods, somewhere like a holiday place. Here a detailed search. I was relieved of my watch, which showed 6.30am, asked for my wedding ring. Roubles, belt and pocket knife taken away.'

Journey's end for the soldiers was the Katyn Forest, sloping towards the Dnieper River and not far from the town of Smolensk. Here, gigantic pits had been dug in the sandy soil, within the leafy groves of fir trees and silver birch. Not far from the pits was a building known innocently as The Little Castle of the Dnieper; in reality it was a summer house, a dacha, of the local NKVD and now served as the headquarters of the killing squads who were about to despatch the cream of the Polish army to their deaths.

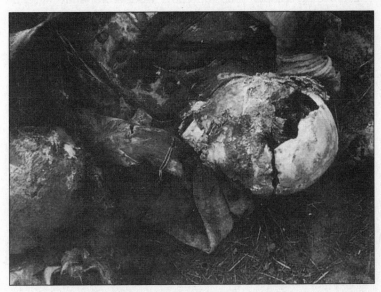

Skulls revealed that execution had been carried out with high-calibre weapons used at point-blank range.

A SINISTER JOURNEY

The prisoners were taken from the railcars in what were known as the *chorny voron* – the police buses that had been a grim feature of Soviet life for years. A glimpse of one of them, in a Soviet street, was enough to send shivers up the back of any innocent observer. These buses were divided into separate steel compartments, each little bigger than a kennel, in which the Polish officers were kept until their turn for execution arrived.

Only one man, a Polish professor, Stanislaw Swianiewicz, saw the killing of his comrades and lived to tell the tale. He was on board one of the trains, but was locked into a compartment by himself, only to be transported to Moscow to face charges of espionage. But he witnessed the scene as his fellow officers were led to their deaths. In the authoritative book *Katyn* by Allen Paul, the professor was quoted: 'wondered what kind of operation it was. Clearly, my companions were being taken to a place in the vicinity, probably only a few miles away. It was a fine spring day and I wondered why they were not told to march there, as was the usual procedure at camps. The presence of a high-ranking NKVD officer, at what was apparently the simple transferal of several hundred prisoners from one camp to another, could be explained if we were actually going to be handed over to the Germans. But, in such a case, why these extraordinary precautions? Why the fixed bayonets of the escort? I could think of no reasonable explanation. But then, on that brilliant spring day, it never even occurred to me that the operation might entail the execution of my companions.' Such an act was unthinkable.

Execution at the pits was to be cold, methodical, production-line work. Machine guns or grenades could not be used; people would run, there would be survivors, there would be an immediate panic among those prisoners awaiting transport from the train to the execution place. Instead the NKVD agents used 7.65mm Walther German police-issue pistols, considered by handgun experts to be the best pistols of their type in the world. NKVD squads would be waiting with fresh guns to replace those that overheated in the ceaseless slaughter, others with mounds of ammunition.

Once taken, one by one from the buses, the individual prisoners were bound in a particularly gruesome manner – a manner perfected over the years by the murderers from the NKVD. The victim's hands were first tied behind his back, then a second cord was tied over his head at neck level with the victim's greatcoat pulled up over it, like a shroud. From the neck the cord was passed down the prisoner's back, looped around the bound hands and tied again at the neck, forcing the arms painfully upwards towards his shoulder blades. Any attempt to lower his arms put pressure on the neck; repeated pressure would result in strangulation.

One by one these brave, noble men were led to the edge of the pits. Many bodies bore the brutal stab-marks of the four-squared NKVD bayonets - proof that, agonizing though their bonds were, they had attempted to struggle for their lives. Each one was despatched with what the Germans called the Nackenschuss – a shot through the nape of the neck which caused instant death and limited blood loss. This method had been perfected in countless cellars and execution dens of the NKVD over many years of Stalinist terror.

They fell into the pits and were stacked like cordwood, one on one, in layers of 12 before lime was sprinkled over them and tons of sand bulldozed back over them. But the tons of sand helped to press the corpses down and literally 'mummify' them as the body fluids and blood was squeezed out. The lime failed to work, so when the advancing Germans discovered the graves of Katyn, the thousands of corpses were well preserved.

On and on went the killing. The NKVD butchers fuelled their spirits with massive quantities of vodka consumed in the nearby dacha. Twelve hours a day for six weeks, nothing but the sound of gunshots echoed from those lonely groves until, finally, 4,143 victims were dead. As the last of the sand was bulldozed over the graves, the butchers planted tiny birch saplings on top.

The remaining 11,000 Polish officers held in other camps were liquidated at killing sites deeper in Russia. Their graves have never been exhumed but there has since been an admission from the now-defunct Soviet Union that all these Polish officers had been annihilated on Stalin's personal orders.

But Katyn was, and remains, the most significant massacre site. It was a known site, yet for decades it was surrounded by lies and duplicity. It justified a deep-rooted hatred of the Soviet state felt by all the people of Poland.

FRIENDS TURN ON EACH OTHER

It was only a matter of time before those arch-enemies, Hitler and Stalin, were to turn on each other. Hitler had written in *Mein Kampf* that Lebensraum – living space – in the east was his single greatest goal. On 22 June 1941 he set out to achieve that with Operation Barbarossa, the attack on the Soviet Union.

Fifteen hundred miles away from Stalingrad, in the dacha where the NKVD executioners planned the killing of the Polish officers, the soldiers in Lt. Col. Friedrich Ahrens' signal regiment were having a relatively quiet war.

Ahrens and his men had a strange foreboding about Katyn Wood, the site of the dacha. They heard rumours from the local people about NKVD executions taking place there, and hidden graves. Then, in February 1943, when the German 6th Army was routed at Stalingrad, a wolf unearthed bones in one of the mass grave sites. Ivan Krivozertsev, a local peasant, approached Ahrens and formally informed him of the dark secrets of the forest. NKVD secrecy and planning had not been hidden from the sharp eyes of the peasants.

The Germans prepared to tell the world of the slaughter of the Polish officers, and Dr Gerhard Buhtz, a professor of forensic medicine from a leading German university, was put in charge of the exhumation and examination of the grave pits, which were opened in early March. For ten weeks the stink of rotten flesh and

Egyptian tobacco – the Germans smoked it to mask the smell of the dead – mingled with the scents of moss and pine sap as the murdered men were disinterred and laid out. Some prisoners of war, American Lt. Col. John van Vliet among them, were taken by the Germans to witness the massacre site. He recalled: 'I sensed a propaganda exercise. I hated the Germans. I did not want to believe them. But after seeing the bodies there, piled up like cordwood, I changed my mind. I told the Allies, after the War, that I thought the Soviets were responsible.'

A priest prays at the graveside for the Polish officers, who were denied the blessing of the last rites at their death.

On 13 April 1943, at 3.10 p.m. Berlin time, the German radio network officially announced the finding of the graves where the Polish officers had been 'bestially murdered by the Bolsheviks'. The world was stunned into silence, choosing to believe that the report was fabricated by the Nazis. But the Polish government-in-exile, in London, had long harboured suspicions that the Russians had copious amounts of Polish blood on their hands.

On 15 April the Soviets counter-attacked, claiming: 'In launching this monstrous invention the German-Fascist scoundrels did not hesitate at the most unscrupulous and base lies, in their attempts to cover up crimes which, as has now become evident, were perpetrated by themselves. The Hitlerite murders will not escape a just and bloody retribution for their bloody crimes.' Three separate commissions were invited to visit Katyn by the Germans. The first was entirely German, the second composed of scientists and forensic experts from Switzerland, Belgium, Hungary and Bulgaria, and the third was entirely Polish. The evidence was mightily in favour of the German viewpoint. Although the ammunition was German, records from the manufacturing plants showed it to be batches sold, before the war, to Lithuania only to be seized later by NKVD police units.

The Soviets claimed that the men were killed by the advancing Germans in 1941 – although not one document with a date later than 6 May 1940 was ever found on a single corpse. The bayonet thrusts on the bodies were of the four-cornered NKVD type. The fact that there were no insects found in the graves indicated cold weather burial, not summer as the Soviets claimed – and besides, all the murdered soldiers wore heavy winter clothing.

But their military fight against Hitler had, for the Allied commanders at that time, a higher priority than a search for justice and truth. Churchill remarked in a cabinet meeting: 'We must not take sides in the Russo-Polish quarrel.' He assured Stalin in a secret communique that he would do his personal best to silence Free Polish newspapers in London over the affair, while he told Wadyslaw Sikorski, the prime minister in exile: 'If they are dead, nothing you can do will bring them back.' President Roosevelt in the White House preferred to believe the Soviet leader's explanation that the murders were committed by the Nazis.

When the Soviets finally overran the Katyn territory in their great push westwards, they took the opportunity to cover up the massacre of the Polish officers. The ponderously named 'Special Commission for Ascertaining and Investigating the Circumstances of the Shooting of Polish Officer Prisoners by the German Invaders in the Katyn Forest' went into overdrive to persuade the world that the murders were the work of the Gestapo and Einsatzgruppen. The Soviets stuck to their story that the officers had been murdered a year later than was actually the case – and as stories of German atrocities throughout the War began to emerge from all over Europe, there were plenty of people willing to believe the Soviets.

By the time the triumphant Red Army rolled into Berlin in May 1945, the myth that the Germans were responsible for Katyn was firmly planted around the world and in the satellite Eastern European nations over which, in Churchill's words, the Kremlin had drawn an 'Iron Curtain'. In Warsaw, the monument to the dead at Katyn blamed the Nazi invaders; at Katyn itself the inscription read: 'To the victims of Fascism. Polish officers shot by the Nazis in 1941.' The Soviets were operating under the maxim that Hitler once used – tell a lie big enough for long enough and it will metamorphose into truth. They denied any reference to the atrocity if it cast suspicion on their forces. Ewa Solska, the daughter of Major Solski whose diary was found on him, wrote 'killed at Katyn' in the box on her university application form which asked for information about her father. She was expelled for giving this information.

Even at Nuremberg, the great post-war trial for the crimes of Nazism, the Soviets were able to bluff the tribunals that Katyn was a Nazi crime. They could not bluff the Polish people, nor the many people around the world who were slowly coming to realize the enormity of Stalin's crimes.

It wasn't until 1990, at a ceremony inside the Kremlin, that Gorbachev, in keeping with the spirit of his Glasnost reforms, handed President Jaruzelski of Poland a box containing NKVD documents and other files, showing that the officers had indeed been murdered by the NKVD. These revealed that the executioners themselves had been 'liquidated' under Stalin's orders, then buried at an unknown grave site somewhere in Russia. Only 400 prisoners of war from the entire Polish officer corps survived, to be taken to Moscow and other Russian cities, where they proved to be willing Communists. Gorbachev labelled the massacre 'one of the gravest crimes of Stalinism'.

Was it all a big mistake on Stalin's part? Some historians believe that his orders may have been 'misinterpreted' by underlings. Stanislaw Mikolajczyk, the successor to Sikorski in London for the Polish government-in-exile, has his view and claims a Soviet bureaucrat secretly gave him the following interpretation of what happened.

A MISINTERPRETED ORDER

'Early in 1940 the Red Army sent a staff officer to find what Stalin planned to do with the Polish officers. A planned swap in which the officers would be turned over to the Germans in return for 30,000 Ukrainians had just fallen through. The Ukrainians were Polish Army conscripts captured by Germany the previous September, and were interned in two camps in eastern Poland. The Germans at first agreed to the exchange but backed out at the last possible moment, telling the Soviets to take the Ukrainians and keep the Poles. Then came rumours in Moscow that the Ukrainian conscripts and the Polish officers would be organized into special units of the Red Army. Senior commanders were aware of such talk but had nothing specific to go on.

'The staff officer was sent to get Stalin's clarification. The staff officer saw Stalin and briefly explained the problem. Stalin listened patiently. When the staff officer finished, Stalin supplied him with a written order. Such orders were common, often requested by subordinates as a matter of self-protection. In this case, said the informant, Josef Stalin took a sheet of his personal stationery and wrote only one dreadful word on it: 'Liquidate'. The staff officer returned the one-word order to his superiors, but they were uncertain what it meant. Did Stalin mean to liquidate the camp or to liquidate the men? He might have meant that the men should be released, sent to other prisons, or to work in the Gulag system. He might also have meant that the men should be shot, or otherwise eliminated. No one knew for sure what the order meant, but no one wanted to risk Stalin's ire by asking him to clarify it. To delay a decision was also risky and could invite retribution. The army took the safe way out and turned the whole matter over to the NKVD. For the NKVD, there was no ambiguity in Stalin's order. It could only mean one thing: that the Poles were to be executed immediately. That is, of course, exactly what happened.'

Many thought Stalin, the Man of Steel, would never have had it any other way.

The soil in Katyn Wood served to preserve the bodies. This was of considerable help when investigators came to identify bodies and buried papers.

ADOLF HITLER

THE HOLOCAUST

*Germany was humiliated by defeat after the Great War.
Despair gripped the nation. But one man promised to
return their pride. All they had to do was build gas
chambers and kill, kill, kill. So began the most shocking
mass murder in the history of the world.*

They met at a place called Wannsee, a charming suburb of Berlin with ornate houses and tree-lined streets that looked out over the lake which gave the area its name. It was 20 January 1942 and the Reich had reached the zenith of its military victories. The swastika flew over the Russian steppes, over the Balkans and Greece, France, the Low Countries, North Africa, Poland, Norway and Denmark. The wars of conquest had ended in total triumph for Hitler's armies so it was now time to put into effect phase two of his doctrine of Nazism. It was time to implement 'The final solution of the Jewish question in Europe'.

No one who followed the rise of Adolf Hitler and his Nazi party was surprised that he had a diabolical plan to eradicate the Jews. Hitler began his campaign of state terror against the Jews soon after coming power. He passed the infamous Nuremberg Laws which stripped them of property, valuables, human rights and political power. Then he organized the terror, which culminated in the *Kristallnacht* 'Night of Broken Glass' – in 1938. This involved the destruction of synagogues and Jewish property throughout Germany during a frenzied night of state-sponsored terror. But Hitler wanted 'a final solution to the Jewish problem' and this was to become a euphemism for mass murder.

That is why at Wannsee, in 1942, SS and Gestapo chiefs, led by Reinhard 'Hangman' Heydrich, gathered at a villa, once owned by a Jewish merchant, to plot the logistics for the collection. transportation and extermination of millions of men, women and children who had no place in the new world order. The men in black and grey uniforms drew up blueprints for the greatest state-sponsored murder in history.

Since the Nazi seizure of power Hitler had experimented with mass-killing techniques at euthanasia laboratories where the mentally ill were killed in gas-vans or by lethal injection. When his armies overran Poland and parts of Russia he walled his Jewish enemies up in medieval-style ghettoes where he allowed starvation and disease to kill the people locked within. In Russia his *Einsatzgruppen* – action squad – SS commandos shot hundreds upon thousands of Jews and other 'undesirables'. But it was not enough. These methods were cumbersome, slow and inefficient. Hitler was determined to bring some Henry Ford principles into the process of mass murder – a production line of death camps that would dispatch the unfortunates at the greatest speed possible.

Herman Goering, Luftwaffe chief whose first task for the Nazis was setting up the dreaded Gestapo, had Heydrich's orders in a letter, written six months before the Wannsee conference. It read: 'I hereby charge you with making all necessary preparation with regard to organizational and financial matters for bringing about a complete solution of the Jewish problem in the German sphere of influence in Europe.'

Heinrich Himmler, head of the SS; Heydrich, head of the SD, the security arm of the same organization; Adolf Eichmann, and Ernst Kaltenbrunner, Heydrich's successor after his master was assassinated in Prague in May 1942, can be said to be the architects of the final solution. They built the concentration camp network that spanned all conquered Europe.

Survivors stand in bitter mourning for their lost families at the memorial erected to the victims of the Holocaust.

Names like Treblinka, Sobibor, Buchenwald, Dachau and Auschwitz – Auschwitz, particularly, the most infamous human abbatoir of them all – have now become household words for evil. In these death factories Jews from all over Europe made a one-way trip to hell. And not only Jews – gypsies, Poles, Slavs, Russian prisoners of war, intellectuals, revolutionaries, homosexuals and artists who did not fit into the racial or political mould were despatched, A new breed of men and women, inconceivable in their cruelty, depraved beyond belief, were recruited to administer these extermination centres.

Such a man was Rudolf Hoess, commandant of Auschwitz where the final solution was to reach remarkable heights of cruel efficiency. Hoess, at his peak, oversaw a complex where men and women lived in filth, were worked like dogs and finally executed when they were no longer of any use to the Reich. Auschwitz, and its annexe camp of Birkenau, where the gas chambers and crematorium were situated, were two miles from the main town of the same name in southern Poland. Every day, in the camps, 12,000 people died in the gas chambers before being burned in the massive crematorium.

Hoess took a scientific delight in solving the problems of mass murder. Auschwitz, like the other camps, had used mass shootings and hangings to eradicate the inmates, but this was precisely the inefficiency that Hitler and the SS wanted to do away with. Later in 1942 a gas made from prussic acid that was used to kill rats and mice in German factories, was deployed for the first time against Russian POWs. The Russians were led into a long, sealed room, the walls of which were lined with showers. But the shower faucets were false and the plugholes sealed. And then they heard the rattle of hard crystals dropped on to a wire grating above their heads, before the room filled with a gas, called Zyklon-B, that was released from the crystals. They were all dead within 20 minutes.

At the far south end of the Birkenau camp two massive gas chambers and adjacent crematoriums were built by the inmates themselves. Trains arriving at a railhead were greeted by one Dr Josef Mengele – about whom more will be said later – the SS

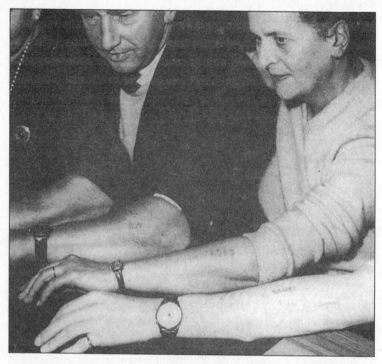

Former inmates of the death camps show the identity numbers tattooed on their arms by the Nazis.

doctor who became supreme arbiter of life and death within the electrified fences of Auschwitz. With a flick of his riding crop he dictated the fate of the inmates. Those who were to work for the Reich on starvation rations, under the blows of whips and cudgels, marched one way while their elderly parents, sisters, brothers and toddlers walked the other.

Loudspeakers told the latter group that they were heading off for showers and delousing before they were to be reunited with their families in barracks. In fact, they were taken to a long wooden hut where they were told to strip and place all valuables in a locker. Then their heads were shaved and the hair collected in giant sacks by other prisoners. Then they were marched in to the giant shower-rooms. But these showers did not flow with water and the naked humiliated prisoners were actually in giant death chambers.

BODILY REMAINS

Afterwards, men working for the Sonderkommando or special commando squads set up by their SS overlords, entered to disentangle the corpses and remove the gold fillings from their teeth. The bodies were then pushed into the ovens, the ashes raked out and spread over nearby woodland or dumped in the River Vistula.

Cruel and inhuman as the killing machine was, death was often the one thing the living prayed for. The camp culture spawned a sadistic, warped race of guards who took morbid pleasure in the mistreatment of their charges. Irnia Greese, the 'Blonde Angel of Hell' from Belsen, delighted in flaying women's breasts with a knotted whip. Karl Babor, the camp doctor of the Gross-Rosen camp, amused himself by burning new-born babies on an open fire. And at Auschwitz there was the infamous Dr Mengele, whose smiling face was always there to greet the new arrivals as they arrived in stinking cattle wagons.

Mengele was a doctor of medicine who betrayed his Hippocratic oath each and every day, while convincing himself that his scientific research in the camp was carried out on mere 'subhumans'.

His greetings at the train ramp for the Auschwitz arrivals had a dual purpose: he sorted out those who could work for the Reich before their deaths, and he sought blue-eyed twins so he could perform experiments aimed at cloning the Nordic supermen which Hitler had decreed were to be the new chosen race. And all the while he salved the shreds of his wicked conscience by claiming that he was saving life for the future! Yet all experts concur that on his personal orders alone some 400,000 Jews were executed. Prisoners, infected with lice, TB, typhus, typhoid and grotesque medieval-style infections – infections bred by the poor diet and insanitary conditions that prevailed in the camps – existed in a twilight zone of brutality that could only be eased by death. When they were no longer able to function in the armaments plants and quarries adjacent to the camps they were eliminated. The gold teeth from the corpses were sent to the Reichsbank in Berlin, their hair was used to stuff mattresses for troops on the Russian front and the fat from their bodies was processed into soap. Such was the efficiency that Adolf Hitler demanded and got from his loyal servants of evil.

Adolf Eichmann, like Mengele, was a classic product of the twisted logic of Nazism. He saw no evil in what he was doing, believed that he was a 'good soldier' who was only obeying orders. Day after day, as Germany was losing the war on all fronts, this son of an accountant rerouted armaments trains headed for the troops with supplies and rations, and cancelled returning hospital trains, so he could use the rolling stock to clear out the ghettoes of Eastern Europe and thus feed the furnaces at the extermination camps. But he was not flamboyant, more a grey bureaucrat and his cruelty only became public after the collapse of the Reich in May 1945.

During the height of the Holocaust 1,000 trains a week were criss-crossing Europe with people destined for the camps. In the middle of 1943 fully a third of all camp inmates assigned to work details died each week. Survival became a matter of cooperating with the SS - by getting a job in a camp clinic, becoming a block captain, seizing any chance to please the SS – anything that might bring a chance of survival. The overwhelming horror of these places was belied by the cynical slogan Himmler placed above the entrance gates of the camps: – Arbeit Macht Frei – Work Brings Freedom. It was a bitter lie.

But the camps were not the only disgraice. As brave German soldiers fought valiantly at places like Stalingrad and Kharkhov, the Einsatzgruppen squads were forever besmirching Germany's name with their mass executions. Herman Graebe, a German civilian engineer working on roadbuilding in the Ukraine, witnessed just such a scene. He wrote: 'Without screaming or weeping these people undressed, stood around in family groups, kissed each other, said farewells, and waited for the sign from the SS man who stood beside the pit with a whip in his hand. During the fifteen minutes I stood near, I heard no complaint or plea for mercy. I watched a family... An old woman with snow-white hair was

Hitler with his mistress, Eva Braun, relaxes in his mountain retreat at Berchtesgaden.

holding a child of about one in her arms, singing to it and tickling it. The child was cooing with delight. The parents were looking on with tears in their eyes. The father was holding the hand of a boy about ten years old and speaking to him softly: the boy was fighting back tears. The father pointed to the sky, stroked his head and seemed to explain something to him.

'At that moment the SS man at the pit started shouting something to his comrade. The comrade counted off about twenty people and instructed them to go behind the earth mound. Among them was the family I have just mentioned. I well remember a slim girl with black hair who, as she passed me, pointed to herself and said: "Twenty-three". I walked around the mound and stood in front of a tremendous grave. People were closely wedged together and lying on top of each other so that only their heads were visible. Nearly all had blood running over their shoulders from their heads. Some were lifting their heads and moving their arms to show that they were still alive. The pit was nearly two-thirds full and I estimated that it contained about one thousand people. I looked at the man who did the shooting. He was an SS man who sat at the edge of the narrow end of the pit, his feet dangling into it. He had a tommy-gun on his knees and was smoking a cigarette. The people, completely naked, went down some steps which were cut in the clay wall of the pit and clambered over the heads of the people lying there, to the place to which the SS man directed them. Some caressed those who were still alive and spoke to them in low voices.'

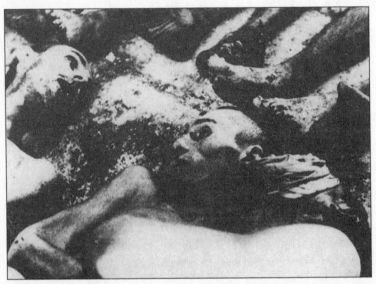

Grim photographs are both proof of, and constant reminders of, the barbaric slaughter of millions of innocent Europeans in the Nazi camps.

A DIGNITY IN DEATH

Towards the end of the war the Nazis increased their frantic efforts to wipe out the estimated nine million Jews within the conquered lands. One of Eichmann's greatest coups in the desperate days of 1944, as the Russians were advancing rapidly throughout Eastern Europe, was to get the Hungarians to hand over half of their population of 800,000 Jews. They were all gassed at Auschwitz – an achievement which Eichmann said gave him 'intense satisfaction'.

Most Jews and other Nazi victims went nobly and quietly to their deaths. They had a dignity that mocked the brutality of their tormentors, yet the Nazis liked to crow that the Jews had continually shown their weakness in life's struggle because they did not fight, but meekly submitted to the sword. But in reality, there was nowhere for these tortured people to go if they had escaped, no prospect of victory over well-trained and well-fed guards.

The Nazis did not have it entirely their own way. At Sachsenhausen many guards were killed in an armed breakout and, in 1944, the Jewish Underground in Auschwitz placed explosives in one of the ovens and blew it to smithereens. The most impressive display of defiance came when Hitler ordered the destruction of the Warsaw Ghetto in 1944. Here, the Jews of Poland were housed, but they refused to be taken to the trains and, with smuggled weaponry, killed SS men.

It took half a division of SS men with full anti-tank and armour facilities to rout the defenders in four months of bitter fighting. It cost the Jews 56,000 lives and kept valuable German soldiers

Herman Goering in prison, awaiting sentence, during the war crimes trial.

away from the fight on the front. Such were the twisted values of Nazism – the defenceless Jew always considered more of an enemy than guns, tanks and armed soldiers.

While they may have salved their own consciences about what took place in the death camps, with the excuse that they were 'only obeying orders', the guilty men knew what awaited them. Auschwitz personnel fled the camp just 24 hours before Russian troops arrived to liberate the wretches left inside. The air was still heavy with the sickly sweet stench of burned human flesh and the crematorium, the one that was still working, had corpses awaiting burning. In a warehouse barracks that the Nazis dubbed 'Canada' because of its vast size, the Russians found a mountain of human hair, gold teeth, underwear, clothing and jewellery – the last destined for the Reichsbank. Hoess had planned to demolish Auschwitz but he left it too late. But Franz Stangl, commandant of Treblinka, managed to destroy his camp. The only testimonies to its existence are the tracks of the railway line, and the deep green hue of the grass over the rich, fertile ground that, in places, is 12 feet thick with human bonemeal.

In the west, it was the Americans and the British who liberated the Nazi charnel houses of Belsen and Buchenwald.

Josef Kramer, the commandant of Belsen, was puzzled by the fury of the ordinary British squaddies who liberated his fiefdom; he could not understand why they were so belligerent towards him. At his trial after the war for his crimes at the Natzweiler, Auschwitz and Belsen camps, he told those judging him: 'I didn't feel anything towards the prisoners. I received orders to kill them and that's what I did. Surely you cannot expect a soldier in wartime to disobey an order?'

But Kramer and all the others – Babor of Gross-Rosen, Mengele of Auschwitz, Heinrich 'Gestapo' Mueller, Adolf Eichmann, Franz Stangl of Treblinka – all tried to escape. They knew that their blind obedience to orders would never stand up in a courtroom whose loyalty was not to Adolf Hitler. Using the services of the ODESSA – the Organization of Former Members of the SS – they drew on secret Swiss bank accounts to pay for new identities and lives in distant lands. Much of the money came from the victims whose butchery they had overseen in the camps. It was a final bitter twist of irony that the SS who had tried, without success, to wheedle from Swiss banks the names of wealthy Jewish clients, now used the same good offices of secrecy for their own flight.

A rogues' gallery of Nazis. From the left, Propaganda minister, Goebbels; SS Chief, Himmler; Deputy Hess and Hitler, all together at a pre-War rally

REFUGE FOR THE WICKED

South America, where military regimes had long expressed solidarity and sympathy with the Nazi cause, was a favourite destination. Eichmann headed for Argentina; Mengele for Brazil; Joseph Schwammberger, commandant of the concentration camp at Przemysl, to Argentina; Alois Brunner, designer of the mobile gaswagons and the brains behind the deportation of 46,000 Greek Jews to Auschwitz, made it to Damascus where he still lives under Arab protection.

Justice for those left behind was swift; many camp guards were executed within days of liberation. The Nuremberg trials despatched many more, including Kramer and Greese. But it was left to people like Simon Wiesenthal, who lost 80 members of his family in the Holocaust, to become the conscience of the world – to ensure that mankind never forgot what revolting crimes had taken place.

Wiesenthal survived the death camps and pledged his life to tracking down Nazi war criminals and bringing them to justice. His determination and diligence led to the capture of Eichman in Argentina and the deportation from South America of Lyon's Gestapo chief Klaus Barbie.

Wiesenthal's small office in central Vienna is called the Documentation Centre and it is a museum to the memory of the slain. Wiesanthal calculated that as many as 14 million were claimed by the Nazis in their war of racial purification. From 22 March 1933, when Dachau, 12 miles from Munich, opened as the Reich's first concentration camp, until the Allies liberated the entire network, Hitler had managed to dispose of over a third of Europe's Jews. Wiesenthal inflated his figures because of the special 'actions' taken by the Russians, the enormity of which has still to be fully understood.

Right up until his death in September 2005, at the age of 96, Wiesenthal was still hunting, still ceaselessly bringing to justice those who perpetrated mankind's biggest mass murder. He felt unable to stop, not while revisionist historians and neo-Nazi sympathizers, on the rise in Europe and Russia, were busy denying that the Holocaust with its death camps ever happened.

Wiesanthal would have died a happy man if he could have captured Alois Brunner, the committed Nazi, who, in 1965, said to reporters from a German newspaper: 'I'm glad! I'm proud of what I did. If I could have fed more Yids into the flame I would. I don't regret a thing – we were only destroying vermin.' Alois Brunner is believed by some to be living in Damascus and working as an advisor to the Syrian government, despite contested reports of his death sometime in 1996. On March 2, 2001, he was found guilty in absentia by a French court for crimes against humanity and was sentenced to life imprisonment.

Simon Wiesenthal would have found some solace in the report he intended to give the Lord when it became time to depart his life 'We will all be called before the Lord for judgement,' he said, 'and we will be asked to give an account of ourselves. One man will say "I became a tailor". Another will say: "I became a doctor". Yet another will say: " I became a jeweller".

'And I will be able to say: " I did not forget you...".

The Power-mad, ruthless Herman Goering started the Gestapo to enforce the more ruthless aspects of Nazi rule.

ALFREDO ASTIZ
THE DIRTY WAR

The new military government promised to return Argentina to its former glory. Instead, they unleashed a gang of sadists upon the nation – men like Astiz who led a dirty war of murder and torture against his own people.

Between 1976 and 1982 Argentina waged a full-scale war within its own borders. The enemy were classified as those who acted or sympathized with anyone who had a viewpoint other than that espoused by the government. The military junta in power called their reign of terror The Process of National Reorganization. But it was a fancy euphemism for mass murder, whereby people vanished into human slaughterhouses, were tortured there and murdered. Coffee-bar socialists, mothers of radicals, babies of dissidents, long-lost cousins of intellectuals who had once read a Communist pamphlet – these were the victims of this 'Process' known to the rest of the world as the 'Dirty War'. And working within this state terror machine were individuals like Lt. Alfredo Astiz.

THE CLEANSING OF SOCIETY

Astiz was a member of the officer corps which took upon itself the burden of 'cleansing' Argentinian society. The military throughout South America has had a long and shameful history of interference in civilian governments but none more so than the Argentinian army. Military rule has dominated Argentina and between 1930 and 1982, the only civilian government to last its full term was that of Juan Peron. For years, after no less than six coups, the men in uniform guided – or rather, misguided – the fortunes of this land rich in minerals, farming and cattle.

When the sophisticated and cosmopolitan citizens of Buenos Aries woke up to the clatter of tank tracks on the cobbled streets of their gracious city on 23 March 1976 they did not panic; they had, after all, heard and seen it all before.

This time, it was a General Jorge Videla telling the people that massive unemployment, inflation running at 800 per cent and a resurgence of left-wing violence had driven the military to grab power. Videla, having seized the radio and television stations, put it to his people like this: 'Since all constitutional mechanisms have been exhausted, and since the impossibility of recovery through normal processes has been irrefutably demonstrated, the armed

The Mothers of the Plaza de Mayo defied arrest, torture and even death as they paraded before the junta headquarters in frequent mass demands for the return of their children.

forces must put an end to this situation which has burdened the nation. This government will be imbued with a profound national spirit, and will respond only to the most sacred interests of the nation and its inhabitants.'

There was a tone of determination in his voice which made the people of Argentina embrace rather than shrink from military government. Leftist guerrillas had, since 1966, been rampant in the countryside, murdering, kidnapping, committing atrocities among the civil population. The country was on an inexorable slide into anarchy as it battled against these guerrilla groups, most notably the Ejercito Revolucionarioa del Pueblo – People's Revolutionary Army – and the Montoneros. There is a school of thought that says that, had these terrorists not created a climate of fear which brought the army out of its barracks and put the torturers in government, 15,000 innocent people might still be alive today. But Videla and his henchmen were welcomed by a tired population who were glad to listen to his ideas on The Process of National Reorganization.

While Videla uttered platitudes and told his own people, and the world at large, that his government would respect human rights, his machinery of terror was being secretly assembled, soon to be unleashed on an unsuspecting population.

The officer corps of the Argentinian armed forces saw themselves as an elite group, imbued with the national spirit as no other body within Argentina. Many proved very happy to oversee the terror required to reorganize their countrymen, but none more so than Alfredo Astiz, who was to develop into an infamous torturer, his name forever linked with this shameful period of Argentina's sad history.

THE DEATH SQUADS

Astiz, a handsome naval lieutenant of wealthy parents, drank deeply from the poisoned chalice offered by Videla. He believed the General when he said that the enemies of Argentina were within its own frontiers. With the zeal of a Spanish Inquisition cardinal, Astiz helped enthusiastically in the founding and operation of ESMA, the Navy Mechanics School in Buenos Aries, which was nothing more than a human abbatoir hiding behind the name of an institute of marine engineering.

Thousands of victims of 'The Process' were brought as prisoners to the Navy Mechanics School where they were subjected to the most horrific beatings and torture, then taken out for execution; very few made it back to families and loved ones. It was not only the navy that organized this kind of torture centre: the army, air force and police were also involved, each one vying for glory as they hunted the 'enemy within'. They operated in squads called patotas and they each found places to turn into centres of hell, where they dragged the dissidents who, they believed, were destroying the Argentinian way of life and its cultural traditions.

One of the few victims to survive after Astiz and his men had captured her has a horrifying story to tell. Twenty-seven-year-old nursery school teacher Isabel Gamba de Negrotti was pregnant

*Dagmar Hagelin, a young Swedish woman, disappeared after
the junta kidnapped her.*

when she was seized at gunpoint by the patotas and taken away in
a green Ford Falcon car – a make of car that came to be indelibly
linked with death – and dumped in the Navy Mechanics School.
The young woman described her ordeal: 'They took me to a room
after arrival where they kicked me and punched me in the head.
Then they undressed me and beat me on the legs, buttocks and
shoulders with something made of rubber. This lasted a long time.
I fell down several times and they made me stand by supporting
myself on a table… While all this was going on they talked to me,
insulted me, and asked me about people I didn't know and things I
didn't understand.

'I pleaded with them to leave me alone, otherwise I would lose
my baby. I hadn't the strength to speak, the pain was so bad. They
started to give me electric shocks on my breasts, the side of my
body and under my arms. They kept questioning me. They gave
me electric shocks in the vagina and put a pillow over my mouth to
stop me screaming. Someone called 'The Colonel' came and said

they were going to increase the voltage until I talked, but I didn't know what they wanted me to talk about. They kept throwing water over my body and applying electric shocks all over. Two days later I miscarried.' She survived the ordeal.

Enemies real and imagined were seen everywhere by officers of the junta. Their paranoia is revealed in a telling comment from Fifth Army Corps Commander General Adel Vilas, that he made some months after 'The Process' had started: 'Up to now only the tip of the iceberg has been affected by our war against subversion… it is necessary to destroy the sources which feed, form and indoctrinate the subversive delinquent, and the source is the universities and secondary schools themselves.'

The junta was going after the children, the students and the trade unionists, the journalists and the teachers – all were swept up in the vortex of terror. Victims were picked up at random and, as these citizens were bundled into the death cars, they would yell out their names and addresses to passers-by who, in turn, would inform families that their relations had joined *los desparecidos* – 'the disappeared'.

Often the military disposed of their victims by pushing bodies, dead or alive, out of helicopters as they flew over rivers. Almost 5,000 people are believed to have met their deaths on these 'NN' – 'No-Name' – flights. Others were buried in mass graves on the pampas or in remote corners of country churchyards, buried without name, sacrament or ceremony.

Inside the Navy Mechanics School, Astiz and other torturers preferred even crueller forms of death and practised bizarre forms of torture and sadism against men, women and children.

Many people who came across Astiz compared him to Dr Josef Mengele, the Nazi death camp doctor at Auschwitz. Astiz, who was fair-haired and blue-eyed, was nicknamed 'the blonde angel' and he revelled in his sadistic work. He was keen from the very beginning of 'The Process' to take on the dirty, murderous tasks that many of his naval comrades refused.

Raul Vilarano, the killer who later confessed to the horrible deeds perpetrated by himself and Astiz, said that he and his cohorts did not work to any pattern at the Navy Mechanics School; rather, they roamed at will, at any hour of the day or night, satisfying whatever grotesque lusts came upon them with any victim they happened upon. Dagmar Hagelin happened to be one of those victims.

These men of the Junta faced murder charges. Clockwise: Jorge Videla, Emilio Massera, Orlando Agosti, Omar Graffigna, Basilio Lami Dozo, Jorge Anaya, Leopoldo Galtieri, Roberta Viola and, centre, Armando Lambruschumi.

Dagmar was arrested on 27 January 1977. She had Swedish nationality even though she was raised in Argentina, and was a gifted 18-year-old classical music student with coffee-table ideas about socialism, but no affiliation with any guerrilla groups or other Communist subversives. As she rang the bell at a friend's house two men – a patota squad from the Navy Mechanics School – appeared and Dagmar ran, only to be shot down in the street. She was dumped in the boot of a Ford Falcon and driven away. The man who had fired the shot was Astiz.

Unlike other 'no-names' who had disappeared, Dagmar did not come from the poor and powerless. Her father ran a profitable business and was on good terms with the Swedish ambassador but, though he used every influence to trace his daughter, his efforts were to no avail. Dagmar, another innocent among thousands, died in the Navy Mechanics School and her remains have never been found. The Swedish ambassador refused to accept honours from his host country when it became time for him to take up another diplomatic posting – he did not want to give credence to a regime that, he was convinced, murdered young girls.

Alfredo Astiz in his role as naval officer signs his surrender to the British during the Falklands War.

The Mothers grew bolder and bolder. They knew they had to attract world attention to their plight if they were to defeat the regime.

Jacob Timerman, a Jewish newspaper editor who was deemed sympathetic to the enemies of the state, was tortured by Astiz but he survived to shame the military men with an account of his suffering in the book *Prisoner Without a Name, Cell Without a Number*. He wrote: 'When electric shocks are applied, all that a man feels is that they're ripping his flesh apart. And he howls. Afterwards, he doesn't feel the blows. Nor does he feel them the next day, when there's no electricity, but only blows. The man spends days confined in a cell without windows, without light, either seated or lying down. The man spends a month without being allowed to wash himself, transported on the floor of an automobile to various places of interrogation, fed badly, smelling bad. The man is left enclosed in a small cell for forty-eight hours, his eyes blindfolded, his hands tied behind him, hearing no voice, seeing no sign of life, having to perform his bodily functions upon himself. And there is not much more. Objectively, nothing more.'

Astiz reached new heights of cynicism and cruelty when he posed as Gustavo Nino, a peasant boy who had lost relatives to the patotas. He infiltrated the ranks of the women who came to be called 'The Mothers of the Plaza de Mayo', the headscarved women who paraded silently in front of the junta's pink palace with the names of missing loved ones on boards hanging from their necks. These women were the true heroines of the Dirty War, defying truncheons and teargas to stage their weekly vigil, a vigil that played a powerful role in bringing the world's attention to the mass killings taking place in what the West had long regarded as the most 'civilized' of the South American nations. However, when the women's ranks were depleted by arrests, when their homes were raided or set on fire, when more members of their family disappeared, Gustavo Nino was always there to comfort them, never letting on that he had been the one who fed the damning information about their families back to his colleagues, who were waiting with the whips and the electric cattle prods and the flames.

For a time Astiz also worked out of his government's naval bureau in Paris, where he spied on exiled Argentinian human rights groups. After he was rumbled in Paris he headed for South Africa on a naval posting, but was hounded out of the country in 1981 when journalists learned of his unsavoury work at the Mechanics School. His superiors decided to pack him off to the war against Britain in the Falkland Islands in 1982.

The military roll their weapons throught Buenos Aires.

THE TORTURER IS FREED

Astiz was captured by Royal Marines and when his name appeared in British newspapers, alarm bells began to ring in the capitals of the world. There were calls for his blood from Stockholm to Paris to the capital of his homeland, where thousands had a righteous claim on his murdering hide. But, under the terms of the Geneva Convention, Astiz was a prisoner of war and could not be handed over to foreign powers who suspected him of domestic crimes. He returned home after the war.

In Argentina, the following year, Raul Alfonsin was sworn in as the democratic president, the forty-first in the nation's history. His mandate was not only to steer the country towards democratic reforms, but also to exorcise the evil perpetrated upon his people by the junta. Some of the guilty men were brought to trial – including the suave torturer, Astiz. But he was never punished, never served time in a prison. At his pre-trial hearing his lawyers refused to admit that he had abducted and killed Dagmar – but in a supreme Orwellian twist said that if he had, it did not matter, because he was operating in a 'wartime' situation. The military really did believe they were at war with their own people. He is now free in Argentina, a man with a wicked past but not a troubled conscience.

A commission was established after the war by the Alfonsin government to probe the terror. It found that the 'final purpose' of the terror was to exterminate the detainees and disfigure the bodies, so they could never be identified. The commission found no common factor to link the victims - they came from every level of Argentinian society. Almost nine thousand of 'the disappeared' have never been found, despite the fact that more than 60 per cent of those seized were abducted in front of witnesses in public places. Three hundred and forty torture centres were unearthed – centres which, according to the junta, never existed. The commission produced a report 50,000 pages long but the government failed to bring any of these state murderers to account.

Democracy now rules in Argentina, the dark days of 'The Process' are over. But the men in the olive green uniforms with the dark glasses are still there, lurking, waiting their next chance. Hebe Bonafini hopes they stay hidden. She was one of the founding members of the Mothers of the Plaza de Mayo and lost two sons and a daughter-in-law in the terror. She said: 'The military went to war against people who spoke their own tongue. They never got the right ones anyway, just children, really, no one who was ever a threat. What happened to us must serve as a warning to all people all the time. It can happen anywhere you know, making people disappear. That is the tragedy of it. It can happen to anyone…'.

SEPTEMBER 11
WORLD TRADE CENTER

On 11 September 2001, terrorists unleashed a shocking air assault on America's military and financial powers by hijacking four commercial jets and then crashing them into the World Trade Center in New York, the Pentagon and the Pennsylvania countryside.

It was the most dramatic attack on American soil since Pearl Harbor and caused the most incredible scenes of chaos and carnage. With the estimated death toll at over 5,300, this was definitely one of the most devastating terrorist operations in American history.

HIJACKED PLANES

The terrorists hijacked four California bound planes from three airports on the Eastern Seaboard. The planes were loaded with the maximum amount of fuel, which suggested a well-financed and well-coordinated plan. The planes were identified as American Airlines flight #11 and United Airlines flight #175, both flying from Boston, Massachusetts to Los Angeles, California. There was a total of 157 people on board the two planes.

At 8.45 a.m. the first hijacked passenger jet, Flight #11, crashed into the north tower of the 110-storey World Trade Center, tearing a gaping hole in the building and setting it on fire.

As if this wasn't horrifying enough, at precisely 9.03 a.m. the second hijacked airliner, Flight #175, crashed into the south tower of the World Trade Center and exploded – both buildings were now burning. They had ripped a blazing path through the Defence Department, bringing the domestic air traffic system to a halt and plunging the whole nation into an unparalleled state of panic.

Immediately the Federal Aviation Administration shut down all New York City area airports, halting all flight operations for the first time in US history. The Port Authority of New York and New Jersey ordered that all bridges and tunnels in the New York area were to be closed.

President Bush put US military forces, both at home and abroad, on their highest state of alert, and navy warships were deployed along both coasts for air defence

The horrors of the attack, however, were not yet over. At 9.43 a.m. American Airlines Flight #77 out of Dulles International Airport, ripped through the newly renovated walls of the Pentagon - perhaps the world's most secure office building. Evacuation of the Pentagon and the White House began immediately.

At 10.05 a.m. the south tower of the World Trade Center collapsed, plummeting into the streets below. A massive cloud of dust and debris formed and slowly drifted away from the building. At the same time as the collapse of the tower, a fourth jet, Flight

The second plane hits the south tower of the World Trade Center.

#93, was reported to have crashed 80 miles south-east of Pittsburgh, shortly after it was hijacked and turned in the direction of Washington.

None of the 266 people aboard the four planes survived. There were even more horrific casualties in the World Trade Center and the Pentagon, which together provided office space for more than 70,000 people.

The spectacular collapse of the historic twin towers and another not so famous skyscraper during the rescue operations caused even more bloodshed. At least 300 New York firefighters and 85 police officers lost their lives.

In a grim address to the nation, President Bush condemned the attacks as a failed attempt to frighten the United States and promised a relentless hunt to find those responsible. 'We will make no distinction', he said, 'between the terrorists who committed these acts and those who harbour them.' Bush also promised that America would continue to function 'without interruption'.

GROUND ZERO

The site of destruction became known as 'Ground Zero'. The extent of the devastation, even the limited view of it that could be seen from outside the perimeter, was a horrifying sign of just how evil mankind can be. However, you could also see many signs of the good side of humanity, in the numerous outpourings of love and support for the victims and their families that surrounded the site. You could see the tributes everywhere – in the yard of a church near the site, and along the fence surrounding the area. There were signs, posters, greeting cards, dolls, stuffed animals, flowers and numerous other messages and items indicating that people all over the world cared about the people who had died in this tragedy. It seemed to show the sheer determination of the people to stand up against the terrorists.

Though it may never feel right to describe the place as clean, the clean-up of the World Trade Center site is now complete. What was just a pile of jagged, knotted steel and concrete, is now a hole, a neatly squared-off, rectangular cavity of 16 acres.

One prominent reminder of the scale of the disaster that engulfed New York on that fatal day was the remains of 'The Sphere' which stood in the fountain. This was once the centrepiece of World Trade Center plaza.

WHO WAS RESPONSIBLE?

Although no one claimed responsibility for the attacks on September 11, federal officials said they suspect the involvement of Islamic extremists with links to fugitive terrorist Osama bin Laden. Bin Laden has been implicated in the 1998 bombings of two US embassies in Africa and several other attacks. There is also a lot of evidence implicating bin Laden's militant network in the attack. Politicians from both parties predicted a major and immediate escalation in America's worldwide war against terrorism.

Following the cataclysmic events of September 11, the US authorities were quick to name Osama bin Laden as their prime suspect. The reasons for their suspicions were many, and the evidence collected during the ensuing investigation seemed to support their theory.

Although the evidence seemed compelling, at least two people weren't convinced. Milt Beardon, a former CIA agent who spent time in Afghanistan advising the mujahedeen during their fight against the Soviets, told ABC's *Sunday Programme* that the attacks may have been the work of Shi'ite Muslims because the hijackers on the aircraft that crashed outside Philadelphia were described as wearing 'red head bands', an adornment known to date back to the formation of the Shi'ite sect. Pakistani journalist, Hamid Mir, also doubted that bin Laden was behind the September 11 attacks, saying the terrorist leader did not have the resources to pull it off.

Despite these doubts, another piece of information provided a chilling insight into what was to come. While recording a segment for the CBS *60 Minutes* programme, the show's producer George Creel, was travelling in a car with Khaled Kodja, a known bin Laden associate, when Kodja told him:

'America is a very vulnerable country, you are a very open country. I tell you, your White House is your most vulnerable target.

It would be very simple to just get it. It is not difficult. It takes only one or two lives to have it, it's not difficult. We have people like this.'

Although the world intelligence community has been aware of bin Laden and his al-Qaeda network for some time, no one was able to predict where and when he would strike next. The organisation is not only more sophisticated than past terrorist groups, but it is controlled and financed by a man who has dedicated most of his adult life to fighting a jihad against anyone he sees as an 'enemy of Islam', particularly America.

Recovering the body of the firefighter's chaplain from the Ground Zero site.

FROM A LARGE FAMILY

Osama bin Laden (Usamah bin Muhammad bin Awad bin Ladin) was born in 1957 or 1958 in Riyadh, Saudi Arabia. He was the seventh son in a family of 52 children.

His father, Sheik Mohammed Awad bin Laden, was a poor, uneducated labourer from Hadramout in South Yemen who worked as a porter in Jeddah. In 1930, the elder bin Laden started his own construction business, which became so successful that his family grew to be known as 'the wealthiest non-royal family in the kingdom'.

Bin Laden, top of the FBI's most wanted terrorist list, he used to live in exile under the protection of Afghanistan's Taliban regime. Since the collapse of the Taliban regime, he has been in hiding. Though his current whereabouts are unknown, most reports indicate that, if alive, bin Laden is probably in Afghanistan or Pakistan.

Although the September 11 attacks shocked the world with their audacity and far-reaching repercussions, one positive factor remains. A large percentage of the world's population was united in a collective resolve to never let it happen again. Perhaps, at least in this case, some good will come out of it and the thousands of victims will not have died in vain.

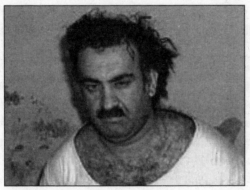

Khalid Sheikh Mohammed following his arrest

THE BIGGEST AL-QAEDA CATCH

The arrest and interrogation of Khalid Sheikh Mohammed was one of the biggest catch is in the global hunt for al-Qaeda suspects. Western security sources said they had no doubts that Khalid played a major role as al-Qaeda's operational commander in the September 11 attacks.

Kuwaiti-born Mohammed was one of three al-Qaeda suspects detained in the city of Rawalpindi near the Pakistani capital

Islamabad as part of Pakistan's support for US President George W. Bush's war on terror.

Nobody but a few Pakistani intelligence agents had heard of Khalid until a 1,200lb bomb of fertilizer, petrol and hydrogen exploded in the underground car park of the World Trade Center in New York on 26 February 1993. This attack, which killed six people and injured more than 1,000, was Khalid's spectacular debut in international terrorism.

Chilling details have begun to emerge regarding Khalid's alleged activities since September 11. He is reported to have commanded Richard Reid, the shoe-bomber now serving life in an American prison for attempting to blow up a US aircraft over the Atlantic. Jose Padilla, who was arrested in Chicago last June on suspicion of planning a 'dirty bomb' attack, is said to have been another one of his protégés. Attacks on an Israeli aircraft and the bombings of the USS Cole in Yemen and a hotel in Kenya in October 2003, were planned by him, according to reports. He has also played an important role inspiring and fostering ties with Asian terrorist groups, particularly those responsible for the Bali bombings.

Witnesses in Pakistan are also reported to have confessed that Khalid personally killed Daniel Pearl, the *Wall Street Journal* reporter who was kidnapped in Karachi 2002.

Some of America's most senior politicians are already saying that the normal rules governing the torture of terror suspects should be set aside because Sheikh Mohammed is the repository of so much important information.

Sheikh Mohammed has already disclosed the names and descriptions of about a dozen key al-Qaeda operatives believed to be plotting terrorist attacks on American and other Western interests. He has also filled in important gaps in what US intelligence knows about al-Qaeda's practices.

The collapse of the south tower at the World Trade Center.

SADDAM HUSSEIN
GENOCIDE OF THE KURDS

*The proud warrior tribes refused to bend before a dictator.
So he took his vicious revenge. He sprayed them with
terrible chemicals, which brought painful and dreadful death
to thousands of Kurdish men, women and children.*

Long before the high-tech war visited on his country by the Allied forces during Operation Desert Storm, Iraqi despot Saddam Hussein had waged another, dirtier kind of war within his own borders. His enemy was the fiercely proud Kurdish tribe, the hot-blooded warrior race that, for centuries, had longed for an independent Kurdistan that would span the border between Iraq and Turkey.

Hussein assembled one of the greatest war machines ever seen, before it was dismantled during the Gulf War. In manpower alone, he had the fifth largest army in the world, plus a formidable array of conventional and chemical weaponry. He needed to ensure that he was the master of the Middle East, but part of his arsenal was developed for a plan every bit as sinister as that hatched by the Nazis. He wanted to wipe out the Kurdish people once and for all. In 1988, before his power was stunted, if not altogether broken by the West, Saddam unleashed his appalling chemical weapons against innocent Kurds, as part of his blueprint for their destruction, killing over 4,000 people. Against his arch-enemy Iran, whom he fought for eight futile years, he used mustard gas.

His chemical weapons programme was one of the most advanced in the world. America and the former USSR had long ago curbed production of chemical weapons, which are forbidden under United Nations rulings and the Geneva Convention. The world did not want to repeat the horrors of the First World War where chemical weapons had been used. But Saddam realized that massive stockpiles of lethal gas would give him a huge military advantage over his enemies.

The technology had not changed a great deal in the years since the Great War – the poison is still delivered by shell and bomb – but the chemical content has. Saddam developed hydrogen cyanide, a particularly lethal gas which causes death within two seconds when inhaled. He also developed new versions of the nerve gases Tabun and Sarin, pioneered by the Nazis during the Second World War, though never used by them. A very small quantity of either of these gases, will, when it falls on skin, cause a human being to go into convulsions, followed very quickly by death.

THE MEANS OF DESTRUCTION

The technology needed for his gas programme was provided by the Western nations that would one day be arrayed against him. As long as Saddam Hussein was keeping the forces of Islamic fundamentalism on the opposite bank of the Euphrates river, the West was happy to give him the means for mass destruction. Western companies salved their consciences by saying that much of the hardware necessary for the production of chemical warfare was for fertilizer factories within Iraq, although any scientist knows that it is but a small step from producing fertilizers to poison gas. Some were merely duped. The Phillips Petroleum Company of Bartlesville, Ohio, was one of the American companies whose security system failed it. Phillips, through a Belgian unit, had sold the Iraqis 500 tons of a complex chemical called thiodiglycol, believing it was for use as a fertilizer. Combined with hydrochloric acid, it makes mustard gas. An understanding of what had been made from their shipment to Saddam hit company executives, when in 1988, they read news reports of Iranian soldiers on a remote battlefield coughing up their lungs, and of corpses covered with horrifying chemical burns.

Germany, Holland and Britain also sold chemical weapon technology and raw materials to Iraq, enabling Saddam to build up stockpiles that sent shivers through his bitterest enemy – Israel. Israel, long before Saddam unleashed his Scud missiles on her cities during the Gulf War, feared a pre-emptive strike with chemical missiles. When Saddam used his mustard gas on the battlefield, it was in limited quantities and aimed strategically at Iranian command posts and communications centres; rarely was it used against civilians. But in his war against the Kurds he had no such qualms.

The Kurds were Saddam Hussein's biggest political problem. They were not impressed by his bellicose speeches, the huge pictures of him that adorned public buildings and stretched over highways; nor did they pay anything other than lip-service to his regime. The Kurds, armed and virtually autonomous in the northern, mountainous region of Iraq, were to be taught a tragic, final lesson that they would never be able to forget.

In March 1988, while the war against Iran was still raging, Saddam received reports from his battlefront commanders that Iranian troops, aided by Kurdish guerrillas, had seized control of the Kurdish town of Halabja. The town was based near a vital hydro-electric dam. The information that Iranian troops were involved gave Saddam reason to unleash his deadliest poisons on the innocent civilian population. Yet he must have known that there were, in fact, no Iranian troops in the town because they had left within hours of taking it.

Iranian soldiers cower in their trenches during the war against Iraq.

THE DEADLY CLOUD

The sun was just rising over the mountain peaks when the first shells began to rain down on Halabja. But unlike the high explosives that the citizens had heard falling along the battlefront with Iran, there was only a soft 'plop-plopping' as the shells dropped without detonating. But soon palls of sickly yellow, white and grey gas began to swell and swirl, drifting like fog through the streets, creeping into every nook and cranny. Saddam had uncorked his evil weapons of Tabun, cyanide gas and mustard gas on the townspeople. Chaos and hysteria reigned as panic gripped the townsfolk. They ran through the streets their skin peeling from their faces when the mustard-sulphur clouds hit them. If they ran into Tabun fumes, they were dead within seconds. A shocking photograph recorded a poignant death during this morning of carnage. It shows a mother clutching her dead baby in the main street, both killed as they ran in a frantic attempt to seek cover from the deadly clouds.

By the afternoon the donkeys and goats in the fields were all dead, the vegetation wilted. The sickly smell of rotten onion mixed with burned garlic hung over the air. It was as if someone had gone in with a giant fly spray and snuffed out the life of all the citizens. Only those who had been working in remote fields survived. In all, 4,000 men, women and children died on that tragic day in Halabja.

Caglayan Cugen, a Turkish doctor who treated survivors who had burns and respiratory problems, said: 'They talked of seeing these blue canisters from which the gas came. There was an odd odour first and then they remember burning in their eyes, blurring the vision as the eyes smart and itch. There followed uncontrollable bouts of sneezing and vomiting. Their breath shortens in the hours following inhalation of the mustard as the inflammation spreads, swelling the internal lining. Many of them had horrible blisters on their necks and thighs, causing huge patches of skin to fall off. Large lesions broke out over their genital areas. They were young and old but they were not soldiers. The youngest I treated was a baby of four months. I could not help but ask what they had done to deserve this.'

Iraq, usually so adept at controlling press coverage within its borders, made the mistake of allowing Western newsmen and foreign relief workers into the area. The pictures of thousands of bodies without any visible wounds whatsoever belied Baghdad's statement that they had been killed in the crossfire of shelling between the forces of Iraq and Iran. It was several months before the Iraqi leadership admitted to the use of the gas as 'a necessary measure to drive out the Iranian infidels'.

A UN official who saw the carnage said: 'The bodies were lying in doorways, in streets, around tables set up for lunch and in cellars where people mistakenly sought shelter from the heavier-than-air gas. Many other corpses were found on the roads leading from the town, where residents had failed to outrun the spreading cloud. The victims seemed to have died quickly, as there were few signs of a struggle. The streets were also littered with the bloated carcasses of cows, dogs, cats, sheep and goats.'

Western newsmen recorded the murder of Kurds in the streets of Halabja.

233

The presence of their despot could not be forgotten by the Iraqi people. His image loomed on billboards across the country.

A TERRIBLE OUTRAGE

Some thirty of the victims were flown for treatment at hospitals in the West, which confirmed that several poison gas agents were indeed deployed on the innocent civilians. Iranian doctors, who treated those refugees who managed to cross over into their country, said their tests had shown that the gases were mustard, cyanide and nerve gas. The injured suffered from the most appalling burns and their lungs were all but destroyed.

Western diplomats in Iraq were appalled at the outrage. 'Halabja was inexcusable in every sense of the word,' said one indignant emissary at the time. 'The use of poison gas against enemy troops is bad enough, but to use it against civilians, and especially your own citizens, is quite unbelievable.'

Steven Rose, a neurobiologist at Britain's Open University, said: 'Despite the fact that Saddam Hussein committed major acts of genocide, the fact is, Iraq got away with it.' There was no pressure to bring this criminal, a man who clearly and openly violated the rules of war, to justice. No less than six separate United Nations missions went to Iraq before and after the Halabja massacre, each time collecting more information on Iraqi chemical assaults. One team was despatched to the town of Halabja and reported: 'This warns us that the use of chemical weapons against the Kurdish people may become more frequent, even commonplace.'

Saddam was well satisfied with this awesome display of his maniacal power. He had cocked a snook at world opinion, defied the conventions of the West – which he viewed as weak – and had dealt a stunning blow to his Kurdish enemies. He felt so good about it that he decided to do it again.

TWO BLEEDING NATIONS

In August 1988 the guns finally fell silent in his war with Iran. It had bled the two nations white, ravaged their economies, decimated their populations and cemented the politics of hate for generations to come. But the onset of peace for Saddam meant he could turn more manpower – and more chemical weaponry – against his Kurdish foes.

By the end of August Saddam had moved some 6,000 troops into the Kurdish region, together with battalions of helicopter gunships, tanks and artillery, all effective methods of launching the gas blitz he intended. The first village to die under his onslaught was Butia.

This has the result of cyanide gas burns which happened when her village was wiped out in a gas attack launched from the air. She fled to Turkey with her husband and three children. They were the lucky ones. Left behind were an estimated 2,000 neighbours, who suffered the same death as the victims of Halabja. She said: 'I was cooking breakfast for my family when I heard the sound of aircraft. I heard bombs whistling and the next thing I knew was that there was something wrong with my eyes. I started to vomit almost immediately. I knew what was happening. We had heard what had happened at Halabja. My family suffered the same effects. We all drank a lot of milk and then we ran. We ran to get as far away as we could. We know that not many made it out.'

REFUGEES FACING DEATH

In the refugee camps along the Turkish border the hordes of burned, coughing survivors of the latest outrage swelled the hospital tents, as medical teams from the West struggled to cope with the aftermath of Saddam's attacks. The refugees were called Pesh mergas by the Iraqis – 'Those who face death' – and there were no apologies from Baghdad for the fate of these victims. It was estimated that along with Butia, two other villages in the Danhuk region of the country were hit, but these suffered few fatalities because the populace were working in far-away fields and strong winds blowing that morning helped disperse the gas away from them.

Kurdish refugees, almost 100,000 of them, moved into Turkey, where they were accommodated in insanitary, overcrowded tented camps along the border. Massad Barzani, one of the Kurdish leaders, appealed to the UN to press Iraq not to use any more chemical weapons. He said: 'It is one thing to be blown to pieces, but it is another to be killed by a weapon you cannot hear and cannot see until it is too late. In the name of humanity, the governments of the west must come together to end this nightmare we are suffering. Many women and children who were gassed, but who survived the onslaught, were later murdered by Iraqi troops to prevent them from spreading information about what dark deeds were done to them. It is a crime against humanity we are talking about here.'

America finally woke up to the atrocities, realizing that Saddam Hussein was becoming more of a liability than an ally in the region. The State Department said it had obtained proof of the latest outrages and called them abhorrent and unjustifiable. Secretary of State George Shultz met with Iraqi's Minister of State for Foreign Affairs, Saddoun Hammadi, to tell him that the continued use of poison gas would severely affect the future of US–Iraq relations.

Hammadi insisted, despite all the evidence to the contrary, that no civilians had this time been killed by gas. Gwynne Roberts, a British television journalist, had himself collected soil samples from some of the villages he visited in Kurdistan and had them analysed by a laboratory. The laboratory report showed significant traces of mustard gas in the samples.

The anger felt by Shultz and other officials was supported by the American people and there was a popular feeling that perhaps America had, after all, been backing the wrong horse in the long struggle between Iran and Iraq. Senator Claiborne Pell, a Democrat from Rhode Island, introduced a bill calling for sanctions against Iraq for what he called its 'anti-Kurdish genocide'. There was a period of an arms embargo after more UN evidence of the chemical atrocities was revealed, but sadly trade with Iraq was soon resumed again.

THE GULF WAR

In August 1990, Iraq invaded Kuwait. At the conclusion of a decade of war against Iran, Iraq was bankrupt and needed money to rebuild. Saddam claimed that oil was being stolen from Iraq through slantdrilling in Kuwait and took his complaint to the US. No action was taken. He further claimed that the border between Iraq and Kuwait had been incorrectly laid down, which meant that the oil companies in Kuwait were stealing even more Iraqi oil. Again, no action was taken. Having been told that the US would not get involved in border disputes, Saddam decided to resolve the problem his own way. Although poor economically, Iraq now had a massive army and arsenal – which the United States had helped stockpile – and on 2 August, Saddam drew it up to the border and stormed into Kuwait, taking the nation and the world by surprise.

It is likely that Saddam did not anticipate the reaction which this move provoked from the US. Or perhaps he had thought that their refusal to get involved in border disputes meant that they would not intervene in this invasion. He was wrong. President George Bush stepped up and declared that 'This will not stand'. The UN Security Council declared war on Iraq and gave the US permission to end Iraq's occupation of Kuwait using any means necessary.

The air campaign began in January 1991, and bombing continued for over a month. During this time, Saddam positioned human shields as defence. The ground attack began in February and was instantly successful, with Iraqi forces either surrendering immediately, or pulling out of Kuwait completely. Before leaving though, those who retreated dropped millions of barrels of oil into the Persian Gulf and set fire to a large amount. The effect on the environment, on people's health and on the landscape was devastating.

With the primary goal of liberating Kuwait achieved, the US pulled their forces out and received much criticism for doing so. Many felt that Saddam was still a threat and should have been deposed. George Bush nevertheless decided to pass the problem over to the UN, and to celebrate the success they had already had. So Saddam remained as leader of Iraq.

In the aftermath of the Gulf War, during which Iraq lost an estimated 100,000 troops, Iraqis rose up against Saddam. But he brutally crushed every rebellion. Conditions worsened when a UN trade embargo was imposed on Iraq by the US, following Saddam's purge of the Marsh Arabs in the south. In retaliation, an assassination attempt was made on President Bush when he visited Kuwait to meet the restored Emir, but it was unsuccessful.

During the administration of President Clinton, Saddam was accused of violating the terms of the Gulf War ceasefire and producing weapons of mass destruction (WMD).

George Bush Snr watches on as his son, addresses the nation. He forced Iraq out of Kuwait during the Gulf War, and his son brought down Saddam Hussein's tyrannical regime in 2003.

GEORGE W. BUSH

This accusation was pursued by President George W. Bush, when he came to office in 2000. Apparently picking up where his father had left off, Bush launched a diatribe against Saddam, declaring that he was ever-dangerous and that only the complete overthrow of the Saddam regime would remove the threat of the employment of the WMD which he alleged that Iraq possessed. When war on

239

terror was declared following the September 11 attacks, Bush's belligerence intensified. Despite the lack of any evidence that Iraq actually possessed WMD, even after numerous inspections had been carried indicating the contrary, Bush declared Iraq to be a threat to national security.

After many months of threats and a long military build-up, the United States finally attacked Iraq on Thursday, 20 March 2003. The war faced strong opposition from France, Germany, Russia, China and the great majority of UN member states as well as world public opinion. The combined military ground force of the US and the UK was around 300,000, and they encountered stiff Iraqi resistance.

THE ATTACK

Named 'Operation Iraqi Freedom', the attack was an attempt to target Saddam Hussein and other Iraqi leaders, using air strikes and ground troops who entered the country by crossing southern Iraq from Kuwait. The following day the major phase of the war began with heavy aerial attacks on Baghdad and other cities. There was also fighting in the north of the country, with some reports that it involved US Special Forces. During the day, a number of oil wells – seven, according to the British government – were reported to be on fire. According to the British government, two of the fires were extinguished by special firefighting troops. The Iraqi government denied that oil wells had been set on fire, saying that it had set fire to oilfilled trenches as a defensive measure against airstrikes.

By 23 March US and British forces succeeded in taking the airport outside of Basra, and were in battle with Iraqi forces for control of the city itself. On 9 April Baghdad fell to US forces. Some Iraqis cheered in the streets after American infantrymen seized deserted Ba'ath Party ministries and pulled down a huge iron statue of Saddam Hussein, ending his brutal 24-year rule of Iraq.

The looting and unrest, especially in the major cities of Baghdad and Basra, became a very serious issue. In Baghdad, with the

The statue of Saddam Hussein in Paradise Square is brought crashing down, as Iraqi civilians and the rest of the world watch on.

notable exception of the Oil Ministry, which was guarded by American troops, the majority of government and public buildings were plundered totally. On 13 April, Tikrit, the home town of Saddam Hussein and the last town not under control of the coalition, was taken by American marines.

With the fall of the Tikrit region, the coalition partners declared the war effectively over on 15 April.

CAPTURE OF SADDAM HUSSEIN

On Saturday, 13 December, 2003, US troops converged on a two-room mud hut, squatting between two houses on a Tigris farm near the village of Ad-Dawr. One room, which appeared to serve as a bedroom, was in disarray with clothes strewn about the place. Inside the hut, dirt and a rug covered the entrance to a subterranean hideaway. The US troops had finally caught up with the man who had eluded them for many months. Saddam Hussein's last hiding place was a miserable 8ft hole dug in the mud. Although Saddam was armed with a pistol, he showed no resistance during his capture. The former dictator of Iraq appeared tired and disorientated when he was pulled from his hiding place, which was found to contain arms and around $750,000 in cash. The US proudly declared 'We got him', and paraded the once proud man, now unkempt and with a scraggy beard, around in front of a world audience. The assumption that the capture of Saddam Hussein would solve all the problems surrounding Iraq was soon scotched. Violence on the streets and attacks against coalition forces continued with the same ferocity and fatalities witnessed prior to Saddam's capture. Saddam, the pathetic, bedraggled man, living in a hole in the ground with only three guns and some cash, certainly was not the powerful figure behind the resistance forces in Iraq. The fact that he probably had very little control or influence is a disturbing and significant fact as it raises the question as to whether these were insurgents vying for power, or Iraqis demonstrating their continued hatred and aggression towards the US.

The first images of Saddam Hussein after his capture. He was dirty and dishevelled, and surrendered without a struggle.

242

MURDER MOST FOUL

DR CRIPPEN
HEN-PECKED KILLER

*Dr Crippen is notorious as the first murderer to be arrested
with the help of Marconi's newly invented wireless telegraphy.
This quiet little patent medicine salesman was hanged in
1910 for poisoning a wife who had treated him shamefully.*

Early in 1900 a slight, modest gentleman enquired about a flat in Shore Street, Bloomsbury. He had a high-domed, bald head, a large sandy moustache, and greyish eyes that bulged behind a pair of gold-rimmed spectacles. With him, and seeming to loom over him, was his wife, a florid, full-figured woman in garish silks.

The oddly assorted pair were American, they explained. They had just arrived on the boat from New York, she to make a name on the music-hall stage, he to manage a patent medicine firm. Their names were Dr Hawley Harvey and Mrs Cora Crippen, and they were to become almost synonymous with twentieth-century murder.

THE MEDICAL MAN

Hawley Crippen was born in 1862, the son of a dry goods merchant in Coldwater, Michigan, who had ambitions for his son to be a doctor. In 1879, when he was just 17, the young Crippen embarked on his medical training.

In subsequent years he was to be reviled as an out-and-out quack, or defended as a highly qualified medic who was simply unlicensed to practise in England. The truth lies somewhere in between.

He received a general scientific background at the California University, Michigan, and then went on to study medicine at the Hospital College in Cleveland, Ohio. Probably, though not certainly, he left without a degree.

In 1883 he sailed for England and spent some time attending lectures at Guy's and St Thomas's hospitals in London, before returning to New York and enrolling at the Opthalmic Hospital there, gaining a diploma in 1885. While in Santiago in 1887 he met and married a woman named Charlotte Bell, and the following year their son Hawley Crippen was born. He was to spend his life in Los Angeles.

The Crippens moved to Salt Lake where, in 1890, Charlotte died. Hawley drifted back to New York. Two years later he met a

39 Hilldrop Crescent, London.

striking young woman of 17 who called herself Cora Turner and was the mistress of a rich stove manufacturer.

Crippen fell in love with her, and for her part she seemed to like the idea of being a doctor's wife. In 1893 he married her and took her with him to St Louis, where he was working as consultant physician to an optician. There he learned that his wife's real name was Kunigunde Mackamotzki. She was the daughter of a Russian – Polish father and a German mother.

Despite the strong prejudice then current among 'White Anglo-Saxon Protestants' against mid-European Catholics, the revelation did little to affect Crippen's passion for Cora.

For her part, Cora was growing dissatisfied with Crippen's earnings as an orthodox doctor, pointing out that there was much more money to be made in the world of 'patent' medicines. One of the best-selling of these was 'Professor Munyon's Pills for Piles'. In 1897, Crippen joined the firm in New York and parted company with mainstream medicine for ever.

When Munyon's opened an office in Shaftesbury Avenue, London, Crippen was appointed first manager. The summer of 1900 saw him and Cora taking the lease on the flat in Shore Street, Bloomsbury.

AMBITIONS

Bloomsbury was at the heart of the London music-hall world. Cora lost no time in introducing herself into the pubs and restaurants in which the music-hall artistes met, and even hired an agent, 'billing' herself under the stage name of Belle Ellmore.

She looked the part. Cora was pretty enough, with dark eyes and raven hair. Her looks, together with her American accent, described as 'twangy', and the stagey clothes she affected, reeked of the American vaudeville theatre of which she claimed to have been a part.

Cora hired herself out as an artiste's agent under her stage name of Belle Ellmore.

The trouble was that Belle Ellmore could not sing – at least, she could not project her voice to reach the far corners of a theatre. Once, during a music-hall strike, she obtained work at the Euston Palace. But she was hissed and booed from the stage, partly for being a 'blackleg' and partly for being dreadful. After that distressing experience, Cora's active theatrical days were over.

Despite this she remained friendly with such artistes as Marie Lloyd. She also became a member and later honorary treasurer of the Music Hall Ladies' Guild, a charitable organization. And she took to wearing expensive jewellery, which she bullied Hawley Crippen into buying.

Ethel LeNeve, Dr Crippen's lover, thinly disguised as a boy for their flight to America.

In 1901, urged on by Cora to 'better' himself, Crippen took an appointment as consultant to a dubious firm of ear specialists named the Drouet Institute. Its bookkeeper-secretary was a 17-year-old named Ethel Neave who shared with Cora a dissatisfaction with her surname and called herself LeNeve. Two years after Crippen joined, the Institute was bankrupted after a charge of negligence was levelled against it – the charge did not involve Crippen. By this time he had fallen in love with Ethel. Under any name, Ethel LeNeve does not seem to have been particularly prepossessing. Despite her pretty face she was a mousey child with a slight limp, who suffered from chronic catarrh.

But, like Cora, she had a strong dominant trait which seemed to appeal to Crippen. And there is no doubt that she loved the by-now infatuated doctor as much as he loved her.

She followed him, as secretary, to the Sovereign Remedy Company, which failed, then to the Aural Company, which also failed, and then back to Professor Munyon's, where he took up his old post as manager.

Later, she became secretary to a dental practice which Crippen set up as an extra source of income at Albion House, New Oxford Street, with a dental surgeon named Dr Rylance.

HEN-PECKED HUSBAND

In 1905, the Crippens left Shore Street and moved north to a leased semi-detached villa at 39 Hilldrop Crescent, off the Camden Road in Kentish Town. By this time Crippen was making money, most of which was spent on entertaining Cora's friends and on buying Cora's dresses and jewellery. However, by now the couple slept in separate bedrooms and were polite to each other only in company. Cora openly had men friends and occasionally took them to bed in the afternoons when Crippen was at work.

When her interest in the new house waned a little, Cora took in four lodgers. She had an antipathy towards 'living in' domestic servants, so she buckled down to the task of being a landlady herself, with the help of a daily cleaner.

Police accompany Dr Crippen and Ethel LeNeve down the gangway of the SS Negantic after his arrest in 1910.

Crippen was ordered up at six in the morning to clean the lodgers' boots, lay and light the fires, and prepare the breakfast – all before he set off for his office at 7.30.

Incredibly, the doctor continued to pay all the household bills, while the lodgers' rents went into Cora's dress and jewellery account.

In December 1906 Crippen came home to find Cora in bed with one of the lodgers, a German. The following day he told Ethel, and for the first time in their four-year relationship she consented to go to bed with him. Their affair was consummated in a cheap hotel one afternoon on Ethel's day off.

Soon after this, Cora tired of the game of being a landlady and dismissed the lodgers. Instead she entertained her friends on two or three evenings a week. For the rest of the time, she and her husband virtually lived in the kitchen. Both of them gave up housework, and cleaning was done only spasmodically.

Over the next four years Crippen continued to live at Hilldrop Crescent, though life with Cora became more and more intolerable. There was no longer any pretence at amiability. Cora mocked him in front of her friends and Hawley Crippen bore it all stoically, buoyed up by his love for Ethel LeNeve.

Cora was by now aware of the affair. At one point Ethel became pregnant and decided to have the baby, thus forcing matters to a crisis. But she miscarried.

Cora's response was to speculate, to a group of her music-hall friends and in her husband's hearing, as to which of Ethel's many lovers was responsible for the child. It may have been at that moment that Hawley Harvey Crippen's patience came abruptly to an end.

THE WORM TURNS

On 1 January 1910 he went to the firm of Lewis and Burrows, wholesale chemists, and ordered 17 grains of the vegetable drug hydrobromide of hyoscine. It was, he said, on behalf of Munyon's – though the American company did not manufacture in Britain. On 19 January he took possession of the drug, which he had seen used to calm violent patients in mental hospitals. It was also an anaphrodisiac – it killed sexual ardour.

On 31 January the Crippens entertained a couple named Martinetti, theatrical friends of Cora's. During the course of the evening Cora picked a quarrel with her husband because he had not shown Mr Martinetti to the lavatory. It was an odd grudge, even for Cora. But, according to Crippen's later evidence, she took it as a 'last straw' and threatened to leave him.

It is doubtful whether Crippen would have worried overmuch if his wife had simply walked out of his life. But she had access, through their joint account, to his savings, and she would also have taken her valuable jewellery and have had a legal right to their joint property. She had threatened before to leave and take 'her' money – though in fact, apart from the abortive nights treading the boards of the Euston Palace, she had never earned a penny in her life.

At 1.30 on the morning of 1 February the Martinettis bade Cora and Hawley goodbye. Cora Crippen was never seen alive again. That afternoon, Crippen called on the Martinettis, as he often did, and remarked that Cora was well.

On 2 February, Crippen pawned for £80 a gold ring and a pair of earrings belonging to his wife. The same evening Ethel LeNeve came to Hilldrop Crescent for the first time and stayed overnight. The same day a letter arrived at the Music Hall Ladies' Guild office, apparently from their treasurer, Belle Ellmore. It said that she was leaving immediately for America to nurse a sick relative and was therefore tendering her resignation.

On 9 February Crippen pawned more jewellery, this time for £115. At his trial Crippen was to point out indignantly that he had every right to dispose of his wife's jewellery in any way he thought fit, since he had bought it.

On 20 February Crippen carried openness to potentially dangerous lengths when he escorted Ethel LeNeve to the Music Hall Ladies' Guild ball. She was decked out in some of Belle Ellmore's finest jewels – a fact not lost on the Martinettis, among other guests present.

Ostensibly Ethel was still simply Crippen's secretary, standing in for his absent wife at a social occasion. But on 12 March caution was thrown to the winds. Ethel moved in permanently to 39 Hilldrop Crescent.

FAKED DEATH. SUSPICIOUS FRIENDS

On 20 March, with Easter approaching, Crippen wrote to the Martinettis to say that he had heard from his wife and that she was seriously ill with pleuropneumonia. He was thinking, he said, of going to the United States to look after her. Contemporary writers have suggested that this may have been his original plan – to go to America and then quietly disappear. But something stopped him, and that something was probably Ethel LeNeve.

At this stage, it seems unlikely that Ethel knew that Cora was dead. But she knew that she was finally with the man she loved and she was not going to let him leave her, even for a short while.

On 23 March, instead of going to America, Crippen and Ethel took a cross-Channel ferry to Dieppe, where they stayed during Easter week.

But from Victoria station he sent the Martinettis a telegram: 'BELLE DIED YESTERDAY AT SIX O'CLOCK. PLEASE PHONE ANNIE. SHALL BE AWAY A WEEK - PETER.' 'Peter' was a nickname for Crippen used by Belle Ellmore's theatrical friends.

When he returned, Crippen was inundated with enquiries from his wife's friends. Where exactly had she died? Where could they send a wreath? Crippen told them that he was having her cremated in America. When her ashes were shipped back 'we can have a little ceremony then'.

Lil Hawthorne, the well-known music-hall comedy singer who had been one of Belle Ellmore's closest friends, was not satisfied. She checked with shipping lines but could find no record of either a Cora Crippen or a Belle Ellmore embarking for the States around

Superintendent Frost, head of the Crippen investigation, discusses evidence with his colleagues.

the first week in February. Lil and her agent husband, John Nash, had to go to New York on business in March and their enquiries there also drew a blank.

On his return to London, Nash confronted Crippen. Under questioning, Crippen broke down and sobbed pathetically. Nash, knowing of the doctor's kindly nature and tolerance of what even her friends had to acknowledge as his wife's often outrageous treatment of him, was almost convinced of the truth of Crippen's story.

And yet if Crippen was so distressed, why was his mistress living openly with him? Eventually Nash went to Scotland Yard and, on 30 June, poured out the whole tale.

INTERVIEWED BY THE YARD

A week later, on 8 July, Detective Chief Inspector Walter Dew, accompanied by Detective Sergeant Mitchell, went to call on Crippen at Albion House. Dew was one of the Yard's most experienced detectives. He was impressed by Dr Crippen's demeanour.

Asked about his wife's disappearance and alleged death, Crippen immediately confessed that the whole story was untrue. In fact, he said, Belle Ellmore alias Cora Crippen had run off to Chicago with an old prize-fighter lover of hers. Crippen had been so ashamed, and so worried about damaging his medical career with a scandal, that he had invented the story of her fatal illness.

Dew spent all day with Crippen, sitting in the waiting room between Crippen's periodic surgery calls to dental patients. In the evening, Crippen took the two policemen to Hilldrop Crescent and showed them over the house, from attic to basement. All seemed perfectly normal.

'Of course,' said Dew, 'I shall have to find Mrs Crippen to clear the matter up.'

'Yes,' agreed the doctor, 'I will do everything I can. Can you suggest anything? Would an advertisement be any good?' Dew thought an advertisement in the Chicago papers an excellent idea, and helped Crippen draft one before finally saying goodnight.

In fact, Dew later admitted, the advertisement was unnecessary. He was convinced by that time that Crippen was telling the truth at last, and that the flighty Belle Ellmore had run off. The investigation was to all intents and purposes finished. However, Crippen had no means of knowing this.

THE FATAL MISTAKE

Despite numerous theories, no one has ever given a satisfactory reason why Crippen, whose nerve had so far held, should suddenly at this point make the mistake of flight. But flee he did.

August 1910 – crowds gathered outside Bow Street Court as
Crippen stood before magistrates.

After carefully putting his affairs in order Crippen and LeNeve took the boat to Rotterdam on the night of 9 July. From there they made their way to Antwerp, where they embarked on the SS *Montrose*, bound for Quebec, under the names of Mr and Master Robinson.

Ethel had had her hair cropped short and was wearing cut-down men's clothes, probably Crippen's, and they kept under cover as much as possible before the ship sailed on 20 July.

Even now, the fleeing lovers might have got away but for a fluke. Chief Inspector Dew had forgotten some minor point during his questioning of Crippen. It was not important and there was no urgency. But on Monday 11 July, finding himself in the vicinity of Albion House, he decided to drop in and check it out. There he was told that Crippen had left.

Suddenly alarm bells were beginning to ring and Dew dashed up to Hilldrop Crescent. All seemed to be in order, but he carried out a thorough search, checking the garden for recent signs of digging and testing the bricks in the empty basement coal cellar with his foot.

All was solid and normal. But Dew was certain that somewhere in this ordinary little house and its garden lay the solution to Cora's disappearance.

On the following day he returned with extra men. Again they searched, digging and probing. Again nothing. On Wednesday the 13th they were there again, but towards evening it began to look as if Dew's instinct was wrong. Then, standing in the brick-floored cellar, he probed one of the cracks with a poker and found that the brick was loose. He prised it out and found loosely packed soil underneath. This time he got a spade, removed the rest of the bricks and dug. Eight inches down he found what he described at the trial as 'a mass of flesh' wrapped in a striped pyjama top.

On preliminary examination by Dr Marshall, the police surgeon, it proved to be a human torso from which the neck and head, arms and legs had been severed. The vagina and uterus had been excised, and the trunk had been neatly filleted – all the bones had been removed – with considerable surgical skill.

On 15 July, Marshall and Dr Augustus J. Pepper, a Home Office pathologist based at St Mary's Hospital, Paddington, removed the remains for further examination. The following day a warrant was issued for the arrest of Crippen and LeNeve.

On 20 July, the westward-bound SS *Montrose* steamed out of Antwerp. Sharing a cabin were a Mr John Robinson and his son, who between them had only one small valise as luggage. The ship's master, Captain Henry Kendal, thought them an odd couple, and kept an eye on them.

Among other things he noticed that 'Mr Robinson' was reading a copy of Edgar Wallace's *Four Just Men*, a famous murder yarn of the time. But he also noticed that the 'son' wore an ill-fitting hat and trousers, which were held together with safety pins at the back, and that the couple held hands in a manner most unusual for a father and son. When he saw a picture of Crippen in a copy of the *Daily Mail* which had been brought aboard just before the *Montrose* sailed, Captain Kendal despatched a wireless message that began: 'Have strong suspicion that Crippen London cellar murderer and accomplice are among saloon passengers...'

The message went out on 22 July, and the following day Dew and Mitchell embarked on the SS *Negantic* at Liverpool just before she sailed. On 31 July, Dew boarded the *Montrose* as she lay at anchor off Father Point, Quebec, and arrested the pair.

Crippen's first words were: 'I am not sorry. The anxiety has been too much.' He was the first murderer to be arrested by wireless telegraphy, for which Marconi had received the Nobel Prize the previous year.

Back in London Dr Pepper, assisted by his colleagues Dr William Willcox and Dr Bernard Spilsbury, had conducted a thorough examination of the remains from the cellar. They contained at least five grains of hyoscine which, as Willcox the toxicologist was to point out, was derived from henbane. When used as a sedative, one-fortieth of a grain had been known to produce 'severe symptoms'.

The defence were to claim that these remains were not those of Belle Ellmore/Cora Crippen, but of some previous murder, coincidentally committed in the house before the arrival of the Crippens. Even this credulity-stretching defence was scotched when pubic hairs on the torso were matched for colouring with Cora's head hair, and Bernard Spilsbury showed that a mark on the skin was not a fold, as alleged by the defence, but the scar of an ovariotomy such as Cora was known to have undergone. At the trial, the piece of flesh and skin showing the scar was handed about, to the judge, jury, defence and defendant Crippen, on a soup plate.

Finally, Crippen was caught out in a direct lie when he claimed that the pyjamas in which the body was wrapped were not his. They were proved to have been bought by him in 1909.

CRIPPEN'S PATCH

The trial had begun at the Old Bailey on 18 October before the Lord Chief Justice, Lord Alverstone, and the jury took 27 minutes to reach their verdict. Crippen was sentenced to hang, while Ethel LeNeve, tried separately, went free.

Crippen's only concern, after his arrest, had been for the welfare of his mistress. He told Dew: 'She has been my only comfort for the last three years.' In jail at Pentonville his courtesy and pleasant nature almost endeared him to his warders. When he asked the Governor that a photograph and two letters from Ethel LeNeve be buried with him, the Governor readily complied.

Crippen was hanged on 23 November 1910. To this day the graveyard within the walls of Pentonville prison in which he and other executed prisoners were buried is known to staff and inmates as 'Crippen's Patch'. Exactly when he killed his wife, and how he disposed of the body, remains a mystery. It was most probable that he poisoned her on either the night of 31 January or the following morning. He then cut her up in the bath, and dropped the missing head and limbs overboard in a suitcase during his subsequent trip to Dieppe.

The other abiding mystery is exactly why, after tolerating his apparently intolerable wife for so long, he suddenly decided to kill her. Many theories have been produced over the years, but none have resolved the mystery satisfactorily.

After her acquittal, Ethel LeNeve emigrated to Canada until the fuss died down, and then quietly returned to England in 1916. She took a job as bookkeeper for a company in Trafalgar Square, and married a man who was said to look remarkably like Crippen. They lived in East Croydon.

In 1954, novelist Ursula Bloom published a book entitled *The Woman Who Loved Crippen*. Afterwards, she was approached by an elderly lady who revealed herself to be Ethel. She told Miss Bloom that she had never ceased to love her little doctor. Ethel LeNeve died in 1967, aged 84.

Dr Crippen in the dock at the Old Bailey during his trial for the murder of his wife.

JEREMY BAMBER

AN IMPATIENT HEIR

The horrific mass killing seemed to be the work of a deranged family member who had then committed suicide. Eventually the real murderer was nailed – but no thanks to the police who jumped to conclusions and destroyed vital evidence.

At 3.26 in the morning of 7 August 1985, the duty officer at Chelmsford police station in Essex received a phone call from a young man calling himself Jeremy Bamber. The caller sounded agitated.

He explained to the policeman that he was calling from his home at Goldhanger and that he had just received a frantic call from his father who lived in the nearby village of Tolleshunt D'Arcy. According to Bamber, his father had shouted: 'Come over. Your sister's gone crazy and she's got a gun…'

Bamber had then heard a shot and the line had gone dead. He had tried to call back, but the telephone was off the hook. What should he do?

The duty sergeant told Bamber to go to his father's farm and wait for the police. Under no circumstances should he enter the building. Within minutes Detective Inspector Bill Miller had assembled an armed squad of 40 men which included Special Firearms Unit marksmen.

The police reached White House Farm shortly after 4 a.m. There were lights in some of the windows but everything seemed peaceful. Marksmen took up their positions and covered every door and window in the elegant Georgian farmhouse. There was still no sign of life.

Minutes later, Jeremy Bamber arrived at the farm. He was hurried over to Inspector Miller who wanted to know what they were dealing with. Was there normally a gun in the house?

Yes, Jeremy explained. His father, Nevill Bamber, was a keen shot and kept a rifle, a high velocity semi-automatic .22 Anchutz, which he used for rabbiting.

What about his sister? From the start, Jeremy made it clear that there was no love lost between them. He stressed that they were not really brother and sister, but that they had both been adopted.

'My sister is a nutter,' Jeremy explained. 'She could go mad at any time… She's gone mad before.'

Sheila 'Bambi' Caffell was a pretty young woman but was dogged by psychological problems.

WAITING GAME

The police kept their vigil for a while longer and then made a series of appeals over a loud hailer. There was no response.

The basic brief in circumstances like these is for police to minimize the risk of loss of life. Since there was a possibility that members of the family were being held hostage, they opted to wait it out.

Bamber, meanwhile, provided police with a detailed picture of the house and family. His adoptive parents, Nevill and June Bamber, 61, lived there and farmed the surrounding 400 acres. His adoptive sister, 27-year-old Sheila Caffell, nicknamed 'Bambi', had been staying with them since March with her six-year-old twins, Daniel and Nicholas. Bambi, Jeremy explained, had a long history of depression and had recently come out of mental hospital after a 'nervous breakdown'.

As dawn broke there was still no sign of life in the farmhouse and the police decided to move in. A squad of ten armed officers inched their way towards the kitchen door. One of the assault team then smashed down the door and the others moved quickly into the building.

But there was no sign of violence – in fact no sign of life at all.

SCENES OF CARNAGE

As the police reached the sitting room, however, they were confronted with a glimpse of the carnage that was to come. The room was a shambles, and lying near the telephone was the body of Nevill Bamber. He had been shot six times in the head, once in the shoulder and once in the arm. He had also been brutally beaten about the head and face. Other officers moved upstairs. In one of the bedrooms they found the bodies of the twins, Daniel and Nicholas. Both had died from multiple gunshot wounds. They had obviously been murdered while they slept; Daniel was still sucking his thumb.

The master bedroom was the scene of more horror. June Bamber was sprawled in her nightdress on the floor beside the door, a Bible lying open by her side. She had been shot seven times, once directly between the eyes.

And by the window was the body of Sheila 'Bambi' Caffell. She was lying on her back in her nightdress. She had one gunshot wound in the throat and another in her jaw. Across her lap was lying a .22 Anchutz rifle, its butt splintered and its magazine empty.

BERSERK

The forensic team, led by Detective Inspector Ronald Cook, moved into the house together with police surgeon Dr Ian Craig. Craig examined each of the five bodies in turn.

Nevill Bamber had multiple wounds to the head and had probably been beaten unconscious before he was shot. Upstairs, the children and June Bamber were quite obviously victims of a surprise attack.

That left Bambi. Dr Craig examined her two wounds. The shot to her throat had severed her jugular vein. The other had passed through her chin and entered her brain. This would have killed her instantly. Bambi had one impact bruise to her cheek but was otherwise unmarked. Her long fingernails had survived the night of violence unscathed.

Dr Craig went downstairs and joined Detective Inspectors Cook and Miller. There was no sign of a break-in and the three men agreed that the most obvious scenario was that Sheila Caffell had gone berserk, murdered her entire family and then turned the gun on herself.

They expressed this opinion to Detective Chief Inspector Tom 'Taff' Jones when he arrived at the farm later that morning. Jones was apparently happy to accept their conclusions.

Having 'solved' the case to their own satisfaction, Cook and his forensic team apparently decided that a detailed examination of the house and its contents was surplus to requirements – a

Sheila 'Bambi' Caffell with her adoptive mother, June Bamber, and her two sons, Nicholas and Daniel. All of them died at White House Farm.

decision that would later attract violent criticism from both the press and the judiciary.

The police did remove the rifle and some other items of evidence, but officers failed to wear gloves, and no fingerprints were ever taken of the dead family members, or of Jeremy Bamber, for elimination purposes. The only rooms that were searched were the sitting room and the two bedrooms where the bodies had been found.

Then, in an act of misplaced kindness to Jeremy Bamber, the police destroyed the very evidence they had already failed to examine properly. They washed bloodstains from the walls. Then they removed bedding and carpets from the living room and bedrooms and burned them on a bonfire.

Jeremy Bamber remained outside while his family's bodies were removed from the scene. He remained calm and subdued. The only person he wanted to see was his girlfriend, Julie Mugford. A police officer was despatched to collect her from her home in Colchester.

When Julie was told of the massacre, she looked grim but made no comment. She was driven to White House Farm and she and Jeremy Bamber held each other as they watched evidence being carried from the house and destroyed.

As police moved the focus of their enquiries to neighbours and friends, everything they heard seemed to confirm what they already suspected. The wealthy and eminently respectable Bamber family had died tragically at the hands of a deranged family member.

The suggestion that Bambi might have been involved with drugs was raised by several of the Bambers' neighbours. The press were quick to accept salacious village gossip as fact, and this case had everything the tabloids could ask for – a glamorous, drug-crazed heiress had apparently murdered her own children and her adoptive parents.

THE SCEPTICS TAKE ACTION

The police and press had effectively convicted Bambi of murder. Not everyone felt comfortable with that idea, however.

Nevill Bamber's nephew, David Boutflour, had been very fond of his adoptive cousin. He was horrified by the allegations being made against her.

Boutflour said the very idea that Bambi could have carried out the killings was preposterous. He knew from police reports that 25 shots had been fired. This would have meant reloading twice in a situation of mayhem, an operation that would have required skill and coordination. 'Sheila', said Boutflour, 'couldn't put baked beans on toast without knocking them over.'

Boutflour's protests fell on deaf ears so he decided it was up to him to obtain evidence that would exonerate Bambi and, he hoped, identify the real killer.

Whitehouse Farm, a monument to upper-middle class respectability, and scene of one of the worst mass murders of recent times.

On Sunday, 11 August, while a service for the Bambers was being held at St Nicholas's Church in Tolleshunt D'Arcy, David and his sister, Mrs Christine Baton, went to White House Farm. They worked their way methodically through the house, looking for possible clues.

Much of the evidence had already been removed or destroyed, but the amateur sleuths found two vital clues. At the back of the gun cabinet David Boutflour discovered a .22 silencer with some specks of blood on it. Christine noticed scratches on the kitchen window-ledge which suggested that the window had been closed and locked from the outside.

Boutflour immediately informed the police of their findings. Detectives were polite but unimpressed, and it was two days before they even bothered to go out to the farm to collect the silencer.

More doubt was cast on the murder-suicide theory two days later by the Home Office pathologist. He reported to detectives involved in the case that, in his opinion, their scenario was absurd.

Firstly it required slender, 5ft 7in Sheila Caffell to bludgeon 6ft 4in Nevill Bamber unconscious. And the 'suicide' shots didn't add up either. The first shot, through her jugular vein, would have rendered her incapable of firing the second into her brain. In addition, the second shot had been fired with a silencer, and there was no sign of a silencer near Bambi's body. And if the rifle had been fitted with a six-inch silencer, the weapon would have been so long that Bambi would not have been able to reach the trigger while the muzzle was pressed under her chin. She could not possibly have fired that shot.

Despite these glaring inconsistencies, detectives ignored the pathologist's findings. No mention was made of them at the coroner's inquest, which was held at Chelmsford on 14 August.

The bodies of Nevill and June Bamber were released to Jeremy Bamber. Two days later friends and relatives of the Bambers returned to St Nicholas's Church for the funeral service. Then the coffins were driven to Colchester for cremation.

A police officer holds up the .22 Anchutz rifle and silencer used in the Bamber murders.

THE TRUTH FILTERS OUT

On 8 September, three weeks after his family's funeral, Jeremy Bamber was arrested – not for murder, but for an unrelated burglary which dated back some six months. He was charged with stealing £980 from a caravan park which he co-owned with his late parents.

The following day, Bamber appeared at Chelmsford court and was refused bail. This was extremely unusual for a first offender accused of a non-violent crime, and it suggests that the police were starting to look at the White House killings in a new light. Jeremy was held in gaol for five days before being released in his own recognizance.

Jeremy left immediately for a holiday on the French Riviera. Surprisingly, he went with a friend, Brett Collins, rather than his girlfriend. This would prove Bamber's most expensive mistake.

A few days after Jeremy left for France, Julie Mugford went to see the Essex police. She told them she was certain that Jeremy had killed his family.

According to Julie, Jeremy had been planning the murders for months. She explained that Jeremy loathed his parents and he resented the fact that he had not been given his inheritance while he was young enough to enjoy it.

Julie said that on the night of the massacre Jeremy had telephoned her and said: 'It's got to be tonight or never.' Julie said she had told him not to be stupid, but that he had hung up. At three the following morning, Jeremy had rung again and said: 'Everything is going well.'

Jeremy Bamber handcuffed to a prison officer as he leaves court in a police van.

At first, detectives were inclined to believe that they were listening to the bitter rantings of a spurned woman. After all, hadn't Jeremy just taken off to France without her? But, as her story unfolded, they were reminded of the pathologist's findings and the evidence submitted by David Boutflour and Christine Eaton. It was becoming increasingly obvious that they had made a terrible mistake.

On 30 September, police were waiting at Dover ferry terminal when Jeremy Bamber returned from his holiday. He was arrested and charged with murdering Nevill and June Bamber, together with Sheila, Daniel and Nicholas Caffell.

GREED AND EXTRAVAGANCE

On Tuesday, 2 October 1986, more than a year after the massacre at White House Farm, the trial of Jeremy Bamber opened at Chelmsford Crown Court. Bamber had secured one of the country's best criminal solicitors, Sir David Napley, and he in turn had briefed Geoffrey Rivlin QC to conduct the defence. Bamber pleaded not guilty to five charges of murder.

The prosecution, led by Anthony Arlidge QC, opened by describing the massacre in graphic detail. He said that he would prove beyond all reasonable doubt that the perpetrator of the five killings was Jeremy Bamber. His motive, Arlidge claimed, was greed. Bamber knew that if all his family died, he would inherit almost half a million pounds.

The prosecution produced a plethora of evidence and expert witnesses. It all indicated that Sheila Caffell could not have committed the murders, and suggested that Jeremy Bamber might well have done so. The evidence against Bamber was, at best, circumstantial. Mr Arlidge chastised the police for their handling of the case, saying that if they had done their job properly his own job would have been made simpler.

On the morning of 9 October, Arlidge put his star witness on the stand. Julie Mugford wept as she told the jury of the months during

May 1986 – Jeremy Bamber arrives at Maldon Magistrates'
Court for the committal proceedings.

which Jeremy Bamber's fantasies of killing his family had
threatened to become a horrifying reality. Her answers during
cross-examination were precise and consistent, and bore an
unmistakable ring of truth.

On 16 October, Rivlin opened the defence. He set out to prove
that Sheila Caffell was a more likely murderer than Jeremy was.
His argument came unstuck, however, when he was unable to
discredit evidence submitted by the ballistics expert and the Home
Office pathologist.

The following day, Rivlin put Jeremy Bamber on the witness
stand. Bamber denied the killings and claimed to have had a loving
relationship with his family. Under cross-examination, however,
Bamber displayed a petulant, arrogant streak which did nothing to
help his case.

Arlidge went to town on Bamber's character, portraying him as a
greedy, vain and idle young man. None of this was very flattering,

but it didn't prove that Jeremy Bamber had killed his family. In the final analysis, it all came down to who the jury chose to believe – Jeremy Bamber or Julie Mugford.

In the afternoon of 27 October, the jury retired to consider their verdict. Two days later they returned a verdict of 'guilty' on all five counts by a majority of 10-2.

Sentencing Bamber to five concurrent life sentences, the judge recommended that he should not be released for at least 25 years.

REIGN OF TERROR
THE BOSTON STRANGLER

In 1963 a serial killer stalked the streets of Boston. His female victims were first sexually assaulted, then strangled and left lying in obscene postures. And this demented psychopath left no clues...

Just before seven o'clock on the evening of 14 June 1962 Juris Slesers, a 25-year-old research engineer, climbed the stairs to his mother's third-floor apartment at 77 Gainsborough Street in Boston. He had arranged to drive her to a memorial service at the Latvian Lutheran church in nearby Roxbury.

Mrs Slesers, a petite 55-year-old divorcee, had fled Soviet-occupied Latvia with her son some 20 years earlier and settled in Boston, where she worked as a seamstress. For the past three months, since Juris had moved out, she had lived alone in this tiny apartment.

Juris knocked on the door and waited. There was no answer. He knocked again, pressed his ear to the metal door and listened. There was no sound from within.

He presumed his mother had popped out to do some shopping and went downstairs. He sat on the front steps and waited. Three-quarters of an hour passed and Juris was becoming concerned. He went back upstairs, hammered on the door and shouted his mother's name. There was still no response.

He put his shoulder to the door, backed up and then rammed it with all his strength. The door sprang open.

Massachusetts State Troopers search for the Strangler.

275

JUST ANOTHER STATISTIC

Inside the apartment it was quite dark, and Juris tripped over a chair which had unaccountably been left in the middle of the narrow hallway. He looked into the living room and the bedroom, both of which were oddly untidy. There was no sign of his mother. He returned to the hallway and headed for the bathroom.

Anna Slesers was lying just outside the bathroom door. She was wearing her blue taffeta housecoat which was spread wide apart at the front, leaving her effectively nude. She lay with her left leg stretched straight out and her right flung at right angles with the knee bent so that she was grossly exposed. The cord of her housecoat was knotted tightly round her neck and then fastened under her chin in the fashion of a crude bow. She was quite obviously dead.

The police, led by Special Officer James Mellon, arrived on the scene within minutes of receiving Juris Slesers's call.

Despite the fact that there was little sign of disturbance, it was immediately obvious to Officer Mellon that he was dealing with homicide. Mrs Slesers had been sexually assaulted and then strangled.

His initial suspicion was that someone had broken into the apartment with the intention of committing a robbery, had found Mrs Slesers in a state of undress – she looked younger than her years – and was seized by an uncontrollable sexual urge. He had raped Mrs Slesers and then strangled her to prevent her from identifying him.

The police conducted a thorough investigation. House-to-house enquiries were carried out. Relatives and friends were interviewed. A few possible candidates for the crime were picked up and questioned.

But the officers made no headway and, gruesome though the crime was, it soon became just another statistic. Boston averaged more than a murder a week at that time and, with a total lack of clues, the police accepted that their chances of ever finding the man responsible for Anna Slesers's death were very slim.

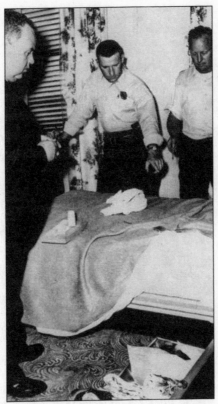

The police search for clues in Helen Blake's apartment.

SEXUAL PSYCHOPATH

At five o'clock on 30 June, two weeks after the murder at Gainsborough Street, Nina Nichols, a 68-year-old retired physiotherapist, returned home to 1940 Commonwealth Avenue in Boston. She had just spent a pleasant few days in the country staying with friends.

As soon as she got into her apartment Mrs Nichols called her sister, Marguerite Steadman, to say that she was back safely and that she would be over for dinner at six o'clock as planned. The sisters chatted for a while but then Nina Nichols cut their conversation short, saying: 'Excuse me, Marguerite, there's my buzzer. I'll call you right back.'

Mary Sullivan, 19, was found strangled on the 5 January 1964 in her Beacon Hill apartment.

Mrs Nichols didn't call her sister back, nor did she arrive for dinner at six o'clock. By seven, her sister was becoming concerned and asked her husband, attorney Chester Steadman, to telephone and make sure everything was all right. There was no reply to his call.

Another half an hour passed and the Steadmans were becoming really alarmed. Maybe she had been taken ill? Chester Steadman called the janitor of the building, Thomas Bruce. Would he go up to Mrs Nichols's apartment and see if she was still there?

Bruce went upstairs, knocked on the door and, when there was no reply, opened it with his pass-key. He never set foot inside. What he saw from the doorway was enough.

The apartment had obviously been burgled. Drawers had been

pulled out and clothes strewn all over the floor.

But there was worse, much worse. Directly ahead of him, Bruce could see into the bedroom. And on the floor, legs spread wide apart, was the nude body of Nina Nichols. Around her neck, tied so tightly that they cut into her flesh, were a pair of stockings. They were knotted under her chin in a clumsy bow.

Police Lieutenant Edward Sherry was soon at the scene with medical examiner Dr Michael Luongo. The similarities to the Slesers murder were immediately obvious to both men.

Nina Nichols had been sexually molested and then strangled. Both women had been left in a grossly exposed state. And then there were the tell-tale bows in the ligatures. There had been no sign of forceable entry to either apartment. Both had been ransacked but apparently nothing had been stolen in either case, despite the fact that high value, easily disposable items like jewellery and cameras had been lying around. And there was no reason to believe that the intruder had been interrupted on either occasion.

The police came to the conclusion that the murderer had never intended to commit a robbery – he had merely wanted to give the impression of committing a robbery. So what were they dealing with? Two murders did not constitute a serial, but Sherry and his colleagues had a gut feeling that there was a sexual psychopath at large in Boston.

They did not have to wait long before their fears were confirmed. On 2 July, two days later, police received a call from the neighbours of Helen Blake, a 65-year-old retired nurse.

Helen had not been seen for a couple of days. Her friends had been concerned and borrowed a pass-key from the building supervisor. They had opened the door of her apartment, seen signs of a burglary and been afraid to go in.

The police entered the apartment and found Helen Blake lying face down on her bed. She was naked except for a pyjama top, which had been pushed up to her shoulders. She had been sexually assaulted and strangled with a pair of stockings. A brassiere was also tied around her neck and fastened under her

Police remove the body of Mary Sullivan from her apartment.

chin in a bow. The medical examiner estimated that she had been dead for about three days.

Police Commissioner McNamara was winding up a conference on the murders of Anna Slesers and Nina Nichols when Lieutenant Donovan told him that Helen Blake's body had been found. As Donovan gave him the details, McNamara expressed the feelings of the whole police department. 'Oh God,' he said. 'We've got a madman loose!'

What McNamara could not know was that these three murders were just the beginning and that, over the next year and a half, a total of eleven women would be strangled and sexually assaulted in Boston. The city would become a town paralysed by terror.

As the public screamed for a solution to the atrocities, the police mounted the greatest manhunt known in modern crime, using every known detection technique, both natural and supernatural. They would use computers, clairvoyants and psychometrists, psychiatrists with hypnotic drugs and truth serums, psychologists, experts on anthropology, graphology and forensic medicine, as they found themselves confronted by a man whose brutality and insanity were matched by enormous cunning. He appeared to be able to gain access to locked apartments, molest and kill women, and never leave a single clue.

EXHAUSTIVE ENQUIRIES

The day after the discovery of Helen Blake's body, Commissioner McNamara cancelled all police leave. All his detectives were reassigned to homicide. There was a round-up of all known sex offenders. And anyone between 18 and 40 who had been released from a mental institution in the previous two years was investigated.

The police held a press conference during which they appealed to women, particularly women living alone, to keep their doors and windows locked, to admit no strangers, and to report any prowlers, obscene phone calls and letters.

Over the next few weeks the police were deluged with telephone calls and letters conveying tips, suspicions and alarms, both genuine and spurious. Lieutenants Sherry and Donovan, Special Officer Mellon and Detective Phil Di Natale, together with scores of other detectives, spent long hours and weekends covering leads and tracing and picking up possible suspects. The police held identity parades and administered lie-detector tests on scores of men. None of them was the strangler.

By mid-August there had been no more killings, and McNamara was beginning to hope that the strangler had sated his hideous cravings. Then, on 21 August, they found Ida Irga.

A 75-year-old widow, Mrs Irga had been dead for two days. She had been strangled by human hands, but a pillow case had also been tied round her neck in a bow. Like the other victims, she had been sexually molested and, in her case, the murderer had added an appalling refinement to his attack. He had placed two chairs widely apart and tied one ankle to each in an obscene parody of a gynaecological examination. Again, the apartment had been ransacked yet no property had been removed.

Ten days later, the strangler struck again. His victim was Jane Sullivan, a 67-year-old nurse. She was found in the bathroom of her apartment; she had been dead for more than a week.

Her body was half-kneeling in the tub, her face and arms submerged in six inches of water so that her buttocks were exposed. She had been strangled with two of her own stockings and placed in the bath after death.

UNBRIDLED HYSTERIA

Three months passed without a strangling but, far from relaxing, the people of Boston built themselves up to a state of unbridled hysteria. Every prowler, every flasher, every obscene phone caller was automatically presumed to be the strangler. A housewife in Brockton dropped dead of a heart attack when she found herself confronted with a stranger on her doorstep. He turned out to be selling encyclopaedias.

The police, with the help of a host of experts, had built up a complex psychological profile of the strangler. He was, they decided, between 18 and 40 years old, white, highly intelligent but psychopathic. He might well be homosexual or bisexual. He probably suffered from schizophrenia. He hated women, particularly older women, and had probably been brought up by a domineering mother. To his actual identity, however, they still had no clue.

When the next killing occurred, on 5 December 1962, even their psychological profile proved at least partially inaccurate. The latest victim, Sophie Clark, could not have been more different from the established strangler 'type'. She was an attractive black student of 20 who shared a flat with two other women. And Patricia Bisset, who was found strangled and sexually assaulted on New Year's Eve, was 23 and white.

It was now obvious that the strangler struck at random and no woman in Boston, young or old, black or white, living alone or living with others, was safe from him.

FURTHER GROTESQUE ATTACKS

On Wednesday, 8 May, 1963, 33-year-old Oliver Chamberlin called round to see his fiancee, Beverly Samans, a graduate student at Boston University. There was no answer when Chamberlin rang the bell of Beverly's apartment, so he let himself in with his own key.

He saw her at once. She was sprawled on a sofa bed in the living room, naked, her legs spread wide apart. Her wrists were tied behind her back with sequin-studded silk scarves. A bloodstained stocking and two handkerchiefs were knotted around her neck.

Beverly, however, had not died of stangulation. She had been stabbed 22 times in the throat and left breast. There was no doubt, however, that this was the work of the strangler, whose body count had now risen to eight.

Three months passed before the strangler struck again. Number nine was a vivacious 58-year-old divorcee called Evelyn Corbin. Strangled, assaulted and grossly exposed, she was found by a neighbour. Again the police found no clues, save a doughnut on the fire escape outside Mrs Corbin's apartment.

Friday 22 November 1963 is a day that no American will ever forget. President Kennedy was gunned down in Dallas, Texas. The following day, the entire nation was reeling from the blow, but for the strangler it was business as usual. This time his victim was a shy 23-year-old, Joann Graff. He strangled her with her own black leotard and left her nude body on a day bed in her apartment.

Christmas came, and the people of Boston did their level best not to let the strangler ruin the holiday season. Indeed, he did not strike over that period. But shortly after New Year Pamela Parker and Patricia Delmore returned from work to find their 19-year-old flatmate, Mary Sullivan, brutally murdered. It was the most grotesque and macabre killing so far.

Mary's body – in the words of the police report – was 'on the bed in a propped position, buttocks on pillow, back against headboard, head on right shoulder, knees up, eyes closed, viscous liquid dripping from mouth to right breast, breasts and lower extremities exposed, broomstick handle inserted in vagina...' Knotted round her neck were a stocking and a silk scarf tied together in a huge, comic bow. A bright greetings card which read 'Happy New Year!' was propped against her left foot.

The public outrage was intense, and two weeks later the Attorney General, Edward W. Brooke Jr., announced that the Attorney General's Office of the Commonwealth of Massachusetts was taking over the investigation.

NO LONGER TOLERABLE

The strangler task force worked tirelessly throughout 1964. There were no further stranglings, but the police force's determination to identify and convict the man responsible was undiminished. But, by the autumn of 1964, the authorities were no nearer catching the strangler. It was now nine months since he had struck and there was a feeling that the killer might have moved from the area, committed suicide or merely quit.

Then, on 27 October, the police in Cambridge, Massachusetts received a complaint from a young housewife. It was destined to open a whole new avenue of enquiry.

She told detectives that she was dozing in bed, after seeing her teacher husband off to work, when a man appeared at the bedroom door. He was about 30, of medium build, wearing green slacks and large sunglasses.

The man had come slowly towards her and said: 'Don't worry, I'm a detective.' The young woman had yelled at him to get out, but the man had leaped forward, pinned her to the bed and held a knife to her throat. 'Not a sound,' he had commanded, 'or I'll kill you.'

The intruder had gagged his victim with her underwear, then tied her ankles and wrists to the bedposts so that she was spreadeagled. He had proceeded to kiss and fondle her body. Suddenly he had stopped, got to his feet and loosened her bonds slightly.

'You be quiet for ten minutes,' he said. 'I'm sorry,' he added and then fled from the apartment.

After she had finished giving her statement to detectives, the young woman spent several hours with a police artist trying to establish a likeness of her attacker. Between them they did a good job. One of the detectives recognized the face immediately. 'That', he said, 'looks like the Measuring Man.'

Police Commissioner McNamara with the special tactical squad he formed to catch the Boston Strangler.

THE MEASURING MAN

This was a character well known to the Boston police. He had been convicted and gaoled in 1960 for breaking and entering and indecently assaulting young women. He had gained his nickname because he had a habit of posing as an artist's agent, calling on young women and taking their measurements for supposed employment as models. The Measuring Man's real name was Albert H. De Salvo.

Thirty-three-year-old maintenance man De Salvo was picked up and brought to the police headquarters at Cambridge. He denied assaulting the young woman, but she identified him immediately. De Salvo was charged and taken into custody. As a matter of routine, the Cambridge police teletyped De Salvo's picture to neighbouring states. The response was astounding.

Messages poured in from New Hampshire, Rhode Island and Connecticut to say that De Salvo had been identified by scores of

285

women as being the man who had sexually assaulted them. In some areas he was known as the Green Man because of his penchant for green trousers.

De Salvo denied everything and refused to answer any questions until he had spoken to his German-born wife, Irmgard. She was duly delivered to him and detectives watched them as they whispered together.

The police got the impression that Irmgard knew her husband had been 'up to something with women'. She confirmed their suspicions by saying aloud: 'Al, tell them everything. Don't hold anything back.'

De Salvo heeded his wife's advice and told detectives: 'I have committed more than four hundred breaks [breaking and entering], all in this area, and there's a couple of rapes you don't know about.'

As the investigation widened, detectives soon realized that De Salvo was not exaggerating. They estimated that in the past two years he had committed sexual assaults on more than 300 hundred women.

Women of all ages crowd into the Middlesex Superior Courtroom, hoping to catch a glimpse of the Strangler.

De Salvo was shipped to Boston State Hospital for observation while he awaited trial for the Green Man offences. Doctors found him to be 'overtly schizophrenic and potentially suicidal', and on 4 February 1965 Judge Edward A. Pecce ordered him to be committed to a hospital for the criminally insane 'until further orders of the court'.

Al De Salvo should really have been caught up in the 'strangler dragnet' three years earlier. But, because of an administrative anomaly, he had been listed on the computer as a breaking-and-entering man rather than as a sex offender. So he had been overlooked when Boston police were conducting routine questioning early in the case. Now they wanted to know if he was involved. But De Salvo was horrified at the suggestion that he might be connected with the killings. 'No, no,' he wept, 'I've done some terrible things with women – but I've never killed anyone.' Detectives were initially inclined to believe him. De Salvo didn't fit their profile of the strangler, and he simply wasn't smart enough to have got away with it.

In hospital, De Salvo befriended a convicted killer named George Nassar. Soon he was using him as a confidant.

He did not come straight out and say he was the strangler, but his hints were sufficiently pointed for Nassar to get a distinct impression that he might be. A $110,000 reward had been offered to anyone giving information that led to the capture and conviction of the strangler, and Nassar saw this as a perfect chance to make a fast buck. He informed his attorney, F. Lee Bailey.

Bailey went to see De Salvo and recorded his confession to all eleven Boston stranglings, plus another two killings which the police had not previously connected with the strangler. Bailey turned a copy of his tape over to the police and the Attorney General's Office.

At first everyone was sceptical about De Salvo being the strangler. Not only did he not fit their profile, he had also gained a reputation as a braggart.

But when he was questioned at length, he started to disclose facts about the killings that only the strangler could have known –

facts that had been deliberately kept secret to catch out the 'confessors'. De Salvo drew diagrams of the various apartments where the killings had taken place, and under hypno-analysis described the actual stranglings in gruesome detail.

Finally, the authorities were forced to accept that he might indeed be the Boston Strangler.

NO CASE

It was now the spring of 1965. The manhunt, now in its third year, was wound down, and the investigation team was reduced to two men. Assistant Attorney General John Bottomley spent the next seven months interviewing De Salvo, talking him through each crime in minute detail. De Salvo proved to have an incredible memory and his descriptions of the various murders left Bottomley in absolutely no doubt that Albert De Salvo and the Boston Strangler were one and the same person.

Bottomley had his confession, but he had no one to corroborate it. De Salvo's victims could not testify against him and there were no eye-witnesses to identify him, and in America no one can be convicted solely by their own uncorroborated testimony. After all that effort, the state still had no case.

De Salvo had committed other crimes, however, for which the police had ample evidence. On the last day of June 1966 Albert De Salvo attended a hearing at Middlesex County Courthouse in East Cambridge, which was designed to determine whether he was mentally fit to stand trial for the Green Man offences.

It was his first public appearance since he had been committed to the institution at Bridgewater on 4 February 1965. Everyone in the court knew that De Salvo was probably the Boston Strangler, yet that case was not allowed to be mentioned.

Dr Mezer and Dr Tartakoff appeared as expert witnesses for the prosecution. They said that in their opinion Albert De Salvo was suffering from a committable mental illness, but was quite capable of standing trial.

Dr Robey, however, who had originally committed De Salvo to Bridgewater, disagreed completely: 'He is suffering from schizophrenic reaction, chronic undifferentiated type with very extensive signs of sexual deviation... My opinion is that I cannot – repeat – cannot consider him competent to stand trial...' Dr Robey added that, in his opinion, De Salvo would react to cross-examination by getting 'in such a state that he would not be making sense'.

Ten days later Judge Cahill accepted the prosecution argument and found Albert De Salvo competent to stand trail. The following year De Salvo was tried and convicted of armed robbery, breaking and entering, theft, assault and sexual crimes against four women, all of whom were lucky enough to live to identify their attacker. He was sentenced to life imprisonment.

While Albert De Salvo was never to stand trial as the Boston Strangler, the system had made sure he would never be free again. As it turned out, the length of his sentence was academic. On 26 November 1973, Albert De Salvo was found dead in his cell in Walpole State Prison. He had been stabbed 16 times. The identity of his killer has never been established.

GEORGE HAIGH

ACID-BATH MURDERS

The dapper 39-year- old charmed the ladies of a London hotel – until one of them disappeared. The suspicions of her best friend led to the conviction of one of the most shocking murderers of the century. Not content with robbing his victims, he also did sickening things to their bodies.

Mr John George Haigh was something of an odd man out at the Onslow Gardens Hotel in South Kensington. In 1949 this genteel establishment in a fashionable part of London was the haunt almost exclusively of elderly, well-heeled, upper-class ladies.

Not that Mr Haigh's presence was in any way resented by the other permanent residents of the hotel. On the contrary, for the most part they found the dapper 39-year-old engineer handsome, charming and meticulously well mannered.

One of his particular fans was Mrs Helen Olivia Robarts Durant-Deacon, a well-preserved, buxom 69-year-old widow. She was quite smitten with 'young Haigh' and confided in him freely.

Mrs Durant-Deacon's husband, a colonel in the Gloucester Regiment, had died some years earlier and left her a legacy of £40,000. It was enough to allow her to live in some comfort for the rest of her life. But, as she explained to Haigh, she wasn't the sort of person to sit around doing nothing.

She was thinking of starting a business, designing and manufacturing artificial fingernails. She had already made some paper prototypes, but she knew absolutely nothing about the technical side of things. Perhaps Mr Haigh, as an engineer, could give her some pointers?

APPOINTMENT WITH DEATH

In reality, Mrs Durant-Deacon's idea was a commercial non-starter in ration-bound, post-war England. But Haigh feigned enthusiasm. Of course he would be delighted to help. Perhaps she would like to come out to his factory in Essex some time, and they could look at some possible materials from which the nails could be made.

At about 3 p.m. on Friday, 18 February 1949, Haigh picked up Mrs Durant-Deacon and drove her down to a factory in Crawley, Sussex. He did not, as he had claimed, own the factory, but he did know the owner, and had the use of a storeroom for his 'experimental work'. The grimy brick shed was cluttered with bottles, vats and drums. It was not what Mrs Durant-Deacon had

The gas mask worn by George Haigh to protect himself from acid fumes.

expected, but Haigh reassured her. Experimental laboratories were always chaotic.

Mrs Durant-Deacon took his word for it and reached for her handbag, which held her designs. As she turned away from Haigh, he pulled a .38 Enfield revolver from his jacket pocket. He calmly shot her through the nape of the neck, killing her instantly.

Haigh then kneeled by his victim's body and made an incision in her neck with a knife. He collected a glassful of her still coursing blood and drank it.

Having quenched this gross thirst, Haigh gathered Mrs Durant-Deacon's valuables – a Persian lamb coat, rings, a necklace, earrings and a gold crucifix – and stowed them in his car.

Now it was time to get rid of the body. The very clutter that had offended Mrs Durant-Deacon was, in fact, the paraphernalia of her destruction. There were vats of sulphuric acid, a specially lined metal drum, rubber gloves and a rubber apron, a gas mask and a stirrup pump. Haigh needed all these things to dissolve his victim's body. He knew precisely what to do. He'd done it before.

He laid the 45 gallon drum on its side and pushed Mrs Durant-Deacon's head and shoulders inside. Then he righted the drum so that the whole body slumped down to the bottom. He donned his rubber apron and gloves, his wellington boots and gas mask and proceeded to pour concentrated sulphuric acid into the drum.

Using the stirrup pump, Haigh adjusted the level of acid to cover the entire body. Once satisfied, all he had to do was wait for the flesh and bone to dissolve. He knew this would take at least two days. So, tired and hungry after his exertions, he drove to Ye Olde Ancient Priors restaurant in Crawley for a little supper, before driving back to London.

NAGGING SUSPICIONS

At breakfast the following morning several residents of the Onslow Court Hotel remarked on Mrs Durant-Deacon's absence. Her closest friend at the hotel, Mrs Constance Lane, was particularly concerned and started to make some discreet enquiries. The chambermaid told Mrs Lane that Mrs Durant-Deacon's bed had not been slept in.

Later that morning Mrs Lane was approached by John Haigh who solicitously enquired about Mrs Durant-Deacon's whereabouts. He said that he had had an appointment with her the previous day, and that Mrs Durant-Deacon had failed to show up.

Mrs Lane already knew about the trip to Crawley. She had seen her friend just as she was about to leave the hotel. She couldn't understand how Mrs Durant-Deacon could have 'failed to show up'. Mrs Lane had never liked Haigh. He was too oily for her taste, and his involvement with Mrs Durant-Deacon had always made her uneasy. Now she had a creeping feeling that something awful had happened to her friend.

Mrs Lane toyed with the idea of going to the police. But she was afraid that there might be some perfectly good reason for Mrs Durant-Deacon's absence and was anxious not to embarrass her friend – or to make a fool of herself. She decided to wait.

The following morning there was still no sign of Mrs Durant-Deacon. Mrs Lane was at breakfast, pondering her next move, when she was again approached by Haigh, expressing concern.

The barrel used by Haigh to dissolve his victim's body.

Mrs Lane was suddenly galvanized into action. She told Haigh that she was going down to the police station and that she would like him to go with her. Haigh had little choice but to agree, so he drove her to Chelsea Police Station.

The report Haigh made to the police was plausible enough. He had arranged to meet Mrs Durant-Deacon outside the Army and Navy Stores in Victoria Street at 2.30 p.m. on 18 February. He had waited there until 3.30. Mrs Durant-Deacon had never materialized and he had driven down to his workshop in Crawley alone.

He was, of course, extremely concerned about Mrs Durant-Deacon's welfare and would do anything he could to help them locate her. The police thanked Haigh for his cooperation and said that they would be in touch if they thought of anything else.

Haigh drove Mrs Lane back to the Onslow Court and hoped against hope that that was the last he would hear of the matter. It wasn't. Four days later, on Thursday, 24 February, Woman Police Sergeant Alexandra Lambourne went to the hotel to gather additional background information on Mrs Durant-Deacon. She interviewed Haigh at some length.

Like Mrs Lane, she was immediately repelled by his superficial charm and his unctuous concern for the well-being of the missing widow. She was an experienced police officer and was convinced that Haigh was lying.

WPS Lambourne had no evidence to support her gut feeling, but she felt strongly enough about it to mention it in her report to her divisional Detective Inspector, Shelley Symes. 'Apart from the fact I do not like the man Haigh and his mannerisms,' she wrote, 'I have a sense that he is "wrong", and there may be a case behind the whole business.'

Symes had sufficient respect for Sergeant Lambourne's judgement to ask the Criminal Record Division at Scotland Yard to run a check on Haigh. Within a matter of hours, they came back to him with a file that showed that John George Haigh had been jailed three times, twice for obtaining money by fraud and once for theft. Further enquiries in London and Sussex showed that he owed substantial sums of money – to the Onslow Court Hotel, among others.

On Saturday, 26 February, Sergeant Pat Heslin of the West Sussex Constabulary, accompanied by Police Sergeant Appleton, went to see Mr Edward Jones, owner of Hurtslea Products, a small engineering company located on Leopold Street in Crawley. Jones told the police that he had known John George Haigh for some years. Over the past few months he had let him use a storehouse at the back of the factory for a nominal rent. Haigh had been using the premises for 'experimental work', but had never said precisely what that entailed.

The police were anxious to look round the shed, but Jones told them that Haigh had the only set of keys. So Heslin picked up a steel bar and prised the padlock off the door. At first glance, the whitewashed interior looked ordinary enough. There was the usual clutter – paint pots, old bits of wood, a couple of work benches, vats of chemicals, protective clothing.

Then something caught the sergeant's eye. On one of the workbenches there was a small hatbox and an expensive leather briefcase. They simply didn't belong.

Heslin looked through the case. He found a variety of papers and documents, including ration books and clothing coupons. The contents of the hatbox were even odder. It contained several passports, driving licences, diaries, a cheque book and a marriage certificate, none of which bore the name of Haigh. At the bottom of the box was the most alarming find of all, a .38 Enfield revolver and a small white envelope containing eight bullets.

The following evening, 27 February, Haigh was invited back to Chelsea Police Station to answer further questions. He appeared totally unconcerned as he was led into an office and given a cup of

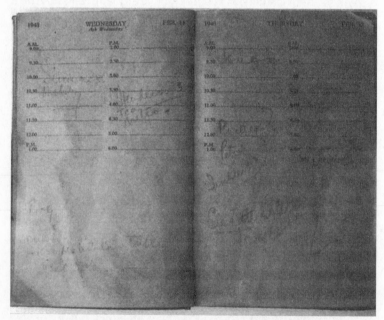

George Haigh's diary was scrutinized by police.

tea. He had dozed off by the time Detective Inspector Shelley Symes, Inspector Albert Webb and Superintendent Barratt arrived to interview him at 7.30.

They came at him well-armed with evidence. Not only did they have the obviously stolen documents from the Crawley workshop, they had also traced Mrs Durant-Deacon's jewellery to a dealer in Horsham, Sussex. His description of the seller matched John George Haigh precisely. As did that of a dry-cleaner to whom he had taken Mrs Durant-Deacon's Persian lamb coat.

THE AWFUL TRUTH EMERGES

Confronted with this, Haigh was barely ruffled. Puffing on a cigarette, he said, 'I can see you know what you're talking about. I admit the coat belonged to Mrs Durant-Deacon and that I sold her jewellery.'

'How did you come by the property?' asked Symes, 'And where is Mrs Durant-Deacon?' Haigh thought for a while before replying. 'It's a long story,' he confided. 'It's one of blackmail and I shall have to implicate many others.'

Just then the telephone rang, and Symes and Barratt were summoned from the room. Left alone with Inspector Webb, the most junior of his interrogators, Haigh changed his tack. 'Tell me frankly,' he asked. 'What are the chances of anyone being released from Broadmoor?'

Webb's immediate reaction to Haigh's extraordinary question was to caution him and advise him of his rights. Haigh dismissed the warning with a wave of the hand. 'If I told you the truth,' he continued, 'you would not believe it. It is too fantastic for belief. I will tell you all about it…

'Mrs Durant-Deacon no longer exists. She has disappeared completely and no trace of her can ever be found. I have destroyed her with acid. You will find sludge that remains at Leopold Road. Every trace has gone. How can you prove a murder if there is no body?' Haigh added, obviously pleased with himself. Webb's first reaction was to disbelieve Haigh's confession. It was simply too fantastic, too grotesque. Haigh was obviously setting himself up for an insanity plea. After all, he had already mentioned Broadmoor.

When Symes and Barratt returned to the interview room, Webb asked Haigh to repeat what he had said. Haigh did so. Symes cautioned him again, but there was no stopping Haigh now. He talked for $2^1/_2$ hours. And Inspector Symes wrote it all down.

He described the events of Friday, 18 February, in meticulous detail. He told how he had shot Mrs Durant-Deacon, how he had drunk her blood, put her in the acid bath, and then gone to the Ancient Priors for tea and poached eggs. He explained how, on Monday, he had disposed of her jewellery for £110. Then he had returned to Crawley and emptied the sludge – Mrs Durant-Deacon's decomposed body – out of the drum with a bucket, and poured it on to some wasteground at the back of the shed.

The police said nothing as Haigh told his terrible story of murder and theft, vampirism and genteel cups of tea. When he had

Police search a cellar in Gloucester Road for clues in the Haigh murders.

finished the story of Mrs Durant-Deacon's death, Haigh moved back in time. By the early hours of 1 March he had confessed to five additional murders.

The first, he claimed, had been committed on 9 September 1944. The victim had been an old acquaintance, William McSwan. He had killed him at a basement flat in Gloucester Road. A year later, he had lured William's parents, Donald and Amy McSwan, to the same flat. There he had beaten them to death.

He had forged Donald's signature to gain power of attorney over the McSwans' estate. While selling one of their properties in February 1948, he had met Dr Archibald Henderson and his wife Rosalie. He had killed them in a storeroom in Giles Yard.

Rosalie Henderson – she died at Haigh's hands along with her husband.

In each case, he had acquired money or other property belonging to his victims by skilful forgery and deception. Years after he had disposed of their remains, he had written forged personal and business letters, 'successfully staving off enquiries from relatives, friends and associates'.

Haigh added that he had destroyed all the bodies by his acid bath method – after drinking a glass of their blood.

The arrest of John George Haigh caused an immediate public sensation. His remand at Horsham magistrates court drew huge crowds – predominantly of jeering women.

BUT WHERE IS THE PROOF?

On 4 March, after being transferred from the Chelsea police cells to Lewes Prison, Haigh sprang more surprises. He asked to see Inspector Webb, with whom he clearly felt some sort of affinity. He confided in the young detective that he had committed three murders which he hadn't mentioned in his earlier statement – a woman and a young man in West London, and a girl in Eastbourne. This brought his total to nine.

The police, however, were having their time cut out establishing a case against Haigh for the murder of Mrs Durant-Deacon. Even though he had admitted to the crime, to be certain of a conviction, the prosecution needed proof that the woman was, in fact, dead and that Haigh really had killed her.

The Home Office pathologist, Dr Keith Simpson, first carried out routine blood tests at the workshop in Crawley. He established that blood stains found there were of the same group as Mrs Durant-Deacon. He then turned his attention to the wasteland where Haigh claimed to have deposited the 'sludge' from his acid bath. Soon he found a stone 'the size of a cherry'. It was a gallstone.

Simpson soon found more human remains, including fragments of a left foot. He managed to reconstruct it and cast it in plaster. The cast fitted one of Mrs Durant-Deacon's shoes perfectly.

He discovered other, non-human remains – the handle of a handbag, a lipstick container, a hairpin and a notebook. All of these could be traced back to the victim. His most sensational find, however – the clincher – was a set of dentures which were positively identified as having belonged to the missing woman.

In Lewes Prison, Haigh was well aware of the forensic evidence being amassed against him, but he still remained optimistic. He was certain that he could escape the gallows by convincing a jury that he was insane. And on being told that the eminent barrister Sir Maxwell Fyfe was to represent him, Haigh was delighted. He wrote: 'I'm very glad to see we have got old Maxy. He's no fool.'

THE MIND OF A KILLER

The trial of John George Haigh for the murder of Mrs Durant-Deacon – that was the only charge ever brought against him – opened at Lewes Assizes on 18 July 1949 and lasted less than two days.

There was no real question as to whether Haigh had killed Mrs Durant-Deacon. The case rested on whether or not he was sane. The defence called Dr Henry Yellowlees, a consultant psychiatrist at St Thomas's Hospital, as an expert witness.

Dr Yellowlees was no doubt an able man in his field, but he was a rotten witness. He was a pompous windbag. 'In the case of pure paranoia,' Yellowlees explained, 'it really amounts, as it develops and gets a greater hold, to practically self-worship, and that is commonly expressed by the conviction in the mind of the patient that he is in some mystic way under the control of a guiding spirit which means infinitely more to him and is of infinitely greater authority than any human laws or rules of society.'

Haigh is beseiged by photographers as he leaves court.

Dr Yellowlees rambled on in this vein for some considerable time. He was frequently interrupted by both Sir Travers Humphry, the judge, and Sir Hartley Shawcross, counsel for the prosecution, neither of whom had the faintest idea what he was talking about.

As for the jury, he had lost them after the first few sentences. It took them only fifteen minutes to return a verdict of guilty on John George Haigh. Sir Travers Humphry was equally speedy as he summoned the black cap and condemned him to death. Haigh was taken to Wandsworth Prison to await execution.

While there was no expression of pity for him from the press, there was a great deal of editorial speculation. How was it, they wondered, that an intelligent boy from a good home – his parents were members of the Plymouth Brethren – could grow into a monster like Haigh?

Haigh himself went some way to answering them. He wrote from prison: 'Although my parents were kind and loving, I had none of the joys, or the companionship, which small children usually have. From my earliest years, my recollection is of my father saying "Do not" or "Thou shalt not". Any form of sport or light entertainment was frowned upon and regarded as not edifying. There was only condemnation and prohibition…

'It is true to say that I was nurtured on Bible stories but mostly concerned with sacrifice. If by some mischance I did, or said, anything which my father regarded as improper, he would say: "Do not grieve the Lord by behaving so." '

On 24 July, five days after his trial ended, Haigh's mother sent him a fortieth birthday card, but he rejected any suggestion that she visit him in prison.

As the day of his execution approached, Haigh's apparently limitless poise began to crumble. He started to suffer from depression and complained of recurrent nightmares about blood.

Despite his depression, Haigh maintained his sense of theatre. He bequeathed his favourite suit and tie to Madame Tussauds, ensuring himself a place in the Chamber of Horrors. He even requested his model should show at least one inch of shirt cuff.

Then Haigh became concerned about the hanging itself. He contacted the prison governor, Major A.C.N. Benke, and requested to rehearse his own execution. 'My weight is deceptive,' Haigh insisted, 'I have a light springy step and I would not like there to be a hitch.'

The governor turned down his request, assuring him that the executioner was highly experienced and that there would be no hitches.

On 9 August, the eve of his execution, Haigh wrote a letter to his parents. It began: 'My dearest Mum and Dad, Thank you for your very touching letter which I received this morning and which will, I suppose, be your last...'

He went on to say that he had found parts of his upbringing very restrictive: 'There was much that was lovely... We cannot change the inscrutible predictions of the eternal... I, that is my spirit, shall remain earthbound for some time: my mission is not yet fulfilled...'

Haigh did not go on to explain what he thought his mission was, nor expressed any remorse for his terrible crimes. In the end, the ultimate mystery of Haigh's life – what was going on inside his mind – would go to the grave with him.

At 9 a.m. on 10 August, John George Haigh was executed. His depression had left him and he was his old self, all swank and swagger, as he faced the gallows. He was buried the same day inside the prison walls, as is the custom in cases of execution.

TED BUNDY
THE CHARMER

Serial killer Ted Bundy terrorized young women throughout various American states and claimed the lives of many young women in vicious sexual assaults and killings. Ted Bundy is estimated to have murdered between 35 and 50 young women in almost a dozen states.

As a youth, Ted was terribly shy and was often teased and bullied in his junior high school. Despite this he was able to maintain a high grade average that would continue throughout high school and later into college. Ted was more popular in high school than he was in junior high. Although he was very shy, Ted was thought of as being well dressed and exceptionally well mannered. He was not known to have dated anyone during this period; it seemed his interests lay elsewhere, such as in skiing and politics. In fact, it was in high school that Ted's interest in politics began to bloom.

Ted graduated from high school in 1965 and won a scholarship to the University of Puget Sound. In 1966 he transferred to the University of Washington, where he began his intensive studies in Chinese. He worked his way through the university by taking on low-level jobs such as a bus boy and shoe clerk. It was in the spring of 1967 he began a relationship that would change his life forever.

Stephanie Brooks was everything Ted had ever dreamed of in a woman. She was a beautiful and highly sophisticated woman from a wealthy Californian family. Although they had many differences, they both loved to ski and it was during their many ski trips together that they began to fall in love. Stephanie was Ted's first love and they spent a lot of time together. However, Stephanie was not as infatuated with Ted as he was with her. She believed that he had no real direction or future goals and it appeared she wanted someone who would fit in with her lifestyle. Ted tried too hard to impress her, even if that meant lying, something that she didn't like at all.

In 1968, after graduating from the University of Washington, Stephanie broke off relations with Ted. Ted never recovered from the break-up. Nothing, including school, seemed to hold any interest for him and he eventually dropped out, dumbfounded and depressed over the break-up. Ted was totally obsessed with Stephanie and he couldn't get her out of his mind. It was an obsession that would span his lifetime and lead to a series of events that would shock the world.

A TIME OF CHANGE

Ted re-enrolled at the University of Washington, to study psychology. It was at this time that he met Meg Anders, a woman with whom he would be involved for almost five years. Meg worked as a secretary and was a somewhat shy and quiet woman. She was a divorcee who seemed to have found the perfect father figure for her daughter in Ted Bundy. Meg was deeply in love with Ted from the start and wanted to marry him one day. She was totally unaware of the infatuation that he still held for Stephanie. Ted, however, was not yet ready for marriage because he felt there was still too much for him to accomplish.

Outwardly, Ted's life seemed to be changing for the better. He was more confident, with high hopes for his future. Ted began sending out applications for various law schools, while at the same time he became active in politics. He worked on a campaign to re-elect a Washington governor, a position that allowed Ted to form bonds with politically powerful people in the Republican Party. Ted also did some voluntary work at a crisis clinic on a work-study programme. He was pleased with the path his life was taking at this time, everything seemed to be going in the right direction. He was even commended by the Seattle police for saving the life of a three-year-old boy who was drowning in a lake.

In 1973, during a business trip to California for the Washington Republican Party, Ted met up with his old flame Stephanie Brooks for a night out. Stephanie was amazed at the transformation in Ted. He was much more confident and mature. They met several times, unknown to Meg. During Ted's business trips he romantically courted Stephanie and she once again fell in love with him.

Ted raised the subject of marriage many times during that autumn and winter. But suddenly it all changed. Where once Ted lavished affection upon Stephanie, he was suddenly cold and despondent. It seemed as if Ted had lost all interest in her over the period of just a few weeks. Stephanie was undoubtedly confused as to the sudden change in Ted. In February 1974, with no warning or explanation, Ted ended all contact with Stephanie. His plan of revenge worked. He rejected Stephanie as she had once rejected him. Stephanie was never to see or hear from Ted again.

A TIME OF TERROR

On 6 December 1973, a young couple stumbled across the remains of a 15- year-old girl in McKenny Park, Washington. Kathy Devine was last seen by friends on 25 November hitchhiking to Oregon, trying to run away from home. Shortly after she began her journey Kathy met her death. She had been strangled, sodomized and her throat cut. A month after the discovery of the Devine girl came the attack on Joni Lenz, which was soon followed by an even more gruesome attack. Lynda Ann Healy didn't show up for work or for dinner on 31 January 1974. Healy's parents immediately called the police and soon after their arrival, they discovered a mass of blood drenching Lynda Ann's mattress. They also found a nightdress close to the bed with blood on the collar.

During that spring and summer, seven more women students suddenly and inexplicably vanished within the states of Utah, Oregon and Washington. There were striking similarities among many of the cases – all the girls were white, thin, single and wearing slacks, had long hair parted in the middle, and they all

Lynda Ann Healy

disappeared in the evening. Police interviews of college students revealed that they had seen a strange man wearing a cast on either his arm or leg. Others reported a strange man in the campus car park who had a cast and asked for assistance with his car. A man wearing a cast was also spotted in the same area where two of the girls mysteriously disappeared.

Finally, in August of 1974 in Lake Sammamish State Park, Washington State, the remains of some of the missing girls were found and two were later identified. It was remarkable that police were able to identify two of the bodies considering what was left. The girls identified were Janice Ott and Denise Naslund who disappeared on the same day, 14 July.

The similarities between the Washington State and Oregon murders caught the attention of local police in Utah, who were frantically searching for the man responsible for these awful crimes. The evidence was slowly mounting and Utah police consulted with Oregon and Washington State investigators. Almost all agreed that it was highly likely that the same man who

Ted Bundy drove around in a Volkswagen Beetle and used such ruses as feigning a broken arm to seek help from women. He would then lead his victims into his car and to their death.

committed the crimes in Oregon and Washington State had been responsible for the killings in Utah.

When Lynn Banks, a close friend of Meg Anders, saw the account of Melissa Smith's murder and the composite picture of the could-be killer in the paper , she knew Ted Bundy must be the man. Meg also had to agree that the sketch of the killer did resemble Ted, yet she couldn't believe the man she loved and lived with could do such horrible things. Hesitantly, she contacted the police on the advice of her friend. She was one of five people to have turned in Ted Bundy's name to police. Her report, along with the others, was filed away and forgotten until a few years later. Police were so inundated with tips that when they came to Ted Bundy, an apparently respectable man, they set him aside to investigate other more likely suspects.

It wasn't until 8 November 1974, that police investigators were to get the break in the case they had been waiting for.

CAROL DARONCH

One rainy night in November 1974, Carol DaRonch was window-shopping in Salt Lake City, Utah when she was approached by a man in his twenties who said he was a policeman. He asked her if she had left her car in the car park and asked for her registration number. The plain-clothes policeman said a man had been arrested for trying to break into her car and asked if she could come and see if anything had been stolen. But she became suspicious as they walked to the car park because he did not seem to know the way.

The 17-year-old then asked him for proof of his identity and he produced his wallet and showed her what appeared to be a police badge. When they got to the car – and found nothing stolen – he asked her to accompany him to police headquarters to make a statement. He led the way to his own car, an old Volkswagen Beetle, and she became suspicious again and asked for his name. The man said he was Officer Roseland of the Murray Police Department. He was so convincing that she got into the Beetle and they drove off.

A LUCKY ESCAPE

She began to panic when she smelt alcohol on his breath and realized he was driving in the opposite direction to the police station. When he stopped briefly in a side street, she reached for the door handle and tried to get out. But he was too quick for her and he snapped a handcuff on one wrist but was unable to secure the other one.

She continued to struggle and he pulled out a gun and threatened to shoot her. Then Carol's instincts took over – she pulled the door open, clambered out and began to run. The man began chasing her, but he stopped when a car turned into the street. He got back in his VW and sped off.

Carol had been lucky, but Bundy was determined to claim a victim. Later that night he abducted and murdered 17-year-old Debbie Kent. And she would not be the last of his victims . . .

Bundy's first victim was Lynda Healy, 21, a psychology student at the University of Washington in Seattle, who was abducted from her basement flat.

Five more young women vanished from the Seattle area in the spring and summer of 1974, but the case did not merit national newspaper headlines until July, when two girls disappeared from Lake Sammamish State Park on the same day.

SEATTLE

It had been a sunny day and the park, 12 miles from downtown Seattle, had been crowded with people walking their dogs, sailing boats and enjoying picnics. Several women reported having seen a man, calling himself Ted, with an arm in a sling. He had been asking for help with his boat. Doris Grayling had accompanied him to his brown VW, but then became suspicious and left.

Two other women, however, Janice Ott, 23, and Denise Naslund, 19, must have fallen for Bundy's trick, and they were never seen alive again. The double murder struck terror into women in Seattle but Bundy, having finished his psychology degree, was about to leave the city and move to Salt Lake City to study law.

It wouldn't be long before Bundy continued his murder spree. In October, he claimed his first Utah victim. Three more killings followed that first murder and another happened in the ski resort of Snowmass in neighbouring Colorado.

Theodore R. Bundy (right) is taken from a Pensacola jail by Pensacola police Captain Raymond Harper, following his arrest on February 15, 1978 for driving a stolen car.

DISCOVERED BY CHANCE

In the early hours of 16 August 1975, Bundy was stopped while driving without lights in a Salt Lake City suburb. Bundy's evasive answers fuelled the suspicions of Utah Highway Patrolman Bob Hayward, who soon discovered a balaclava, a stocking mask, an iron bar and a pair of handcuffs on the floor of the car.

Bundy was arrested but he remained cool under pressure and explained away the items, saying he needed the balaclava and mask for skiing and had found the handcuffs in a rubbish bin. A search of Bundy's flat uncovered a brochure from a hotel in Snowmass.

Bundy denied having been to Colorado but by now the police were beginning to see through his harmless, self-confident exterior. Bundy was ordered to attend an identity parade and was picked out by Carol DaRonch and two other witnesses. It seemed that Ted Bundy had been caught.

He was convicted of the aggravated kidnapping of Carol DaRonch and was jailed for 15 years. In June 1977 he jumped out of the window of a court building and escaped, only to be recaptured eight days later. The authorities in Colorado were confident they could put him on trial for the murder of Caryn Campbell, the girl who was killed in Snowmass at the height of the skiing season.

But in December 1977 Bundy escaped again – this time by cutting a hole in the ceiling of his cell with a hacksaw blade and this time he would not be caught so easily.

BUNDY ON THE RUN

Bundy fled east and by mid-January was in sunny Florida, 1,500 miles from chilly Colorado. By now he had adopted a new identity. Bundy was no longer the dapper, mild-mannered Republican, he had become an unkempt fugitive from justice, whose murderous urges were out of control.

On 15 January he broke into a sorority house on a university campus in Tallahassee, Florida. He strangled 21-year-old art history student Margaret Brown and beat to death Lisa Levy, 20, after assaulting her. Two other girls who lived in the house had also been beaten with a wooden club but they survived.

A month later Bundy claimed what would be his final victim, 12-year-old Kim Leach. She was abducted from a high school gym, sexually assaulted and strangled. Bundy's days as a free man were, however, numbered.

RECAPTURED

Bundy was finally arrested in the early hours of 15 February 1978, as he drove a stolen car, an orange VW, towards Pensacola, and in June 1979, he went on trial for the sorority house murders. Bundy protested his innocence and conducted his own defence.

The evidence for the prosecution – including evidence from a dentist that his teeth matched bite marks found on Lisa Levy – was overwhelming and the jury found him guilty, sentencing him to death.

Bundy spent the next ten years on Florida's Death Row, using legal tactics to delay his execution and offering confessions to his crimes in exchange for a reprieve. After years of living in denial - insisting on his innocence – Bundy finally confessed to the murders of 28 women. However, many believe the number of deaths to be much higher.

No one will ever really know how many women fell victim to Ted Bundy; it would be a number he would take to his grave. After countless appeals, Ted was finally executed on 24 January 1989.

DONALD NEILSON
THE BLACK PANTHER

For three years police pursued a man who committed 16 robberies and four murders and terrorized a large part of England. But the real Donald Neilson was very far from the hooded 'Black Panther' image of popular imagination.

On the evening of 13 January 1975, 17-year-old Lesley Whittle was at home alone and went to bed early. She lived with her widowed mother, but on this particular night Mrs Dorothy Whittle was out for the evening. When she did return to her comfortable home in the village of Highley, Shropshire at 1.30 a.m., Mrs Whittle made a point of checking her daughter's bedroom. Lesley was sound asleep.

HOODED FIGURE CLAD IN BLACK

Shortly after Mrs Whittle herself retired to bed, a man forced the lock on the garage door. He was dressed from head to foot in black and was wearing a hood. Working silently and in total darkness, the intruder cut the telephone line and then moved into the house. Passing through the living room, he climbed the stairs and made his way directly to Lesley's room.

Lesley Whittle was woken by a hand shaking her roughly. She looked up to see the black-clad figure standing over her, pointing a sawn-off shotgun in her face. Lesley lay transfixed as the intruder taped her mouth and indicated that she should get out of bed. He led Lesley downstairs and outside to a waiting car, a green Morris 1300. He laid her on the back seat, bound her wrists and ankles and placed tape over her eyes.

The intruder then removed his hood, got into the driving seat and set off on a 60-mile trip to his hiding place. He drove down the M6 motorway, turned off at Junction 16 and drove to Bathpool Park, near Kidsgrove. He parked the car alongside the access shaft of the town's drainage system, removed the manhole cover and forced Lesley to climb 65 feet down a rusty ladder.

When they reached a tiny platform, on which he had installed a foam rubber mattress, the kidnapper removed Lesley's dressing gown, placed a wire noose around her neck and clamped it to the wall. Below, the access shaft fell away. If Lesley were to slip she would hang.

The kidnapper then made his next move in an elaborate plan to extort money from his victim's family. He uncovered Lesley's eyes, proffered a memo machine, and instructed her to read two messages that he had written on a pad.

Lesley did not know her kidnapper. She had never laid eyes on him before in her life. His name was Donald Neilson.

The name would have meant nothing to her. It would have meant little to the police either, even though they had been chasing him for more than three years, during which time he had been responsible for armed robberies and the murder of three sub-postmasters. Yet they only knew him by a nickname.

No one knew it yet, but Lesley Whittle had been kidnapped by the 'Black Panther'.

HOAXES AND MISTAKES

On the morning of 14 January, Mrs Dorothy Whittle woke to find her daughter missing. She was more puzzled than alarmed. Lesley had been safely tucked up in her bed at 1.30. Nothing bad could have happened to her since then. Mrs Whittle checked round the house and then tried to telephone her son, Ronald.

The phone, of course, had been cut. But, assuming it was merely out of order, Dorothy Whittle drove to her son's house at the other end of the village.

Neither Ronald nor his wife Gaynor had seen Lesley that morning. Mrs Whittle was now becoming uneasy.

Gaynor drove back home with Mrs Whittle, and the two women checked the house more carefully in the hope of finding a note. They found a note all right, but it wasn't from Lesley.

In a cardboard box, resting on a flower vase in the lounge, they discovered a long roll of Dymo tape. There were three messages carefully typed into the coloured plastic. The messages were ransom demands.

The first read: 'No police £50,000 ransom to be ready to deliver wait for phone call at Swan shopping centre telephone box 6 p.m.

Lesley Whittle's disappearance prompted a nation-wide hunt.

to 1 a.m. if no call return following evening when you answer give your name only and listen you must follow instructions without argument from the time you answer you are on a time limit if police or tricks death.'

Despite the warning in the note, Mrs Whittle did not hesitate to call the police. Within an hour the case was being led by the head of West Mercia CID, Detective Chief Superintendent Bob Booth.

He was in no doubt that this was a professional kidnapping. Lesley was a logical target. Two years earlier she had been the beneficiary of a large and highly publicized inheritance.

Booth advised the Whittle family that their best chance of getting Lesley back alive was to comply fully with the kidnapper's demands.

While Ronald Whittle, who owned a successful coach company, was raising the money, Booth had his own elaborate arrangements to make. He installed taps on the phones at Mrs Whittle's home and the phone box at Kidderminster.

After midday, Booth and his detectives were joined by a team of kidnap specialists from Scotland Yard. Shortly after 5 p.m. Ronald Whittle, armed with a white suitcase full of money, installed himself

The boot of Neilson's Morris car yielded a host of clues for police

318

in the phone box at Kidderminster and waited.

The police, who were watching Whittle from a discreet distance, hoped to have the whole episode dealt with that night, but it was not to be. A freelance journalist had somehow got wind of the operation and started making a nuisance of himself.

Rather than alerting the kidnapper to the fact that the police were indeed involved, Booth decided to abort the mission.

The following evening, Ronald Whittle returned to the phone box with the money. Shortly after 8 p.m., the police called him out again. They had received a call from a man claiming to be the kidnapper and had been given delivery instructions for the ransom money. The call, however, proved to be a hoax.

Meanwhile, another drama was unfolding. Donald Neilson left his hideout in the drains of Bathpool Park and did a dummy run of the route he had mapped out for the ransom carrier. He travelled to Dudley in Worcestershire, stopping at various telephone boxes to conceal more Dymo tape instructions.

In Dudley itself, he decided to check over the final drop-off point, the Freightliner depot. He was browsing around when he was challenged by the night supervisor, Gerald Smith.

Neilson shot Smith six times. He then ran from the scene, abandoning his stolen Morris car.

When local police investigated the shooting, they failed to check the car. This was a tragic oversight, because the boot of the car was a positive treasure trove of clues.

Amazingly, Gerald Smith survived the shooting – though he died 14 months later as a result of his wounds – and was able to give the police a description of his assailant. What he told them left police in no doubt that he was the victim of the 'Black Panther'.

At 11.45 p.m. on the night of 16 January, the third day of the kidnap, Leonard Rudd, transport manager of Whittle's Coaches, received a telephone call. On the other end of the line was Lesley Whittle's recorded voice instructing the courier to take the ransom money to a phone box at Kidsgrove.

Ronald Whittle was extensively briefed by Detective Chief Superintendent Lovejoy of Scotland Yard.

Whittle reached the Kidsgrove telephone box shortly after 3 a.m., and waited there for half an hour before discovering another Dymo message. It read: 'Go up road to Acres Nook sign. Go up Boathouse Road turn right into public footpath dead end go into entry service area. Drive past wall and flash headlights looking for torchlight run to torch instructions on torch. Go home wait for telephone.'

Ronald Whittle got back into his car and followed the directions. After a few minutes he arrived at Bathpool Park. He flashed his headlights and waited for the torch signal. It never came.

Donald Neilson had been watching as Ronald Whittle arrived and was immediately suspicious. He could smell police.

Certain that he would never now get his hands on the ransom money, he flew into a rage. As soon as Whittle had left he climbed back down the drainage access shaft, pushed Lesley Whittle off her precarious platform and left her to hang by her neck until she died.

By dawn, he was on the train north to his home in Bradford.

A press conference given by the police during the hunt for the 'Black Panther'.

VITAL NEW EVIDENCE

Most of Booth's and Lovejoy's efforts now centred around the village of Highley, where the abduction had taken place. Everyone in the village and the surrounding area was interviewed. But this revealed absolutely nothing.

And then, on 23 January, a week after the last abortive attempt to deliver the ransom money, a police constable patrolling the Freightliner depot at Dudley became interested in a green Morris 1300. He noticed it had been parked in the same spot for several days.

The car was towed into the police station and searched. The boot revealed startling new evidence. There were a tape recorder containing a tape of Lesley Whittle's voice, a gun, torches and a foam mattress. A ballistic examination of the gun confirmed that it had been used in the 'Black Panther' raids.

As the days passed, Detective Chief Superintendent Booth felt sure that Bathpool Park was probably the most important location they had encountered in their investigation, and he was determined to search it thoroughly. To this end, he planned an elaborate ruse.

On the evening of 5 March, Booth appeared on a television news programme with Ronald Whittle and the two men acted out a pre-rehearsed confrontation. Whittle described how he had gone to Bathpool Park on the night of 16 January. Booth, pretending this was the first he had heard of the abortive rendezvous, flew into a rage and stormed out of the studio. The effect was to make Booth look extremely foolish. In fact, the deception gave him the excuse he had been looking for to search the park.

At dawn the following day, the police moved into Bathpool Park. At first their search yielded nothing. But then, two schoolboys came forward with a torch they had found there a few weeks earlier. Wrapped around the handle was a strip of Dymo tape which read: 'Drop suitcase into hole.'

On the next day, Friday, 7 March, Police Constable Paul Alien removed the manhole cover of the drainage system and climbed slowly down. He had descended about 20 feet when he paused and shone his torch downwards. He was confronted with the grisly spectacle of Lesley Whittle's naked body, hanging from its wire noose.

Police sniffer dogs search for clues in the murder of Lesley Whittle

UNITED AGAINST THE PANTHER

Up to this point, different teams of police had been working on 'Black Panther' murders in Accrington, Harrogate and Langley, as well as the team investigating the kidnap of Lesley Whittle. There had been close cooperation between the forces, but now it was decided to form a single 'Black Panther' task force under Scotland Yard's murder squad.

The murder squad took over Kidsgrove police station, and 800 officers were drafted in to interview every one of the town's 22,000 population.

In an attempt to solicit help from the public, a local actor was dressed in black and drove the green Morris along the route thought to have been taken by the 'Panther'. The reconstruction was shown on national television and attracted more than a thousand phone calls. Scores of names were submitted but the name Donald Neilson was not among them.

Nine months passed, and the murder squad were no nearer identifying the 'Black Panther'.

On Thursday, 11 December, Donald Neilson finally obliged them. It was 11 p.m. and Constables Stuart McKenzie and Tony White were sitting in their Panda car in Mansfield Woodhouse, Nottingham, when they caught sight of a man with a holdall loitering outside the Four Ways public house.

McKenzie did a U-turn and pulled up alongside Neilson. White got out of the car and asked him what his name was and what he was doing. Neilson smiled, gave them a name and a local address, and said he was on his way home from work. Still suspicious, White asked him to write down his particulars.

Suddenly Neilson produced a sawn-off shotgun from under his coat. He forced White into the back seat of the Panda car and got into the front passenger seat himself. He instructed McKenzie to drive to Blidworth, a village six miles away.

As they drove, White in the back noticed the shotgun waver away from his partner's side. He lunged forward and grabbed the barrel of the gun. McKenzie slammed on the brakes; the shotgun went off, blowing a hole in the roof of the car.

The Panda screeched to a halt outside a fish and chip shop, which was still open. As the two constables wrestled with Neilson, two customers, Keith Wood and Roy Morris, rushed over to help.

Despite his diminutive stature, Neilson fought ferociously and it took all four of them to subdue him. A few minutes later, other police cars arrived on the scene. Donald Neilson was driven the 70 miles to Kidsgrove police station.

Neilson was questioned for 12 hours before he finally admitted to the abduction of Lesley Whittle.

The burning question for the police was, just who was this man Donald Neilson? For a man who had terrorized an entire region, he did not cut a very impressive figure – 40 years old, 5ft 4ins tall, and slightly built.

Yet, over the previous ten years, he had committed more than 400 robberies – 16 on sub-post offices – and had killed four people. All this, and he had never so much as been questioned by police.

The secret of his 'success', the police were to discover, was discipline and meticulous planning, qualities he had developed courtesy of Her Majesty's armed forces. In 1955–7 Neilson had spent his National Service in the King's Own Yorkshire Light Infantry, where he rose to the rank of lance corporal and served in Kenya, Aden and Cyprus.

At the time of his arrest, Neilson was living a quiet life with his wife Irene and their 15-year-old daughter Kathryn at their terraced house on the outskirts of Bradford. He made a modest living as a jobbing carpenter and, according to his neighbours, had no enemies and few friends.

WHEN LIFE MEANS LIFE

The trial of Donald Neilson began on 14 August 1976 at Oxford Crown Court. In addition to the murder of Lesley Whittle, Neilson stood charged with the murder of three sub-postmasters – Donald Skepper of Harrogate, Derek Askin of Accrington and Sidney Gray–land of Langley – all of whom had been shot to death in 1974. He was defended by Gilbert Gray QC and entered a plea of not guilty to all four charges.

Neilson's behaviour in court was nothing short of extraordinary. He maintained his military posture throughout the trial, standing smartly to attention and answering questions with a brisk 'Yes, sir' or 'No, sir'.

Neilson seemed to have the idea that by being calm, precise and matter-of-fact he could persuade the court that he was the victim of a ghastly misunderstanding. At no time did he show one iota of sadness or remorse.

When it came to the murder of the three sub-postmasters, Neilson again tried to portray himself as the victim of misfortune. On all three occasions, he claimed, the gun he was carrying had gone off accidentally.

All in all, it was one of the most feeble defences ever presented to a British criminal court, and the jury wasted no time in returning a verdict of guilty on all charges.

Sentencing Donald Neilson to life imprisonment, Mr Justice Mars-Jones would not set a minimum number of years. 'In your case,' he said, 'life must mean life. If you are ever released from prison it should only be on account of great age or infirmity.'

The diminutive figure of Donald Neilson, head covered, is led away from the committal proceedings.

GARY HEIDNIK

THE BABY FARMER

Gary Heidnik believed God wanted him to people the world. So he kidnapped women to start his 'baby farm', feeding them on dog food and human flesh. Was he insane, or, as the judge said at his trial, merely 'possessed of a malignancy in his heart'?

On the freezing cold night of 24 March 1987, Philadelphia police received a telephone call from a box in the neighbourhood of Sixth and Girard Streets. The caller, who identified himself as Vincent Nelson, was excited but apologetic, as if he found the story he had to tell difficult to believe.

His ex-girlfriend, Josefina Riviera, a half-black, half-Puerto Rican prostitute, had turned up at his house after a long absence. 'She was... you know... talking real fast about this guy having three girls chained up in the basement of this house and she was held hostage for four months... She said that he was beating them up, raping them, had them eating dead people just like he was a cold-blooded nut... I thought she was crazy.'

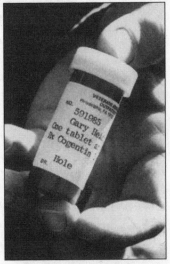

Medicine prescribed for Heidnik by Dr Hole.

HORROR IN THE BASEMENT

The police switchboard operator was inclined, on the evidence, to side with the latter point of view. Nevertheless he despatched a patrol car. Officers David Savidge and John Cannon picked up Nelson and the distressed Josefina and took them to the precinct house.

There, a brief examination of Josefina's skinny body convinced the police that something untoward had happened to her. Her ankles, in particular, bore the marks where shackles had eroded the flesh.

She managed to tell them that her captor was named Gary Heidnik, and that he was due to pick her up in his new grey and white Cadillac Coupe de Ville, with his initials 'GMH' on the door, at the gas station on Sixth and Girard.

Officers Savidge and Cannon cruised around to the filling station. There, sure enough, was the Cadillac. The driver was a greasy-haired man with cold blue eyes, dressed in a fringed buckskin jacket and gaudy shirt. After admitting that he was Gary Heidnik, he was taken to the Philadelphia Police Department Sex Crimes Unit for further questioning.

At 4.30 a.m. on 25 March, a squad of officers bearing a search warrant, crowbars and a sledge hammer arrived at Heidnik's address – 3520 North Marshall Street.

The foetid stench hit them as they broke the locks of the door. Following Josefina's instructions they made their way down to the basement, where their torches picked out the terrified faces of two black women huddled under a blanket on a dirty mattress. The women were shackled, chained, filthy and naked apart from skimpy vests, and they cringed and whimpered in the light.

When they were calmer, they indicated a shallow pit in the floor. In it was another black woman, naked and with her hands handcuffed behind her back.

But when the officers examined the kitchen, they began to believe that starvation would have been the lesser of two evils. In an aluminium pot were boiled human ribs, while the fridge contained a jointed human arm. Officer Savidge, hardened as he was, had to run outside for air.

Back at the precinct house, Josefina Riviera slowly began to piece together a statement. She explained that Gary had a notion of starting a 'baby farm' in his basement. A religious freak, he claimed that God had commanded him to collect women so that, 'like a bee to flowers', he could move from one naked woman to another, impregnating them.

Josefina herself was 25 years old and had been brought up in an orphanage by nuns. Since her early teens she had worked the streets as a prostitute.

On 26 November 1986 Josefina met Gary Heidnik for the first time. Heidnik took her to a McDonald's where he had a coffee, ignoring Josefina. Finally he suggested they go back to his house in North Marshall Street.

Josefina Riviera (right) leaves court with another of Heidnik's victims, having given evidence at his trial.

As he parked in the garage she noticed a 1971 Rolls Royce, and in the house itself the hallway was papered with $1 and $5 bills. But again, these signs of opulence were spoilt by the squalor of the bedroom, which contained only two battered chairs, a table and a big waterbed.

The pair then stripped and the sex act was over in minutes. Gary handed her a $20 bill and Josefina reached for her jeans. Then her nightmare began.

THE 'BABY FARM'

Heidnik leaped from the bed, grabbed her wrists and handcuffed her. Before she realized what was happening he dragged her out and down several flights of stairs to a dim and filthy cellar, lit only by narrow windows set near the ceiling. Metal heating pipes ran around the room and he shackled her ankle to one of these, using a U-shaped link and a length of chain. Then he slapped her down on to an evil-smelling mattress, placed his head in her naked lap, told her to be quiet and slept. Josefina noticed a shallow pit in the centre of the room. This, covered by boards, was to be used by Heidnik as a 'punishment pit'.

Three days later Heidnik went out again. He was looking for his former lover, a slightly retarded black girl of 25 named Sandra Lindsay. Some time before, Heidnik was to explain to Josefina, he had paid Sandra $1,000 to have his baby but she had aborted it.

That evening he came back with the terrified Sandra, and she too was stripped and shackled. The women, forced to perform various sexual acts, were told by Heidnik that they were the nucleus of his 'baby farm'.

The following day the two girls had a moment of hope when they heard pounding on the front door. Gary told them later that the callers had been Sandra's sister, Teresa, and two cousins, searching for her in her old haunts.

Over the next few weeks, more women were lured back to join Heidnik's 'baby farm'. Lisa Thomas, aged 19, was picked up on 22 December. On New Year's Day 1987, 23-year-old Deborah Dudley became his fourth victim, while his fifth and youngest, 19-year-old

Searching for evidence of Heidnik's crimes in the basement of his house.

Jacquelyn Askins, joined the unwilling harem on 18 January. Another girl, Agnes Adams, known on the streets as 'Vickie', was tricked by Gary Heidnik into going back with him through her acquaintance with Josefina. She arrived the day before the latter's escape.

Every day, Heidnik beat the girls and forced them to perform sexual acts with both him and each other. He fed them a curious diet of bread, dog food and ice cream, which he kept in a deep freeze in the corner of the cellar. Later, another ingredient was to be added.

At some time during the New Year Sandra Lindsay annoyed Heidnik. To punish her, he strapped her by one wrist to an overhead beam and then forced her to eat lumps of bread, holding her lips together until she swallowed. For a week the half-witted girl dangled feverishly from the beam, until finally she choked on a piece of bread and died.

He carried the body upstairs. Soon the girls in the cellar heard the whine of an electric saw, followed by the pungent odour of cooking flesh.

That night Deborah Dudley had a bout of rebelliousness and physically fought Heidnik when he tried to force himself upon her. In reply, the furious man unshackled her and dragged her upstairs.

A few minutes later she came down, silent and shocked. When she could speak, she told the others: 'He showed me Sandra's head in a pot. And he had her ribs in a roasting pan, and a bunch of her other body parts in the freezer. He told me if I didn't start listening to him, that was going to happen to me too.'

But despite the horror of what she had seen, Deborah rebelled again. This time she was thrust down into the pit in the floor and water was poured in on top of her. Then Heidnik made Josefina push a live electric wire through a hole in the boards covering the pit. Deborah gave one terrible scream. When the boards were removed, she lay dead in the water.

The streetwise Josefina, however, had a streak of cunning. Gradually she worked at winning Heidnik's trust, until he began taking her out on little expeditions to McDonald's and even buying her clothes and wigs. Finally, she begged him to let her see her three children who, she claimed, she had left with a babysitter. Instead she ran to her old boyfriend, Vincent Nelson.

What kind of a monster had the Philadelphia police netted?

Police sift through the debris in Heidnik's house.

BACKGROUND OF A MANIAC

Gary Michael Heidnik had been born on 21 November 1943 in the suburb of Eastlake in Cleveland, Ohio. At the age of thirteen he became fascinated with things military – he had been a keen Boy Scout – and with his father's profound approval enrolled at the Staunton Military Academy in Virginia, There he scored consistently high marks until, quite suddenly, he dropped out.

In October 1961, as soon as he was old enough, Gary Heidnik joined the US Army. After basic training he was transferred to Landsthul in Germany.

Less than a year later he developed nausea, dizzy spells, headaches and blurred vision. Doctors noticed a series of nervous tics, including sudden head spasms, and he developed a habit of saluting in an exaggeratedly smart fashion at inappropriate moments.

Despite recording his IQ as up to 148 – a 'near genius' level – the army psychiatrists could do little to help Gary out of the slough into which he had fallen. In January 1963 he was given an honourable discharge and, with it, a pension of almost $2,000 a month.

Heidnik being brought into the sheriff's office after his arrest.

Neither the army nor his civilian psychiatrists noticed Gary Heidnik's extraordinary sexual drive. Even in his forties, shortly before his arrest, he was regularly having sex four times a day, and he spent a great deal of money on prostitutes and sex videos. His only other material interest was in cars.

After his discharge from the army, what friends he had were invariably black. The prostitutes he consorted with were also black, and, with rare exceptions, like Josefina Riviera, simple-minded. And it was among these women that he looked for mothers – the mothers of his children.

His obsession that God wanted him to father children led Heidnik, on 12 October 1971, to start a religion to be known as the United Church of the Ministers of God. Gary was the Church's 'Bishop', and his brother Terry a member of the board. The Church was registered with the state, and under US law was exempt from taxes.

The congregation was largely comprised of black physical and/or mental cripples. All the evidence shows that Heidnik treated these people with generosity and kindness.

In 1977 he impregnated an illiterate black girl named Aljeanette Davidson. She had an IQ of 49 and was completely under Heidnik's thrall. The baby girl was immediately fostered by the state.

The viewing of Deborah Dudley's body.

334

Undeterred, Heidnik hatched a wicked plan. Aljeanette's sister, Alberta, was 35 and had for 20 years been an inmate of an institute for the mentally handicapped in Harrisburg, Pennsylvania. Gary took Aljeanette to see Alberta, and the elder sister was delighted when her sister's kindly boyfriend suggested they go for 'an outing'.

Alberta failed to return and the institute officials became worried. Days later the hospital authorities, accompanied by police, broke into the house in North Marshall Street and found the wretched Alberta crammed into a garbage bin in the cellar.

Because she was not deemed fit to give evidence, Heidnik could only be tried on the comparatively trivial charges of assault and abduction. But Judge Charles Mariarchi spotted something 'evil and dangerous' about Heidnik.

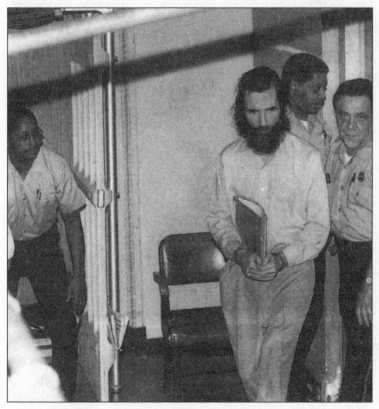

Heidnik is led into court for his trial at city hall in Philadelphia.

Heidnik spent most of the sentence in mental hospitals. For at least six years after his release from jail, Gary Heidnik vanished from all official records except those of the stock market. When he registered his Church in 1971 its total assets were $1,500, but 12 years later, despite its founder's curious habits, the funds had multiplied to $545,000.

TRIAL BY JURY

His trial opened at City Hall, Philadelphia, on 20 June 1988 before Judge Lynne M. Abrahams. The charges against Heidnik were murder, kidnapping, rape, aggravated assault, involuntary deviate sexual intercourse, indecent exposure, false imprisonment, unlawful restraint, simple assault, making terroristic threats, recklessly endangering another person, indecent assault, criminal solicitation, possession, and abuse of a corpse. The judge proved very dubious of arguments presenting Heidnik's acts as 'excusable' because of his alleged mental sickness.

In a three-hour stint in the witness box, Josefina Riviera told how Heidnik had set up his basement baby farm 'because the city was always taking his babies away'. She described in graphic detail the horrors of life in the Heidnik basement.

Food consisted of crackers, oatmeal, chicken, icecream, bread, water, and – after the murder of Lindsay – dog food 'mixed with minced body parts'. Very occasionally, their captor would take one of the girls upstairs for a bath, have sex with her, and then bring her down again.

The tiny figure of Jacquelyn Askins presented the most forlorn figure on the witness stand. She was so small that Heidnik had used handcuffs to shackle her ankles, and his lawyers tried to suggest that a degree of compassion had been shown in the extra length of chain he had used to link them. 'Oh no,' said Jacquelyn, 'he did that so I could open my legs for sex.'

After two and a half days the jury brought in a verdict of guilty on all counts. Heidnik was sentenced to death on two charges –

the death penalty was in abeyance in Pennsylvania – and a total of 120 years' imprisonment on the rest.

He was, said Judge Abrahams, possessed 'not of an illness in his head, but a malignancy in his heart. I don't want any parole order to put Mr Heidnik back on the streets as long as he's breathing,' she concluded.

In January 1990 the State Supreme Court refused Heidnik's request to be executed, and almost simultaneously the US Bankruptcy Court divided his $600,000 among his creditors. Each of his surviving victims was awarded $34,540 for her bizarre ordeal.

Friends and relatives of the victims hurry from the courtroom after the jury finally returned their verdict of guilty on all charges.

DENNIS NILSEN
A QUIET CIVIL SERVANT

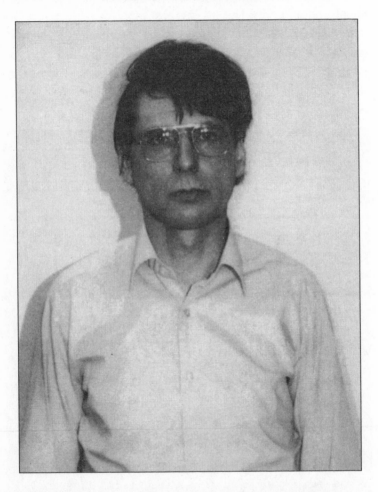

Was it fear of desertion that caused Dennis Nilsen to become a mass murderer in the most gruesome of circumstances? And was he merely evil, or was he himself one of life's victims – a schizophrenic?

At 6.25 on the morning of 8 February 1983, Michael Cattran parked his Dyno-Rod van outside 23 Cranley Gardens in the north London suburb of Muswell Hill. It was a routine call. Jim Allcock, one of the residents of No. 23, had phoned to say that the drains had been blocked for five days. After a quick examination of the interior plumbing, Cattran decided the problem lay outside the house itself. He walked round to the side of the house and removed the manhole cover.

The smell was nauseating as Cattran climbed down the 12-foot inspection shaft. At the bottom he found a glutinous greyish-white mass.

Cattran told Jim Allcock that it was nothing serious and that he would be back shortly to straighten things out. When he called his boss, however, he voiced his real suspicions. The matter that was clogging the drains at 23 Cranley Gardens was, in his opinion, human flesh.

Cattran and his boss returned to Muswell Hill the following morning. To Cattran's surprise, the glutinous mass had vanished. He knew that, even though it had been raining the previous day, the drains could not possibly have cleared themselves. Cattran reached deep into the drainpipe and pulled out several pieces of meat and a number of bones.

Cattran explained the mystery of the missing sludge to Jim Allcock and another tenant, Fiona Bridges. They told him they had heard someone moving the manhole cover in the early hours of the morning. They thought it might be Mr Nilsen who lived above them in the attic flat. Cattran and his boss decided it was time to call the police.

Detective Chief Inspector Peter Jay arrived on the scene shortly after 11 a.m. and collected the meat and bones for forensic examination. At Charing Cross Hospital, it took pathologist Professor David Bowen only minutes to confirm that the meat was indeed human flesh and that the bones were from a man's hand.

THE TENANT OF THE ATTIC FLAT

Police attention immediately focused on the occupier of the attic flat, Dennis Andrew Nilsen, an executive officer at the Kentish Town Jobcentre, who lived alone with his dog, Beep. The other tenants had seen him leave for work that morning at his usual time of 8.30.

Peter Jay, together with Detective Inspector McCusker and Detective Constable Butler, waited outside 23 Cranley Gardens for Nilsen to return.

When he walked up to the front door at 5.40, Peter Jay intercepted him. Nilsen, a polite, quietly spoken man in his late thirties, seemed surprised but not alarmed when Jay introduced himself and his colleagues as police officers.

A police constable stands guard at the back of 23 Cranley Gardens, Muswell Hill, where Dennis Nilsen rented an attic flat.

The four men went inside the house and climbed the stairs to Nilsen's tiny flat. Once inside, Jay told Nilsen about the human flesh that had been found in the drain outside. Nilsen feigned horror, but Jay was not remotely convinced. 'Stop messing about,' he said. 'Where's the rest of the body?'

Nilsen didn't even bother to protest his innocence. 'In two plastic bags in the wardrobe. I'll show you,' he said, unlocking the doors. The awful stench from the cupboard confirmed that Nilsen was telling the truth.

He arrested Nilsen, charged him with murder and shipped him off to Hornsey Police Station.

En route, Inspector McCusker asked Nilsen if there was anything he wanted to say. Nilsen replied, 'It's a long story. It goes back a long time. I'll tell you everything. I want to get it off my chest.'

'Are we talking about one body or two?' McCusker asked Nilsen.

'Fifteen or sixteen,' Nilsen replied calmly. 'Since 1978... Three at Cranley Gardens and about thirteen at my previous address, 195 Melrose Avenue in Cricklewood.'

Black plastic bags in Nilsen's wardrobe contained the remains of two bodies.

CONTENTS OF A WARDROBE

Detective Chief Inspector Jay returned to 23 Cranley Gardens with Detective Chief Superintendent Chambers and the pathologist, Professor Bowen. They removed the two stinking black plastic bags from Nilsen's wardrobe and took them to Hornsey mortuary.

When Bowen opened the first he found it contained four smaller shopping bags. In the first of these was the left-hand side of a man's chest with the arm attached. The second contained the right-hand side of a chest. The third held a torso and the fourth an assortment of human offal.

In the other black bag, Bowen found two human heads and another torso with the arms attached but missing the hands. One of the heads had most of the flesh boiled away.

Nilsen told the police that one of the heads belonged to a young drug addict called Stephen Sinclair. The second he knew only as 'John the Guardsman'. He could put no name to a third victim whose remains were later found in a tea chest at his flat.

Nilsen seemed willing, even anxious, to help the police. On

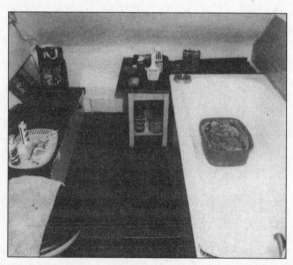

Two bodies had been dissected in Nilsen's bath, and the remains of Stephen Sinclair had been hidden under it.

11 February, three days after his arrest, he accompanied Peter Jay to the ground-floor flat at 195 Melrose Avenue which he had occupied from l976 to 1981.

He told Jay that he had cut up the bodies and burnt them on a series of huge bonfires in the back garden. He even pointed out where the fires had been and where they should look for human remains.

Using this information, forensic teams started the laborious task of sifting through the earth for evidence. A day later they had found enough human ash and bone fragments to establish that at least eight people had been cremated in the garden.

Despite his willingness to cooperate with the police, Nilsen was unable to identify many of his early victims. None of them had ever been more than casual acquaintances. They had been, for the most part, young, homeless homosexuals – social misfits, drug addicts or alcoholics, men who could simply disappear without anyone knowing or caring. However, based on dates and physical descriptions given by Nilsen, and comparing them with missing persons' records, the police were eventually able to identify six victims with reasonable certainty.

The question now for the police and Nilsen's lawyer was not whether Nilsen was a mass murderer, but rather why he had killed more than a dozen young men. On this point, Nilsen could not help. 'I am hoping you will tell me that,' he said.

A cooking pot use by Nilsen to simmer the head of one of his victims.

343

FOUR YEARS OF CARNAGE

Nilsen was questioned for the next few weeks, during which time he gave a meticulous account of his four years of carnage. It was a story so monstrous and grotesque that it made even case hardened police interrogators physically ill to listen to it.

It had all started on New Year's Eve 1978. Nilsen had met a young Irish boy in a pub in the West End and taken him back to his flat in Melrose Avenue. After seeing in the New Year, the two men had gone to bed together. They were both stupefied with drink and no sex took place between them.

In the morning, according to Nilsen, he woke to find the young Irishman still asleep beside him. He was suddenly overcome with terror that the boy would want to leave as soon as he too awoke. Nilsen desperately wanted him to stay and could only think of one way to ensure that he did so.

Nilsen picked up a tie from the floor, straddled the boy's chest, placed the tie around his neck and pulled. The boy woke and a mighty struggle ensued before he finally passed out.

But he was not dead yet. So Nilsen went to the kitchen, filled a bucket with water and held the boy's head under the water until he drowned.

Nilsen then bathed the boy's body, dressed it in clean underwear and socks, took it back to bed with him and masturbated. For the next week, Nilsen went off to work as usual. He returned each evening to his dead companion who would be sitting in an armchair, waiting for him.

After eight days, Nilsen prised up some floorboards and hid the corpse. It remained there for seven months before Nilsen dissected it and burnt it on a bonfire in his back garden.

On the evening of 3 December 1979, almost a year later, Dennis Nilsen was cruising the gay bars of Soho when he met a 26-year-old Canadian tourist, Kenneth Ockendon. Ockendon, who was staying at a cheap hotel in King's Cross, was due to fly home the following day.

Nilsen persuaded him to accompany him back to Melrose Avenue for a meal. He could stay the night if he wanted and pick up his things from the hotel the following morning.

By the early hours of the morning the two men were in Nilsen's sitting room, both much the worse for drink. Nilsen was watching Ockendon as he listened to music through a set of headphones.

His feelings of imminent desertion were similar to those he had experienced a year earlier.

Police remove human remains from Nilsen's flat at Melrose Avenue.

So Nilsen walked behind Ockendon's chair, grabbed the flex of the headphones and strangled him with it. Again he washed the body, dressed it in clean underwear, placed it next to him in bed and went to sleep.

Ockendon's corpse remained his constant companion for the next two weeks. Nilsen spent the evenings watching television with

Having confessed his crimes, Nilsen is remanded at Highgate Magistrates' Court in north London.

the body in an armchair next to him. When he was ready for bed, he would wrap it in a curtain and place it under the floorboards for the night.

Unlike the Irish boy, Ockendon's disappearance caused a considerable stir. Several of the tabloids carried his picture and Nilsen felt sure that his days were numbered. But the police didn't come. And over the next 18 months 11 more young men were destined to die at Melrose Avenue.

By the end of 1980, Nilsen had accumulated six bodies. Three were stowed under the floorboards, while the others were cut up, stuffed in suitcases and stored in a garden shed.

At the beginning of December, Nilsen built an enormous bonfire which was constructed in part from human remains wrapped in carpet. He crowned the fire with an old car tyre to disguise the smell of burning flesh.

At the end of 1981, Nilsen was planning to move. By this time he had accumulated a further five bodies and, shortly before he left, he had another massive fire.

No. 23 Cranley Gardens, Nilsen's new home, presented some real problems for a mass murderer of his ilk. It was an attic flat with no floorboards and no garden – in fact nowhere decent to hide a body at all. But this didn't stop him.

Within weeks of his move to Muswell Hill, Nilsen strangled John Howlett with an upholstery strap and then drowned him. Graham Allen was the next to die. Nilsen couldn't actually recall killing him, but thought he had strangled him with a tie while he was eating an omelette.

On 26 January Nilsen met his last victim. Stephen Sinclair, a drug addict and petty criminal, was wandering the streets of Soho looking for a handout. Nilsen offered to buy him a hamburger and then persuaded him to go back to Cranley Gardens with him.

Two weeks later, Michael Cattran of Dyno-Rod found what was left of Stephen in the drain outside 23 Cranley Gardens.

NO EMOTION, NO REMORSE

On 24 October 1983, Dennis Andrew Nilsen stood before Mr Justice Croom-Johnson at No. 1 Court in the Old Bailey. He was charged with six murders and two attempted murders.

There was no doubt that Nilsen had committed the offences. What the court had to evaluate was Nilsen's mental state at the time he committed them.

If Nilsen had pleaded guilty, as he originally intended, he would have saved the jury a considerable ordeal. Instead, they were forced to spend two weeks listening to detailed evidence of Nilsen's gruesome acts.

Detective Chief Superintendent Chambers spent almost an entire day reading out a transcript of Nilsen's confession. The graphic descriptions of decapitations and dissections, of the boiling and mincing of human flesh, and of necrophilia, sickened and enraged the jury. Nilsen, for his part, sat through the evidence without betraying a single vestige of emotion.

The prosecution called three witnesses to give evidence that Nilsen had attempted to kill them. Paul Nobbs, a university student, told how he had been rescued by Nilsen from the unwanted attentions of another man.

Nilsen had taken him back to Cranley Gardens and had shown him genuine kindness. He had not tried to ply him with drink or force him to have sex. He had even suggested that he call his mother so that she would not be worried. Nobbs had gone to bed alone but had woken in the early hours of the morning with a splitting headache. He had looked in the mirror and had seen that his eyes were completely bloodshot and that there was a bruise around his neck.

Nilsen had feigned concern, saying that Nobbs looked awful and should go straight to a doctor.

At the casualty department of the hospital he went to, Nobbs was told that he had been partially strangled. He had realized that Nilsen must have been his attacker, but had been reluctant to report the incident to the police because he felt sure that he would not be believed.

The defence made much of Nobbs's testimony. It demonstrated that Nilsen could behave perfectly normally one minute and then be possessed of murderous impulses the next, without provocation or reason. It proved, they said, that Nilsen was clearly insane.

If Nobbs's story was difficult to credit, Karl Strotter's encounter with Nilsen was nothing short of fantastic. Strotter had met Nilsen in a pub in Camden Town. He was depressed after the break-up of a relationship and, like Nobbs, he described Nilsen's behaviour towards him as sympathetic and undemanding.

They had gone back to Cranley Gardens together and Nilsen had put him to bed in a sleeping bag. Strotter described what happened next: 'I woke up feeling something round my neck. My head was hurting and I couldn't breathe properly and I wondered what it was.

'I felt his hand pulling at the zip at the back of my neck. He was saying in a sort of whispered shouting voice, "Stay still. Stay still." I thought perhaps he was trying to help me out of the sleeping bag

Two that got away: Douglas Stewart (left); Karl Stotter (right). Both testified at the trial that they had been victims of attacks by Dennis Nilsen. Their evidence was vital for the prosecution as it argued that Nilsen was not technically insane.

because I thought I had got caught up in the zip, which he had warned me about. Then I passed out.

'...the pressure was increasing. My head was hurting and I couldn't breathe. I remember vaguely hearing water running. I remember vaguely being carried and then felt very cold. I knew I was in the water and he was trying to drown me. He kept pushing me into the water... I just thought I was dying. I thought: "You are drowning. This is what it feels like to die." I felt very relaxed and I passed out. I couldn't fight any more.'

Strotter said he was amazed to awake lying on a sofa with Nilsen massaging him. Nilsen had then helped him to the underground station and wished him luck.

This apparent detachment from reality was echoed in Detective Chief Inspector Jay's evidence as he described Nilsen's behaviour during his interrogation. He was, Jay said, relaxed, cooperative and matter-of-fact. He did not, however, show any remorse. It was as though he was talking about someone else.

Both the prosecution and defence trotted out their 'expert witnesses', a mandatory feature of insanity pleas. Two equally

Nilsen's face bears the scar from an attack by a fellow prisoner.

well-qualified psychiatrists proceeded to give directly conflicting evaluations of the mental condition of the accused, thus effectively cancelling one another out in the eyes of the jury.

The judge spent four hours summing up, addressing himself in particular to the question of Nilsen's personality. 'A mind can be evil without being abnormal,' he advised the jury. 'There must be no excuses for Nilsen if he has moral defects. A nasty nature is not arrested or retarded development of the mind.'

The implication of what Mr Croom-Johnson was saying was obvious. Dennis Nilsen was, in his opinion, evil rather than insane, and the jury should therefore find him guilty of murder.

The jury retired on the morning of Thursday, 3 November 1983. Despite the clear guidance given by the judge, they returned the following morning to say that they were unable to reach a consensus about Nilsen's state of mind at the time of the various murders.

Mr Croom-Johnson said that he would accept a majority verdict. At 4.25 that afternoon the jury returned to court with a verdict of guilty on all six counts of murder, by a majority of ten to two.

The judge condemned Dennis Andrew Nilsen to life imprisonment, with the recommendation that he should serve no less than 25 years.

Nilsen spent the first nine months of his sentence in Parkhurst Prison on the Isle of Wight.

In the summer of 1984 Nilsen was transferred to Wakefield Prison. He remains there to this day, sharing his cell with a budgerigar called Hamish.

SAM SHEPPARD
A TRAVESTY OF JUSTICE

A well-respected citizen is arrested for the brutal murder of his pregnant wife. Vital forensic evidence is ignored and the trial is a travesty of justice. In this, as in so many murder cases, there are no winners, only losers.

Saturday, 3 July 1954 – the eve of Independence Day – was a busy one for Dr Sam Sheppard, though his wife, $4^1/_2$-months pregnant Marilyn, took things rather more easily. Dr Sheppard was on call at his father's Bay View Hospital in Bay Village, Cleveland, Ohio and split his day between work and socializing with their close neighbours, Don and Nancy Ahern.

THE FATAL EVENING

The Aherns' two young sons and 7-year-old Chip Sheppard ate first, while their parents sat on the porch overlooking the lake and sipped drinks. Later the Ahern boys were sent home and Chip went to bed, after which the four adults spent a relaxing evening.

By midnight Marilyn and Sam were drozing. The Aherns decided to go home to bed. Before leaving, Nancy Ahern locked the lakeside door of the house for Marilyn. Then she and her husband went out by the main door on to the road. Marilyn had gone upstairs to the bedroom, Sam was snoring on the sofa.

At 5.45 a.m. John Spencer Houk, a businessman friend of Sheppard's who was also mayor of Bay Village, was awakened by the shrilling noise of his bedside telephone. Sleepily he picked it up and heard the voice of Sam Sheppard: 'For God's sake, Spen, come quick! I think they've killed Marilyn!'

The Sheppards' clap-board house in Bay Village, Cleveland, Ohio.

SCENES OF VIOLENCE

Houk's house was just 100 yards from that of the Sheppards. He and his wife arrived at 5.55 a.m. to a scene of chaos. The roadside door was open and Sheppard's medical bag lay inside, its contents scattered around. A desk drawer hung open, and the immediate impression was of a burglary. Sam Sheppard sat, stripped to the waist, in his den. His trousers were wet and his face was bruised. His neck was contorted with agony.

Houk pounded upstairs and into the Sheppards' bedroom. Marilyn lay on her back, her legs protruding from the bottom of the bed. Her face, hair and pillow were plastered with blood from over 30 deep head wounds.

Three minutes after sunrise Patrolman Fred Drenham arrived. He was closely followed by Richard Sheppard, one of Sam's elder brothers, and his wife, and by the other brother Stephen and the local Chief of Police, John Baton. At 6.30 a.m., as police began

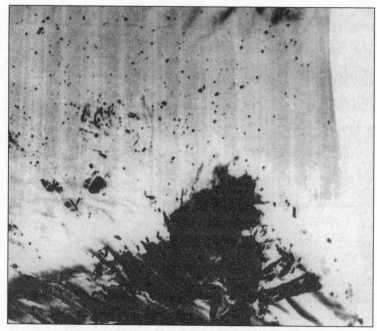

Marilyn Sheppard's blood splattered pillow.

354

their systematic work at the murder scene, Sam was driven by Stephen and John Baton to Bay View Hospital for a check-up. Nurses who tended Sam were later to testify that his lips were badly cut and swollen, and his front teeth were loose.

By 9 a.m. Sam had been fitted with a neck brace and was heavily sedated. He was, however, able to answer questions from the coroner of Cuyahoga County, Dr Samuel Gerber, who had already made a brief visit to the house. At 11 a.m. Detectives Robert Schottke and Patrick Gareau of Cleveland Police took over the questioning.

The two detectives had already noted that there had been no signs of forced entry into the Sheppard house, and the only fingerprint was a thumb-mark which subsequently turned out to be Chip's. Sam's corduroy jacket, which the Aherns had seen him wearing the night before, was neatly folded and lying on the sofa. No bloodstained weapon had been found and, despite the confusion, the detectives were pretty sure that the motive had not been burglary.

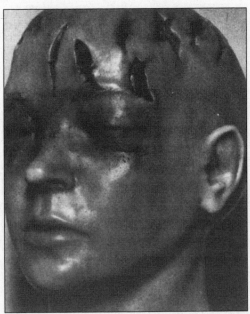

A model shows the horrific wounds inflicted on Marilyn Sheppard's Skull.

They were not happy that Sheppard had been taken to his family-run hospital, and they were certainly not happy with his uncorroborated story. As Schottke was to tell him: 'The evidence points very strongly at you. I don't know what my partner thinks, but I think you killed your wife.'

By that evening the murder was headline news, not merely because of its bloody drama but because it involved the Sheppards, one of Ohio's most prominent and controversial medical families.

PROMINENT MEDICAL FAMILY

Samuel Holmes Sheppard was born in Cleveland on 29 December 1923, the youngest of Dr Richard and Ethel Sheppard's three boys. Richard Sheppard was a general surgeon who was beginning to gain a reputation as an osteopath, at a time when this holistic form of medicine was little known in the United States.

Newsmen pack the courtroom during the trial.

Academically Sam was not particularly bright, but he had an ability for hard work which got him through his exams. In 1943, as an alternative to military service, he began to study medicine at the Western Reserve University in Cleveland, at Hanover College, Indiana, and finally at the Osteopathic School of Physicians and Surgeons in Los Angeles.

In the meantime he had met and fallen in love with Marilyn Reese, and in November 1945, when she was 19, the couple were married at the First Hollywood Methodist Church in Los Angeles.

In 1948 Sam graduated as a doctor of medicine, and he and his wife intended to stay in California. Sam's father, however, had that same year founded the Bay View Hospital back in Cleveland, and Sam, with his two brothers, was pressured into joining the family 'firm'.

Within months, business was booming. By 1954 Bay View was one of the most prestigious hospitals in the state.

Now, despite their suspicions, the police were reluctant to arrest one of the Dr Sheppards of Bay View. As his attorney, William Corrigan, told him: 'The only way to convict yourself, Sam, is by opening your mouth.'

PRESS CAMPAIGN

There was one man, however, who was unimpressed by Sheppard's status in the community. He was Louis Benson Seltzer, editor of the *Cleveland Press*, and well known for his hard-hitting campaigns against crooked politicians and 'soft' police departments.

On 21 July, seventeen days after the killing, the *Cleveland Press* ran a splash headline: 'Why No Inquest? Do It Now, Dr Gerber.'

Dr Gerber, the 57-year-old coroner for Cuyahoga County, had felt Seltzer's righteous wrath before. The next day he called an inquest. Gerber refused witnesses the right to counsel, and when William Corrigan protested he had him thrown out to tumultuous cheers.

Sam Sheppard waived his right not to give evidence and was

questioned for eight hours by Gerber. Among other things, Sheppard denied having committed adultery with a mystery woman in California named only as 'Miss X'. Finally, on 30 July, he was arrested, even before Gerber recorded his verdict that Marilyn had been murdered.

Sheppard's statement at the time of his arrest was essentially the same as he had made shortly after the crime was committed. He said that he had been awakened, as he lay on the sofa, by his wife's screams from upstairs. He refused to guess what time it might have been.

'I charged into our room and saw a form with a light garment,' he said. 'It was grappling with something or someone…'

He and this person had wrestled, until Sheppard was knocked out from behind. When he regained his senses he saw on the floor his own police surgeon's badge – he was unpaid police surgeon for the Bay Valley force – which he normally kept in his wallet. He took Marilyn's pulse 'and felt that she was gone'.

After checking that his son Chip was still asleep and safe,

Police search Dr Sheppard's medical bag after the murder.

Sheppard had heard a noise, ran downstairs and saw 'a form rapidly progressing somewhere'. Sheppard had chased the figure down from the porch to the lake, where he had grappled with a large man with bushy hair. The man had caught his neck in an armlock, and he had passed out.

When he came to he had woken up on his face by the water's edge. His T-shirt was missing, though he could not recollect what had happened to it.

Also missing from his wrist was his gold watch, which was later found, spattered with Marilyn's blood, in a duffle bag in the Sheppards' boat-house by the lake. This watch was to be the centre of vigorous controversy later. Sheppard had then staggered back to the house.

TRIED FOR FIRST DEGREE MURDER

The trial of Sam Sheppard on the charge of first degree murder began in the Court of Common Pleas, Cleveland, on Monday 18 October 1954. But because of delay in jury selection - many admitted that they had firm ideas on the case – it did not properly get under way until 4 November. The judge was Edward Blythin, and Sheppard pleaded not guilty.

The main thrust of the case against Sheppard was indicated by prosecuting counsel John Mahon in his opening address: 'The state will prove that Sheppard and Miss X talked together about divorce and marriage. No one was in that house that morning on 4 July attempting to commit a burglary. No evidence has been found that any burglar or marauder was there.'

The Aherns were called early in the trial. Don said that he had never seen the placid Sam Sheppard lose his temper, though Nancy introduced a hesitant note when she said that, though she was sure Marilyn was very much in love with her husband, she had never been sure of Sam's feelings towards Marilyn.

Dr Samuel Gerber, the coroner, caused a sensation when he spoke of a 'blood signature' on the yellow pillowcase under

Marilyn's battered head. 'In this bloodstain I could make out the impression of a surgical instrument,' he said. The instrument, he suggested, 'had two blades, each about three inches long with serrated edges'.

No weapon of any kind had been found at the house, but, said Gerber, 'the impression could only have been made by an instrument similar to the type of surgical instrument I had in mind'. Curiously, he was not asked to specify just what the mysterious instrument was.

On 1 December came another sensation when Miss X entered the witness box. She identified herself as Susan Hayes, a 24-year-old laboratory technician who had worked at the Bay View Hospital and met Sam there in 1951.

They had begun their affair in California, after she had left Bay View to work in Los Angeles in 1954. She admitted that they had slept together, as well as made love in cars. 'He said that he loved his wife very much but not as a wife, and was thinking of getting a divorce,' she testified.

This evidence meant that Sam was not only a perjurer – he had

Police examine evidence during the investigation of the case.

denied adultery at the inquest – but guilty of the then criminal offence, under Ohio law, of adultery.

On the stand, Sam now admitted lying at the inquest, saying that he had done so to protect Susan Hayes rather than himself. In any case, he went on, he had never truly been in love with her, and had never discussed divorce with either her or his wife. He admitted that he had committed adultery with women other than Susan Hayes, but refused to name them. Summing up for the prosecution, Thomas Parrino, an assistant prosecutor, said: 'If the defendant would lie under oath to protect a lady, how many lies would he utter to protect his own life?'

Corrigan's defence was, on the face of it, poor. He made no mention of one or two curious pieces of evidence which might have helped Sam.

Tooth chippings had been found on the bedroom floor, which belonged neither to Sam nor to Marilyn. There was firm evidence that Marilyn had bitten her attacker savagely, though Sheppard bore no bite marks. There was the business of the mysterious surgical instrument. And there were wool threads, found under Marilyn's nails, which matched no clothing in the house – not hers, not Sam's, not Chip's. Above all, there was the blood-spattered watch.

Instead, Corrigan took up the prosecution's sex theme and made a negative mess of it. 'Is sex the only thing in a marriage?' he asked. 'Sheppard wandered from the path of rectitude. That didn't prove he didn't love his wife, his home, or his family.'

After a briefing from Judge Blythin on the laws governing circumstantial evidence, and the difference between first and second degree murder, the jury retired. They returned on Tuesday, 21 December after over four days' deliberation. Their decision was that Sam Sheppard was guilty of second degree murder and Judge Blythin sentenced him to life imprisonment. After what must have been a melancholy Christmas for the Sheppard family, William Corrigan retrieved the keys of Sam's house from the police and handed them over to Dr Paul Leland Kirk. One of the country's leading forensic scientists, he had undertaken to do independent tests.

EXHAUSTIVE FORENSIC WORK

Dr Kirk began work in the Sheppards' house in January 1955, and after studying the results in his California headquarters produced a 10,000-word report three and a half months later.

Among the detailed facts examined in the report the most important was Dr Kirk's emphatic assertion that a fourth person, other than Sam, Marilyn or Chip, had been in the house on the night of the murder. Blood on the wardrobe door demonstrably did not match that of any of the Sheppards. And teeth fragments on the carpet showed that Marilyn had bitten her attacker very deeply, though, as had been shown at the trial, Sheppard bore no such scars.

Dr Kirk was able to show that whoever delivered the death blows to Marilyn would have been covered in her flying blood, but the only

Susan Hayes. It was revealed that she was
Sam Sheppard's mistress.

stain on Sam's clothing was a spot on the knee of his trousers – gained, he claimed, when he had knelt to take his wife's pulse.

Furthermore, bloodstains on the walls showed that the killer had struck with his left hand, while Sam was right-handed. The blows had undoubtedly been made with a blunt instrument such as a piece of piping, which made nonsense of the coroner's 'surgical instrument' theory.

'No actual proof of a technical nature was ever offered indicating the guilt of the defendant,' he concluded.

Despite what seemed to be Kirk's irrefutable report, Judge Blythin refused, on 10 May 1955, to grant a retrial. Six weeks later the Ohio Court of Appeals praised 'the originality and imagination' of Dr Kirk, but nevertheless turned down an appeal for a new trial.

The following summer, on 31 May 1956, the Ohio Supreme Court upheld Sheppard's conviction by five votes to two. Hope was raised, however, by the two dissenting judges, who expressed the view that there had been little real evidence to prove Sheppard guilty, and that Judge Blythin had accepted gossip as evidence.

But on 19 December the highest judicial body in the land, the United States Supreme Court, refused to review the case on technical grounds. Again, however, doubts were expressed about the conduct of the Ohio judiciary.

A CONVICT'S CONFESSION

Sheppard's hopes were raised once more six months later when, in June 1957, a convict named Donald Wedler, who was serving a ten-year sentence for a Florida hold-up, confessed to the murder. He claimed that he had been in Cleveland, Ohio on the day of Marilyn's killing, and after taking heroin had stolen a car and driven around looking for a house to burgle.

He had found a suitable one, a large white house on a lake front, had broken in, crept past a man asleep on a settee and gone upstairs.

A woman in an upstairs bedroom had awakened as he was preparing to rifle her dressing table, and he had beaten her repeatedly with an iron pipe. Then, as he fled downstairs, he had encountered a man, whom he had struck down with the pipe, before flinging the impromptu weapon into the lake and driving away.

The coroner was quick to point out discrepancies in the story. Sheppard had said that he was struck down from behind in the bedroom, not on the stairs, and Wedler had made no mention of a struggle in the garden by the lake. Nor was Wedler a burly man with the 'bushy' hair mentioned by Sheppard – he was slight, though he did have unruly, curly hair.

What interested Sheppard's lawyers most was the fact that a lie-detector expert who tested Wedler was quite certain that he was telling the truth, 'or what he believed to be the truth'.

Unfortunately, there were many imponderables about the Wedler story. As a heroin user, he might have been telling the truth and have confused the details, but equally he might have invented the whole thing after reading newspaper accounts of the case and convinced his drug-addled mind that he was the murderer.

In the end, it was the plethora of newspaper speculation surrounding the original event that led to a successful appeal – but only after Sheppard had served ten years in jail. In 1961 Williarn Corrigan died, and in his place Stephen Sheppard hired a smart, fast-talking young attorney from Boston named F. Lee Bailey.

RETRIAL AT LAST

In April 1963, after a series of legal moves, Bailey lodged a petition with the US District Court, a federal rather than state body, that the case be reopened. This time he was successful. After almost a year's deliberation, Judge Carl Weinman delivered his verdict on 15 July 1964. The original trial, he said, had been a 'mockery of justice'. He ordered Sheppard to be released pending a retrial.

Lawyer F. Lee Bailey immediately swept into the attack. Quoting the exhaustive inquiry undertaken by Dr Kirk, he compared it with the muddled and pathetic attempts of the Cleveland Police, whose search for clues, he forced them to admit, had been perfunctory to a degree. Their check for fingerprints had been particularly casual. They had not even tried to get prints from the bloodstained watch found in the duffle bag, and had also ignored a keyring and chain which accompanied it.

Bailey produced a photograph of the watch, which had blood speckles across the face such as could have been caused had Sheppard been wearing it when he battered his wife to death. But, as Bailey pointed out, there were also speckles of blood on the back of the watch and the inside of the wristband, which certainly could not have got there if he really had been wearing it under such conditions.

On 6 June 1966, the United States Supreme Court overturned Sheppard's conviction, and he walked free.

Sam Sheppard outside Ohio Supreme Court.

UNANSWERED QUESTIONS

There were, of course, still questions that remained unanswered. One was the old Sherlock Holmesian puzzle of the dog that did nothing in the night.

For if an unknown intruder had indeed broken in, why had the family dog Koko not barked a warning? Although neither police nor defendants thought fit to bring their suspicions into the open, privately they admitted that, if Sam did not kill his wife Marilyn, then it was someone who knew her, and the house, well.

As Harold Bretnall, a New York private detective hired by the Sheppard family, wrote in a report dated 1955: 'The answer to the Sheppard case riddle lies in Bay Village.' At the first trial, the jury had heard part of a statement made by Sam to detectives, in which he had said that Marilyn had 'spurned lovers – potential lovers... three that I know of and I am pretty sure more'.

Although not named at the trial, the men had, it was claimed, been identified to the investigating officers. Bretnall also claimed that a pair of Marilyn's bedroom slippers bore evidence that she had left the house during the night of 4 July 1954 while she was wearing them. 'Marilyn Sheppard was murdered by someone who was a frequent visitor to the Sheppard home,' wrote Bretnall.

The blood-speckled watch, too, posed unanswered questions. For if it had been splashed with Marilyn's blood, it must surely have been lying on the bedside table when she was killed – when it should have been downstairs on her husband's wrist. Did he come to bed, leaving his corduroy jacket downstairs, place his watch on the bedside table and batter his wife to death?

Or did he come to bed, take off his watch, hear an intruder, put on his trousers to investigate, get himself laid out – and then inexplicably lie to the police about his movements?

FURTHER TRAGEDY

One thing was sure: Marilyn's death and Sam Sheppard's ruined career were not the only tragedies involved in the drama. Sam's mother Edith was deeply shocked by the event and took an overdose of sleeping pills during the first trial. She recovered at the family hospital.

But on 17 January 1955, soon after her youngest son was convicted of murder, she shot herself. Eleven days later Sam's father, Dr Richard Sheppard, died at the age of 65 of a bleeding gastric ulcer. Almost exactly eight years after Mrs Sheppard's suicide, Marilyn's father, Thomas Reese, also shot himself.

Soon after his release, Sam married Ariane Tebbenjohanne, who had supported his cause. In December 1967, after a vigorous fight to regain his medical licence, it was granted and Sheppard joined the staff of the Youngstown Osteopathic Hospital, Ohio. His appointment lasted a year, until a malpractice claim was made against the hospital. The insurance company refused to pay out until Sam resigned.

On the day of his resignation, 3 December 1968, Sheppard was sued for divorce by Ariane. She claimed that she had suffered mental and physical cruelty at the hands of 'that maniac'.

Sheppard had authorized a ghost-written autobiography entitled *Endure and Conquer*, but most of the proceeds went to pay F. Lee Bailey's legal fees. While fighting once more to re-establish his medical career, he took up wrestling. In October 1969 he married his manager's daughter, a 20-year-old named Colleen Strickland.

For a while his wrestling career and the third marriage seemed to prosper, but Sheppard was consuming heavier and heavier amounts of vodka. On 5 April 1970 he died of liver failure.

RUTH ELLIS
SPURNED IN LOVE

On a summer's day in 1955 a woman walked out of the condemned cell in Holloway Prison to await the hangman's noose. Having shot to death a lover who had treated her appallingly, Ruth Ellis became the last woman in Britain to be executed.

For most of the year, the north London suburb of Hampstead keeps to itself on the edge of its leafy and spacious Heath. But at Easter the area's tranquillity is jovially disrupted. Outsiders flock in, as they have done for 150 years, to enjoy the fun of the fair. Lights and music flicker and boom across the green slopes, and the balmy spring air is scented with the pungent odour of fried onions from the fast-food stalls.

On the evening of Easter Sunday, 10 April 1955, everything was running true to form. Downhill from the fairground, the Magdala pub in South Hill Park was packed and boisterous. Just after nine o'clock two young men parked their grey-green Vauxhall Vanguard van and crossed the road to push into the saloon bar. Twenty-six-year-old David Blakely and his friend Clive Gunnell had been to the fair and were now after a quick drink before buying beer to take out to a nearby party.

As they re-emerged, neither of them noticed the slender blonde standing with her back to the wall of the pub. She was 29, her name was Ruth Ellis, and she had had a stormy relationship with Blakely which had lasted for two years. That evening, her pale, pretty face was grim behind her horn-rimmed spectacles as she called out: 'David!'

Blakely had been intent on avoiding Ruth all day. Now he ignored her. 'David!' she said again, sharply. Clive Gunnell looked up and saw that she was holding a .38 Smith and Wesson service revolver which was levelled at his friend.

David Blakely turned from the door of his van, opened his mouth, and then dropped his car keys and the bottle of beer he was holding as the first bullet slammed into his white shirt. A second bullet knocked Blakely on to his back.

'Clive!' Blakley's voice was a gurgled choke.

'Get out of the way, Clive,' said Ruth, deadly calm. She pulled the trigger again. Blakely, crawling on his stomach by now, was slammed into the tarmac. She positioned herself beside him and then she fired twice more, sending fragments flying from the back of his jacket. David Blakely lay prone and still.

Ruth unfocused from what she had done, looked Gunnell blankly in the eye, raised the pistol to her own temple and pulled

The Magdala pub on Hampstead Heath, outside which Ruth Ellis shot David Blakely.

the trigger. Amazingly, the 'four-inch Smith', renowned for its reliability, did nothing.

She lowered the gun to her side and almost absent-mindedly tried the trigger again. The sixth and last bullet splintered the pavement, whined off up the road and clipped the hand of a passer-by, Mrs Gladys Kensington Yule.

Ellis and Gunnell stood facing each other. The whole bloody little drama had lasted less than 90 seconds, but those six shots were to reverberate for an unconscionable time in criminal history.

Someone had already called for the police and an ambulance when Ellis herself seemed to come out of a trance to tell a young man nearby: 'Fetch the police.'

'I am the police,' said Alan Thompson, an off-duty Hampstead officer who had been drinking in the pub. He took the pistol from her hand – inadvertently smudging latent prints, as it later proved – and led her off to await the squad car.

By the time it took to deliver Ruth into the hands of Detective Chief Superintendent Leonard Crawford at Hampstead's Haverstock Hill police station, David Blakely was being declared dead on arrival at nearby New End Hospital.

When cautioned by DCS Crawford, Ruth Ellis was detached and composed. 'I am guilty,' she said. 'I am rather confused.' Then, little by little, she began to spill out her story…

FROM FACTORY WORKER TO CLUB HOSTESS

It had begun a quarter of a century earlier in Rhyl, North Wales, where Ruth was born the daughter of dance band musician Arthur Neilson and his wife Bertha on 9 October 1926. When Ruth was 15 the family moved to Southwark in south London, and the girl found work in the local OXO factory. She was ordered to take a year off work after contracting rheumatic fever. As part of her convalescence she took up dancing.

By 1943 she was working as a dance hall photographer's assistant when she met a Canadian soldier named Clare, and in September 1944, she bore him a son, christened Andria. Unfortunately Clare proved to have a wife back home, and Ruth, her mother Bertha and her older married sister Muriel were left to care for the boy.

In 1945, with the war in Europe ending and Ruth in her nineteenth year, she found another kind of career when she met Morris Conley.

Conley was a property racketeer, pimp and gangster who was to be dubbed 'Britain's biggest vice boss' by the press. But he did not attempt to draw Ruth into prostitution. Astutely, he spotted her greater potential as a club hostess.

At that time Britain's licensing laws were stringent. Pubs were permitted to open for only nine hours or less a day.

To beat the drinks ban, afternoon and late-night drinking clubs were set up, often in seedy basements and garret rooms. Usually there were rooms off the main bar where the prostitutes who were an integral part of such places could entertain their clients.

Conley owned a number of these dives in Soho, Bayswater and Kensington. Most were sleazy, but a few, like his Court Club in Duke Street near Marble Arch, catered for the raffish 'officer classes' with money to spend. He set Ruth up as hostess at the Court, and her rather tinsel good looks and natural wit were soon drawing in a fast set of hard-spending drinkers.

Ruth herself was soon earning up to £20 a week – about ten times the national average. For a time, she and her infant son lived well.

SHORT-LIVED RESPECTABILITY

Despite her lifestyle, Ruth Neilson's maternal instincts, though erratic, were strong. She yearned for respectability not only for herself but for Andria. When she met George Johnston Ellis, a 41-year- old-dentist with a practice in Surrey, she thought she had it within her grasp.

Ruth had a brief and not very successful stab at modelling.

Ellis was a bore and a drunk, but Ruth pursued him, moved in with him and finally, in November 1950, married him.

In October 1951 the couple had a daughter, Georgina, though by then the marriage was over. Ruth now had two young children to support. After recovering from Georgina's birth, she went back to London. Morris Conley was delighted to see her, and in October 1953 he made her manageress of his Little Club in Brompton Road, Knightsbridge.

A NEW JOB AND NEW ADMIRERS

She was paid £15 per week plus commission, with a £10 per week entertainment allowance. and a rent-free two-bedroom flat above the club rooms. Even if the job lacked respectability, it was security of a sort. But among her first customers were two men destined to be fatal to her very existence.

Desmond Cussen was a rich and well-established businessman, with a large car and an elegant bachelor flat in Devonshire Place, near Baker Street. Aged 32, he had had several minor affairs, but when he set eyes on Ruth Ellis it was love at first sight.

For her part she was fond of him – with his money and status he fitted her needs very nicely. But within hours of their first meeting a complication in the shape of a handsome young drone named David Blakely was to enter the picture.

The first time Blakely came to the Little Club he was drunk and abusive. Ruth had him thrown out, commenting: 'I hope never to see that little shit again.'

But Blakely came back to apologize and Ruth let him buy her a drink. Within a month, Blakely had moved into Ruth's flat above the club.

David Blakely was 24 when he first entered Ruth Ellis's life. He had been born on 17 June 1929 in Sheffield, the fourth child of a Scottish doctor. In 1940 his parents divorced, and David's mother married a well-to-do racing driver named Humphrey Cook, who imbued his stepson with a love of his sport.

Blakely's real father had left him £7,000 – then a considerable sum. Between about 1951 and his death David was to spend all of that and more on his dream, a prototype racing car that he called the Emperor. The Emperor was probably his only real love, though Ruth Ellis learned this too late.

So Blakely moved into Ruth's rooms above the Little Club and they began a turbulent affair. Blakely had a fiancee, Linda Dawson, the daughter of a rich Halifax millowner, whom he tried to string along for a while, but he lost her as his life became more and more centred on Ruth.

Ruth Ellis's first judgement of Blakely had in fact been the correct one. Most of his acquaintances thought him a 'little shit' and he proved it by living off his new mistress, cadging drinks from her club and openly flirting with her female customers.

The pair had violent rows, but Ruth tolerated Blakely's behaviour until it started driving customers away. She had a confrontation with Morris Conley about it and, favourite or no, she was fired.

The .38 Smith and Weson revolver with which Ruth Ellis committed murder.

Meanwhile, Desmond Cussen had proved a faithful friend to Ruth, constantly by her side whenever she felt the need of a shoulder to cry on. When Conley threw her out of her job and her flat, it was he who took her into his own apartment along with Andria – Georgina had by then been adopted. Cussen and Ellis slept together but her benefactor was by no means possessive. He allowed her to go on seeing Blakely and even connived at the pair sleeping in his flat.

A CYCLE OF BETRAYAL, VIOLENCE AND RECONCILIATION

In August 1954 Blakely finally broke off his engagement with Linda Dawson. Ruth thought, wrongly, that this was for her benefit. Blakely took her to Buckinghamshire and his family, but she was treated there as a London tart. And she discovered that he was in any case sleeping with other women.

One of these was Carole Findlater, wife of Anthony 'Ant' Findlater, a skilled amateur mechanic who worked on Blakely's Emperor. He and Clive Gunnell, another skilled mechanic, were almost as keen as Blakely on the expensive racing car.

After every betrayal there followed gin-soaked acrimony, violence and finally reconciliation. But it was a punishing cycle which must have damaged Cussen almost as much as the two principals.

In any case, in January 1955 he paid for a one-bedroom service flat at 44 Egerton Gardens, Kensington. Ruth – and by tacit agreement Blakely – could now have privacy, of a sort, for their rows.

That spring, Ruth discovered she was pregnant. Her divorce from George Ellis was almost final and Blakely was free, but when she brought up the subject of marriage his response was to beat her so badly that she miscarried. The usual boozy, tearful remorse followed, with Blakely sending a bunch of red carnations and a note of apology.

Ruth Ellis with long-time friend Desmond Cussen.

On Good Friday, 7 April, they spent what was to be their last night together. Over breakfast Blakely gave her a signed photograph proclaiming his love and finally proposed to her. They parted with Ruth blissfully happy and with Blakely promising to take her to drinks with the Findlaters that evening. But he failed to keep his promise.

Instead, he went alone to meet the Findlaters at the Magdala. He told them that Ruth had him trapped, that he wanted to leave her, but that he feared the consequences. And he had a sympathetic audience. Both Ant and Carole thought Ellis a grasping, vulgar woman, totally unsuitable for their friend. They suggested that Blakely stay with them for the Easter holiday.

The following morning was Easter Saturday and the fair on Hampstead Heath was in full swing. Blakely, the Findlaters, Clive Gunnell and other friends spent a jovial day.

Ruth Ellis spent a distracted one. On the previous evening, she had insisted that Cussen drive her to Hampstead in search of Blakely, but she was turned away from the Findlaters' house in Tanza Road, just up from the Magdala.

Now she returned, banging vainly on the Findlaters' front door and ringing them from a telephone box nearby – only to have them hang up on her. In the afternoon she began to kick Blakely's Vanguard van, screaming at the top of her voice, and the police were called to send her away.

Finally, on Sunday evening, she took a taxi to Tanza Road, spotted Blakely and Gunnell getting into the van and followed them to the Magdala. She had a revolver in her bag...

ARREST AND TRIAL

That, in essence, was the story Ruth Ellis told DCS Crawford. She remembered little, she said, about Sunday afternoon, other than that 'I intended to find David, and shoot him.'

And therein lay the whole case, as far as the police were concerned. Ruth Ellis had cold-bloodedly gunned down her lover in front of a pub full of witnesses and then admitted to the crime. But where had she got the gun? Unfortunately PC Thompson, in taking the weapon from her, had accidentally wiped all prints from it.

However, Ruth said that she had had the gun and ammunition for three years. It had been left with her as a pledge against a bar bill by one of her customers. The police were satisfied with her story.

So Ellis was charged with murder and removed to Holloway women's prison to await trial.

On 11 May 1955 she was arraigned at the Central Criminal Court of the Old Bailey before Mr Justice Barrie. The defence team was a distinguished and formidable one: Melford Stevenson QC, Sebag Shaw and Peter Rawlinson. Melford Stevenson asked for, and was granted, an adjournment of 40 days in order to look for a precedent that would allow his client to plead guilty to manslaughter provoked by jealousy.

Unfortunately, no precedent could be found. Accordingly, when the trial proper began on 20 June, Ruth was advised to plead not guilty in the hope that her story would sway the jury to pity. But Stevenson had reckoned without Ruth's vanity.

Throughout her stay in Holloway, her main concern seems to have been that mousy roots were beginning to show through her platinum hair, and the day before her trial the Governor, Dr Charity Taylor, allowed her to bleach it. The result was that when she appeared in court she cut an impossibly glamorous figure in her smart black suit. Her lawyers were convinced that her dazzling appearance alienated half the jury before the evidence was heard.

As it was, the trial lasted barely two days. On 21 June the jury took just 23 minutes to return a verdict of guilty and made no recommendation for mercy. Ruth Ellis was sentenced to death by hanging.

PUBLIC OUTRAGE

Back in Holloway she refused her solicitor, Victor Mishcon, permission to appeal on her behalf, though he wrote in vain to the Home Secretary begging for mercy. Instead she asked her brother, Granville, to smuggle in poison so that she could kill herself. He refused.

Granville Neilson, in fact, rightly mistrusted Ruth's story of how she had come by the fatal gun and spent his time in a frantic search for its real owner.

Meanwhile the general public – women in particular – launched an outcry against the sentence. Letters were written to MPs and petitions were launched.

It was all to no avail. As the clock began to strike nine on the morning of 13 July 1955, Ruth drank a last glass of brandy and walked steadfastly to the Holloway gallows.

There is no retrospective doubt that Ellis's death was a turning point in the anti-hanging campaign, though another decade was to pass before the rope was abolished completely.

Ruth and Desmond enjoy an evening out with friends.

THE MISSING DETAILS EMERGE

It took even longer for what seems to have been the real truth to emerge. On the night before her death, Ruth summoned Victor Mishcon to the condemned cell and dictated her account of what she said really happened on that fateful Easter Sunday.

Desmond Cussen, she said, had given her the gun. The pair had been drinking Pernod in Cussen's flat while Ruth poured out her misery. Cussen drove her and the boy Andria out to Epping Forest, where he had shown her how to load the weapon and had given her tips on aiming and firing.

Later that afternoon, after having more to drink, she had taken the loaded pistol and demanded that Cussen – not a taxi, as she had stated - drive her to the Findlaters' house in Tanza Road. From there she had made her way to the Magdala.

If this was true, what were Cussen's motives? He was certainly besotted with Ruth, lavishing money, presents and offers of marriage upon her. He had never refused her slightest whim. Perhaps he was simply going along blindly, as usual, with her wishes.

Or as has been suggested, did he simply give her the gun, knowing that in her mood of jealous, drink-fuelled rage she would kill his rival Blakely? In which case, was he also convinced that she would be acquitted?

Desmond Cussens visited Ruth Ellis every day during her remand in Holloway Prison, bringing her flowers, chocolates and other presents. But as soon as the guilty verdict was pronounced he broke all contact with her. He died 20 years after his troubled lover, in Australia, without apparently ever having told his side of the story.

Huge crowds gathered outside Holloway Prison on the morning of Ruth Ellis's execution.

EVIL WOMEN

PAMELA SMART

MISTRESS OF MURDER

She was a teacher, a person of some standing and authority. She was a wife. But Pamela Smart was also crazy for sex with a teenage boy, so maddened by lust that she was driven to commit a gross and ugly murder.

Pamela Smart was young, she was beautiful and she was ambitious. She lived in the small town of Derry, New Hampshire on America's eastern seaboard, and she was restless. Bored with her life as a teacher, bored and unhappy as a wife, she sought excitement in a love affair with an adolescent boy. But this illicit passion was to lead her and her young lover to disaster and tragedy.

Shortly after 10 p.m. on 1 May, 1990, police patrolman Gerald Scaccia received an urgent call to investigate a crime at number 4E in Misty Morning Drive. Derry Scaccia had been cruising for the usual drunks and speeders when his despatcher announced an emergency call at the address – something about a body. He found a sobbing Pamela Smart sitting on the stoop of a neighbour's house. Hysterical with grief, she pointed into the open doorway of her own home, saying: 'He's in there - my husband's in there.' Scaccia entered with his flashlight, saw a man lying face down, his heels toward him in the hallway of the residence. He turned the body over and was about to begin mouth-to-mouth resuscitation when he spotted the small circle in the man's temple, a wound caused by a bullet, fired at point-blank range from a snub-nosed .38 revolver.

Neighbourhood sympathy for the young widow was widespread. Friends appeared, to comfort the popular and personable high school teacher whose husband, Greg, had been so cruelly murdered just six days before their first wedding anniversary. Pamela, who was a director at a media studies' centre that managed a number of projects in local schools, was interviewed by the police. She explained that she had been at a school meeting that night. She and Greg had moved to Derry a few months earlier. He worked as an insurance salesman with the Metropolitan Life Company and, no, she did not know why anyone would want to kill him. But a detective at the interview said: 'There was something strange about her. Her world had fallen apart and, well, she seemed very, very calm about it all. I thought it was a bit weird. Call it a cop's intuition. There was nothing I could put my finger on at the time.'

The doomed husband, Greg Smart, on his wedding day in 1989.

Captain Loring Jackson was the officer put in charge of the investigation. He was to uncover a story of manipulation, obsession, greed, sex and lust. Just as his detective had felt, so Jackson, too, was puzzled by the widow's apparent calm, and there were aspects of her husband's murder that did not fit the story she was telling; nor was there was any sign of a burglary. A diamond ring had been left on the murdered man's hand. There was no cash in his wallet, but all his credit cards were there.

In the days following the killing, numerous rumours began to circulate about Pamela and Greg Smart, that the couple dabbled in drugs and held wild parties at the house. Pamela telephoned a local television station so that she could make a public statement, denying the truth of these rumours. She seemed very composed for one so recently and tragically bereaved, thought Jackson. He was very annoyed when, just two days after the murder, Mrs Smart described to reporters the crime scene. She revealed details that the police would have preferred to remain confidential, as they tried to track the killer.

PAMELA'S VERY YOUNG VISITORS

Four days after the murder, Dan Pelletier, a detective on the homicide squad, took an anonymous phone call from a woman who claimed that a minor, named Cecelia Pierce, was the person the police should interview in connection with the killing. The caller then claimed that Pamela had confided to Cecelia her plot to kill Greg. The detective remembered that Pamela had supplied a list of the people who had been in her home a month prior to the murder. Cecelia Pierce was on that list, and the police were now interested to note how many other very young people visited the school teacher in her home. Billy Flynn, for instance, was a visitor.

Billy Flynn was 15 when he met Pam Smart in her role as teacher, when she came to Winnacunnet High School to organize a series of lectures on the dangers of drug and alcohol abuse.

Erotic poses from the sexually-bored Pamela Smart.

A female friend recalled that the first time Billy saw Pamela, he turned and said: 'I'm in love.' People noticed that Pamela enjoyed flirting with her students; and the police were to hear that she seemed to favour Billy Flynn.

Cecelia Pierce was also close to Pamela, pleased because the 22-year-old woman did not treat her as a big child, as her mother and other teachers did. Cecelia worked with Smart on the drugs and alcohol project, and was soon confiding her romantic problems to the older woman. It seemed Pamela knew how to empathize with the adolescents she taught.

Pamela Smart began a love affair with Billy Flynn. Her marriage to Greg, the man she met when she was a college student, was volatile, and they had violent rows. Billy Flynn would never forget his first sexual experience with Pamela. He visited the older woman at her home when her husband was away. She put the steamy Kim Basinger film $9^1/_2$ Weeks on to her video recorder. Then, leading Billy to the bedroom, she mimicked the striptease act performed by the actress in the film. To the music of Van Halen's 'Black and Blue', they had sex. Later, again copying a scene from the film Billy rubbed Pam's body with ice cubes before they made love again.

Later he would say: 'I was kind of shocked. It's not every day that a teenage kid gets to do this with an older woman who says she likes him a lot. I was totally infatuated with her. I was in love with her.'

BILLY'S JEALOUS HATRED

They made love in her Honda car, at her office in school and at her home. She was compiling an anti-drugs film for a Florida orange juice company, and as Billy was her student on this project, he was able to skip school. They spent a lot of time together. She gave him sexy pictures of herself in a bikini, which he kept in his wallet, and the boy began to develop a jealous hatred of his lover's husband, Greg. Pamela portrayed Greg as evil, a man who cheated on her, abused her. She wanted to get rid of him... have him killed. Soon, the idea of murder took root in Billy Flynn's mind. Pamela told him that, if she were free of her husband, she could be with Billy for ever.

Pamela Smart was not only persuading Billy Flynn to kill her husband. She also influenced Cecelia Pierce, manipulating the girl into feeling a strong dislike of Greg Smart.

Billy told the police that it was Pam's idea to make the murder look like the act of a violent burglar. He said that Pam even revealed details of the plan to Cecelia Pierce, who treated such conversations as part of some sort of macabre game of love enjoyed by Pam and Billy.

Pamela Smart tried to convince the police that her husband had been killed by burglars, but they arrested her for conspiracy to mrder.

Stephen Sawicki, in his book *Teach me to Kill*, a study of Smart, analysed the motives: 'Perhaps it had become something of a perverse game that had nothing to do with reality for Billy and Cecelia. Maybe it was the thrill of flirting with danger, a dance along the edge of a precipice. Or maybe it was simply the lack of a sound-minded adult that the kids felt comfortable with, someone who could point out just how crazy it had all become. Whatever the case, being around Pam, even with all the strange talk of murdering her husband, offered a form of sustenance. Pam provided it in different ways for the boy and the girl, but when it came right down to it, their needs were the same. Both Cecelia and Billy deeply wanted to feel that they were good and loved and special. It was madness, but without abhorrence the kids continually accepted the small steps that in the end pointed to death.'

As Billy's infatuation for Pamela grew, so did his determination to kill her husband. He enlisted the aid of Patrick Randall, 17; Vance Lattime, 18, and Raymond Fowler, 19. All were promised a reward by Pam and Flynn, a little something for their trouble – a stereo, some cash or some other item of value from the house. Pam's only stipulation was that they hid her beloved shih-tzu dog, Halen, away from the murder scene – she thought that witnessing the death of his master might disturb the animal.

A TOWEL WAS ALREADY SPREAD ON THE CARPET

The quartet's first attempt to kill Greg Smart failed when, travelling in Pam's Honda, they lost their way to the Smarts' address. They planned to hide inside the house, waiting for Greg's return from work, then killing him on arrival. However, when they finally arrived he was already at home.

On the second occasion there were to be no errors. This time, Flynn and Randall were dropped off near the house, and then changed into tracksuits they had bought for the occasion. As they started to move towards the home of Greg Smart, a couple appeared near the corner ahead of them. The two boys started jogging, pulling the tracksuit hoods over their faces. They broke into the house through the metal doors of the basement, and they began to vandalize the master bedroom, the bathroom and the lounge, hoping to create the scene of a frantic burglary. The other two accomplices, Lattime and Fowler, were waiting in a nearby plaza with a getaway car.

The killing took a few seconds. Greg was ambushed in the hallway of his own home. Grabbed violently by the hair and pummelled in the face by Randall, the man was brought to his knees. 'Don't hurt me, dude,' pleaded Smart, as Randall waved a long-bladed knife in front of his eyes. Randall told the police that he did not have the stomach to murder in cold blood. It was Flynn who pulled a gun out and shot Greg Smart, who dropped dead on to a towel that had been spread on the carpet. Pamela had made it quite clear she did not want blood on her precious hallway tiling and carpet.

The anonymous phone call that led the police to these confessions came from Louise Coleman, a friend of Cecelia Pierce. Thirty-one and pregnant, Louise had been told by Cecelia that she knew of a woman planning to 'snuff her husband for the insurance money'. Louise thought at the time that Cecelia was acting out some kind of fantasy, or that her wires had become crossed. When Greg Smart was murdered, Louise felt it was her duty to tell the police about Cecelia's conversations.

A month after the murder, Captain Jackson was convinced that Pam was guilty. Her own behaviour combined with the gossip indicated that she was not innocent. She was, once again, hanging around with her adolescent friends – which, under the circumstances, smacked of impropriety. Captain Jackson decided to enlist the aid of Greg's father, Bill. Smart Snr was appalled by Pam's callous indifference to the murder of his son, her husband,

Throughout her trial, Pamela Smart tried to maintain a posture of wounded innocence. She did admit that the evidence seemed to be against her, but this, she said, was merely coincidence.

and he realized that, probably, Pamela had killed his son. He would co-operate with the police in their investigations.

The police questioned Cecelia again and again. But the girl was loyal to Pamela Smart and although Cecelia had nothing to do with the murder, she refused to say anything against the woman whom she believed was her closest friend. However, the young killers were unable to resist boasting of their exploit, and soon their school was abuzz with gossip. One of the students, Ralph Welch, did not view the adventure as part of a game, and after Randall and Fowler boasted to him of the murder, Welch told Vance Lattime's father that his gun had been used in a murder and that his son was involved. Lattime checked his weapon and noticed it was dirty, although it had been clean when he had put it away in his gun cabinet. He went straight to the police. Soon the four boys were rounded up for questioning.

CECELIA AGREES TO WEAR A 'WIRE'

Pam's wicked world was falling apart, but she was determined that she would not crumble. The boys gave their statements, in which Flynn admitted his role as killer, while the others claimed that they thought it was a game, that they had no idea they were part of a murder plan, but they all implicated Pam, insisting that she made Flynn kill her husband. But it was not enough to arrest Pamela Smart. The boys' claims needed to be supported by evidence of her part in the crime.

'We had to get some proof,' explained Captain Jackson after the investigation. 'We needed Pamela Smart to convict herself. Luckily, Cecelia Pierce came around for us after two more interviews. Like the rest she realized that what had happened was ugly and filthy and vile. She finally, finally helped us nail Pamela Smart.'

Cecelia agreed to wear a 'wire' to record her conversations with Pamela Smart, in a bid to get her to implicate herself in the death of her husband. Cecelia was coached by lawmen to ask leading questions. Pamela Smart must have been very concerned that now her accomplices, the boys, were in custody, telling police of her role in the drama, but she maintained a facade of calm composure. In the first few conversations with Cecelia she gave nothing away and even denied that she was having an affair with Billy. But as the conversations proceeded, the police coached Cecelia and told her to mention to Pam that the district attorney wanted to interview her over a love note that she had written to Billy. This was the conversation between Pam and Cecelia:

Pam: 'All I can say is that no matter what they try and make you talk about if I were you I didn't know a damn thing.'

Cecelia: 'Well, all I know is that I had to come and talk to you because I… I mean I don't know what to do. I have to go talk to the district attorney. I'm just sick of lying you know.'

Pam: 'Well, you know, I'm just telling you that if you tell the truth, you're gonna be an accessory to murder.'

Cecelia: 'Right.'

Pam: 'So that's your choice. And not only that, but what is your family going to think'? I mean, they're like, 'Cecelia, you knew about this.' You know?'

Cecelia: 'Yeah.'

Pam: 'Nothing was going wrong until they told Ralph.'

Cecelia: 'No.'

Pam: 'It's their stupid-ass faults that they told Ralph.'

Cecelia: 'I can't even believe they told him.'

In another conversation she tried to keep Cecelia on her side: 'I think I've been a very good friend to you and that's the thing, even if you send me to the f***ing slammer or you don't or if anybody sends me, it's gonna be you and that's the big thing, and that's what it comes down to. But what good is it gonna do you if you send me to the slammer? Because if you think that's gonna be the end of your problems… don't think it's the end of your problems. It's gonna be like your whole family going: "You knew about a murder, how could you have lived like that?" And the newspapers are gonna be all over you. And you're gonna be on the witness stand a million times, you know?'

THE GOOD NEWS - AND THE BAD NEWS

Pamela Smart began to incriminate herself in these conversations with her good friend – someone whose destiny was closely tied up with her own. In one of the final wiretaps Pamela said: 'Bill coulda told them all I'd pay them. I don't know what Bill told them to get them to go, and then that was just a lie. You know. They're not going to have any proof. There's no money. So they can't convict me 'cause of a sixteen-year-old's word in the slammer, facing the rest of his life. And me, with a professional reputation and a course that I teach. You know, that's the thing. They're going to believe me.'

Pamela Smart was taken by surprise when Detective Dan Pelletier entered her school on 1 August and confronted her in her office with the words: 'I have some good news for you and I have some bad news for you. The good news is that we have solved the murder of your husband. The bad news is that you are under arrest for first degree murder.'

When she was arrested, the boys admitted they had been involved in the murder plan and told the police that they did it because of Billy's love affair with Pam. But Pamela maintained that she was innocent, the victim of a teenager's infatuation. She said she had never encouraged Billy Flynn, had never slept with him and had not solicited any of them to commit murder. But it was clear in the first days of her trial in March 1991, that her story was difficult to believe; she may have been adept at manipulating impressionable youngsters, but she did not impress the prosecutors or jurors given the task of weighing up the facts.

Billy Flynn gave damning witness when he was under oath. He told how he had loaded the weapon with hollow-point ammunition, bullets designed to cause maximum destruction to a human target. He said he held back a moment after aiming the gun at Greg's head. 'A hundred years it seemed like,' he sobbed. 'And I said: "God forgive me".' He paused before admitting: 'I pulled the trigger.'

Pamela Smart treated her court appearances as a fashion show and bemoaned the fact that there was so little time to fix her make-up. The court revelations of her sordid sex games with youngsters did not shake her demeanour and she maintained her plea of innocence to the end.

SHE TOOK MORE THAN GREG'S LIFE

The recordings made by Cecelia were played in court. Pamela Smart did not sound like a grieving young widow. The court heard her boast that her position in the community would give her an edge over her accusers. Smart's lawyers denounced the state case against their client as 'toxic soup', claiming Flynn and his cohorts were no more than deranged thrill-killers who had murdered Greg Smart because he was a romantic rival. The jury of seven women and five men took just 13 hours of deliberation to decide that Pamela Smart had set out to teach the boys the business of murder and that she was guilty as charged. Judge Douglas R. Gray imposed the mandatory sentence of life, without the possibility of parole, on Pamela Smart; Billy Flynn and Patrick Randall received sentences of not less than 28 years each, while Vance Lattime was given 18 years. Raymond Fowler's case has yet to be tried.

Pamela Smart could not believe it when the verdicts were read out. She turned to her attorney and said: 'First Billy took Greg's life. and now he's taking mine.' But Captain Loring Jackson, who has met a fair cross-section of criminals in his 25 years' service with the police, was not impressed. He said: 'She not only took Greg's life but she also took away the lives of these bright, impressionable young men when she enlisted them in her scheme of murder. She is cold, calculating, manipulative, self-centred, totally unfeeling for anybody but herself. I have never met such a cold person as her. I think life in prison is, for this young lady, very, very fitting.'

ROSEMARY
ABERDOUR

THE LADY IS A THIEF

She was plump, generous and fun-loving. She was also a lonely little fraud. Rosemary Aberdour gave herself a grand title and stole a vast sum from a charity. She spent it on parties, inviting all the friends that money could buy, but the only return on this investment was a prison sentence.

There is no denying it – when Rosemary Aberdour lived it up, she did it in style. She bought herself a Bentley turbo car worth £50,000 and promptly hired a chauffeur to go with it. In the course of a few years, she splashed out an amazing £780,000 on parties, once setting up an entire funfair in London's docklands. She bought a string of luxury cars, including a Mercedes and five other smaller models for her staff, at a cost of over £200,000. In one lavish week Rosemary poured 240 bottles of Dom Perignon champagne into a bathtub for a friend to bathe in.

SWINDLING IN STYLE

There were Caribbean yachting holidays, shopping trips to London jewellers and clothes purchased from the best couturiers in London and Paris. Once, in London, when her black labrador dog Jeeves was looking a little ill, she decided to take it for a walk... in the Scottish hills. So she hired a chauffeur-driven car to take the dog for walkies in Scotland. Excess was the motto of her life. But so was cheating, for 'Lady' Aberdour was nothing more than a swindler, a fake aristocrat who deceived many good and trusting people, so that she could use their money to finance her lifestyle.

Flanked by family and legal men, Aberdour makes her way into court as a common criminal.

She fiddled almost £3 million from a hospital charity before she was detained as a guest of Her Majesty, in surroundings that bear little resemblance to those she left behind.

Her rise to riches was the result of a carefully orchestrated plot. Rosemary Aberdour was born in 1961, neither titled nor rich, but with lashings of that essential ingredient necessary for any good thief – greed. The daughter of Kenneth Aberdour, an Essex radiologist, and his wife Jean, once a secretary at the National Hospital, Rosemary was brought up at Witham, near Chelmsford, and had an ordinary education at a local school. She was a bright child who left school with several 'A' levels and then trained as an accountant with a city firm. After working in various jobs, she landed the plum job of book keeper to the National Hospital Development Foundation in 1987. It was the beginning of her trek down the pathway of deceit.

During the first two years in this position, Rosemary worked exceedingly hard – and honestly – raising cash for a new wing and for medical equipment. The National Hospital, in London, is recognized internationally as a centre for the treatment af multiple sclerosis, Parkinson's and Alzheimer's diseases, epilepsy and strokes. One of Rosemary's early successes came after she convinced the hospital trustees that the annual Queen's Square Ball, which got its name from the hospital's Bloomsbury address, could be promoted as a profitable fundraising event.

Rosemary grew up in a semi-detached home in Worchester Park, Surrey but she wanted the secluded luxury of a house hidden in private gardens. She stole the money to pay for her dreams.

HAVING A BALL FOR CHARITY

The ball was little more than a staff party, but Rosemary knew that, if society folk and celebrities could be persuaded that this was a grand charity ball, worth the expense of the highly priced tickets, the hospital would make a good deal of money. The Queen's Square Ball was so successful that Rosemary organized three more similar occasions, as well as other fundraising events, some of which were attended by the Princess of Wales, the charity's patron.

Rosemary won the respect of the charity's bigwigs, who were impressed by her remarkable energy and genuine talent for persuading the rich and famous to donate large sums to the National Hospital Development Foundation. She was very persuasive, as her words in a society brochure reveal: 'I have gained great motivation from meeting patients who show immense courage in coping with their illnesses, often against incredible odds.' However, Rosemary was to lengthen those odds when she stole the money that should have been used to treat these sickly patients, to top up her own income.

SHE BEGAN TO DOCTOR THE BOOKS

She crossed the line into criminality in 1988, when she began filching small amounts of the cash donated to the charity. Because she was held in such high esteem by the trustees of the charity, Aberdour had wide control of the charity's finances. There were several accounts in banks and building societies in which cheques, donated to the charity, were deposited. Aberdour became a signatory on these accounts when she organized the first revamped Queen's Square Ball. However, other signatures, like those of Richard Stevens, the charity director, were required on each cheque and Rosemary began to forge these. Initially, she took enough money to pay for a car. She simply doctored the books so that the amounts she stole never appeared in the charity's legitimate accounts. She quickly realized that this was a very easy way to siphon off cash for her own purposes, and the horizons of her world were broadened considerably.

The bulk of the cash disappeared between April 1989 and 1991, when she was caught. And as the money flowed into special bank accounts she had set up for herself, Rosemary Aberdour set about spinning a web of lies to give herself a completely new persona.

John Young, the chairman of the charity, recalls the day he became aware of her metamorphosis. He was used to seeing Rosemary arrive at work in her modest saloon, so he gave a double-take when she pulled up outside the offices in a gleaming Bentley, complete with chauffeur and bodyguard. 'We might have thought the queen was arriving,' he said to her jokingly at the time. Aberdour replied gravely: 'You must understand that I have inherited £2 million and I have to have a minder because I might be kidnapped.'

She informed anyone who cared to listen that her windfall also gave her the right to assume the title of 'Lady' Aberdour.

After her enormous inheritance, 'Lady' Aberdour began to collect the trimmings necessary for her new status in life. She moved to a Thameside penthouse, complete with indoor swimming pool that had an ivy-covered swing suspended from its atrium roof. There were maple wood doors, pink marble bathrooms, outstanding views of the Thames and celebrity neighbours like the actress Brigitte Neilsen. Her lavish bedroom was swathed in blood-red and gold silks, while a cushion, placed on an antique chair, had been embroidered in her own hand. It read: 'I love old money, young men and me.' The chandelier in the living room – in the corner of which nestled a baby grand piano – was worth £10,000. In a valuable antique cabinet in her bedroom she kept her supply of bargain-basement Marks and Spencer knickers. Careful to avoid old friends and family, who might blow the whistle on her, Rosemary Aberdour began to cultivate the 'right' people who would appreciate the finer things in life that she now enjoyed.

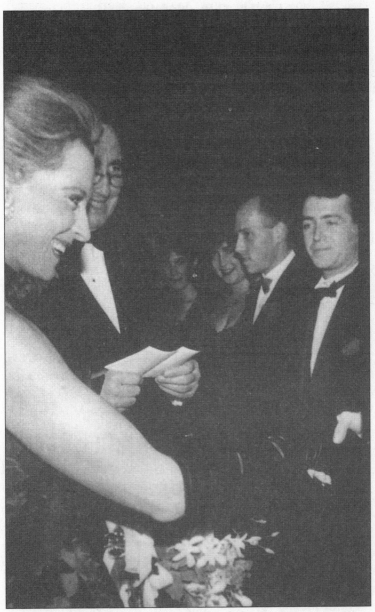

At the Red Ocotober Ball in 1990, Rosemary, third from the right, waits eagerly in a line-up to shake the hand of Princess Michael of Kent.

WILD TWO-WEEK PARTY

Rosemary Aberdour was a brilliant party hostess. At one party, held in the thirteenth-century Thornton Watlass Hall in North Yorkshire, the revels continued for two weeks, with new guests coming and going every two to three days. A fleet of rented cars ferried the guests to and from airports and railway stations, and bottles of vintage champagne were cracked open for every arrival. It took weeks to fix the ancient mansion after the Bacchanalia had ended.

Tim Mudd, who ran the estate, said: 'They damaged silver and furnishings and left owing a great deal of money to local tradespeople. The saddest thing was that they put silver salvers worth thousands of pounds in the oven, melting the lead which secured the handles. Some became stained with carrot juice – so they cleaned the silver with scouring pads, totally ruining it. On Hallowe'en night she staged the biggest party of the lot and totally tore the place apart. One room was stripped of all its antique furniture and another was turned into a dance hall. There were imitation dead bodies everywhere and "live" bodies which jumped out of coffins. The bill for that one alone must have run to thousands a head.'

ROSEMARY AS QUEEN OF THE CASTLE

There were other memorable events. To mark the birthday of a girlfriend, Aberdour hired Conwy Castle in North Wales. To get there she rented a helicopter, and she planned an elaborate medieval-style pageant to greet it on arrival. The pampered labrador, Jeeves, was not allowed in the chopper but joined his mistress later… after a newly hired flunkey had driven him down the M4 in the Bentley. As the helicopter bearing Aberdour and her friend landed, minstrels, in elaborate costume, blew a triumphant fanfare on the battlements while a menacing black knight, replete with mock-armour, approached the giggling girls. They were saved by a dashing 'white' knight who fought his 'black' counterpart to a fake death. Rosemary was then playfully crowned 'Queen of the Castle'.

Following this little display – estimated cost, £10,000 – she flew her friend on to another castle, where the reception committee consisted of a brass band and a full Welsh male voice choir. The whole day ended with bucketloads of champagne and gourmet food. The estimated cost of the fantasy jaunt was £40,000.

To her frequent hangers-on and staff, it soon became apparent that the plump charity queen was an unloved, lonely person who hoped to buy friendship with her lavish generosity. Rosemary handed out Caribbean and Indian Ocean cruises, and invitations to the best parties in London. She housed her London butler, Manuel Cabrera, a Filipino who worked for her for 18 months, in a luxurious flat. He claimed that although she had a fiancé, British Army Captain Michael Cubbins. Rosemary also entertained a boyfriend. It was Cabrera's job to help her keep this secret and to prevent the two men from bumping into each other.

Her parents were driven away in shock after Rosemary was given a prison sentence.

A £60,000 VALENTINE'S PARTY

Cabrera described his employer: 'When Michael and Rosemary got engaged he gave her a fantastic diamond ring but she didn't like it, and bought herself another for over £8,000. She seemed to think money could always buy happiness. She meant to throw a hen party in the Grenadines but she didn't go because it would have meant leaving Michael – so she paid for all her girlfriends to go, but she stayed home. Once she had an incredible beach party at her flat where the whole place was emptied of furniture and the floors were covered with sand. The bath was filled with bottles of Dom Perignon champagne that were just poured in one after the other. Another time she had a Valentine's party – and that was really one to remember.'

She called it the St Valentine's Day Massacre party and she spent £60,000 on it. Guests were handed exotic cocktails as they entered her flat, then were led to tables groaning under the weight of fabulously cooked food. After the meal, guests went upstairs to her swimming pool where they were invited to change into costumes especially laid on for them. Pink heart-shaped balloons festooned the place and the fun began with a jolly water fight that ended in more champagne, more frolicking and more indulgence. It was a never-ending cycle of fun for 'Lady' Rosemary.

The National Hospital Development Foundation hoped to collect £10 million intended to pay for a complete refurbishment of the hospital. So clever was Rosemary Aberdour at juggling figures in the foundation's accounts, that twice the accounts passed the scrutiny of top city auditors and were declared to be perfectly in order. Nothing could have been further from the truth. Aberdour used to give the auditors her accounts in sections, allowing herself time to move funds from one to the other, so that no discrepancies would show in the section she sent to the auditors. It seems foolish that the trustees of the charity allowed her this access to, and control over, their finances. But they trusted her and she abused their faith.

THE REAL LADY ABERDOUR

With such a successful system of fraud, greed grew fat and demanding. 'Lady A' became more and more extravagant, stealing £1 million in the first six months of 1991. In an ironic, callous twist, she signed over a cheque for £100,000 from a personal account – money she had diddled from the charity – and 'donated' it to the hospital. It was an act of great magnanimity from the aristocrat who worked so hard for them and her generosity was not lost on the grateful trustees.

Such extensive embezzlement would not, of course, go unnoticed for ever. But long before the fraudster was rumbled by her bosses in London, there was, on a Scottish estate, a Lady Aberdour who was aware that something strange was afoot when her husband, Lord Stewart Aberdour, began receiving thank-you mail from guests who attended parties at strange venues, not in his home. Christmas cards, addressed to his wife, were signed by people neither the lord nor his wife had ever met.

Michael Cubbins and Rosemary's vicar leave the Old Bailey. They both attended Rosemary's Trial to give her some comfort and support.

'WHO WAS THIS WOMAN IMPERSONATING MY WIFE?'

'There was one incident', said Lord Aberdour, 'when I was at a shooting weekend and this chap came up to me and said: "I met your wife recently – she's hosting the most amazing parties." He had never met my wife, Mady, so he just assumed she was this person. I was perplexed. I said: "My wife's up in Scotland having a baby so I don't see how you could have done." I told him he must have met someone who was pretending to be Lady Aberdour. I thought about turning up at one of her parties and exposing her as a fake. Another time I saw an article in a Sunday newspaper describing this woman as my daughter. When letters started arriving I sent them back to the post office saying "person not known at this address". When you discover someone is an impostor there is not really very much that you can do.'

Two weeks before she was caught. Rosemary, a hopeless romantic, hired a grand hotel in Sussex, then rented the services of a professional video company. She dressed as Scarlett O'Hara, one of her favourite screen heroines, and kitted her friends out as other characters from *Gone With The Wind* to create her own version of the screen classic. She spent £50,000 of charity funds on this little lark.

When her tissue of lies and deceit finally unravelled, it did so rapidly. One careless slip on her part caused her downfall – and saved the remaining cash in the bank accounts for the hospital. Rosemary Aberdour grew complacent, becoming less meticulous about covering her tracks. In June 1991, she left her office for a few days to take another of her fabulous holidays. But on her desk she left, unhidden, a copy of a £120,000 cheque which had been drawn from one of the Foundation's building society accounts. With this copy was a letter authorising the transfer of the cash to a Barclays Bank account which was one of five used by Aberdour to 'launder' the charity cash. Both the letter and the cheque copy were found by Richard Stevens, the charity director. He knew that the building society account did not have Aberdour as a signatory to it and realized with horror that the signatures on the cheques were crude forgeries of the legitimate signatories' writing.

TREASURES AND RARE WINE

The following day, 14 June, Fraud Squad officers visited Aberdour's apartment to take stock of the Aladdin's Cave of furnishings and fittings that graced her home. Box after box of papers and other evidence relating to her mammoth swindle were removed from the flat, as neighbours of the fake aristocrat stared. The police inventory of luxury goods found in the Battersea apartment ran to 37 pages and included over 300 bottles of old and rare wine.

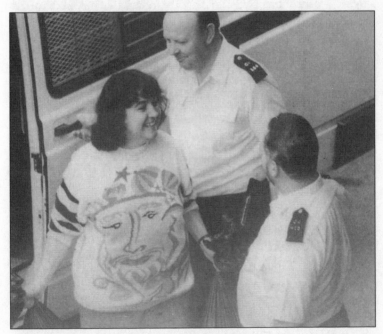

Rosemary returned from her refuge in Brazil and was whisked off from the airport in a police car that took her to for questioning at the Fraud Squad headquarters.

But there was no sign of the fraudster. She had fled Britain after hearing that Fraud Squad officers had been to her apartment. In the footsteps of Great Train Robber Ronnie Biggs, she escaped to Rio de Janeiro, as the horrified trustees of the charity began to realize the massive scale of her fiddling. From a rented flat near the Copacabana Beach, Aberdour contacted her parents and called her fiancé Cubbins in Germany. There were numerous telephone conversations, over several days, during which they tried to persuade her to return to Britain. Finally, the Ministry of Defence allowed Cubbins leave from his regiment to fly to Rio, in a bid to bring her back to face the music. An old schoolfriend, called Sarah Boase, was also instrumental in trying to coax her back.

As she was taken off to start her prison sentence, Rosemary Aberdour managed a smile for the press.

LAST FEAST BEFORE PRISON

Finally, Rosemary agreed but her journey back was in the high style that she had grown accustomed to. She forked out, presumably with charity money, for business-class seats for herself and her fiancé. On board she tucked into fillets of beef and fine wine… the last meal before prison food faced this woman, ruined by her own greed. When the aircraft landed in Britain, detectives and security men escorted the ashen-faced Rosemary to an ante-room in the terminal building. She was cautioned by Fraud Squad officers. Then the woman who was used to being chauffeured in a green Bentley limousine, was sandwiched between two burly detectives in the back of a Montego police car. She was driven off to face questioning at the Fraud Squad headquarters, in Holborn, Central London.

There followed a drastic change in lifestyle for the bogus aristocrat. Stripped of her Hermes and Chanel creations, Rosemary was clad strictly in prison flannel for Rosemary when she was remanded without bail, although she was allowed to visit home for Christmas.

SHE LIVED IN A FANTASY WORLD

Rosemary Aberdour came to settle her account – not with the charity, but with justice – in March 1992, when she appeared at the Old Bailey. She pleaded guilty to 17 charges of fraud and remained motionless as a litany of her crimes was read out in court by the prosecution; a £65,000 surpise party for a friend, £80,000 for the rental of a yacht in the Caribbean, £780,000 in all on parties, £134,000 on personal staff and £280,000 on cars.

In her defence, Graham Boal said: 'She is not an ordinary criminal or a sophisticated fraudster, stashing away funds. She had absolutely nothing to show for her crimes, nothing except shame, remorse, poverty and the courage to answer the indictment.' He said all the so-called friends who had wined and dined off her had evaporated like so many champagne bubbles. Aberdour had poured money down other people's throats. He said that she suffered from an impenetrable lack of self-esteem, insecurity and immaturity. He said she was a victim of the hard-bitten and glossy world of high-society fundraising. 'Eventually,' he said, 'the fantasy world became reality. Self-deception started to take over.' He added: 'This binge, this gorging, became a disease.'

The prosecution painted a rather different picture. Brendan Finucane said: 'It is clear many people were taken in by her, close friends and even her boyfriend. Thousands of pounds were given away to hangers-on and spongers. She had started humbly and then had grander designs. She was bound to be caught and fled to Brazil when the crime was discovered.'

The grand riverside block where Aberdour installed herself using money she swindled from charity funds.

Sentencing Aberdour to four years in jail, a sentence perceived as remarkably light by many at the charity, Mr Justice Leonard said: 'You spent the money on gross extravagance. It is said the motivation which brought you to these offences was complex or unusual. So it was, I am sure, but for two and a half years you went on milking this fund. You were trusted and you abused that trust.'

Rosemary Aberdour was certainly a rogue, and one of the greatest swindlers in British criminal history, but there is a certain sadness in her story, for the money she stole was used to buy friendship. Even as a schoolgirl, it is reported, she had used bribery to attract loyalty and company.

But there is one man who would have liked to befriend her. He has issued an invitation to 'show her the sights' of the Rio de Janeiro she missed. Ronnie Biggs, holed up in the Brazilian sunspot ever since his jailbreak from a London prison, said: 'I could have given her so much pleasure around town before she went back. It's the perfect place for a girl who loves parties and she would never have had to flash that much cash.

'I don't think she's mad to give herself up. In the circumstances I think she did the right thing. She is a young woman and has her whole life ahead of her. But you can be sure I will not be on the next plane. When she comes out I hope she comes to visit me – I'll show her what a true friend can be.'

IMELDA MARCOS
THE STEEL BUTTERFLY

Imelda grew up in poverty, but her beauty lifted her out of the slums. A powerful politician wooed and married her. Imelda Marcos became a wildly greedy woman who robbed her own kind to pay for her extravagances.

The wife of the last of the great dictators walked free from court after a trial that ended in humiliating defeat for the American government. As Imelda Marcos emerged blinking into the Manhattan sunlight on 2 July 1990, she carried in her heart a dark secret… the whereabouts of the missing millions she and her husband had milked from his impoverished land. Ferdinand Marcos ruled the Philippines in the manner of a robber baron. He used foreign aid and stole national treasures to finance a luxurious lifestyle. But he did not escape the consequences of his greed, for he died in exile and shame. His wife Imelda, dubbed the Steel Butterfly by peasants who gazed in awe at her extravagance and her ruthlessness, survived to face charges of fraud, grand larceny and racketeering. She had the dubious honour of being the first wife of a head of state to stand trial in the USA.

SHE HAD NO REGRETS

At her trial she gave no hint of the repentance that her accusers expected: rather they were subjected to Imelda's arrogant boasts about her lifestyle. From the first day she stepped into the dock in New York to face charges of racketeering, conspiracy and fraud and a possible sentence of 50 years in prison, she happily revealed the fabulous wealth she had enjoyed as wife of the president. Imelda and Ferdinand had viewed the Philippines as their personal fiefdom and appropriated, for their own use, bundles of aid-dollars donated by America. But their rule came to an end when Cory Aquino ousted the Marcos couple from power and then pressed the USA to put the pair on trial. But Imelda Marcos, however, was moved neither by the accusations nor the anger of her people. She did not regret her old life. Instead of feeling shame over her wealth, Imelda flaunted it. 'I get so tired of listening to "one million dollars here, one million dollars there," ' she yawned in court. 'It is so petty.'

When Imelda Marcos was found not guilty of the charges brought against her, observers thought that heads would roll in the

413

US Justice Department because, it was felt, they had not properly prepared the case against Marcos. The Justice Department spent £20 million preparing this case and they had all the resources of the State Department, the FBI and the CIA behind them. But they lost their case.

SACKS OF MONEY WERE DELIVERED TO HER HOTEL ROOM

The American government was under pressure from Marcos's successor, Cory Aquino, who hinted that the important US military bases in the Philippines might be in jeopardy if Imelda Marcos was not prosecuted by the US government.

But the Justice Department was hindered in its investigations by the Swiss banking system that prides itself on its total secrecy regarding clients' finances, while allowing the clients the same discretion – they do not have to reveal the source of their money. Vital documents relating to the Marcos personal accounts, hidden in the vaults of banks in Geneva and Zurich, were not released to the US prosecutors, despite damning testimony from Philippine National Bank officials, who could show documents and who claimed that, although she had never earned a penny during her rule, Imelda had had sacks of cash delivered to her hotel in New York every time she visited the city. But there was not enough evidence against the woman and she was found not guilty.

Despite her acquittal, the Philippine government insists that Marcos and Imelda may have salted away as much as £7 billion worth of national treasures, hard currency and bullion in banks and investments around the world. The arrest of the billionaire arms dealer, Adnan Khashoggi, on charges that he 'laundered' the Marcos fortune so that the US government would not be able to trace the money, were also dropped. His case only served to further the speculation that the Marcos couple were thieves on a fabulous scale.

In 20 years of power, initially as a democratically-elected politician but later as a despot who imposed martial law, Marcos and his Steel Butterfly drained the national economy. America supported his regime on the strategic Pacific islands because they saw the Philippines as a bulwark against communism. They maintained important military bases in the country, and pumped in millions and millions of dollars intended to improve the economic growth of the 62 million inhabitants of the islands.

Instead, these funds fell into the personal piggy bank of the state leader and his wife.

Imelda, a former beauty queen, became a symbol of grotesque greed to her fellow Filipinos, most of whom lived in frugal poverty. At the height of her career as 'leader's wife', she was spending £300,000 a week on clothes. Designer gowns from Paris and Rome were jetted over to her and she spent weeks touring Europe on shopping expeditions. After one shopping trip, she filled three sea containers with goods. Shoes were her quirky addiction. Three thousand pairs of Gucci, Christian Dior and Karl Lagerfeld designs were found in her wardrobes.

While she spent, her husband – a wily, shrewd politician – was gradually dismantling the democratic state which the world believed he was protecting.

Imelda, former beauty queen, who became more famous for her greed than her looks.

A PRESIDENT WITH A PAST

Marcos was born on 11 September, 1917, the son of a lawyer and school teacher, in a small town 250 miles from the capital of Manila. He trained as a lawyer and qualified for his bar exam with flying colours. In 1939, he was arrested on charges of murdering his father's political rival and was sentenced to life imprisonment. But in a retrial, when he cleverly conducted his own defence, the charges were dropped. During the Second World War, he claimed that he led guerrilla fighters against the Japanese conquerors, although this is disputed. Nevertheless, the story helped him become a representative in the Philippines Congress when he was only 31 years old, the youngest politician in the country. In 1954, after an 11-day courtship, he married Imelda. Ferdinand Marcos said that her love for him 'drove me to the pinnacles of success'.

In 1965, after the general elections, he became the President of his country. Ironically, he won on an anti-corruption platform. Throughout his 20 years in office, his salary never varied. He received £3,300 a year, yet he lived in great opulence. He rode in

Ferdinand and Imelda Marcos with the Pope during his visit to the Philippines in the eighties.

armour-plated Rolls-Royces, channelled millions of aid-dollars to secret bank accounts in Rome and Switzerland, while his financial advisers purchased, on his behalf, properties all over Europe and in New York. As his own greed increased, his patience with democracy wore ever thinner. He won re-election in 1969 in a campaign tainted by allegations that he had practised vote rigging, intimidation and corruption. Three years later, in 1972, Marcos dispensed with democracy in the Philippines and imposed martial law on the country.

HANDMADE LAVATORY PAPER

The attempted assassination of a senior military figure was the excuse for suspending democracy, though it has been claimed that the assassination was only a pretence, something Marcos set up so that he could justify his political move. Under the new martial rules, thousands of political enemies and dissenting journalists were thrown into jail, tortured and murdered. Then Marcos lifted martial law in 1981 to hold another election. However, his political opponents boycotted these elections, saying that to participate in the farce would only give Marcos a credibility he did not deserve. So the man held on to his immense political power. However, although his power was unchallenged, he became increasingly paranoid. His secret police continued to fill the prisons with rivals, while all political parties were kept under surveillance or infiltrated by Marcos informers.

During these dark days, the Steel Butterfly lived in bizarre luxury. Every detail of her style was richly excessive. Every roll of lavatory paper was handmade, silk-screen printed in Thailand and cost seven pounds. There was a storeroom of them in Manila's Malacanang Palace, and each of the building's 14 bathrooms was graced by two rolls of this exquisite tissue. When she fled her homeland in 1986, she took her collection of pearls that, when it was spread out, covered 38 square feet. She even coined a word for her own excesses – 'Imeldific'. Guests at the palace were treated lavishly. They got to keep the contents of the wardrobes in the rooms where they stayed as visitors. These wardrobes were stashed with furs, clothes and jewellery. In the main dining room, in a silver tureen, Imelda kept a great mound of Beluga caviar, renewed every day. And when she felt very generous, she would airlift a planeload of pals to New York for a little shopping. She could afford it. She headed 30 lucrative government corporations and she used the money for her own purposes. According to Filipino government investigators, Imelda, at one stage, was sending so many suitcases stuffed with cash to a bank in Geneva that the bank cabled her and asked her to stop because she was over loading the staff with work.

THE YOUNG IMELDA SANG FOR CANDY

If Imelda ever noticed her fellow citizens, including those from the seamy side of town, the barrios, where people lived next door to open sewerage ditches and had no running water, she still behaved as if she were royalty and she expected people to bow. But Imelda understood poverty. She came from a poor family and as a child had sung to American GIs for gifts of candy. She earned a living as a singer when she was a young woman. Her big break came in 1954 when she won a beauty contest and was introduced to the politician who would make her his Pacific empress.

Imelda preferred – naturally – to forget her poor youth. She banned a book called *The Untold Story of Imelda Marcos*, written by Filipino journalist Carmen Pedrosa. Pedrosa's book revealed that Imelda was once as poor as the people she now ruled over, and had been obliged to sleep on milk crates in the garage of a relative's house after her mother pushed her out of the family home. 'She did not want her poor origins ever to be known,' said Pedrosa. 'She conveyed a completely different image of herself, that she had been born with a silver spoon in her mouth. And that was important to them – because if the Marcoses had been born with wealth there would be no questioning of that wealth. When she went into the barrio, she was regarded as a celebrity. She would wear a gown in places where people didn't even have a toilet. She was just living a fantasy life in a very poor country.'

THE CIA VERDICT

The fantasy was almost shattered in 1972 when an assassin stabbed her with a foot-long dagger, as she was handing out awards at a beauty contest, but she only sustained a flesh wound. This incident reinforced Imelda's strange belief that 'God has great things planned for me and is watching carefully over me at all times.'

The CIA had their own impressions of Imelda Marcos. During the seventies, the agency prepared a character analysis of the woman, which was not flattering but accurate. It read as follows: 'Mrs Marcos is ambitious and ruthless. Born a poor cousin of landed aristocracy, she has a thirst for wealth, power and public acclaim, and her boundless ego makes her easy prey for flatterers.

Imelda Marcos playing stateswoman at her desk in the Plaza Hotel in the Philippines.

Although she has little formal education, she is cunning.'

Imelda's relatives prospered with her. Her brother, Benjamin Romualdez, masterminded the takeover of the Manila Electric Company. Brother Alfredo ran the national, government-controlled gambling industry. Initially Marcos outlawed gambling, but legalized it when he realized that huge profits could be made from this form of entertainment. William Sullivan, the US Ambassador to Manila from 1973 to 1977, said: 'When I was there foreign investors did not come into the Philippines without distributing shares to Imelda or some of her cronies. That was the way business was done.' American officials described the country as being run by two factions – the FM faction loyal to Ferdinand Marcos and the FL faction loyal to the first lady of excess, his wife, Imelda.

Imee, her beloved daughter, got in on the act too. A vice-chairman of a Filipino bank tells a story about four business people who had fallen behind with their kickbacks to the Marcos

Imelda was incredibly greedy. Her numerous homes were filled with vast amounts of valuable objects and furnishings.

gang. The four were summoned to the palace in 1985, where they were confronted by Imee. She had become her mother's book keeper, and she sat in front of the four, with a notebook on her lap and armed secret servicemen at her side. Rather than face the niceties of a torture chamber, they promptly paid the illicit funds to Imee. The first lady preferred to spend her money on jewellery and clothes and she lavished gems and couture collections on herself, whenever she felt depressed or sad. Documents drawn up by the Aquino government list some of Imelda's treasures: diamond bracelets, brooches and earrings valued at £1 million; 167 racks of designer dresses valued at £2 million; five fur coats, 400 Gucci handbags and a mere 68 pairs of handmade gloves.

But other documents were to make that lot seem like the remnants of a jumble sale.

MULTI-MILLION SPENDING SPREE

On one day in Switzerland in the late seventies, Mrs Marcos spent £9 million during a shopping spree. She gobbled up diamonds, rubies and pearls, along with a diamond-and-garnet-encrusted watch for her husband. Another US customs document proved that in seven days in May and the beginning of June 1983, she squandered £4 million on a shopping orgy in New York. Imelda also spent a great deal of money on diamonds, shopping at Cartier, Van Clef & Arpels and Tiffany. She then splashed out a further £21,000 on towels and bedsheets. Finance for these spending sprees came from the New York branch of the Philippine National Bank. Bank official, Willie Fernandez, testified at Imelda's trial that between 1973 and 1986 he personally authorized transactions of £24 million for Mrs Marcos.

'The call would come in: "Ma'am needs two hundred and fifty thousand cash", ' said a bank official who was granted anonymity at her trial. 'The money was carried to her in a big, over-sized attache case.' The prosecution called the bank 'Mrs Marcos's private piggy bank'.

The goodies inside her Manhattan townhouse made one angry customs official declare: 'Such opulence made me feel sick to the pit of my stomach.'

VALUABLE ITEMS JUST TOSSED ASIDE

Alan Ehrlichman. the auctioneer hired to sell the contents of this house for the Philippine government, described valuable crystal glasses found hidden in an oven; rare biblical manuscripts from the twelth century were stuffed under an old boiler; two gilt mirrors which belonged to Marie Antoinette's husband, King Louis of France, were found broken and mysteriously lying in water in the bath; hand-embroidered bedlinen had been left lying in damp piles which attracted mildew: 24-carat gold-plated taps were tarnished and dripping in every bathroom.

Ehrlichman said: 'It broke my heart. Many collectors aspire to work of that calibre but never attain it. Here's somebody who owned it who had no respect for it. It's a sacrilege. If two words summed up what I felt about it those words would be opulence and waste.' The house also had jacuzzis in every bathroom and a discotheque where Imelda would gyrate while her bodyguards would sidle up to her to ask her for a dance.

A stitched pillow on one of the many sofas in the room bore the inscription: 'To be rich is no longer a sin. It's a miracle.' Another read: 'I love champagne, caviar and cash.' And then there were also three baby grand pianos in her New York house.

Yet Imelda rarely stayed in this house, valued at £7 niillion. She preferred the comfort of a suite at New York's Waldorf-Astoria Hotel. But Ehrlichman said that while she wallowed in opulence, the servants were treated disdainfully and lived five beds to a room in the basement.

Between 1980 and 1986, Imelda drew on another account in New York. This was held in the name of her secretary and was credited with a whopping £19 million. She also used her wealth to commission expensive portraits of herself and her family from New York artists. One of them is a version of the Renaissance artist Botticelli's 'Birth of Venus'. His painting shows the goddess rising from a shell. In her version, Imelda is shown rising from the shell with her arms extending to embrace the world. She commissioned portraits of Nancy and Ronald Reagan, her husband Ferdinand Marcos, and General MacArthur – the wartime leader who liberated the Philippines from the Japanese occupation.

THE TIDE TURNED AGAINST THE MARCOSES

But the politics of the Philippines were changing. On 21 August 1983, Senator Begnigno Aquino, who had been imprisoned and then exiled by Marcos, returned to Manila. He was shot dead by a Marcos assassin, as he stepped from the plane at the airport in Manila. Marcos claimed that the murderer was a communist agitator, himself shot by government forces just after he had shot the returning exile. No one believed this story. Marcos sought to quieten the growing unrest of his people by calling for an election in 1986. After the votes were counted, Marcos declared himself the elected winner. However, Cory Aquino, the widow of the murdered exile, had won the support of the Philippine army and had convinced the United States that Marcos was a corrupt and unworthy figure.

Finally, confident that she had the full support of the army, Aquino toppled the Marcos regime. The Marcoses, with their entourage, fled their homeland on 26 February 1986 as, outside the palace gates, the mob bayed for their blood. Only hours after the deposed leader and his wife had left, this mob broke into the palace and were astonished by the excessive consumerism that they now confronted. The opulence that the Steel Butterfly and her husband had enjoyed was photographed for the world's amazement. Pictures of Imelda's shoe collection also showed closets the size of bungalows, built to hold her vast number of acquisitions.

The Filipino people wanted their money back and an international treasure hunt was launched. Jovito Salonga, the Filipino lawyer charged by his government to find the loot, said: 'They stole and stole and stole. And then they stole some more.

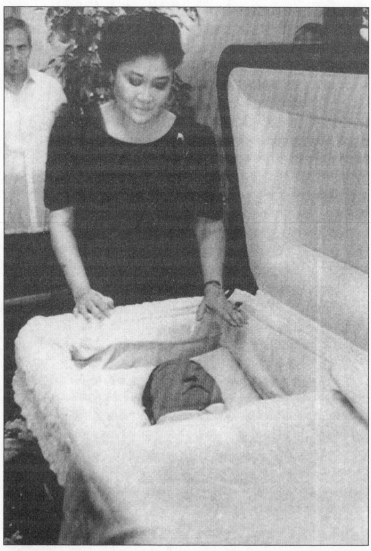

Ferdinand Marcos died in Honolulu. His wife says her last farewells

Not only did they take what was not theirs, they also seized businesses and created monopolies, granted exclusive import licences and guaranteed bank loans for associates and relatives, loans that they never paid back. As new businesses rose the first payments were delivered to the boss, Marcos, and it got so crazy that I would estimate that even he doesn't know how much he was worth. The time has come to return their ill-gotten gains to the Filipino people.' Salonga maintained that between them, they ran off with something in the order of £7–9 billion.

Imelda remained proud and arrogant and revealed herself as rather stupid, if cunning. When she arrived in Hawaii, seeking a refuge after fleeing Manila, she declared shamelessly: 'They call me corrupt, frivolous. I am not at all privileged. Maybe the only privileged thing is my face. And corrupt? God! I would not look like this if I was corrupt. Some ugliness would settle down on my system. My people will judge me innocent.'

FAIRY-TALE OF JAPANESE TREASURE

The Marcoses called it a 'despicable act' when the US government slapped racketeering charges on them. The CIA and FBI had built up an enormous list of crimes with which to charge the pair. They were charged with, among other things, fraudulent use of foreign aid, with the connivance of members of their family who controlled major Western-funded public works projects in the Philippines. 'There wasn't one pie, one cash register, one scam going that this duo didn't have their sticky fingers in,' said international money expert, John Stapleford. 'They were rotten to the core but blessed with a supreme arrogance which made them think that they really could get away with anything.'

Marcos was horrified that America turned against him. Imelda said they had been 'shamed' by their old ally. Shortly before his death in September 1989, Marcos came up with a novel explanation for his wealth, 'I discovered the treasure of Yamashita,' he said. 'That is the key to it all.' Lieutenant General Tomoyuki Yamashita was the Japanese commanding officer of the occupying forces in the Philippines during wartime. He is said to have stashed priceless works of art and gold bullion in secret caves. However, he was hanged in 1946 as a war criminal and he died without revealing the whereabouts of his hoard. But investigators on the trail of the treasure say it was just one more lie from Yamashita, a man who had spent his life evading the truth and destroying those who tried to tell it. The treasure is as much myth as reality and there is nothing to prove that Ferdinand Marcos ever laid his hands on anything other than all the money he stole from his own impoverished countrymen.

In July 1987, two US lawyers posing as Marcos allies, telephoned the exiled despot and claimed to be interested in representing him. They taped a telephone conversation in which he claimed to have £7 billion worth of gold bullion lying in secret vaults on the island of Mindanao. He didn't make any claim at this time that this gold was part of the fabled wartime booty of the Japanese general, Yamashita.

In 1991, Imelda and her son, Ferdinand Jnr., spoke at a political rally in Manila. There was bitter rivalry between the 'reformist' Aquino faction and those who favoured the Marcos family.

THE AMERICANS ARE UNKIND

Before she stood trial, Imelda, whose tears flowed freely during numerous press conferences, said: 'I have only one dream now. I am not asking for justice any more, I am asking for a divine human right to die, to be buried in my own country. I am shocked by all this inhumanity shown by America, they have not been nice to us – us who were such good friends to them.' She believed this statement.

Imelda was left alone to face the music when Marcos, suffering from a disease of the kidneys, died. 'He settled with a higher authority,' one embittered State Department official said. 'She faced earthly justice – and won.' The secrecy of banking laws protected her from detection, but there is no one in the Philippines or in the American intelligence agencies who believes that justice was done.

IMELDA'S 'DIVINE' MISSION

The Steel Butterfly returned to the land she looted, where she risked facing further criminal charges. She had lost none of the arrogance that was her chief characteristic. She took to calling herself a goddess, a deity who confronted mortal challenges and troubles and won. She explained: 'I must be a deity because I was given a divine mission, to return to my homeland, which I did. An ordinary mortal would not be able to stand what I did.'

MA BARKER

MACHINE-GUN MAMA

*She was a rare person – a woman who was a leader of
men and dangerous gangs; a woman who bred criminals,
deliberately teaching her sons to be wicked delinquents.
Ma Barker has secured her place in the annals of crime, for
her story is that of a truly evil person.*

Ma Barker was a mother who taught her children the three 'Rs' - reading, writing and revolvers. She had been brought up in the same rural area that Jesse James used to roam, and she was steeped in criminal lore. She taught her four sons - who became, under her tutelage, one of the most feared and ruthless criminal gangs in American history - to despise authority and follow the maxim that all laws were made to be broken. Unlike their contemporaries such as Pretty Boy Floyd and John Dillinger, who, although notorious, did not make much money from their crimes, the Barker boys did steal vast amounts of money and were very careful about publicity. They acted with stealth and skill, as they roamed across the United States, from the mid-west to Texas in the far south. And they had no qualms about killing. They were social misfits, encouraged by their own mother to live as habitual criminals.

Ma Barker was born Arizona Donnie Clark in Springfield, Missouri, in 1872, the daughter of a hard-drinking, illiterate ranch hand and a God-fearing mother who taught her to read the Bible and play the fiddle. She left school when she was ten, although she never adandoned her habit of reading lurid penny crime sheets which chronicled the exploits of the James gang and other villains of the Old West. Arrie, as she called herself, was particularly excited whenever she caught sight of Jesse, riding tall in his saddle at the head of his gang. In 1892, when she was 20 years old, she went into a kind of mourning when the evil Dalton Gang were riddled with police bullets during their last vicious bank robbery in Coffeyville, Kansas. She was a rare person – a woman who was a leader of men and dangerous gangs; a woman who bred criminals, deliberately teaching her sons to be wicked delinquents. Ma Barker has secured her place in the annals of crime, for her story is that of a truly evil person.

GET·DILLINGER!
$15,000 *Reward*

━━━ A PROCLAMATION ━━━

WHEREAS, One John Dillinger stands charged officially with numerous felonies including murder in several states and his banditry and depredation stamp him as an outlaw, a fugitive from justice and a vicious menace to life and property;

NOW, THEREFORE, We, Paul McNutt, Governor of Indiana; George White, Governor of Ohio; F. B. Olson, Governor of Minnesota; William A. Comstock, Governor of Michigan; and Henry Horner, Governor of Illinois, do hereby proclaim and offer a reward of Five Thousand Dollars ($5,000.00) to be paid to the person or persons who apprehend and deliver the said John Dillinger into the custody of any sheriff of any of the above-mentioned states or his duly authorized agent.

THIS IS IN ADDITION TO THE $10,000.00 OFFERED BY THE FEDERAL GOVERNMENT FOR THE ARREST OF JOHN DILLINGER.

HERE IS HIS FINGERPRINT CLASSIFICATION and DESCRIPTION. ———— **FILE THIS FOR IDENTIFICATION PURPOSES.**

John Dillinger. (w) age 30 yrs., 5-8½.
170½ lbs., gray eyes, med. chest, hair, med.
comp., med. build. Dayton, O., P. D. No.
10587. O. S. E. No. 559-646.

F.P.C. (12)

	M	9	R	O	O
	S	14	U	OO	8
13	10	O	O	O	
u	R	w	w	w	
5	11	15	I	8	
u	U	u	w	u	

FRONT VIEW

Be on the lookout for this desperado. He is heavily armed and usually is protected with bullet-proof vest. Take no unnecessary chances in getting this man. He is thoroughly prepared to shoot his way out of any situation.

GET HIM

DEAD

OR ALIVE

Notify any Sheriff or Chief of Police of Indiana, Ohio, Minnesota, Michigan, Illinois.

or THIS BUREAU

SIDE VIEW

Ma Barker copied the murderous methods of John Dillinger and taught her sons to do the same. The police eventually killed Dillinger on 22 July, 1934.

TRAINED IN VIOLENCE

By the end of the year, her grieving for the Daltons was mitigated by her marriage to George Barker, a common labourer every bit as coarse as she was. Weak and ineffectual, he winced under the savagery of his wife's tongue – particularly vicious after she had been drinking whiskey. He was a hag-ridden husband, dominated by his wife. But they managed to produce four healthy sons – Herman in 1894, Lloyd two years later, Arthur in 1899 and Fred in 1902. Every single one of them was trained in violence... and they were all to die by the gun, just as their mother did. They started life in Aurora, Missouri, and were known as 'The Four Horsemen of the Apocalypse' by their Sunday school teachers.

In 1908, perhaps driven out by the neighbours who believed that she had given birth to sons of the Devil, Ma moved her brood and her milksop spouse to Webb City, Missouri. There was money in this town, where recently gold had been discovered in the surrounding hills.

But Ma's dream of wealth was sadly at odds with the reality of their impoverished life; the Barkers continued to live in grinding poverty, in a shack made of tar and paper with no running water or electricity. It was the perfect breeding ground for the kind of resentment that turns a dissatisfied young person to crime.

'MY BOYS ARE MARKED'

Ma had a pathological hatred of authority and of those who made the slightest criticism of her crooked brood. Policemen, in particular, were regarded as prime suspects in a universal conspiracy against her sons. In 1910, when Herman Barker became her first son to get arrested for stealing, she astonished the neighbourhood policemen at the Webb City police station when, instead of berating her delinquent young son, she turned on the officers of the law with a tirade against them: 'My boys are marked.' she screamed at them. 'You'll burn in hell before you lay another filthy pig hand on a Barker boy!'

In 1915, after more run-ins with the law, the family upped and left for Tulsa, Oklahoma, where her husband had found a job as a railway worker. They still lived in soul-destroying poverty, and her sons continued to confront the law. These boys went through the whole catalogue of juvenile crime – from breaking and entering, to stealing cars and mugging.

NEW AND DEADLY FRIENDS

Ma Barker herself developed friendships with a motley assortment of bums, heels, conmen, robbers and murderers. She became very attached to an ex-con, called Herb Farmer, who ran a hideout for villains on the run in nearby Joplin, Missouri, and she met many big-name criminals of her day, men like bank robber Al Spencer, Frank Nash, Ray Terrill and Chicago hold-up men Francis Keating and Thomas Holden. Soon numerous shifty criminals sought refuge in her house, and these visitors regaled the impressionable

The Dalton Gang, laid out like big game safari trophies, were shot by the police during a bank raid.

boys with tales of murder, robbery and general mayhem. Psychiatrist James Alien, who has made a study of Ma Barker, said: 'This woman saw in the hoodlums and robbers that hung out at her home a reincarnation of the bandits that she idolised as a child. She was incapable of instilling in her offspring a respect for the natural laws and rules of society; she portrayed the underside of life as a kind of romantic, Robin Hood affair, which of course, to wayward young boys with limited education and even shorter attention spans, was exactly what they wanted to hear.'

The Barker boys, by the time they reached adolesence, were carrying guns and were deeply involved in the underworld. Ma Barker took great delight in hearing of the boys' exploits at the family dinner table, and was happy to dispense advice on how they could best become stick-up men or jewel-store robbers. In 1917 the Barkers were members of the Tulsa Central Gang, a loose-knit consortium of teenage hoods who robbed banks, post offices and country gas stations. Ray Terrill, who spent many hours with Ma plotting bank raids, took Herman with him on a number of minor robberies. After these outings, Ma would turn her son's pockets out to make sure he was not holding back her share of the spoils. Once she found a 50-dollar bill in the top of his sock and laid into him with the butt-end of a .38 police issue revolver.

In 1922 she kissed goodbye to the first of her crooked brood after Lloyd was caught during a raid on a post office, when he shot and wounded a guard. Nothing she could say or do would persuade the court that her boy was innocent and she was inconsolable when he was sentenced to 25 years hard labour in Leavenworth Jail, the state's penitentiary. Arthur was next in line for justice when, also in 1922, he was convicted of murdering a nightwatchman in a Tulsa hospital. Arthur was trying to steal a supply of drugs to satisfy his morphine addiction. He got 20 years in jail, despite an attempt by Ma Barker to bribe another man to plead guilty to Arthur's murder charge.

After Arthur went to jail, Ma Barker abandoned her husband, George, and descended into deviant sexual practices with young girls. 'Hell, when Freddie and the others weren't knocking off banks, they were running around trying to find young girls for Ma,' said James Audett, a reformed bank robber who had once been part of the Barker gang and was an expert on the family. 'The boys would bring the girls, all under-aged, to Ma and when the old lady was through with them, she would tell Freddie and Alvin Karpis, an associate of the gang, to get rid of them. Those two crackpots would just up and kill these poor girls and dump their bodies in lakes nearby. God, there were bodies of young girls floating all over those lakes because of crazy old Ma Barker. Disgusting. The whole bunch of them made me so sick that I only went on two jobs with them. They couldn't keep regulars in the gang because of the way they lived.'

'THEY WERE ALL KILL-CRAZY LOVERS'

'That was the key to them. Ma became a lesbian, and all the boys – with the exception of Arthur – were homosexuals, and there ain't nothing worse than a homosexual bank robber and killer. You see, if one of them saw a cop coming at them with a weapon they would shoot to kill because they thought their lover might be bumped off. They were protecting their lovers as well as themselves. Freddie killed a lot of people to save his sweetheart Karpis. They were all kill-crazy lovers.'

In 1926, Freddie received a fifteen-year sentence for the armed robbery of the main bank in Windfield, Kansas – a raid that had been organized by Ma. The only son not in jail was Herman. Ma, saddened by the loss of her sons, was never tempted to make Herman go straight, in order to keep him free; instead she encouraged him to join the Kimes-Terrill gang, a mid-western mob who specialized in stealing entire safes from banks. They would drag the safe out with a pulley and a truck, then blow it open. This method worked successfully on many raids but, in 1926, Herman was shot when a posse of policemen surrounded the gang during a raid on a Missouri bank. He scuttled home to Ma's hideout in Tulsa where, even as she tended to his wounds, she plotted new methods of robbing banks and stores. On 18 September 1927, Herman held-up a grocery store in Newton, Kansas, before fleeing town at the wheel of his getaway car with an unknown accomplice. On the outskirts of town, Sheriff John Marshall raised his gun to fire at the speeding vehicle, but was cut down by a hail of Thompson sub-machine-gun fire from Herman. Marshall died instantly.

The next day in Wichita, Herman was alone when he drove his car into a police trap. He emptied his machine gun and pistol at the law officers – then he withdrew a bullet he called his 'lucky piece' from his waistcoat pocket. It was his last round and, although he was wounded by return fire from his cop pursuers, he chose to blow his own brains out.

SHE DEVOTED HER LIFE TO FREEING HER SONS

Ma Barker was convinced that Herman had been executed by police, claiming: 'A Barker don't do things like that. Barkers weren't raised to kill themselves for pigs.' But an autopsy proved that he had, indeed, ended his short, violent life.

She maintained her lust for young girls, but knew that she needed a man to look after her while her boys were in jail. She took up with a penniless alcoholic, Arthur Dunlop, saying: 'A drinking man's better 'n no man at all.' Now Ma Barker divided her time between writing petitions to governors and prison wardens, asking for clemency for her sons, and maintaining a safe haven for villains on the run. She also began 'fencing' – selling stolen goods - for the rabble who stayed with her. J. Edgar Hoover, the legendary head of the FBI, would later say of her: 'It was the suicide of Herman, and the imprisonment of her other three sons, which changed her from an animal mother of the she-wolf variety to a veritable beast of prey. She slipped deeper into depravity and villainy.'

The money she received from the desperadoes she was hiding, plus her take from the sale of stolen gems and other valuables, soon meant that she no longer needed the spurious protection of

J.Edgar Hoover, crime buster extraordinaire, who ruled the FBI with an iron fist for fifty years. He went to war against the mobsters with astonishing success.

Arthur Dunlop, although she continued to live with him. She ignored his presence, however, as she devoted her life to freeing her sons. Ma said: 'I gotta have at least one of my poor babies free. At least one… it's all I ask. Who would deny a poor woman at least one of her brood?' In 1931, her pleas for clemency finally paid off when Freddie was released from jail. He brought with him his cell-mate and partner-in-crime, Alvin Karpis, who, by a freak quirk, had also wangled his way out of hard time. It was about the worst mistake the authorities could have made.

Now admitted lovers, the duo embarked on a Ma-inspired wave of terror. Karpis later explained: 'What I wanted was big automobiles like rich people had and everything like that. I didn't see how I was going to get them by making a fool of myself and working all my life.' Such an attitude delighted Ma Barker, so it was no surprise that Karpis became a surrogate son, replacing Herman in her affections.

Freddie had fallen deeply in love with Karpis and, in jail, they made a pact that they would never bluff their way past lawmen after doing a job, nor risk a high speed chase. They would simply kill and take their chances.

In the summer of 1931, with the Great Depression ravaging the lives of millions of ordinary Americans, the pair embarked on a crime wave, robbing several jewellery and clothing stores. Captured twice and confined in small-town jails, they escaped easily and continued their spree. They often returned home to Ma with details of their exploits, and to give her a share of the spoils. They persuaded Ma to move with them from Tulsa to set up their crime HQ in a farmhouse in Koskonong, Missouri. Karpis – a skilled electrician, thanks to his years in the federal slammer – rigged the house with an elaborate alarm system to keep cops at bay. Under the aliases of Dunn and Hamilton, the two lovers roamed the mid-west states. In July of that year they successfully held up a hardware store and took $1,000 before making their getaway. Two days later, however, Sheriff Charles Kelley spotted them sitting in a car, dividing up the loot. He pulled his gun to arrest them, but they fired first and he fell dead on the road. It was time for the Barkers to hit the road, and find someplace safe until the heat died down.

Ma cleared out of the Missouri farmhouse, and headed for St Paul, Minnesota, well known as a place where gangsters could hide from the law. Once more, she set up a refuge for gunmen, while she became closely associated with the well known hijackers Jack Pfeifer and Harry Sawyer. Ma planned the hijackings of long distance trucks and Freddie and Karpis carried them out. The goods were fenced through Pfeifer and Sawyer, and Ma used her share to pay lawyers in her fight to free her other sons from prison. Now poor Arthur Dunlop, overshadowed and detested by the criminal family into which he had married, was no longer wanted. His bullet-riddlen body was found floating in the icy waters of Lake Freasted, in Wisconsin, towards the end of 1931. It was Freddie Barker who pulled the trigger on his own stepfather. Freddie and Karpis had, by now, acquired some criminal clout of their own, and no longer relied on Pfeifer and Sawyer. Many hoodlums and gunslingers were prepared to work for Freddie and Karpis, and the pair began to run their own gang. Between 1931 and 1933, they robbed dozens of banks, killing numerous people along the way, including a marshall called Manley Jackson. Several armed guards and policemen were also killed. Ma Barker and Freddie were now among the most-wanted criminals in America, for they had stolen an incredible $500,000 in cash and had murdered many people.

In October 1932, Arthur Barker was released after being paroled. Now Ma had two sons to run her business in crime. In May 1933 Ma had a brainwave. She had tired of bank robberies and plotted a kidnapping. She reasoned in her warped brain that, just as she herself would pay any amount of money and pull any string to get a loved one out of jail, so a wealthy family would hand over any amount of cash to get one of their brood back. Teaming up with Fred Goetz, a member of the old Al Capone gang, wily Ma Barker hatched a plan to seize William Hamm, the head of a wealthy brewing dynasty.

MA'S FIRST KIDNAPPING

On 15 June 1933 after Hamm left his brewery in St Paul, he was snatched by Freddie and Karpis. He was ordered to sign a ransom note, was fitted with a pair of goggles stuffed with cotton wool, and driven for several hours to the Ma Barker hideout, where he was

Fred Barker, the beloved son who died on 16 January, 1935, after a four-hour gun battle with FBI agents in Florida. Arthur Barker was killed when he tried to escape from Alcatraz prison in California on 13 June, 1939.

placed under the machine-gun guard of Goetz. For three days the brewer's family consulted with police, and their own consciences, before deciding to pay the ransom. On 17 June, the ransom was thrown from a car speeding along a dark road on the outskirts of St Paul; the plot hatched by Ma Barker had worked perfectly and William Hamm was returned safely to his family.

The Barker brothers, with Ma as the mastermind, then resumed their old trade of robbing banks. In August 1933 they hit a payroll truck in St Paul and stole $30,000. But in the subsequent shootout with cops, one policeman died and another was seriously wounded. Another policeman was killed in a botched Chicago raid a month later.

MA AS MASTERMIND

Ma decided to go back to kidnapping, believing that the ease with which they ransomed Hamm was proof that this was a lucrative, and relatively safe, criminal pursuit. Feeling the heat after their numerous killings, with the Barker names on thousands of FBI wanted posters, Ma proposed the kidnapping of Edward Bremer, a wealthy Minneapolis banker.

Ma masterminded the snatch meticulously, spending several months on the crucial planning stages before unleashing her boys to do the dirty work on 17 January 1934. Bremer dropped his 8-year-old girl off at school that morning and began driving to his office. He was ambushed at a traffic light by Arthur, who held a gun to the victim's head.

Bremer was forced to sign a ransom demand for $200,000. The Bremer family did not contact the police, but their attempts to pay the ransom were botched on several occasions. Meanwhile, the psychopathic Arthur Barker tried to kill Bremer but his brother Freddie stopped him with the words: 'Sure, blow his brains out, but you know what Ma will think about that!' The mere mention of the one and only person Arthur feared was enough to make him put his twin revolvers down. Edward Bremer lived to be reunited with his family after the ransom cash was delivered on 17 February 1934.

PLASTIC SURGERY FOR MA BARKER AND HER BOYS

Karpis and Freddie Barker, together with Ma, now chose to have plastic surgery to alter their appearances and so elude the law. They selected a doctor called Joseph Moran, who was also an alcoholic. Moran drugged them with morphine before setting about his crude surgery. Ma was about to undergo her operation when she saw the results that Moran had achieved on Freddie. Moran was murdered by Freddie and Arthur on Ma's orders.

Ma insisted that the gang should split up, so she sent Arthur to live in Chicago. She rented a house in the rural backwater of Oklawaha, in Florida, where Karpis and other gang members were regular visitors. In 1935, following an underworld tip-off, Arthur was arrested outside his Chicago apartment by FBI agents. In normal circumstances he would have reached for his gun and started blasting away – but he had left his weapon indoors and was captured without a struggle.

A search of his apartment revealed a detailed map and directions to the hideout in Florida, used by Ma and Freddie. This was a welcome breakthrough for the police who alerted FBI agents. An armed siege of the hideout was carefully planned.

THE END OF MA BARKER AND HER SONS

On 16 January 1935, agents surrounded the house and one inspector, wearing a bullet-proof jacket, drew the short straw: he actually had to approach the house and tell Ma to surrender. She opened the door the merest crack and hissed through yellowing teeth: 'To hell with you, all of you.' As she closed the door the quaking law enforcer heard her say: 'Let the damned Feds have it – shoot!' Ma, the cool brains behind the murderous brawn of her thieving sons, went to an upstairs window to begin firing a gas-powered automatic rifle at the men ringing her lair. While Freddie opened up with a sub-machine gun, the FBI returned automatic fire and poured tear gas shells into the house. For 45 minutes, the air crackled and hissed with the sound of gunfire and splintering wood.

Finally, when the return fire from the house quietened and stopped, a handyman, who worked for the Barkers, volunteered to go check on the outlaws. He found Ma Barker with three bullets in her heart, Freddie dead from 14 machine-gun bullets. Ma Barker's reign as the berserk gangland matriarch was over.

Her two remaining sons were to die violently. Arthur was killed by guards in the Alcatraz fortress jail in San Francisco Bay on 13 June 1939, as he tried to escape. Lloyd served his full 25-year stretch for murder and was freed in 1947. He married soon after his release but his wife stabbed him to death in 1949. It was a fitting end to the story of the Barker boys who did everything for a wicked woman, their own Ma.

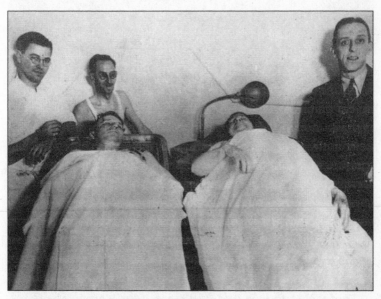

Side by side for all eternity – Ma Barker, right, and her son, Fred, after they died resisting FBI agents. Few mourned their passing.

ULRIKE MEINHOF

QUEEN OF TERROR

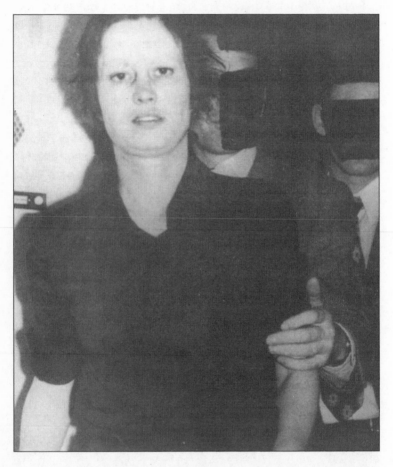

*One of the most enigmatic political figures of our time,
Ulrike Meinhof was well educated, bright and the radical
darling of the national media. But she chose to become an
outcast, a fanatic and a ruthless killer. Hers is a very
mysterious tale.*

Not all of Germany's post-war children shared in the vision of the economic miracle, the rebuilding of their shattered industries and bombed-out cities to heights greater than those achieved by the Third Reich. Nestling in the schools and universities, in certain strata of the intelligentsia and the academics, the seeds of a new revolution were being nurtured by a breed who looked to the east and, in particular, the German Democratic Republic, hiding behind its wall and its wire, as the model state of the future.

These coffee-bar radicals and middle-class communists believed that capitalism was a dead concept and that the time for the true proletarian revolution had arrived. But their vision held no hope for such a utopia to be achieved by peaceful means – the new Jerusalem was to be forged with guns and blood. Into such a maelstrom of fury and fire fell Ulrike Marie Meinhof to be indelibly linked in history with Andreas Baader when they formed the Baader–Meinhof gang which scorched its way across Germany to become one of the most successful terror groups the world has ever known.

A QUICK WIT AND READY CHARM

She was born in Lower Saxony on 7 October 1934, a child of the misfit generation called 'Hitler's Children'. Spawned in his rise to power, old enough to see him bring her country to its knees, she lived through the conflagration and came out of it an orphan. Her father died from cancer at the outbreak of war and her mother in 1948. A foster mother took care of her during her high-school years – a period when she matured into an intelligent, thoughtful young woman, highly gifted in classes, polite to all she met and possessed of a quick wit and ready charm. She was also a pacifist who devoured works by Bertrand Russell and Vera Brittain. Her views were shaped by her mother: but also by the turbulence of the era which left its stamp on her young mind.

By the time she was 23 and studying for her post-graduate doctorate at the University of Münster she had embraced many ecological, left-wing and pacifist causes, including ban-the-bomb campaigns and calls for Germany to resist growing militarism from the right. It was mainstream stuff – even Willy Brandt, the anti-Nazi socialist who went on to become Chancellor of the Federal Republic, was a supporter of similar trends. In 1959, her reputation as a chic radical and avant-garde academic was established. As Ulrike knew how to keep an audience interested, she was asked to speak at an anti-bomb conference in the capital, Bonn. It was there that she met Klaus Rainer Rohl, the Marxist editor of the student newspaper *Konkret*. They fell in love and were married in 1962, and Ulrike gave birth to twins the following year.

Although she was committed to her domestic life, her husband and family, Ulrike's infatuation with the politics of the Left began to deepen. In the permissive sixties, as England swung to a beatnik sound and 'free love' were the two words on everyone's lips, the old order of capitalism and class seemed to her due for destruction. But even as she steeped herself more and more in left-wing ideology she prospered within the system she was one day to despise.

She and Rohl led comfortable lives. Rohl began to translate some pornographic Swedish books into German at a considerable profit while Ulrike's income expanded as she took on the editorship of *Konkret* and increased its sales. In their avant-garde world they attracted an eclectic mix of friends – some rich, some poor, but all imbued with a passion to change the world. She became a successful talk-show host and a radio personality, wheeled out to give the 'alternative' viewpoint whenever an issue of the day was being dissected by the media. And not once, during these years of comfortable affluence, with a white Mercedes parked outside her door and her cellar stocked with fine Rhine wine, did Ulrike Meinhof for a moment consider that violent upheaval was the only answer to all the ills of society.

Towards the end of the sixties, two events occurred that went a long way to derailing her peaceful and ordered world. The first occurred in 1968 when she divorced her husband – a committed womaniser who finally indulged in one affair too many. The second was the trial of a young revolutionary – Andreas Baader.

The brooding good looks of Andreas Baarder helped attract many women to his violent cause.

Baader, born in Munich on 6 May 1943, was a believer in a violent solution to the class struggle that he saw confronting modern German society. Work-shy, handsome, appealing to women, he drifted in his twenties to Berlin where he was a regular in the agitprop demonstrations that happened daily in the old imperial capital against everything from squatters' rights to increased students' fees. In 1967 Gudrun Ennslin, a committed communist, left her husband with her young child to live with Baader, whom she had met at a student demo. It was during this period that Andreas Baader began to evolve his philosophy of anger and class hatred, leading him to call for an armed guerrilla war against the state – his so-called 'People's War'.

ULRIKE'S FIRST STEP TOWARDS TERRORISM

However, their very first act of armed resistance went badly wrong. He and Ennslin planted incendiary bombs in Frankfurt department stores in a protest at the Vietnam War. They were seen escaping, soon tracked down and put on trial. It was while the trial was going on that Ulrike Meinhof began to speak out for him and for the action he had taken. The committed pacifist had taken the first step towards becoming an urban terrorist – absorbing the attitude that any human life is worth taking if the cause is worthy enough.

Baader, Ennslin and two other guerrillas who were caught torching the department stores were sentenced to three years each for arson. In June 1969, after serving 14 months each, they were released pending the outcome of an appeal, but Baader, his lover and one other militant fled to France. When they were re-captured on an Interpol warrant in 1970 and sent back to jail in Germany, the flame of righteous indignation burned deep within Ulrike Meinhof. Now living in Berlin and her credentials with the Left firmly established, her apartment became a meeting place for political sympathizers. In 1970 Ulrike committed herself to the path of terrorism when she plotted with Baader cohorts to spring him from jail.

There was a group in sympathy with Baader and his cause. It was known as the Red Army Faction, a Marxist cadre founded by Horst Mahler, a lawyer who defended Baader at his trial, and was committed to the violent overthrow of the West German state. Linked to an underground network of revolutionaries via university and communist party contacts, the Red Army Faction also had contact with Middle Eastern terror groups.

On 14 May 1970, Baader was freed in an audacious escape from the Institute of Social Studies in Dahlem. The prison authorities had allowed him to further his academic studies at the institute, although he was kept under guard. After the getaway Mahler, Meinhof, Baader and Ennslin fled to a terrorist training camp in Jordan where they hoped to learn advanced terrorism.

STUDYING WITH THE PLO

Under the tutelage of the Palestinian Popular Liberation, Meinhof was an adept pupil. She learned how to roll out of a fast-moving car without seriously injuring herself and how to aim accurately with a recoiless pistol. But the relationship between the Arab hosts and their German guests was a frosty one: each side accused the other of behaving arrogantly. Apparently the Arabs were particularly annoyed by Baader, who refused to take part in commando exercises saying they were 'unnecessary' for the kind of war he was planning back in Europe.

On 9 August, tension between the two groups reached breaking point and the Germans were asked to leave the training camp. Ulrike wanted to stay longer – she was particularly interested in bombs and how to fuse them correctly and she was reluctant to depart before she had completed her bomb-making course. But the Palestinians insisted and the gang slipped back into Germany, where they were hidden in the flats and houses of the radical friends whom Ulrike had cultivated during her political activities with the Left.

The scene of devastation at Frankfurt Airport after a bomb was planted by terrorists. Three people were killed and twenty-eight injured.

ULRIKE SENT HER SONS TO THE TERRORIST CAMP

Ulrike was so convinced by the cause of the Red Army faction that she arranged for her seven-year-old twins to be packed off to the terror camp in Jordan that she had just left. She wanted them to become fighters in the Palestinian conflict with Israel. This ambition was, she explained, the ultimate expression of her love for them. The children travelled no further than Palermo, Sicily, on their journey to the Middle East when they were stopped by police, who promptly arrested the terrorist who was acting as their escort. Weeks later the camp their mother had chosen as their new home was reduced to rubble in an air strike by King Hussein's forces.

Ensconced in their safe houses and apartments, Ulrike and her colleagues set about planning the 'People's War'. First, they needed that essential tool - money. Mahler coordinated a series of bank raids intended to provide the loot needed to buy explosives, false papers, arms and the places needed to store these goods. In one day they hit three banks, but Ulrike was disappointed because she netted just £1,500. There were more robberies and a mixture of bravado with clinical planning ensured their repeated successes.

Karl-Heinz Ruhland, a working-class car mechanic, was brought into the gang because he was able to supply them with a constant stream of getaway cars. The elitist, intellectual fighters looked down on this lowly working-class recruit, but he was to be the first of two lovers Ulrike chose from the men of the Red Army Faction. Gossips said her sexual choice demonstrated her belief that the class system was dying and that she did not recognize it anyway. However, Ruhland had his view. 'I am a worker she has studied,' he said later. 'But although she is intellectually far above me, she never reminded me of that.'

Ulrike became the quartermaster for the group, securing weapons from Palestinian contacts and planning raids on government offices for official paperwork and stamps. These latter were used to forge documents that would give the gang access to places like army camps and government research facilities. The raids on the banks continued and the money – some £100,000 in 1970 – mounted up. But while the institutions of capitalism were being hit, the pillars of the system were not. The People's War had yet to define its targets clearly.

In October of that year Mahler was arrested when he blundered into a police trap, and leadership of the gang fell to Baader. Slightly unbalanced and prone to erratic mood swings, Baader needed the intellectual and analytical mind of Ulrike to help him keep his guerrilla army together.

THE CRAZY GANG JOINS THE RED ARMY FACTION

In 1971, after the gang robbed two banks in Kassel and escaped with £15,000, police pressure to capture them became intense. Germany's Kriminalpolizei – known as the Kripo and the equivalent to the CID – formed a taskforce assigned to eradicate them. One by one, the members of the Red Army Faction were arrested. At one stage just Baader, Meinhof and six others remained free, but there was no lack of willing recruits to their twisted cause. Some of these came from a revolutionary group calling itself the SPK. Soon the blood would start flowing, as the gang switched from robbing banks to wiping out human lives.

Christian Stroebele (left) Kurt Groenwald (centre) and Rolf Clemens Wagner (right) were drawn to the Baader-Meinhof cause. They deliberately cultivated an 'ordinary' appearance to avoid suspicion from both the neighbours and police but Wagner is believed to have played a major role in the killing of Hans Schleyer.

The SPK – Socialist Patient's Collective – was the warped brainchild of Dr Wolfgang Huber of Heidelberg University, who taught that mental illness was created by the state: change the political system and psychiatric illnesses would disappear. He schooled his patients in explosives, in surveillance techniques, in judo and other forms of unarmed combat. His wife Ursula assisted him. By mid-1971 the SPK, a bunch of psycopathic killers, believed that they had found their spiritual home with the Red Army Faction. The Kripo gumshoes trailing this network of misfits called them the Crazy Gang.

On 22 October 1971, a patrol car in Hamburg spotted Margrit Schiller, an SPK member, walking out of a railway station. She met two comrades. The patrol officers, Helmut Schmid and Heinrich Lemke, chased them into a park. But the trio were heavily armed and the policemen presented just the kind of target these crazies favoured. Schmid died with six bullets in him. Lemke was lucky to escape with only a leg wound.

A NEW RECRUIT LIQUIDATED

The killing of the policeman gave added impetus to the police in their determination to capture the Red Army Faction. Margrit Schiller was arrested two days after the killings. She carried a considerable amount of weaponry and a book written by Meinhof called 'The Church Black Book Volume 1'. It contained a list of pastors, doctors, journalists and lawyers who could be relied upon to give aid and succour to the Red Army. This book, with its damning list, caused an outrage in a Germany that was disgusted by the ruthless violence of these urban guerrillas.

Nevertheless, the killing continued. On 22 December 1971 Herbert Schoener, a policeman, was shot dead as the gang robbed a bank in the Rhineland town of Kaiserslautern. Aged 32, with a wife and small children, Schoener was shot three times and was severely wounded by flying glass before he died. The robbers seized £33,000 in loot, but the bloodshed and the screams were too much for Ingeborg Barz, a 19-year-old girl who had recently joined the gang. She wanted to go home to her mother in Berlin. perhaps resume her job as a typist in a small clerical firm and try to forget her life as a revolutionary and forget the screams of the children frightened in that bank raid. But Meinhof decreed a policy of 'liquidation' for any member of the Red Army who wanted to desert. Gerhard Müller, a gang member who would later turn state's evidence against his former comrades, said Meinhof flew into a rage when she heard Ingeborg say she wanted to leave. Müller said that Ulrike Meinhof drove Ingeborg to a remote gravel pit near Aachen, where Andreas Baader executed the girl.

ULRIKE'S 'BABY BOMB'

More policemen were killed – one of them with dum-dum bullets fired by a Crazy Gang member. Meinhof, meanwhile, perfected a series of pipe bombs and a device called a 'baby bomb'. Thisconsisted of an explosive device slung from shoulder straps, so that it lay on a woman's belly and gave her the appearance of being pregnant. Meinhof, the brains of the bombing campaign, mapped out targets at government offices near Hamburg, Heidelberg, Augsburg, Munich and Frankfurt.

At Frankfurt, on 11 May 1972, Jan-Carl Raspe, now Ulrike's lover and a leader in the group, Baader and Ennslin planted several pipe bombs in the American Army's 5 Corps HQ. The explosion was devastating, killing a Lieutenant Colonel and wounding thirteen other civilians and military personnel. The US Army was deemed a target by Ulrike because she said America 'pulled the

The chilling faces of evil. These are some of the women warriors enlisted in the Red Army.

strings' in Europe, and also for its involvement in the Vietnam War, a conflict that the Red Army was opposed to for obvious ideological reasons.

The following year the campaign was stepped up. Five policemen were injured in Munich's CID offices when time bombs left in suitcases exploded. In May, the wife of a judge who had signed arrest warrants for the terrorists, was seriously wounded by a bomb that went off as she turned the key in her car ignition. On 19 May 1972, Ulrike personally planted the bombs that ripped through the offices of the right-wing publisher Axel Springer in Frankfurt. Three more Americans died a week later in a bombing at a barracks in Heidelberg. Ulrike's bombs were perfected in their design by Dierk Hoff, a mechanical genius who swopped his occupation as a sculptor to become a political terrorist. He rnanufactured timers so sensitive that armaments manufacturers would later ask for the designs so that they could be applied to commercially manufactured ordnance.

The police were frustrated that they could not find the core of the gang, even though several lesser members had been captured and several more killed in shootouts on motorways and outside banks. At the height of their terror campaign, the Red Army could still count on some 35 safe houses and a fleet of 40 cars with false number plates to ferry them around Germany with ease and privacy.

THE DEADLY AMBUSH

The ease with which they operated and the carnage they left behind caused acute embarrassment and concern to the West German government. They knew that often Meinhof slipped across the border to East Germany to replenish arms supplies, but it was extremely difficult to trace her because of the multitude of aliases under which the gang leaders operated. Ulrike Meinhof was the brains behind the entire operation, even though much of the blood was spilled by Baader and Raspe.

Seven days after the Red Army committed the murders in Heidelberg, people leaving their homes in a Frankfurt suburb to go to work, did not give a second glance to the corporation workers unloading turf outside a row of garages in a neat suburb. There was a patch of scrubland nearby and observers thought that the council labourers were at long last going to lay grass on it. In fact, the labourers were Kripo marksmen, and the turf was to be used as a barricade if they needed such protection. The Kripo had received a tip off that in one of the garages was a Red Army weapons cache. After a lengthy wait the police swooped on the site and found a formidable weapons dump – but none of the gang. They replaced the explosives and guns with harmless substitutes and waited for their quarry to show.

At 5.50 a.m. on I June, a Porsche drew up in the street where the police marksmen waited and three men got out. Two walked to the garage while the third, Raspe, the lover of Ulrike Meinhof, waited nervously as he scanned the gardens nearby. Years as a criminal fugitive had taught him well: he smelled something was up and decided to flee. He let off a hail of bullets but he was brought down by a rugby-tackling lawman.

Andreas Baader and Holger Meins were in the garage when tear gas bombs were hurled at them. The two terrorists fought back but Baader took a bullet in his right leg. Eight minutes after the first tear gas bomb was released Meins appeared with his arms in the air. Moments later, police stormed the garage where Baader lay with blood pumping from his wound.

THE LAST REFUGE

A week later Gudrun Ennslin was seized in a Hamburg boutique. She was picking out sweaters to try on and carelessly threw her leather jacket on to a chair while she went into the changing room. An assistant, who picked it up to fold it neatly, felt the unmistakeable coldness of a gun barrel. She told the manageress who feared that the woman might be a robber and she in turn called the police. When they arrived Ennslin went for the weapon but after a fierce fight the female terrorist was overpowered.

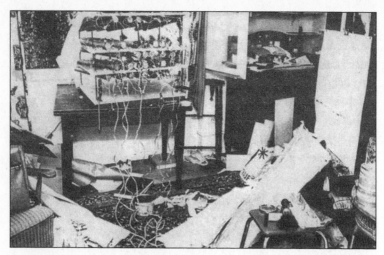

A 42 barrel home-made rocket launcher. The Red Army held a couple hostage in their own flat, then aimed this weapon across the street at the home of Germany's chief prosecutor but the police apprehended the gang before they launched the rocket.

Only Ulrike remained at large, the ideological force behind the Red Army Faction and therefore the most wanted member of the group. She knew the organization was badly damaged by the police activity. Her lover had been arrested, her co-leader arrested, her 'family' dead, dispersed or incarcerated. Even her friends on the political left had deserted her, for they were now thoroughly frightened and disgusted by the violence and robbery that she and her group had practised.

Desperate for refuge, after a safe house in Berlin fell under police suspicion, Ulrike and Gerhard Müller turned up at the home of Fritz Rodewald, a left-wing schoolteacher who, initially, had been sympathetic to her cause. But Rodewald was a socialist, not a terrorist. He was a respected president of a teacher's union, a man with a family and a position in the society she wished to destroy. He took the advice of friends and called the police.

When Kripo squads swooped on the apartment, Ulrike was unpacking her luggage. Nestling among her clothes were three 9mm pistols, two hand grenades, one sub-machine gun and one of her beloved bombs. Gerhard Müller was to become the state's witness against her. But she struggled like a wildcat when the police seized her and eventually had to be sedated. Her face looked puffy when the mugshots were taken at the police station but, in fact, life on the run had been unkind to her; Ulrike had lost three stone and now weighed less than seven stone.

The capture of Ulrike Meinhof was the final nail in the Red Army coffin. She had been the driving force behind the whole operation; she was much admired by her kind, and many guerrilla groups sprang up to commit numerous terrorist acts, including bombing the West German embassy in Sweden, in an effort to free her. On 21 May 1975, in the ultra-secure £5 million Stammheim Prison, the trial of Meinhof, Baader, Ennslin and Raspe opened – Meins would have joined them but he had starved himself to death in captivity.

The industrialist Hans Martin Schleyer was kidnapped on 13 Ocober, 1977. He was photographed beneath the Red Army emblem before the Baader-Meinhof gang killed him.

FOUR THOUSAND MARCHED AT HER FUNERAL

For a year the trial dragged on, a litany of bank robberies, murders, arsons and explosions. The defendants said nothing save that they did not recognize the court. Finally, Ennslin broke in May 1976 and admitted that the gang had carried out a series of murder-bombings. Four days later Ulrike tore her yellow prison towel into strips, tied it to the bars of her cell and slowly strangled herself to death.

The agitprop brigades that she had once so proudly led poured into the streets of several European capitals, claiming that she had been murdered by her guards during the night, although independent examinations of her corpse proved that she had ended her own life. It was an unexpected end to the woman who intellectualized terrorism, who once wrote in a training manual for her fellow guerrillas: 'We women can do many things better than the men. We are stronger and much less anxious. This is our People's War and we must all fight it alongside the men. Violent revolution is the only answer to society's ills.' When this misguided follower of the Left was buried in Berlin, 4,000 sympathizers, many of them masked, marched to her grave.

Her death unleashed new waves of terror that culminated in the murder of industrialist Hanns Martin Schleyer and the seizure of a Lufthansa airliner bound from Majorca to Frankfurt in October 1977. Eventually the plane landed at Mogadishu after a five-day ordeal in which the captain was murdered and the 86 passengers terrorized. A German commando team, under the guidance of British SAS officers, stormed the plane. Three of the four terrorists were killed outright with one wounded, but no passengers were hurt.

The news caused Raspe, Baader and Ennslin, now all serving life sentences after being found guilty of the kidnappings and murder, to kill themselves – the men with smuggled pistols, Ennslin by hanging.

When police issued the list of wanted terrorists in connection with the killing of Schleyer – murdered in the hours after the failure of the Mogadishu hijacking – it was significant that half of them were women from the same background and class as Ulrike Meinhof.

Jillian Becker, who chronicled Meinhof's life, said: 'She was an ambitious, love-hungry child. Her education bred both a puritan and a rebel in her, the one never reconciled to the other. She was drawn to Utopian Communism.'

But those who fought her would say that somewhere within her was a bitter hatred, and not a longing for love or the need for affection, that turned her into the terror queen of Europe.

A US Army personnel office after a Red Army firebomb attack in 1981

CHARLOTTE BRYANT

KILLING KILLARNEY KATEY

Kate was an Irish beauty who was generous with her charms and beauty. The soldiers loved her. But her obsession with sex drove her into a bizarre marriage and the dreadful role of poisoner.

Her real name was Charlotte McHugh but to scores of British troops garrisoned in her native Ireland she was Killarney Kate. A native of Londonderry, Charlotte was a woman of ill-repute who dispensed her favours to the hated troops then stationed in her homeland. The time was the early twenties, and sections of Dublin were still in ruins after the abortive Easter Rising by the Irish Republican Army.

Kate's was a dangerous profession made doubly risky by the clientele she sought out. The nationalist militants seeking to overturn Westminster rule to establish an Irish free state did not take kindly to one of their own indulging men whom they regarded as the enemy. But Kate was a free-spirited, determined young woman who brooked no advice and slept with whomsoever she chose – and she chose British troops, for the simple reason that they had money to spare.

A SPECIAL QUALITY

She had hair as black as coal, a milky white complexion, full breasts and bright green flashing eyes, and she provoked, not exactly love, but certainly lust in the occupying army. Killarney Kate captured the imagination of many a man and long, long after she swung from a gibbet for her crime, the memory of her lived on in many a soldier's head and heart. She braved the threats of tar and featherings from her countrymen, as she boldly flaunted her profession. It could, murmured the Irish sages and righteous gossips who watched her grow up, only end in tragedy.

Regiment after regiment, platoon after platoon, soldier after soldier visited Killarney Kate for her services. But Kate was bored and restless in her native land, fearful that her future offered only more of the same for the rest of her life, and she was searching for that one special soldier who would one day take her to England, where she would bury her past and live happily ever after.

OVER THE WATER

She thought she had realized her dream when she met Frederick Bryant, an easy going military policeman in the Dorset Regiment. Bryant had served in the last great battle of the First World War when he was shot in the legs during the closing days of the campaign. His wounds were to cause him pain throughout his life. But all physical and mental pain were forgotten when he met the beautiful Kate, who stole his heart. In him she saw the passport across the water to the land she dreamed about, with cities like London and Manchester.

In 1925 he was discharged from the army and married Kate in Wells, Somerset. They started their life together on a local farm where he was employed as the head cowman. All went well for the first few months, but rural life in England turned out to be every bit as hard as country living back in Ireland. They lived in a rented cottage with neither electricity nor running water, ate poor food and barely had enough money for the necessities, let alone any of the luxuries that Kate had dreamed about.

Kate turned once again to prostitution while her husband toiled 12 hours a day, often in remote areas of the farm. Her 'gentleman callers' brought her luxury gifts like sides of beef and bottles of champagne while, with the money she earned, she became one of the best customers at the little village shop in the hamlet of Over Compton. Even though she bore five children for poor cuckolded Fred, she never let her motherly duties interfere with her profession. Local legend has it that she enjoyed sex every bit as much as the men who pleased themselves with her. Her neighbours, of course, painted a black picture of her, but she was never troubled by their wagging tounges. Indeed her motto was: 'To hell with fishwives – and their simpering menfolk too!' Fred, who knew about his wife's activities, appreciated the money she brought to the domestic budget.

But this sweet, if strange, life came to an end when Kate fell madly in love with one of her callers. On 11 December 1933, she entertained a gypsy called Bill Moss. She believed that she had met a man as darkly mysterious, as sensual as herself. Moss was classically handsome and very charming. She said of him: 'Bill was more of a man than all the rest of them put together. There was a magic between us. It was like trying to hold back the sea at high tide: I couldn't deny what was passing between us even if I had wanted to.' The high tide washed over them – and caught in its backwash was Fred, who, perhaps wanting to please his wanton wife, invited the swarthy ne'er-do well to stay in their home.

When Fred went to work in the mornings Moss jumped from his place on the settee into the marital bed. Pretty soon this arrangement came to an end: Kate declared her love for the gypsy wanderer and Fred was consigned to the couch. They were evicted from their cottage when Fred's employer heard the village tittle-tattle about the strange arrangement. The threesome were to be evicted from other homes. Once, Fred walked out on Kate but he soon returned, to live with Kate and Moss in the bizarre three-way relationship.

The last home that Kate shared with her husband, Fredrick Bryant.
The cottage was near the Dorset village of Dover Compton

However, in May 1935, Fred began to suffer from a mysterious illness. He thought, at first, that the shrapnel inside his body was affecting him. Several times that month, and in subsequent months, he was doubled up in agony, unable to move, and was seized by the most excruciating cramps. Doctors diagnosed an acute case of gastroenteritis, brought on by his rugged outdoor life and poor diet. Fred began to suspect that Bill Moss was the cause of the illness but then gypsy Moss suddenly moved out, apparently no longer in love with Kate. However, Fred's home was soon occupied by another intruder.

A LADY FRIEND

Kate had struck up an intense friendship with a woman called Lucy Ostler, a widow with six children. Fred suspected that his wife's sexual urges had taken a lesbian turn. He was determined that this new 'friend' would not take over where the gypsy left off. But on 21 December 1935, Mrs Ostler spent the night in his cottage. Fred, however, was too ill to argue. That night the excruciating cramps returned and he was rushed to hospital but died the next morning. The surgeon at the hospital could not diagnose the cause of the abdominal pain that brought death. Fred had been a healthy, well-built man, burdened by hard work but nevertheless fit. The surgeon ordered an autopsy: the results revealed that the old soldier, who had survived the bombs and bullets of the Western Front, had been poisoned with arsenic.

Kate and her children were placed in the care of the local authorities, while the police searched the cottage and questioned neighbours about Fred and Kate's marriage. The investigation went on for many weeks, but there was no evidence to reveal the poisoner. However, after both Kate and her new friend, Mrs. Ostler, were hauled off to an identity parade to be scrutinized by a pharmacist, who had reported selling arsenic to a woman several weeks before Fred's death, Mrs Ostler brokedown.

THE GREEN TIN

Although neither she nor Kate were picked out in the line-up, Ostler went to the police and blurted out her story: 'There was a green tin in her (Kate's) cupboards. She pointed at it and said: "Don't touch that. I must get rid of it." I asked her what was inside it but she refused to tell me. A few days later I was cleaning under the boiler, raking out the old ashes, and I saw the tin, all burned and charred. I threw it into the yard because the ashes were to go on to the compost heap. It's probably still there now.'

Luckily for the police it was – and, even in its charred state, clearly recognizable as the container that the pharmacist claimed he had sold to a woman. The tin was sent for scientific analysis to University College London where it was confirmed that the tin contained traces of arsenic.

Kate was arrested, charged with wilful murder and told that, if found guilty, she could expect the maximum penalty as prescribed under the legal system – death by hanging. The prosecution built

The kitchen of the cottage where Kate, her husband, her gypsy lover, Bill Moss and Kate's five children lived

its case on the bizarre lifestyle that Kate enjoyed with her husband, Fred Bryant, and Bill Moss, and then with Mrs Ostler. Both these lovers appeared as chief prosecution witnesses, perhaps for fear that otherwise they would be linked with the crime. Moss, whose real name was Leonard Edward Parsons, had tangled with the police previously on account of some petty crimes he had committed, and perhaps he did not wish to incur their displeasure once more. When the trial began on 27 May 1936, Kate found Ostler and Moss arraigned against her, as were her two eldest children, Lily aged ten and Ernest, twelve. Both had been deeply fond of their father and were extremely aggrieved by their mother.

It seemed that no one would support poor Killarney Kate. Sir Terence O'Connor, the Attorney General, led the prosecution and set the trial's tone when he announced: 'The prosecution contends that the prisoner destroyed her husband, in order that her marriage might be at an end… crime for which there can only be one penalty and one we heartily endorse: death.'

Fredrick Bryant in his Dorset Regiment uniform. He was to suffer all his life from wounds sustained in the First World War.

THE POISON STORY

Ostler's testimony came first. She said on the night that Fred died, she heard him coughing in the main bedroom. Kate was sleeping on a chair in the sitting room, the same room that Ostler was occupying. Later, she claimed, she heard Kate trying to get Fred to drink some beef extract. 'A few minutes later I heard him vomiting,' she said. 'Later he was taken so queer he had to go to hospital.' She said that Kate wept when she learned her husband had died. But Ostler told the court that she found this strange, claiming that Kate once confided that she hated Fred. Ostler said: 'In that case, I said to her, why didn't she go away and she said she couldn't provide for the children and didn't want to leave them behind.' Perhaps Ostler's most damning evidence was her testimony that she used to read aloud murder accounts from 'penny dreadful' magazines to Kate, who was illiterate. She told the court that she read the story of how a woman in America had poisoned her husband. According to Ostler, Kate's ears had pricked up at this story and she had turned to her friend to ask: 'How do you think I would get rid of someone?'

However, outrage was expressed in court and in the press about the prosecution's use of Kate's children to testify against her. But called they were, although their evidence was of limited use: it centred on a small blue bottle which they alleged Moss used to threaten their mother.

Kate's passionate eyes burned into her former lover as he was led into the witness box, yet Moss's testimony centred on his affections for her, though he repeated a conversation he had had with her concerning a tin of weedkiller. 'It was one day in 1935,' he said. 'I was standing outside the kitchen door when I heard Mr Bryant say to his wife, "What's this?" "It's weedkiller," she replied.' With these words, Moss managed to suggest to the court that Killarney Kate had contemplated weedkiller as a means of killing her husband before she switched to the more lethal poison, arsenic.

The burnt tin of poison that proved to be damning evidence at Kate's trial. It is flanked by undamaged tins of the same brand.

Expert Home Office testimony seemed to confirm Kate's long, premeditated campaign against her husband. Dr Gerald Lynch, the department's senior analyst, said samples taken from Bryant's corpse showed that he had been slowly and systematically fed the poison over many months. He painted a picture of a man who had done no harm to his wife and, indeed, had gone out of his way to accommodate her special needs and desires, slowly dying in agony from a malady that he could not fight and that he could not understand.

A QUICK JUDGMENT

In all, there were 30 witnesses against Kate and not one in her defence. She presented a pathetic figure in the dock, a lost case who, unable to read and write, seemed baffled by the weighty and majestic court proceedings unfolding before her. She denied, as best she could in her simple terms, that she had murdered her husband in order to win back Moss. Under further questioning, she said that her relationship with Mrs Ostler was merely a friendship and did not elaborate upon it.

All Kate could do was refute the suggestion that she had murdered her husband. But the others had no motive to kill him. Moss had returned to his wife. Mrs Ostler had been in Fred's cottage for only one night and was not around him to administer poison over a prolonged period. The trial at Dorchester Assizes took two weeks, and the jury were out for an hour. When the jury foreman appeared, he pronounced the word 'guilty'. Kate took this calmly but became hysterical when, moments later, Mr Justice MacKinnon donned the black cap and solemnly announced that she would die upon the scaffold at Exeter jail. In a state of collapse, the frightened prisoner was led by prison warders into the condemned cells beneath the court.

An appeal was lodged and the defence introduced testimony from a professor in London who was an expert on the effects of arsenic. Unfortunately, it was evidence that fell on deaf ears. Lord Chief Justice, Lord Hewart, said: 'This court sets its face like flint against attempts to call evidence which could have been made available at the trial. Moreover, in this case, it is clear that there has been no mistake. The court will not listen to the opinion of scientific gentlemen bringing their minds on evidence that they have not heard.' But even though the appeal was dismissed, the public

Kate pictured with Ernest, one of the five children she bore Fredrick Bryant. She was, by all accounts, a loving if carefree, mother.

HOW MRS. BRYANT FACED DEATH SENTENCE

DORSET POISON TRIAL DRAMA

CONVICTED MURDERESS

Four-day Ordeal

MUTE EVIDENCE OF ARSENIC TIN

CAMERA DODGER

TWO MEN WARDERS "AS THE JUDGE CALLED HIM"

FATEFUL SCENES ON FINAL DAY OF THE TRIAL

THE JUDGE'S SUMMING UP

A Simple Question For The Jury

IRRELEVANT

A WOMAN'S AGONY

Beer and Barley

THE VERDICT

A SMILE

HOW MRS. BRYANT SENTENCE

The local papers gave full coverage to the trial of a murderess. It was unusual to have a woman accused of this crime, and the fact that a mother of five children was sentenced to death caused a horrified reaction throughout the country.

468

conscience had been aroused by the proceedings. Questions were raised in Parliament and there was a public call for a retrial. There were press articles about the fate of her children, and of how Kate, in her condemned cell at Exeter jail, had turned to God. Her repeated assertions of her innocence were also widely reported. So vociferous was she in protesting against the wrongful judgment that a leading member of the campaign against the death penalty pledged £50,000 in the poor woman's defence.

The majesty of the law, as represented by Mr Justice MacKinnon, frightened the accused, an illiterate country woman.

DON'T LET THEM KILL ME

Kate was learning to read and write and composed a moving, if simple, letter to King Edward VIII in which she stated: 'Mighty King. Have pity on your lowly afflicted subject. Don't let them kill me on Wednesday. From the brink of the cold, dark grave, I, a poor helpless woman, ask you not to let them kill me. I am innocent.' This sad appeal brought no personal response from the king. Did His Majesty even see the letter?

At 8 a.m. on 15 July 1936, Killarney Kate saw dawn come up for the last time. She was led to the scaffold by two warders and the condemned woman listened as a chaplain read the service for the dead. Five minutes later she was pronounced dead.

Was she guilty? The question has echoed down the years. There was no motive to drive the lover, Moss alias Parsons, to murder Fred and, as the poison was apparently administered over a long period, no time for the new acquaintance Mrs Ostler to have been the culprit. Criminal historians have looked back time and again on the case of Charlotte McHugh, the girl known to soldiers as 'Killarney Kate'. Charles Skipple, a criminologist in the United States, who specializes in studying doubtful verdicts, said: 'I think she did it. Her's was the classic defence that echoes in jails around the world, "I'm innocent." And yet she couldn't prove that innocence while the jury obviously believed the proof of the guilt. It's the way of the world, the system we live by. Imperfect, of course, but all we have and all we shall probably ever have.'

PARTNERS IN CRIME

BONNIE & CLYDE
A KILLING LOVE

*The true story of Bonnie and Clyde is far more sinister than
the movie. He was a homosexual and she a nymphomaniac,
both were obsessed with guns and violent death and thrived
on the publicity that surrounded them, even sending pictures
of themselves to newspapers. Their small-time hold-ups
were only an excuse for an orgy of killing.*

Few villains achieve in their own lifetime the status of folk hero. Robin Hood of Sherwood Forest was one who did, and in our own times so did Ronnie Biggs, the Great Train Robber whose bravado and contempt for the law has earned him a certain popular respect. However, time adds lustre to even the most vicious criminals, and their evil is forgotten as myth gives them the glamour of brave individuals, outsiders who defy the constraints imposed by those in power.

Two such misplaced criminals were the professional thieves and murderers Bonnie Parker and Clyde Barrow, who went on the rampage during the Great Depression in America. Although they were ruthless killers, they have been immortalized in film, song and popular legend. They weren't very good robbers – most of their thefts were from gas stations, grocery stores and small-town diners. But they displayed a brutality and worked with a wild audacity that has earned them a place as heroes in the myth of folklore.

Semi-literate and wholly without compassion, they roamed the Great Plains states of Missouri, Kansas and Oklahoma in their quest tor easy cash. They loved their guns and their violent acts, cloaking themselves in the mystique of their mission and recorded themselves for posterity in photographs.

With Buck Barrow, Clyde's brother, and other bandits, they formed the Barrow Gang, a nomadic outlaw tribe that criss-crossed state lines, terrorizing the small businessmen and farmers who were every bit as much victims of the Great Depression as themselves.

Their relationship was an odd one, for Barrow was a homosexual, Parker virtually a nymphomaniac. Together they found a kind of love, a bond between misfits, focussed on firearms and violent death.

Clyde was born on 24 March, 1909 into extreme poverty in Teleco, Texas. One of eight children, his older brother Buck – who would later take orders from him – taught Clyde how to steal and hot-wire cars. After petty crime as a juvenile, and time spent in a boys' reform school, Clyde graduated to robbing roadside restaurants and small, country filling stations.

The shattered Ford V8 in which the gangster pair met their death.

Often there was no more than a handful of dollars and some loose change to steal from these places but Clyde reasoned they were safer to rob than banks. His brother was sent to prison in 1928 after he was caught on a raid on a diner. With the heat on him Clyde drifted to Texas. In January 1930, feeling peckish while wandering around Dallas, he dropped into a café called Marco's and was served a hamburger by a vivacious and pretty waitress. Her name was Bonnie Parker.

Born on 1 October 1910, was the daughter of a bricklayer, Parker a petite blonde package of boredom – 'bored crapless', as she confided to her diary at the time. She listened to the tall tales that the customer spun her about life on the road. Later that night she met him for a date, but there was no sexual interest on his part. Rather, they fuelled their friendship with each other through tales of robbery and mayhem. Parker, married to a convict serving 99 years for murder, moved into a small furnished apartment in Dallas with Barrow.

Guns became the consuming passion of this strange pair. Parker was thrilled by the pistols that her beau wore bolstered beneath his coat, and they took regular trips to the farmland outside Dallas for target practice with revolvers, rifles and sub-machine guns. Soon Parker was every bit as good a shot as Barrow was. Parker undoubtedly saw in her trigger-happy new friend the means of escape from the life of menial work that bored her so much.

They soon took to robbery, she would drive the getaway car – despite the fact that Clyde was a much better driver – while Clyde ran into the stores and cleaned them out at gunpoint. He would then run back to the car, jump on the running board and cover them as the car raced away. The thrill of these escapades was almost sexual for Parker, who could never find satisfaction with Barrow. He had confessed that he became homosexual in the reform school and she satisfied her considerable sexual needs with a series of one-night stands and with the men who would later drift in and out of the Barrow Gang.

Three months after they teamed up Clyde was behind bars, having left his fingerprints all over the scene of a burglary in Waco, Texas. He was arrested at the Dallas apartment and sentenced to two years, but he didn't stay to complete his sentence. His brother Buck had broken out of jail and Clyde wrote a coded letter to Bonnie asking her to spring him. Together, she and Buck travelled to Waco, with Parker wearing a .38 police issue revolver strapped to her thigh. She escaped the attentions of prison guards due to an incompetent search and contrived to slip the weapon to Clyde. He managed to break out that same night and rode freight trains across the plains states to Ohio.

Clyde Barrow stayed free for just a week before he was arrested again and this time sent to Eastham Jail, the tough Federal penitentiary from which his brother had escaped. His mother, Cummie Barrow, deluged the state governor with pleas for leniency; pleas that were answered on 2 February 1932 when he was released on parole. The prison was a crucial turning point in his life – after experiencing it he vowed to Parker, who waited to greet him at the gates, that he would rather die than ever go back inside. He had been tortured in the jail dubbed 'The Burning Hell', beaten with a whip and made to perform exercises until he dropped. He also killed a man, Ed Crowder, a cellblock informer, with a lead pipe, but authorities at the penitentiary did not credit him with the killing until after Clyde's death.

Parker was the next to go to prison after they stole a car and were pursued by police. Clyde escaped after crashing into a tree and running across fields, but Parker was caught and sentenced to two months. While she was inside, Clyde continued to rob the small-town stores and highway gas stations. In Hillsboro, Texas, he murdered 65-year-old John Bucher in his jewellery store after taking just ten dollars from the till. It was when Bonnie was released that their wild and cold-blooded killing spree began in earnest.

On 5 August, 1932 Clyde murdered two lawmen, Sherriff Charles Maxwell and his deputy Eugene Moore. He intended to rob the ticket seller at a barn dance in Atoka, Oklahoma, when the lawmen saw him loitering suspiciously. 'You better come out into the light boy, so I can see you better,' said Sherriff Maxwell, the last words he ever spoke. Clyde lifted up his overcoat and shot the two men at point-blank range with two automatic weapons.

This photo of Bonnie was to become a famous image of the wild outlaw girl, and Clyde cuddling his beloved firearms. The pair often sent photographs of themselves to the press for they delighted in their notorious fame.

A BUNCH OF NUTTY KILLERS

The bizarre couple then began their deadly odyssey across America. They robbed an armoury in Texas of an arsenal of sub-machine guns, ammunition, small arms and rifles. They fired indiscriminately into a dozen state troopers who had set up a roadblock in Texas, wounding several. They held up liquor stores, gas stations and grocery outlets, all for a few dollars. They even kidnapped a sherriff, stripped him and dumped him on the roadside with the parting words: 'Tell your people that we ain't just a bunch of nutty killers. Just down home people trying to get through this damned Depression with a few bones.'

On the road they lived like old-fashioned outlaws, sleeping by camp fires, surviving on wildfowl they shot and peanut butter sandwiches. At night they would get drunk on bootlegged bourbon whiskey and Parker would write turgid romantic poetry that bemoaned their lot in life – that they were persecuted by the establishment and that in reality they were a new breed of hero. A sense of foreboding hung over the two of them; both sensed that they were not long for the world and that they would die young and die violently.

In the autumn of 1932, Bonnie and Clyde headed for New Mexico with gunslinger Roy Hamilton who had joined them, but they decided that pickings were not as rich there as Texas, so headed back. Hamilton, an accomplished robber, was also as perverted as the duo he now allied himself with. He regularly slept with Bonnie ... and with Clyde. This bizarre triangle seemed to suit them all.

They killed indiscriminately and often. Clyde murdered a butcher with eight bullets when the man lunged at him with a cleaver after Clyde had stolen $50 from his store. He murdered Doyle Johnson in Temple, Texas, when he tried to stop them stealing his car. Two lawmen, staking out a house in Dallas for another robber, were gunned down when Clyde turned up instead. And together they kidnapped gas station attendant turned apprentice-robber William

Jones, who was to travel with them for the next 18 months. This fellow traveller would later give lawmen many details of the criminals' life.

Like gypsies, they criss-crossed the south-west, continuing to hold up shops and garages. They picked up brother Buck again, together with his wife Blanche, and the robberies increased. In Kansas they robbed a loan company office where Bonnie saw her wanted poster for the first time. She was so excited that she and Clyde were 'celebrities', she fired off a dozen letters to prominent newspaper editors, complete with snapshots of her and Clyde that they had taken on the road. She perpetuated the myth that they were fighters against authority – authorities like the banks that were foreclosing on poor farmers and businessmen. She made no mention, of course, of the pathological delight they both took in killing.

At this time she was working on a turgid, autobiographical poem. 'The Story of Suicidal Sal' which would later reach the newspapers.

We, each of us, have a good alibi,
For being down here in the joint.
But few of them are really jusfied,
If you get right down to the point.
You have heard of a woman's glory,
Being spent on a downright car,
Still you can't always judge the story,
As true being told by her.

As long as I stayed on the island,
And heard confidence tales from the gals,
There was only one interesting and truthful,
It was the story of Suicide Sal.

Now Sal was a girl of rare beauty,
Though her features were somewhat tough,
She never once faltered from duty,
To play on the up and up.

She told me this rule on the evening,
Before she was turned out free,
And I'll do my best to relate it,
Just as she told it to me.
I was born on a ranch in Wyoming,
Not treated like Helen of Troy,
Was taught that rods were rulers,
And ranked with greasy cowboys…

The poem was interrupted at this point due to a police raid on a hideout they used in Joplin, Missouri. Bonnie and Clyde, Buck and Blanche fired more than 1,000 machine-gun bullets at the police coming to get them, killing two of them. Later she finished the poem and mailed it.

Then I left my home for the city,
To play in its mad dizzy whirl,
Not knowing how little of pity,
It holds for a country girl.
You have heard the story of Jesse James,
Of how he lived and died,
If you are still in need of something to read,
Here's the story of Bonnie and Clyde.
Now Bonnie and Clyde are the Barrow gang,
I'm sure you have all read
How they rob and steal
And how those who squeal
Are usually found dying or dead.

There are lots of untruths to their write-ups,
They are not so merciless as that;
They hate all the laws,
The stool pigeons, spotters and rats,
If a policeman is killed in Dallas,
And they can't find a fiend,
They just wipe the slate clean,
And hang it on Bonnie and Clyde.

If they try to act like citizens,
And rent them a nice little flat,
About the third night they are invited to fight,
By a sub-machine gun rat-tat-tat.

A newsboy once said to his buddy:
'I wish old Clyde would get jumped,
In these awful hard times,
We'd make a few dimes,
If five or six cops would get bumped.'

They class them as cold-blooded killers,
They say they are heartless and mean,
But I say this with pride,
That once I knew Clyde,
When he was honest and upright and clean,
But the law fooled around,
Kept tracking them down,
And locking them up in a cell,
Till he said to me
'I will never be free
So I will meet a few of them in hell.'

The road was so dimly lighted,
There were no highway signs to guide,
But they made up their minds,
If the roads were all blind,
They wouldn't give up till they died,
The road gets dimmer and dimmer,
Sometimes you can hardly see,
Still it's fight man to man,
And do all you can,
For they know they can never be free.

They don't think they are too tough or desperate,
They know the law always wins,
They have been shot before,
But they do not ignore
That death is the wages of sin.

From heartbreaks people have suffered,
From weariness some people have died,
But take it all and all,
Our troubles are small,
Til we get like Bonnie and Clyde.

Some day they will go down together,
And they will bury them side by side,
To a few it means grief,
To the law it's relief,
But it's death to Bonnie and Clyde.

Those in authority were appalled by the public's interest in Bonnie and Clyde. The pair were written about in popular magazines, their images were in all the papers. Here, 'souvenirs' of their vagabond life are assembled – stolen car plates, clothing and baggage.

The robbing went on. They switched mostly to small banks in the rural towns of Indiana, Minnesota and Texas. A marshall was killed in cold blood outside the town of Alma and a 200-strong posse set off after the gang. They were holed up in a rented log cabin at a country park near Platte City in Missouri but the manager became suspicious when they paid the rental in small change – the loot from several of their nickel-and-dime gas station hold-ups. The manager of the Red Crown Cabin Camp alerted police who, upon hearing the description of the guests, assembled a small army to lay siege to the rented cabin. It was 24 July 1933.

In the ensuing confusion they escaped, leaving three officers dead. But Blanche had taken a slug in her leg, Clyde was grazed on the head, Bonnie was grazed with a bullet in her ribs and Buck … Buck was dying from a rifle bullet in his head.

NO PLACE TO GO

They escaped to a woodland area between Dexter and Refield in the rural state of Iowa where they did their best for Buck. But because they were always on the road, and without a network of contacts like those used by contemporary gangsters such as Ma Barker and John Dillinger, there was no place to hole up and get the medical attention Buck badly needed.

They were debating how to leave the wounded Buck when Clyde intuitively sensed a movement in the trees. Suddenly bullets began to rain down on their campsite. They returned fire with rifles and machine guns, even the mortally wounded Buck fired more than 1,000 rounds at the lawmen. Bonnie and Clyde managed to bolt into thick undergrowth and escape but Buck was riddled with bullets. The posse found Blanche prostrate across his corpse, weeping inconsolably.

With the heat on, the duo headed back to the north and Minnesota, reasoning that there would be less trouble in a state where they had committed relatively few crimes. They were practically bums now, stealing washing from clothes-lines and foraging for scraps of food. Jones, the kidnapped garage attendant, was with them and he later told police: 'This was not the life I expected when I joined up with them. We was nothing better than hobos.'

In October, fed up with his diet of raw vegetables stolen from fields, Jones hopped on a freight train back to Texas, was arrested, and told police about the antics of the gang, making sure he disassociated himself from the killings. 'It's them two,' he said. 'I ain't never seen anyone enjoy killin' as much as they do.' The following month Bonnie and Clyde drifted back to Texas for a meeting with his mother at a roadside picnic spot. But the pair barely escaped with their lives – his mother had been followed by a sherriff's posse who ringed the site. Once again alerted by some kind of sixth sense, Clyde drove straight past the rendezvous site. The back of the car was struck by bullets and both he and Bonnie were wounded in the legs but not seriously.

After pulling off a few more small robberies, they teamed up again with Hamilton – after springing him from a jail with minor thugs Joe Palmer and Henry Methvin – and the Barrow Gang was back to strength once more. The FBI, because of the murders and the transportation of weapons and stolen cars across state lines, was now in on the hunt and the officers were instructed to shoot-

Police hold a distraught Blanche Barrow after they shot dead her husband, Buck Barrow.

to-kill and ask questions afterwards. J. Edgar Hoover, celebrated head of the FBI, warned his men that Clyde was a 'psychopath – he should be killed like a rattlesnake'. Even other gangsters, knowing about their bloodlust, decided that there should be no honour among thieves. Charles Arthur 'Pretty Boy' Floyd, the gangster, was furious when he learned that the psychopathic pair had entered territory that he regarded as his own in the Cookson Hills, northern Minnesota. 'Don't feed them and don't give them shelter.' he ordered his cohorts and criminal associates. 'Stick the law on them if you can. They are vermin and have nothing to do with our people.'

Public opinion was rapidly turning against them. The banks they robbed were forced to close because they were suffering in the hard times, as were the businesses they raided. Soon the newspaper readers who had adored her romantic poem realized that there was nothing Robin Hood-like about their exploits. They were simply greedy and ruthless killers.

KNOW THINE ENEMY

Soon only Methvin was left with the gang. Hamilton had argued with Clyde and gone his own way. Palmer dropped out with chronic stomach ulcers. The heat was on like never before, particularly in Texas where a lawman called Frank Hamer, who had gunned down 65 notorious criminals during his career, was given the task of hunting down Bonnie and Clyde.

Hamer analysed every move they made, drew up maps and charts of all their movements over the previous years and discerned a pattern of sorts in the type of places they hit and the routes they took. 'I wanted to get into their evil minds,' he said, 'Know thine enemy was my maxim and I learned it well.' Several times during the early months of 1934 Hamer and his men came upon campsites that the duo had abandoned just hours before, but he was determined to stay on their trail.

In April that year, after hiding out on a farm in Louisiana, they returned to Texas to see Bonnie's relatives and hopefully lie low. But, as they neared the outskirts of the town of Grapevine, motorcycle police Ernest Wheeler and Harold Murphy rode past them. When they crested a rise in the road in front, Clyde pulled the car over and stopped. The motorcycle cops, their suspicions aroused, turned around and came back towards them. As they drew level with the car Clyde murdered them both with both barrels of a shotgun. Two weeks later in Oklahoma, when their car got stuck in mud. they were approached by two police officers. One died with a revolver bullet in the chest; the other was luckier – he was slightly wounded.

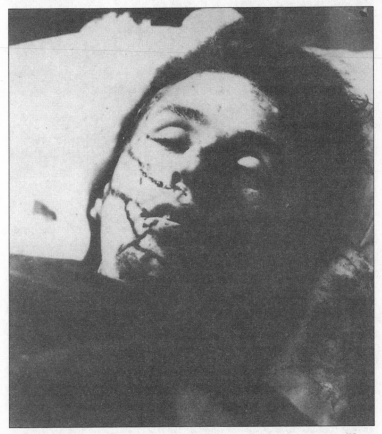

Bonnie Parker at peace at last after a wild and dangerous life.

Her family gave Bonnie a fine funeral ill-suited to a killer.

The key to capturing the outlaws lay with Methvin, who was still running with them. His father Ivan offered to help trap them if Hamer would agree to granting his son a pardon. Hamer, needing Bonnie and Clyde more than him, agreed to the deal. Henry Methvin, seeing a way out for himself, agreed to cooperate with his father when he next contacted him. Henry slipped away from a hideout shack in Shreveport, Louisiana, which was promptly surrounded by Hamer's armed Texas Rangers. Soon a posse had hidden themselves along the road leading to the shack; they were armed with Browning machine guns, high-powered rifles and numerous grenades and tear gas bombs.

At 9.15 a.m. on 23 May 1934, the V8 Ford which the couple had been using for the past week – they changed licence plates every day – crested a rise in the road leading from the hideout. Clyde was at the wheel, his shoes off, driving with bare feet. He wore sunglasses against the strong spring sunshine. Next to him sat his deadly moll in a new red dress she had bought with stolen loot some weeks previously. Stashed in the car were 2,000 bullets. three rifles, twelve pistols and two pump-action shotguns.

A FRIGHTENED DECOY

Methvin Snr had agreed to be a decoy. His truck was parked at the edge of the road and Clyde drew level with it. Clyde asked him if there had been any sight of his son. Methvin, almost quaking with fear, saw a truckful of black farm labourers coming down the road and he panicked, diving for cover beneath his own vehicle. A sherriff with the posse named Jordan suddenly yelled for the duo to surrender. But this was like a red rag to a bull for this homicidal pair. In one swift motion Clyde had his door open and a shotgun in his hand. Bonnie was equipped with a revolver.

This time there was no escape. A murderous rain of fire battered the car. More than 500 bullets slammed into the bodies of the gangsters and they were literally ripped to pieces. Clyde was slumped backwards, his foot off the clutch pedal. The car was still in gear and it inched ahead, coming to a halt in a ditch. The posse of lawmen continued to pour fire into the wreck for four whole minutes after it had come to a stop.

As newspaper headlines around the world shouted the news of their deaths, local residents were charged a dollar a head to view the mangled corpses on a morgue slab. Thousands paid to look.

Ray Hamilton, the robber who ran with them, was eventually executed less than ten years later for other murders. Just before his death, he accurately described Bonnie and Clyde: 'They loved to kill people, see blood run. That's how they got their kicks. There was many times when they didn't have to kill, but they did anyways. They were dirty people. Her breath smelled awful and he never took a bath. They smelled bad all the time. They would steal the pennies from a dead man's eyes.'

The Parker family tried its best to paint Bonnie in a different light. The horribly inaccurate inscription on this murderer's tombstone reads thus: 'As the flowers are all made sweeter, by the sunshine and the dew, so this old world is made brighter, by the likes of folk like you.'

JUAN & EVITA
THE CORRUPTIBLE PERSONS

Proud dictator Juan Peron and his nightclub singer Evita presided over an evil and repressive regime. They brought their country to the verge of bankruptcy as they looted millions from charities and the state to fill their Swiss bank accounts. And they did it all in the name of the Argentinian people they claimed to love.

They were a most unlikely double act, this notorious nightclub singer and the ambitious army colonel, but together they shaped the course of South American politics and still enjoy near-mythological status to this day. Sir Andrew Lloyd Webber's musical *Evita* was not the only reason that Eva Duarte, mistress of Juan Peron, became a household name. In the southern hemisphere, in the land of the pampas, Peronism has become more than a political movement; it is almost a religious affirmation, and to those who supported them Juan and Evita were the demi-gods who put Argentina on the world stage.

However, it was, mostly, a clever show without real substance, for while the illusion created by this glittering twosome was lapped up by the masses, they used the people's ill-judged support to mask their own corruption – a corruption which channelled untold millions from the national coffers into Swiss bank accounts. They also supported the Fascist movements in Europe during wartime, clamped down on the press which opposed them, and even launched an anti-Church campaign aimed at those ministers within the Catholic hierachy whom they regarded as enemies.

The succesful politicians who promised to turn Argentina into a paradise for the workers. But Eva and Juan fulfilled little of their socialist programme.

While Peronism may still make the gauchos and the housewives of Buenos Aries misty-eyed for 'the good old days' it was in reality nothing more than a cover for a well-ordered fleecing of the state. It is an indisputable fact that before their rule Argentina was one of the wealthiest nations in the world; afterwards, the nation was ruined and bankrupt.

Before there was an Evita for the crowds in Argentina to cheer there was Colonel Juan Domingo Peron. Born in Lobos in 1895 to poor immigrant stock, he rose through the army ranks thanks to dilligence and ability. Equipped with charm, athleticism and that essential Argentinian characteristic, machismo, he was destined to go far. But he was also a moral and physical coward, a man who shunned reality if he thought confronting it would be unpleasant. He could not endure being unpopular and many of his ludicrous economic policies were pursued so he could enjoy the applause of the mob while he followed them through.

In 1943 Argentina was under the rule of President Ramon Castillo – at least until June that year, when the military decided to stage a coup. It was led by colonels calling themselves the Young Turks, Peron among them. The colonels claimed that the Ramon government was supporting the Allies in the war. This was alien to the Fascist temperament of the officer corps, many of whom were of Italian extraction and saw Mussolini in Italy as their kind of leader. At the time of the coup Peron was one of the keenest pro-Fascist officers among the colonels and worked in the Ministry of War, but by the end of October he was promoted when he was granted the critical job of running the Labour Department in the new military junta.

The labour movement in Argentina was split between trades unions and those workers on the ranches and in the slaughterhouses who had no organization. Peron set out to mould the workers into a single, military-like unit, with the discipline and style of the black shirts he admired at rallies in Nazi Germany and Fascist Italy. Many workers' leaders had suffered cruelly under previous regimes, while the men they represented were mercilessly gunned down in the streets if they dared to strike.

Peron used his considerable charm to become the friend of the unions, the affable big brother who would ease their economic and social woes. Months earlier these same men had been called communist scum and filth by the military but Peron believed flattery was a better way of attaining what he wanted from them.

What he wanted from them was subservience to the government. He made it, for instance, mandatory for wage negotiations between workers and bosses to go through his office.

Eva uses the state radion to thank the nation for electing her husband as president. He stands on the left, while the Interior Minister, Angel Borlenghi sits to the right.

Kickbacks from the unions and the bosses were discreetly channelled into the seven-figure bank account he held in Switzerland. The more astute union leaders realized what he was up to but he outflanked the old guard. He ordered free paid holidays, a month's bonus at Christmas for the meat packers and other fringe benefits. While the workers cheered at this short-term philanthropy, the bosses bemoaned the loss of their managerial rights, and the unions felt emasculated. They were both victims of Juan Peron's attempt to create a permanent Argentinian military dictatorship based on the solid support of the masses.

As the dictatorships that the Argentinian military so admired crumbled in Europe, so the movement for freedom and openness in Argentina grew. In August 1945, the military lifted a state of emergency that had existed throughout the war years – causing a half-a-million-strong demonstration the following month on the streets of the capital from a populace seeking greater freedom and human rights. It was a frightening display of people-power and sparked a draconian response from Peron, who ordered waves of arrests. However when disputes arose within the ranks of the military themselves (the air force officers standing with the workers while the army were against them), Peron played a gambling ruse that he was doomed to lose. He went on radio urging workers to 'rise up' and follow his path of liberation. It was a valiant but vain plea which ended with his own arrest and imprisonment.

With him when he was arrested in his apartment in the Calle Posadas was his mistress Eva Duarte. Fierce and brave, she yelled abuse at the soldiers, while reliable sources have it that her colonel fell to his knees and begged for mercy. Eva, the nightclub singer who literally slept her way to the top, rallied support for Peron among the unions that he had helped so much and rioting broke out in the streets. For 48 hours, Buenos Aries was paralysed until the military backed down and Peron was released, his stature greater than ever.

With the adulation of the workers ringing in his ears, Juan Peron realized that his dreams of a neo-fascist workers' militia had evaporated; instead he saw in the cheering descamisudos – the shiftless ones – the roots of a new workers' revolution. So, believing this to be his chance, he resigned from the army and offered himself up as the leader of a new labour party. His first step towards domination of the workers was to ruin the unions of the shoemakers and the textile workers, two proud and disciplined welfare groups who were not convinced by his scheme to bond workers to his state. Within six months they were finished, their leaders driven into poverty and exile. To gain credence for the free elections which were to be held in 1946, Peron also had to win over the Catholic Church hierachy, especially because of his relationship with Eva Duarte – 'This woman Duarte', as the newspaper *La Prensu* called her. Eva, born in 1919 into great poverty, was his real love and several years earlier he had divorced his wife, hoping to marry his 'Evita'. He persuaded the Church to recognize his marriage to her in 1945, to view it as reparation for his sin of keeping her as a mistress. The Church gave its blessings to the man who would soon be ruler.

In 1946 he attained his dream in one of the few fair elections ever held in Argentina. He gained the backing of the workers to take over the Casa Rosada, the pink palace of the national leaders, with Eva at his side; the country was his for the taking. Peron came to power with great expectations placed upon him. The country was rich, it had been spared the war which had torn apart the Old World, business was booming and there was plenty of money in the bank. What went wrong?

'Indisputably, Peron operated his system extremely badly,' said historian H.S. Ferns in his authoritative study *Argentina*. 'Like a spoiled child he wanted everything and he wanted it at once. He revealed himself totally incapable of making choices and establishing the priorities which are necessary for the operation of any economic system. He taught the community to believe in the instantaneous and total pay-off, so that no one had any order of expectation.' Another study of Argentina, *The Mothers of the Plaza*, by John Simpson and Jana Bennett, says: 'It was all, essentially, a form of charity with Peron. Peron made working-class people feel they had dignity and an importance in the national life of Argentina. The purpose was not to give power to the working class, but to encourage the working class to give power to Juan Peron.'

His brand of socialism bound the workers and the bosses to the state as never before, while he wasted vast quantities of the nation's money by nationalizing the run-down railways at super-inflated prices. He became a master of the pay-off, offering kickbacks to critics and bosses, while he remained the darling of workers who had never had it so good. But they never had it so good at the expense of a government that was rapidly paying out more than it was taking in. Peron's largesse in handing out holidays, pensions and bonuses was laying the foundations for Argentina's 800 per cent inflation rates of the 1970s and 1980s.

Eva Peron could rally crowds, while winning over the army and the church.

By 1949 his plans were badly adrift; inflation and unrest followed as a government of bribes and torture was exposed. Peron reacted harshly, arresting dissidents, purging churchmen and formulating a law that made it a serious offence to insult the president or any of his public servants. He milked the agricultural aid programme for his own benefit and left the grain farmers and the beef herders increasingly impoverished. Newspapers that criticized him and Evita were closed down - like the honourable and influential *La Prensa*, which was seized and turned into a pro-government trade union sheet.

Evita, during these years, manipulated businessmen and landowners to contribute into what has been called the biggest political slush fund in history. The Eva Peron Foundation did, indeed, build schools, educate children, feed the hungry and shelter the homeless. However, the enormous amount of money that rolled in was administered by people who had to answer to no one but her. Her emissaries travelled to every factory, every workshop, every building site to take the tribute demanded by their new Cleopatra. Those who didn't 'contribute' voluntarily soon found their premises judged unfit by factory inspectors and were closed down.

Experts estimate that Evita stashed away as much as $100 million in hard cash into secret Swiss bank accounts from this fund, flown out twice a month to Geneva in suitcases. Gwyneth Dunwoody, the British MP, said: 'With the euphemistically-titled Foundation behind her, Eva Peron handed out Christmas gifts for needy children to hospitals and schools, while ceaselessly driving home the message that it was because of the Peronistas that these remarkable benefits were available.

'What she omitted to say was that the Foundation, which had initially been billed as a society to be supported by voluntary contributions, was rapidly taking on the air of a Godfather organization. She did not hesitate to demand payment from every worker who obtained a rise and from every business that claimed that it needed the government's assistance.

'Every possible source of finance was milked so that this myth of Eva caring for the workers could be promoted. She was not a gentle and gracious woman – she relied on her own regime and army and police power to keep her where she wanted to be. In an organisation with astonishingly few accounts, the amounts of money that were spent were directly connected with what was useful for the Peronista regime. She was no Joan of Arc.'

Rapt attention on the faces of the leaders as they watch a boxing match.

MORE MONEY LESS LOVE

John Barnes, author of the book *Eva Peron*, says that after her death, investigators of defunct bank accounts traced to her found an estimated $14 million worth of money and jewels that she had literally forgotten she had. No doubt, much of this was stolen from the contributions to the Eva Peron Foundation.

'The love of the people feeds me,' Evita gushed, as large amounts of this unchecked and uncounted money were creamed off into her secret bank accounts. Whole government departments were taken over by her, many of them running 24 hours a day, to keep the Foundation supplied with untraceable money. On the goverment front, Colonel Peron bought off politicians to vote through legislation diverting $5 million worth of public funds into her Foundation. To this day, no one knows exactly how much was stolen from Argentina by the Perons, but it ran into the hundreds of millions of dollars.

She was as vain as she was greedy. Newspapers that did not print mentions of her glittering balls and glittering guests suddenly found that their supplies of newsprint had dried up. Although the workers cheered her and were solidly behind her, as they were behind her husband, she never gained the acceptance she craved from the upper classes. She knew the whispers surrounding her rise from the streets, the 'favours' she paid to men who helped her singing career.

Her revenge against the snobbish elite knew no bounds – once she paid a fishmonger and gave him the necessary permits to sell fish outside the snooty Jockey Club in Buenos Aries for a whole long, hot summer. She saw conspirators everywhere and, when a union boss had the temerity to tell her that she would be better off at home in the kitchen than meddling in politics, she had him arrested and tortured with electric cattle prods. Another man, Victor Belardo, was arrested because he answered correctly the jackpot question on a radio quiz show – and then announced that he would give his money, a large amount, to a charity that was not affiliated with or overseen by her omnipotent Foundation.

The Perons accumulated further millions from kickbacks they received for import – export permits. Traders literally had to grease their palms with millions of pesos – and do so willingly – in order to trade with the outside world.

Evita became a master of stage-managed rallies, copycat versions of those which the deposed dictators of Europe used to hold so regularly. Weeks before one particular event she invited Argentinian women from all over the country to bring their children to her to receive bicycles and dolls, a symbolic gesture to show that she cared for them, and that as the 'mother of the country' so all the children were hers to love and treat. It was a scene of chaos when they arrived outside the palace, so much so that police had to break up the crowds and at least two mothers went home without their offspring – the children had been trampled to death by the mob.

In 1951 Peron's grip on political power was faltering but his live-now-pay-later generosity with the workers still earned them both enormous support. He nearly lost this, however, in the 1951 elections by offering up his wife as the vice-president on his ticket. Much as the people adored Evita, this was still the land of machismo. The thought of Vice-President Evita sent a shiver through the ranks of the military, upon whom Peron relied so much, and also troubled the workers deeply. A new slogan appeared on city walls – 'Long Live Peron – As A Widower!' Other graffiti depicted Evita naked, walking like a giant over masses of Lilliputian men. Juan Peron bowed to the pressure of the Church and the military and his beloved Evita did not appear on his election ticket.

Shortly before the elections, which Peron was in danger of losing, there was another attempt at a military coup, this time put down by Peron and by the workers who idolized him. It ensured his victory in the October polling, giving him 62 per cent of the vote, 10 per cent more than he had gained in 1946. And this, despite the faltering economy, the looted millions and the alienation of the ruling class.

But the following year one half of the double act was gone – Evita died from cancer. Juan Peron used her demise to canonize her in the eyes of an adoring people. She was only 33 and had recently toured the world, capturing hearts and minds for her country. Nevertheless, her death averted the fall from grace and power that would ultimately have been her lot. By dying, she became to her impoverished admirers a memory of diamonds and furs, not a woman who left her nation stripped of its wealth and teetering on the brink of bankruptcy while her detractors screamed under torture in filthy jails.

Economic conditions deteriorated after the death of Evita. The emperor was beginning to be seen without his clothes by the adoring masses burdened under hyper-inflation and suffering increasing harassment from his secret police and torturers. Moreover, the Catholic Church, long the traditional dispenser of charity in the country, was beginning to feel aggrieved at having lost its place in society to the Foundation. The universities had been wrecked by semi-literate oafs who were given their posts by corrupt officials in return for kickbacks. Peron's goonsquads burned down the Jockey Club, which had spurned his late wife in the past, and he robbed the magnificent library and art gallery for his own pleasure.

In 1955 it all literally came crashing down when the air force bombed the Casa Rosada – missing him, but killing hundreds of civilians in the process – and armed gangs took to the streets, ransacking shops, businesses and even churches. The army garrison at Cordoba rose against him and there were no workers who believed in his Utopia anymore to save him. He went into exile aboard a Paraguayan gunboat.

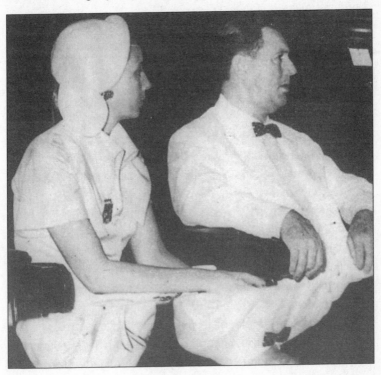

Eva Peron died a young woman. This photograph was taken shortly after she had undergone surgery.

A DAZZLING ALADDIN'S CAVE

In much the same way as the mob was allowed to look over the spoils of office of dictator Ferdinand Marcos in the Philippines years later, the poor of Argentina were given a glimpse of how their Evita had really lived when the portals of her stupendous palace were opened to the public after Peron's flight.

'It was a show which would outdazzle Aladdin's cave,' wrote *Daily Express* correspondent Jack Comben when he gazed at her riches. 'Glass shelves laid tier upon tier in the chandeliered brilliance of Peron's palace displayed gems which are estimated to be worth two million pounds. Diamonds almost as big as pigeons' eggs glittered and flashed. There was a two-inch thick collar encrusted with diamonds.

'I saw at least four hundred dresses – all perfect of their type and all expensive. And experts calculated that Evita owned enough shoes to last her for four hundred years. But all the treasures, the clothes, the pictures, are supposed to be only a fraction of what Peron and his wife acquired during nine years of power. The government believes he sent most of his fortune out of the country to Switzerland. And Peron was once quoted as saying: "The only jewellery I ever gave to my wife was a wedding ring".'

These events, had they occurred in any part of the world other than South America, would have been ended then. In 1973, however, after almost 20 years exile in Spain, Peron returned to power in Argentina with his third wife. Nostalgic, perhaps, for the good old days that never really existed, the people embraced the man who threw in his lot with the workers. They forgot all his sins, the massive amounts of money and assets that he had looted from them in the past.

He died in 1974, the reins of power passing to Isabelita Peron, whom he had married in 1961. She excelled both her husband and his previous wife in the corruption stakes. Arrested in 1976 after she was deposed as president, she was charged with stealing $1 million intended for charity, convicted of embezzling cash from a charity and for using government buildings for her own ends and was jailed. She was released in 1981 after serving two-thirds of her prison sentence.

Despite all this, the name Peron can still elicit nostalgia in Argentina – a land where 'strong' evokes a greater response than 'just'.

An Italian admirer sent this stone statue of Eva to the people of Argentina. It arouses mixed feeling among the citizens: some adore her memory, others despise her greed.

PARKER & HULME
THEIR SECRET WORLD

Pauline Parker and Juliet Hulme were anything but normal schoolgirls. These teenage lesbian lovers bashed in the head of Pauline's mother who had tried to separate them. Were they criminally insane or just murderous little minxes?

x

x

502

There is much in 'Partners in Crime' that dwells on the madness generated by two people that would not have occurred had the partnership never been formed. Normal lives and pattens of behaviour vanish, as two personalities, each bland and safe on its own, ignite into intrigue and danger when combined.

Such was the madness that descended on two adolescent girls in New Zealand in the 1950s – girls who retreated into their own special world of aloofness, superiority and forbidden sex, a world that held murder.

When Juliet Marion Hulme and Pauline Yvonne Parker were brought before the Crown in Christchurch, New Zealand, in 1954, the case received worldwide attention because of its morbid themes. Like the case of Loeb and Leopold, psychologists were at pains to try to explain the fusion of two normal minds into a single entity bent on misery and death. For that is what happened to Juliet Hulme and Pauline Parker when their perfect world was threatened.

The childish face of Juilet Hulme hid a passionate nature and a wilful nature.

In order to prevent separation from one another, they plotted and carried out the murder of Mrs Honora Mary Parker. Mrs Parker, 45, Pauline's mother, was bludgeoned to death by the two, who tried to cover their tracks by claiming she had fallen. But in the end their own inflated ideas of their intelligence and skill failed them badly and the most basic police methods proved that they were the

The distinguished father of Pauline, Dr H.R.Hulme, Rector of Canterbury University College, Christchurch. He intended to take his daughter away from her friend.

killers. The full extent of their wickedness and depravity revealed at the trial shocked this colonial outpost as nothing before or since.

It was on 22 June 1954 that the two hysterical girls, covered in blood, shattered the tranquillity of afternoon tea at a sedate Christchurch restaurant when they burst through the doors. 'Mummy's been hurt,' blurted out Pauline. 'She's hurt, covered with blood.' Tearfully they begged the manageress of the restaurant to phone for the police while they gulped down sugared tea in an apparent attempt to ease their shock. Some of the customers went with police and the girls to a beauty spot in a nearby park close to a small bridge over a stream. Lying in a pool of blood, her face unrecognizable, was Mrs Parker. Her head was brutally battered. It was a bad fall.

Initially the girls told police that Mrs Parker had fallen and slipped on a board. 'Her head just kept banging and banging,' blurted out Pauline to police, in a none-too-convincing explanation of why her mother came to have some 49 serious head wounds, any one of which would have been enough to render her unconscious. The officers knew that they were dealing with something far more sinister than an accident and both young girls – Pauline was 16 and Juliet 15 years and 10 months – were taken into custody for further questioning.

As they were led away, a sharp-eyed policeman found near the pathway, a few feet away from the body of Mrs Parker, a brick wrapped in an old stocking. It was found to be covered in blood and great clumps of her hair were stuck to it. Clearly, this and not a board or a plank of wood had been the instrument which despatched the unfortunate woman. Later, a pathologist examined the corpse and said there was bruising around the throat consistent with her having been held down as blow after blow rained down on her head.

Once in custody Pauline confessed almost immediately to the murder. She said she had made up her mind a few days before the event to kill her mother during an outing in the park and that Juliet, who was walking with them, was not implicated in the crime. She told detectives: 'She knew nothing about it. As far as I know, she believed what I had told her, although she may have guessed what had happened but I doubt it as we were both so shaken that it probably did not occur to her.'

But while she was being questioned, one of the officers guarding her turned his back to her, and she tried to burn a piece of paper on which she had written: 'I am taking the blame for everything.' This was seen as a message that she intended to smuggle to Juliet – who, on learning of the abortive bid to contact her, changed her story immediately and confessed to being a willing accomplice.

Juliet Hulme photographed at the time she was involved with Pauline but before they turned into killers.

IT WAS TERRIBLE, BUT INSANE?

'I took the stocking,' said Juliet, 'and hit her too. I was terrified. I wanted to help Pauline. It was terrible – she moved convulsively. We both held her. She was still when we left her. After the first blow was struck I knew it would be necessary for us to kill her.'

There would have been no need for a protracted criminal trial, along with all its publicity, had the pair pleaded guilty to murder. Instead, they chose to plead guilty of murder by insanity – something the Crown was not prepared to accept. While in custody they had both seemed perfectly aware of what they had done, had both shown little remorse and had both only wanted to return to their 'perfect world'. Their insistence on a plea of insanity meant that the spotlight would now be directed at their dark world.

In his opening speech the prosecutor Mr Anthony Brown ominously told the jury: 'I feel bound to tell you that the evidence will make it terribly clear that the two young accused conspired together to kill the mother of one of them and horribly carried their plan into effect. It was a plan designed solely so they could carry on being together in the most unwholesome manner.'

Brown went on to explain how something 'unhealthy' had developed between the two girls; how they had met at school as friends but then their relationship had deepened and broadened into something much more than girlish camaraderie. He remarked that it was a relationship 'more commonly seen between members of the opposite sex, and of a more advanced age', than that seen between two schoolgirls. Mr Brown painted a portrait of two girls sharing an unnatural love, unhappy when apart, disturbingly attached to each other when together.

Mrs Parker, not surprisingly, was most unhappy about the relationship and was doing her best to break it up when she met her end. She had been in touch with Juliet's father, Dr Hulme, Rector of Canterbury University College, New Zealand. Earlier that year he had resigned his post with the intention of taking a new position in Cape Town, South Africa. He agreed to take Juliet with him, to get her away from Pauline. The date agreed for his departure was 3 July – and the two girls vowed to kill Mrs Parker before then, her punishment for engineering their separation.

'Their first idea was to carry out this crime in such a way so that it appeared that it was an accident which befell Mrs Parker,' said Brown. They persuaded Mrs Parker, having pretended for a couple of weeks prior to her death that they no longer cared about being separated, to take them on a picnic to the country. Juliet Hulme brought along the brick from the garden of her home and the deed was accomplished. All this was corroborated in a sensational diary kept by Pauline Parker and in notes passed between the two – correspondence which the Crown said was definitely the work of people who were quite aware of what they were doing.

'In it', said Brown, waving Pauline's leather-bound diary before the jury, 'she reveals that she and Juliet Hulme have engaged in shoplifting, have toyed with blackmail and talked about and played around in matters of sex. There is clear evidence that as long ago as February she was anxious that her mother should die, and during the few weeks before 22 June she was planning to kill her mother in the way in which she was eventually to be killed.' It was damning evidence.

The girls ran to the Victoria Tearooms, crying that Mrs Parker had fallen and was badly hurt.

On 14 February, he read: 'Why, oh why, could mother not die? Dozens of people, thousands of people, are dying every day. So why not mother and father too?' Later, in April, she wrote: 'Anger against mother boiled up inside me. It is she who is one of the main obstacles in my path. Suddenly a means of ridding myself of the obstacle occurred to me. I am trying to think of some way. I want it to appear either a natural or an accidental death.'

In June it continued: 'We discussed our plans for moidering [*sic*] mother and made them a little clearer. Peculiarly enough I have no qualms of conscience (or is it just peculiar we are so mad!).' On

Mrs Hulme broke down frequently during the trial of her daughter for murder. She refused to speak about the case for many years after the event.

22 June, the actual day of the crime, Pauline penned this entry: 'I am writing a little bit of this up in the morning before the death. I felt very excited like the night before Chrismassy last night. I did not have pleasant dreams, though.' She did not elaborate on these.

The reading of the diary stunned amd shocked the court. The two looked for all the world like normal schoolgirls and yet they had plotted and committed murder. There was even more damning testimony about them which showed that they were sneering, arrogant vixens who enjoyed illicit, adult pleasures wrapped up in a fantasy world of their own making. And much of this damaging testimony was delivered by Juliet's mother.

THE STRANGE DEBORAH AND LANCELOT

Mrs Hulme told the court how the girls were planning to publish a novel (although they hadn't yet written one) and practised writing in strange letters to each other using romantic pseudonyms. Juliet was often called Charles II, Emperor of Borovnia, then she changed to Deborah and then Bialbo. Pauline Parker, at the start of this bizarre correspondence, had called herself Lancelot Trelawney, a Cornish mercenary.

The letters were initially full of romance as they created a fantasy world into which they escaped, but soon the tone changed to something far more sinister. They became violent, sadistic, with maidens raped and knights tortured as the girls' own lust for each other became ever more urgent. Soon they were sleeping together and even indulged in bondage. One said: 'I loved how we enacted how each saint might make love in bed. We have never felt so exhausted... but so satisfied!' It is no suprise that their parents wished to see the girls parted permanently.

Further details emerged of how they spent their days when they were supposed to be in school. They often slipped away to a country barn where they frolicked in the hayloft as lovers, finishing their day by washing each other in a country stream. They talked of going to America, of becoming rich and famous and buying a house together where they would have eunuchs as servants.

Juliet said she wanted to be 'safe' with Pauline – as a child she was brought up in the East End of London at the time of the London Blitz, something which traumatized her deeply. One of their 'games' involved Pauline cradling her as she made noises like bombs exploding around her. And all the while they played out this weird relationship, all schoolfriends and other playmates were excluded; it was, as described in one of Juliet's missives to Pauline, 'their perfect world', one to which no other was admitted.

Initially, Mrs Hulme, who had emigrated with her husband and Juliet when the child was five years old, welcomed her friendship with Pauline because it seemed to bring her out of her shell. 'Had I known where this would lead, I would have killed it stone dead there and then,' she sobbed.

Another entry in Pauline's diary, and one which was instrumental in proving their sanity, was the one that read: 'Prostitution sounds a good idea to make money and what fun we would have in doing it! We are so brilliantly clever, there probably isn't anything we couldn't do.' Were these, said the prosecution, the words of a pair who claimed they did not know what they were doing? Further,

It was on this pathway, near the planking, that the two girls bludgeoned the mother to death.

when Pauline was called to testify, her own arrogance virtually destroyed their defence. When asked if she knew that it was wrong to murder she sneered: 'I knew it was wrong to murder and I knew at the time that I was murdering somebody that it was wrong. You would have to be an absolute moron not to know that something was wrong.'

Lawyers for the two girls said there was no question that they were the killers but that they should not hang – a possibility, despite their age because they were being judged as adults – because of the abnormality of their minds. One medical expert, a Dr Medlicott, pointed out that each of the girls had suffered bad physical health as toddlers and that their siblings were also prone to illnesses, suggesting somehow that this contributed to the unbalanced state of their young murderers' minds.

Discussing the bizarre relationship between them the doctor told the court : 'Juliet told me: "I do believe that we are indeed geniuses.

The trial aroused tremendous interest. Crowds clamoured outside the court for a glimpse of the young lesbian killers.

I don't wish to place myself above the law – I am apart from it." And when I performed a medical examination upon Miss Parker she turned to me and said: "I hope you break your flaming neck." In my opinion they are aggressive, dangerous, but most certifiably insane.'

It was not an opinion shared by expert Dr Charles Bennett who told the court: 'I find that they probably, very probably, knew what they were doing and knew it was wrong in the eyes of society at large. But I doubt very much if they gave any consideration whatsoever to what society thought of them at all.'

In the end, after a careful summing up by the judge, it was left to the jury to decide whether the girls were mad or not. Mr Justice Adams said: 'The important word is the word "knowing". It has to be considered at the very moment of the commission of the crime. Were their minds so confused that they did not know this act was wrong? This is what you, ladies and gentlemen of the jury, have to consider.'

Consider it they did and in just two and a quarter hours returned a verdict of guilty. There was a fleeting smile flashed between the two girls, these supreme egoists, when they were spared the rope by a merciful judge and ordered to be detained at Her Majesty's Pleasure – which meant indefinitely. But in a move which, to many, seemed to mock justice, they were freed just four years later after intense psychiatric counselling. They remained friends but the spark from that earlier relationship had been extinguished by the separation.

Herbert Rieper – he was with Pauline's mother for twenty-five years although he never married her – never recovered from her death. He never forgave the girl, and when his daughter was freed he said: 'It still doesn't make up for robbing a person of their life. It was evil between them that did it. Pure evil.'

BRADY & HINDLEY
THE MOORS MURDERS

Ian Brady and Myra Hindley arouse revulsion and hatred like no other murderers in British history. Together in an evil pact, they systematically tortured and killed more than six children. The real death toll is still unknown, forever locked up in the killers' deranged minds.

He was a 27-year-old stock clerk who idolized Hitler and sank into horrible fantasies after drinking bottles of cheap German wine which transported him back in his imagination to the rallies and the marches of the Third Reich. Although the expression had not yet been coined in the Swinging Sixties, she would no doubt have been called a bimbo: a 22-year-old peroxide-blonde typist who nurtured fantasies of eternal love. And, indeed, she did find immortality of a kind with the man with mesmeric eyes and a quick temper. Together they have gone down in British criminal history as the most wicked of the wicked, for they were the childkillers, Ian Brady and Myra Hindley.

Even today, in a world hardened by violent crime, their vile acts set them apart as monsters of a very special breed. At 16 Wardle Brook Avenue, on the sprawling Hattersley council estate and on the wild Pennine Moors, children abducted by these two died a gruesome death before being buried in unmarked graves. But death was not all these perverts visited upon their innocent victims who should never have accepted the lifts home they offered.

They were sexually assaulted, they were photographed and, in the case of one victim, her screams were even tape-recorded… screams that would later be heard in a criminal court, a shocking testament to evil.

Police search for clues in the garden of the Hindley-Brady residence.

Ian Brady and Myra Hindley are a classic case of partners in crime. Separate and alone, they were ordinary, if stunted, characters who might have lived their lives without ever plunging into the abyss of madness and depravity. Together, they fell prey to what the French call a *folie à deux* – the madness generated between two people. She was the girl he could impress; he was the errant knight for whom she would have sold her soul. In reality, they were bound by perversion and a taste for cruelty. Together they have left an imprint on Britain's national conscience that has not been faded or eroded by the passage of years.

Brady and Hindley forged their relationship after meeting at work. He was a winkle-pickered youth with a fondness for crime B-movies and Nazi philosophy. An illegitimate child who had never known his father (widely believed to have been a reporter on a Glasgow evening newspaper), he was brought up in the Gorbals slums of the city. His mother, coping with both the stigma of being unmarried and the burden of being poor, put him in the care of a family called Sloan when he was small, during the formative years of his life.

The kindness they lavished on him was misplaced; he became a cold, sneering, surly youth who shunned kindness as weakness, compassion as foolishness. Brick by brick, he built a wall around himself and convinced himself that he was better than everybody else and that society was against him.

After serving terms in Borstals as a teenager for housebreaking, he was finally given a chance to escape going to the 'big house' – adult prison – by a Glasgow judge who insisted that he live with his real mother. She, by the time he was a teenager, had moved back to Manchester with her new husband, an Irish labourer, but was willing to take a chance, putting her unhappy young son back on the straight and narrow. Here Brady's teenage rebelliousness metamorphosed into something altogether more sinister.

He began buying Nazi books like *The Kiss of the Whip*, which glorified the persecution of the Jews, and to drink heavily. Alternately in and out of work, in trouble with the law for drunkenness, he managed to land a job as a stock clerk at

Millwards Ltd, a chemical and soap company in Manchester. Here the partnership in evil would be irrevocably forged when Myra Hindley was introduced to him on 16 January 1961.

Within weeks they had become lovers. Her diaries at the time show the student of crime as a pathetically ordinary, normal, unsophisticated suburban girl who confided on paper her childish

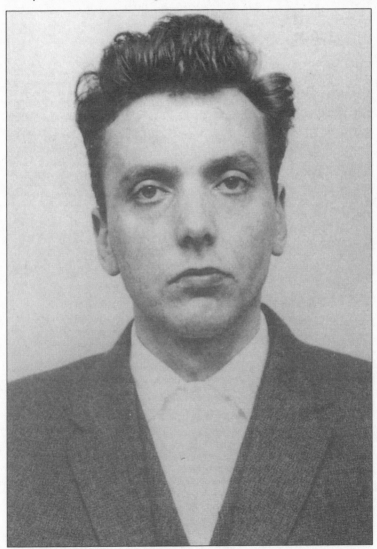

Ian Brady's image reveals an ill-tempered and defiant personality.

hopes and fears: 'Not sure if he likes me. They say he gambles on horses. I love Ian all over and over again!' Then: 'He has a cold and I would love to mother him.' Other times she is frustrated or cross with him, and determined to end their fledgling love affair.

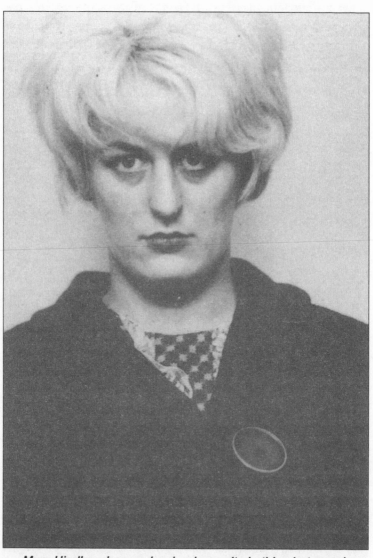

Myra Hindley shows a hard, grim vanity in this photograph taken while she was on trial for killing small children.

Yet in the end he became her first lover, on a sofa-bed in the front room of the house she shared with her grandmother. It happened after they had seen one of his favourite films – *Judgement at Nuremberg*, a story of Nazi atrocities.

From these beginnings grew the seed of perversion and corruption. Brady's book collection of pornographic and sadomasochistic material had swelled now and his needs were more than conventional love-making. Soon he was taking lurid pictures of his girlfriend, complete with whips, a hood and even her pet dog. She took pictures of him, too, surrounded by mirrors as he admired his body. But the thrill of this soon wore thin. Fuelled by the German wine he habitually drank, he drew her into his evil web of fantasy, when he talked of becoming a gangster and of her becoming his moll while they robbed and pillaged like a latter-day Bonnie and Clyde.

They did not have the courage for this, however; it was only Dutch courage inspired by the wine. But they did find the courage to satisfy their expanding sexual perversions, if courage is what is needed for two adult people to lure, humiliate, abuse and then murder little children.

No one knows at what precise moment they slipped over the edge and fantasy became action. Did they decide about it over tea, as the buses taking their neighbours to work roared along outside? Or perhaps it happened on one of their weekend excursions to the wild and lonely moors that ring Manchester. But Ian and Myra, the loving couple did cross the line between perversion and murder on Friday, 12 July, when Pauline Reade, aged 16, accepted a lift from them on her way to a social-club dance in Gorton.

Then on 23 November 1963, they crossed it again when little John Kilbride, aged $12^1/_2$, accepted a lift from them at the marketplace in Ashton-under-Lyne. On Tuesday, 15 June 1964 Keith Bennett, aged twelve, became their third victim when he took a ride on a busy Manchester road after setting out to buy some sweets. On 26 December 1964, Leslie Ann Downey, born on 21 August, 1954, died at the age of ten years and four months after she climbed into their car parked at a fairground near Ancoats.

THE HOME OF MURDER

After the disappearances of these children, there were the usual appeals for help, the usual sad pictures of the missing kids were plastered all over their neighbourhoods and beyond. No clues linked their disappearances to each other, there was no reason to believe an evil pied piper was claiming them one by one. It took the brutal murder of an innocent teenager in the front room of the home Brady shared with his accomplice, to lead the police to uncover the horrific crimes of this couple.

On the morning of 7 October 1965, David Smith, married to Hindley's sister Maureen, made a frantic 999 telephone call at 6.07 a.m. from a phone box on the edge of the housing estate where Hindley and Brady lived. He was a young man with a stammer, who was already known to the police for a string of petty offences, and he blurted out a tale of murder perpetrated, he said, the previous evening in the living room of Brady's house.

Smith said the victim, later identified as 17-year-old Edward Evans, had been axed to death by Ian Brady to 'impress' Smith. Brady had often talked of robbery and murders with Smith but Smith had put it down to an overworked imagination fuelled by the wine. This time the fantasy became reality before his very eyes. Brady had murdered a boy and Smith was asked to help clean up the blood after witnessing the ghastly scene.

In a calm monotone, he described how the young man had been lured to the house by Hindley, was set upon by the axe-wielding Brady and was finally finished off by a length of electrical flex with which Brady throttled him. Brady asked Smith to help him in his macabre clean-up afterwards, saying: 'This one's taking a time to go. Feel, Dave, feel the weight of that. That was the messiest yet.' Afterwards, with the glow of a sexual, murderous frenzy bathing them, Ian Brady and Myra Hindley made love as Edward Evans's mutilated body lay upstairs.

A FATAL DELIVERY OF BREAD

Police decided that there was more to Smith's tale than hysteria or mischief. The house in Wardle Brook Avenue was approached and Police Superintendent Bob Talbot put on the white coat of a local breadman, borrowed his loaves and knocked on the door of number 16. Hindley answered it; Brady was inside on a divan writing a letter to his bosses at Millwards. The letter was an excuse to explain why he wouldn't be at work that day – he claimed he had hurt his ankle. In reality, he was planning an excursion to his private cemetery on the moors to make room for one more corpse.

Talbot, upon being greeted by Myra Hindley at the doorway, pushed past her into the house announcing that he was a police officer. Hindley tried to block his entrance to the bedroom but Brady, nonchalantly still lying on the divan, told her: 'Ye'd best give him the key.' Once inside the bedroom Superintendent Talbot discovered the corpse of the young man who died for their thrills.

With Brady in custody, charged with murder, the police re-interviewed Smith who told them that Brady had boasted of killing 'three or four others'. These others were allegedly buried on the

Scenes outside the courtroom as Lesley Anne Downey's uncle lunged at the man who murdered the child. Police restrained him but the public did not.

bleak, beautiful Saddleworth Moor outside Manchester. Talbot logged the numbers carefully in his orderly policeman's brain, for he believed he had seen in Brady's arrogant eyes and surly manner the mark of a very dangerous predator indeed.

Brady told police a bland story. He said he had met Edward Evans, the victim, in a Manchester pub. The youngster had come to his house afterwards, they had rowed and, unfortunately, he had killed Evans with a hatchet. Talbot's superior officer, Arthur Benfield, Detective Chief Superintendent for the whole of Cheshire, was down at the police station by noon to investigate the drunken death but he was worried by the boast of 'three or four others'.

A search of the house revealed notebooks with ruled columns in which Brady had written down a series of what appeared to be coded instructions. There was 'meth' for method, 'stn' for station, 'bulls' for bullets, 'gn' for gun. After staring at it long and hard, Benfield realized he was looking at a shopping list for murder weapons. But whose murder?

Days later, as he sifted through the paraphernalia of Brady's bedroom, he came upon a tattered school exercise book filled with scribblings and graffiti. There was a list of names that apparently meant nothing, jotted down by the day-dreaming clerk during moments of boredom. But Benfield read through all the names nonetheless – Christine Foster, Jean Simpson, Robert Uquart, James Richardson, Joan Crawford, Gilbert John, Ian Brady, John Sloan, Jim Idiot, John Birch, Frank Wilson, John Kilbride, Alec Guineas, Jack Polish, J. Thompson. John Kilbride... the name hit Talbot like a hammer blow and suddenly the feeling washed over him that he was on to a monstrous crime, something bigger than he had ever imagined.

The search of the house brought to light the pornographic photographs Brady and Hindley had taken of each other and the sadomasochistic and Nazi book collection. And there were other pictures, too, of Hindley and Brady taken on the moors. One in particular caught his eye, that of Myra sitting on the ground, looking wistfully at the gorse and peat beneath her, staring at nothing in particular except the ground as if... as if she were staring at a grave.

Brady played mind games with the police, claiming the stories he told Smith were lies to build up an 'image'. He said there were no more bodies and that the name Kilbride in the exercise book was an old chum from Borstal days. Police made door-to-door enquiries in their neighbourhood.

The police had two lucky breaks. Everyone was eager to help catch the murderers, and the police received vital information from a neighbour's 12-year-old daughter who had accompanied Auntie Myra and Uncle Ian on excursions to the moors to 'help them dig for peat'. Then, a car hire company confirmed that they had rented a car to a Myra Hindley on 23 November 1963, John Kilbride's last day alive. The police used photos removed from the couple's bedroom to locate the burial places of the murdered children. They were helped by the girl who, though she had been taken to the moors by the pair, had survived the trip.

A CASE OF LEFT LUGGAGE

The body of Lesley Ann Downey was found by the police searchers on 16 October, ten days after the death of Edward Evans. Police thought that they would find the body of John Kilbride but they only found the little tartan skirt belonging to the trusting little girl. Two days later another policeman on the team made an even more startling discovery. Hidden in the spine of Myra Hindley's communion prayer book was a left-luggage ticket for two suitcases at Manchester Central Station. Once retrieved, they yielded up more pornographic books, small-arms ammunition, blackjacks, wigs, tapes and photos of moorland views.

And other pictures. Pictures of a little girl with her eyes bulging in terror, naked save for her socks and shoes, bound and gagged. Talbot felt the tears well up in his eyes as he looked into the helpless face of Lesley Ann Downey.

Later, the tapes were played. The first one was a hotch-potch of

Hitler marches and the BBC *Goon Show*, interspersed with a documentary on Hitler's life. Then the second one was played – the tape that numbed the policemen present, would later make hardened journalists weep and would finally nail Brady and Hindley for the cruel and evil monsters they were. 'Don't... please God help me. Don't undress me will you... I want me mam...' Interspersed with screams, pleas and futile whimpers, against the barking commands of Hindley and Brady, these were the final words of Lesley Ann as she met her unspeakable end at the hands of the sinister people who had given her a lift at the fair.

On 21 October the body of John Kilbride was found in the spot where Myra had been photographed with her beloved dog Puppet. John's underpants had been pulled down to below his thighs, knotted hard in the back to prevent him from moving his legs. He had been sexually assaulted and buried face down. Britain and the world were inflamed with anger at the killers now branded the Moors Murderers. Myra Hindley was now under arrest to face charges of murder along with her lover, Ian Brady.

The trial gripped the public attention as no other had done when the pair came before Chester Assizes on 19 April 1966. Both pleaded not guilty to murder and maintained an arrogance and swagger throughout that earned them the hatred of prosecutors, police, journalists, the judge and the parents of the dead.

Patricia Carins, second on the right, the lesbian warder who plotted to free her lover, Hindley.

In the Evans case, Brady maintained that it was Smith's idea to 'roll a queer' for money and that he had participated in the killing. In Lesley Ann's case, Brady gave the court a totally implausible story that he had taken photos of her after she had been driven to their home by men he didn't know and that he turned her over to them afterwards. In the case of John Kilbride, he denied murder and sexual assault.

It was the tape, however, which dominated the proceedings and for which they will always be damned. Emlyn Williams, in his authoritative chronicle of the crimes and aftermath *Beyond Belief* wrote: 'This tape was to become the most scaring object ever to lie on the exhibits table below a judge at a murder trial… the tape began. And played for seventeen intolerable minutes. To listen to it was made doubly dreadful by the very nature of the invention which made the experience possible. In the course of murder trials, for centuries dreadful things have had to come to light, not only visually but mumbled by unwilling witnesses. Never before, however, has the modern phenomenon of preserved sound been put to such a grisly use as was "the Moors tape".' The courtroom listened in shocked horror and disbelief to the pleading of the little girl as she begged for life and her mam, to the backdrop of Christmas carols and the barking commands of Brady for the child to pose in immodest positions.

Brady, when asked why he kept the tape recording, said it was because it was 'unusual'. It was a gross answer.

Hindley, in particular, became the focus of public curiosity. Men like Brady – well, there have been many perverts and murderers down the ages, men who have killed to sate their demonic urges. But women were supposed to be the gentler sex, the givers of life, the nurturers of children. How could she have slipped into such an abyss? She gave little indication that she had a 'feminine' heart at her trial. Scrutiny of testimony during examination by the Attorney General Sir Elwyn Jones shows that she had little remorse for what had taken place, even though she pleaded not guilty to all charges. The following is an extract from the trial.

Attorney General: Time and again you were driving into this child's ears your orders, 'put it in'.

Hindley: I just wanted her to not make a noise.

Attorney General: Then you say, 'Will you stop it. Stop it.' Did you think there was the most terrible threatening note in the second order to stop it, Miss Hindley?

Hindley: No, it was a desperate tone.

Attorney General: Then one hears the poor little child making a retching noise. This thing was being pushed down her throat, was it not?

Hindley: No,

Attorney General: Who do you say undressed this child?

Hindley: Herself

Attorney General: Can you therefore explain the child's saying: 'Don't undress me will you?' That was precisely what you were trying to do with the child?

Hindley: No, I was not.

Attorney General: A little further on Brady is saying: 'If you don't keep that hand down I'll slit your neck.' That is why you do not want to be landed with hearing that, is it not?

Hindley: No.

Attorney General: Then when the child was whining you say, 'Sh. Hush. Put that in your mouth again and…'. Then there follow the words 'packed more solid'. Why did you want the mouth to be packed more solid?

Hindley: Why more solid? I don't know.

Attorney General: That was preparatory to suffocating her in due course, was it not?

Hindley: No.

But no one in the court believed they were innocent. On 6 May 1966, both were found guilty of murdering Edward Evans and Lesley Ann Downey, Brady further found guilty of the murder of John Kilbride with Hindley being an accessory after the fact. Brady was jailed for life on each of the three murder charges, Hindley for life on the Downey and Evans murders with a further seven years for her part as an accessory to the Kilbride slaying.

They were driven off to separate prisons with the screams of the mob outside ringing in their ears, and the lovers were never to see each other again. Hindley appealed her conviction but three appeal judges ruled against her.

The grisly saga of the Moors Murders might have ended then but the disappearances of Pauline Reade and Keith Bennett remained unsolved. Police officers who had worked on the case felt in their bones that these two monsters had something to do with the disappearances of these two but there were no photographs or tape recordings to link them with the youngsters.

These suspicions continued down the years as Myra Hindley became a model prisoner, then was involved in a lesbian love affair that sparked a failed escape plot. She became an Open University graduate, converted to Christianity and established communication with Lord Longford, the prison reformer who is one of very few people who believed that Myra Hindley had been rehabilitated and deserved to be released.

The correspondence between her and Brady was furious and passionate in the first months of separation, but time cooled the

Police with long poles search near the site where they unearthed the body of Lesley Anne Downey. They were looking for other victims.

love while Brady slipped deeper into madness before he was finally moved, in November 1985, to a maximum-security hospital. But he was not so mad as to be incapable of thwarting the long-cherished dream that his former lover clung to throughout her long years of captivity.

The Bleak burial grounds of two murdered children.

A LOVER'S FURY

When Brady heard of Myra's attempts to be released, he broke his silence regarding the deaths of Reade and Bennett, prompting police to visit Myra Hindley in her jail cell. On 15 December 1986, Myra Hindley returned to Saddleworth Moor, her first breath of the moors since the terrible events of more than two decades previously. Her memory, perhaps faded with time, perhaps by the enormity of what she had done, failed to pinpoint any graves, although she was sure she had the right area. But police searched diligently and in June the following year the body of Pauline Reade was discovered. Pathologists analysed that she had been sexually assaulted and her throat slashed from behind.

Her confession to the Reade and Bennett murders effectively stifled any hope that Myra Hindley would ever be freed and she was said to have resigned herself to death in jail. After unconfirmed media reports that Hindley was suffering with advanced lung cancer, she did eventually die in prison at the age of 60.

Brady's mental degeneration continued. Declared clinically insane, in the winter of 1987 he mailed a letter to the BBC containing sketchy information about five further murders, including unsuspected Moors victims, a man murdered in Manchester, a woman dumped in a canal and two victims gunned down in Scotland. He remains alive in the high security Ashworth Hospital on Merseyside. After failing several attempts to starve himself to death, he remains on continual hunger strike being force-fed through a plastic tube.

Other victims of the killings are the families of the murdered children. Mrs Ann West, mother of Lesley Ann, was a vociferous campaigner for Hindley to stay behind bars. On the twenty-fifth anniversary of her child's death she wrote to Home Secretary Kenneth Baker, saying: 'Though a generation has passed since those evil monsters were put behind bars the horror of their crimes remains as fresh as ever. I beg you to turn a deaf ear to those well-meaning but tragically misguided do-gooders who would now set them free on compassionate grounds. Ignore, at all costs, those who would forgive and forget. For just as there is no parole for we who still grieve, so must there be no parole for them.

'Every night I am haunted anew by the memory of that courtroom. I can still hear the taped screams of Lesley Ann begging for mercy…

'The enormity of those murders has not diminished. They killed for sick and twisted kicks, and showed no compassion. They are not fit to mix with humans. I implore you to make sure they do not.'

THE WESTS
HOUSE OF HORRORS

On 24 February 1994, police began to dig up the garden at
25 Cromwell Street to look for Heather West, daughter of
Rosemary and Frederick West. On 13 December 1994,
Frederick West was charged with 12 murders. Rose also
received life imprisonment on each of the ten counts of murder.

Young women would go and stay at 25 Cromwell Street, either as nannies, lodgers or friends, but very few of them made it out of the West house alive. It was slowly becoming a House of Horrors.

FRED'S CHILDHOOD

Frederick West was born in 1941 to Walter and Daisy West, who lived in Much Marcle, a village about 120 miles west of London. After Fred, Daisy had another six children during the following ten years.

As Fred grew older, he developed a close relationship with his mother, doing everything she asked. Fred also had a good relationship with his father whom he admired as a role model.

Police guarding 25 Cromwell Street as evidence is being removed.

While being a scruffy-looking boy, Fred inherited some of his mother's features, a rather large mouth with a gap between his big teeth, resembling the looks of a gypsy.

At school, Fred was always in trouble for which he was frequently caned. His mother, Daisy, would then go to the school and yell at the teacher, which made Fred the victim of many jokes.

At the age of 15 and virtually illiterate, Fred left school and went to work as a farmhand. By the time he was 16, he had become very aggressive to the opposite sex and pursued any girl that took his fancy.

Fred, recognized as a notorious liar, claimed that his father had sex with his daughters using the excuse 'I made you so I'm entitled to have you'. Then at 17, he was seriously injured in a motorcycle accident. After a week in a coma, a broken leg and having a metal plate inserted into his head, Fred was left with one leg shorter than the other. This head injury may have resulted in Fred being prone to sudden fits of rage and the loss of control over his emotions.

After this accident Fred met a pretty 16-year-old called Catherine Bernadette Costello. Nicknamed Rena, she had always been in trouble with the police since early childhood and was an accomplished and experienced thief. They quickly became lovers. The affair ended months later as she returned to Scotland. Then, after thrusting his hand up a young woman's skirt while on a fire escape at a local youth group, Fred fell, banged his head and lost consciousness. It may be that he suffered brain damage due to his two head injuries and this could have been the cause of a lasting impact on his behaviour.

After being fined for theft in 1961, Fred was accused of getting a 13-year-old girl pregnant. He couldn't understand that he had done anything wrong, but as this girl was a friend of the family, it caused a scandal and he was told to find somewhere else to live. Working on construction sites, it wasn't long before he was caught stealing and having sex with young girls.

At the age of 20, although he got off without a prison sentence, Fred had become a convicted child molester and petty thief; a complete disgrace to his family.

ROSE'S CHILDHOOD

Daisy Letts was hospitalized in 1953, due to her deepening depression and trying to cope with a violent husband, three daughters and son. She was given electroshock therapy. Shortly after this treatment she gave birth to Rosemary, in Devon in November 1953. Her mother suffered from severe depression and her father, Bill Letts, was a schizophrenic. Bill was a violent and dominant man, demanding obedience from both his wife and children, and enjoyed looking for reasons to beat them. The family was short of money because Bill was not an ideal employee and only maintained a series of unskilled and low-paid jobs.

The house in Northam, Devon where Rose West lived as a child.

Rose had developed a habit of rocking herself in her cot and as she became older, she would swing her head for hours until she reached semi-conciousness. Being quite pretty, if a little chubby, she was called 'Dozy Rosie', although she was smart enough to become her father's pet. But at school, due to cruel jokes and teasing, Rose was recognized as an ill-tempered, aggressive loner.

In her teens she walked around naked after baths, fondled her brother and became sexually precocious. As boys were not interested in her she focused her attentions on the older men of the village.

During 1968 Rose was raped by an older man who had taken advantage of her innocent ways. Then at the beginning of 1969 Daisy, her mother, took 15-year-old Rose and moved in temporarily with one of her other daughters to escape from Bill. At this time Rose began to spend a lot of time out with men. Later that year, Rose moved back home with her father.

As Rose Letts was neither very smart nor good tempered girl, she became unfocused towards any productive goal except finding a lover older than herself.

Rosemary as a child.

THE FIRST VICTIM

In 1962 Fred was allowed to move back home in Much Marcle. Rena Costello returned from Scotland in the summer and they met up immediately, continuing their relationship. Although Rena was pregnant by an Asian bus driver, she and Fred secretly married and moved to Scotland. Charmaine was born in March 1963. They both wrote to Fred's parents, stating that their baby had died at birth, therefore they had adopted a child of mixed race.

Fred's interest in normal sex was limited, although he had a voracious appetite for oral sex, bondage and sodomy. As an ice-cream man, his apparent politeness and sincerity attracted teenagers around his van. This led to many sexual encounters. With his growing number of infidelities, Rena and Charmaine were pushed out of his mind.

FRED AND ROSE

Rena gave birth to Fred's child in 1964, and they named her Anne Marie. During their turbulent marriage, the Wests embarked on a friendship with Anna McFall. Then Fred, Rena and their two children, as well as Anna, moved to Gloucester where Fred found work in a slaughterhouse. This is probably where Fred developed a morbid obsession with blood, corpses and dismemberment.

As the marriage fell apart, Rena returned to Scotland alone. When she returned to Gloucester in July 1966, she found Fred living in a trailer with Anna McFall. Due to pressure from Anna to marry her, Fred responded by killing her and her unborn child sometime in July 1967. He slowly and methodically dismembered her and the foetus, cutting off her fingers and toes, and burying her body somewhere near the trailer park.

Rena then moved back in with Fred, earning money as a prostitute, while he began, openly, to fondle Charmaine. Then in February 1968, after his mother's death, Fred committed a series of petty thefts, which caused him to change his job frequently. In November 1968, while on one of these many jobs, Fred met Rose Letts, his future wife. Although Rose's father did not approve of Fred, she carried on seeing him until she found herself pregnant with his baby. At the age of 16, Rose left home to take care of Charmaine, Anna Marie and Fred.

CHARMAINE

Rose gave birth in 1970 to Heather. While Fred was in jail, Rose was left at home with all the children whom she treated quite badly. Then one day during the summer of 1971, Charmaine went missing. Although this happened while Fred was in prison, he probably helped to bury her body under the kitchen floor of their home in Midland Road, removing her fingers, toes and kneecaps; the guilty crime would only be discovered 20 years later. It was only a matter of time before Rena came looking for Charmaine. When she found Fred, he got her drunk, then strangled her dismembered her body and buried her, as he had done with Anna, cutting off her fingers and toes.

Fred and Rose married in Gloucester registry office in 1972, then Rose gave birth to a daughter, Mae West. As the family increased in size, they moved to 25 Cromwell Street, where Rose also had room for her prostitution business. As the cellar was soundproof, they used it as a 'torture chamber'. Anna Marie, their eight-year-old daughter was the first victim, her mother held her down and her father raped her. The pain was so bad that she could not attend school.

CAROLINE OWENS

The couple hired a nanny, 17-year-old Caroline Owens. They abducted, raped and threatened her but she got away and reported this to the police. There was a hearing. On this occasion Fred, 31, and Rose, only 19, were found not guilty.

LYNDA GOUGH

Lynda Gough, a friend who helped take care of the children, became the next victim. She was dismembered and buried in a pit in the garage, having had her fingers, toes and kneecaps removed. A terrible pattern was already well established.

CAROL ANN COOPER

In August 1973, Stephen, their first son was born. Fred and Rose abducted 15-year-old Carol in November, abusing her sexually until they strangulated or suffocated her. They dismembered and buried her body in the growing graveyard of 25 Cromwell Street.

LUCY PARTINGTON AND THE REST

The cellar was enlarged and the garage was transformed into an extension of the main house, all done by Fred at strange hours of the day. On 27 December 1973, Lucy Partington went to visit her disabled friend but had the misfortune to bump into Rose and Fred. She was tortured for a week and then murdered, dismembered and buried under one of Fred's many construction projects at 25 Cromwell Street.

During the period from April 1974 to April 1975 another three women became victims like Carol and Lucy. They were Therese Siegenthaler, 21, Shirley Hubbard, 15 and Juanita Mott, 18. The Wests buried these bodies under the cellar floor. Juanita had been gagged by a ligature made from a pair of white nylon socks, two pairs of tights and a bra, then tied up with plastic-covered rope, the type used for a washing line. Tied up so tightly that she could hardly move, she was probably suspended from the beams in the cellar. As for Shirley Hubbard, her body was wrapped entirely with tape; a plastic tube had been inserted up her nose, allowing her to breathe.

Leading into the cellar at 25 Cromwell Street.

Fred continued to get into trouble with the police for theft and stolen goods, which he needed to maintain his home improvement projects.

The Wests took in lodgers. One of these, Shirley Robinson, 18, a former prostitute, developed a relationship with them and later became pregnant with Fred's child. Rose had also become pregnant, but by one of her black clients. Rose became uncomfortable with this situation and wanted Shirley to leave. Seven months later, Tara was born to Rose in December 1977. Shirley and her unborn baby became the next victims and were buried in the garden of Cromwell Street. Yet another baby girl, Louise, was born to the Wests in November 1978, making a total of six. Fred's daughter, Anne Marie also became pregnant by Fred, although this was terminated.

After Rose's father died in May 1979, the Wests raped, tortured and murdered their next victim, Alison Chambers, who was only 17. She was also buried in the garden at Cromwell Street. The rest of the children in the West household were aware of strange happenings. They knew that their mother was a prostitute and that Anna Marie was continually raped by her father. Anna moved in with her boyfriend, so Fred made advances towards his other daughters, Heather and Mae. Heather was beaten for trying to resist her father's advances. Rose gave birth to Barry, Fred's second son, in June 1980, followed by Rosemary junior, who was not Fred's, in April 1982. She also had Lucyanna in July 1983, who was half-black like Tara and Rose junior. With all these children to contend with, Rose became extremely bad tempered.

After Heather broke the silence and told her girlfriend of the abuse from her father, she too was murdered. This happened after an argument with her father got out of control. Fred grabbed her round the neck, she went blue and stopped breathing. After trying to revive her, he dragged her to the bath and ran cold water over her. After taking all her clothes off and drying her, he tried to fit her in the rubbish bin. But as she did not fit, he strangled her with tights just to make sure she was dead, and then cut her up into smaller pieces. Stephen, Fred's son, helped his father dig a hole in the back garden for Heather's dismembered body.

Anne Marie daughter of Fred and Rena Costello.

Katherine Halliday began to participate in the Wests' prostitution business, although this did not last long as she became very alarmed at their collection of suits, whips and chains and left abruptly.

Due to one of Fred's young rape victims talking, Detective Constable Savage, who had experience in dealing with Rena, was assigned to his case. On 6 August, 1992 police arrived at Cromwell Street with a warrant to look for child abuse and pornography. Fred was arrested. While the police had enough evidence to bring child abuse charges against Fred, Detective Constable Savage was curious as to the disappearance of Charmaine, Rena and Heather.

The Wests' children were put into care and with Fred in prison, Rose attempted suicide but failed. After rumours emerged that Heather was apparently buried under the patio, the house and garden were searched. Fred confessed to killing his daughter when human bones, other than Heather's, were found in the garden. The police began to dig up the garden and it was only a matter of time before they found the first remains of a young woman, dismembered and decapitated.

Fred then told the police of the girls in the cellar, admitting to murder but not rape. In the cellar, nine sets of bones were discovered, although the police could not identify them, and Fred was no help as he couldn't remember the victims.

Rena, Anna McFall and Charrnaine's bodies were found,

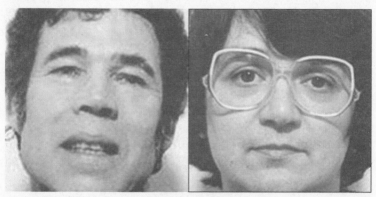

Fred West (the last photograph before his death) and Rosemary West.

although Mary Bastholm was not.

At the joint hearing, Fred tried to console Rose, but she brushed him off, telling the police that he made her sick.

GUILTY

Fred was charged with 12 murders on 13 December 1994. After being devastated by Rose's rejection, Fred hanged himself with his bedsheet on New Year's Day at Winson Green Prison, Birmingham.

On 3 October 1995, Rose went to trial linking her to the murders and sadistic sexual assaults on young women. Among the witnesses were Caroline Owens, whom they had hired as a nannie in 1972, along with Anna Marie. The defence, led by Richard Ferguson QC, tried to show that Rose was unaware of what Fred was up to, and that the evidence of sexual assault was not the same as evidence of murder. But after she had taken the stand, the jury were left believing that she had ill-treated her children and was completely dishonest.

The most dramatic evidence was given by Janet Leach, who witnessed Fred's police interviews. During these interviews, Fred had said how he had involved Rose with the murders and that Rose had murdered Charmaine and Shirley Robinson on her own. After this testimony, Janet Leach collapsed and was admitted to hospital.

It did not take the jury long to find Rose guilty of murdering Charmaine, Heather, Shirley Robinson and the other bodies all buried at Cromwell Street. With ten counts of murder, the judge sentenced Rose to life imprisonment.

THE ROSENBERGS

THE A-BOMB SPIES

Noone ever thought there was anything special about Julius and Ethel Rosenberg, until they were tried and executed in the electric chair as spies. This ordinary couple were at the heart of a traitorous network which passed the secrets of America's first atomic bomb to the Soviet Union.

Julius and Ethel Rosenberg were the children of dispossessed Russian Jews who went to the New World determined to make a different and better life. Julius and Ethel were both born in the USA. Of course, as they matured they also nursed their hopes and their dreams. Their dreamhowever, was not the same dream as that of their family and neighbours; it was one that could only be fulfilled by an alien creed hostile to their homeland, the government of the United States.

For Ethel and Julius Rosenberg were America's 'atomic spies', the suburban couple enmeshed in a plot to sell America's nuclear secrets to their Kremlin enemy. The Rosenbergs were the only communist agents ever to be executed in peacetime and, while apologists and historical revisionists have argued down the years that the pair were the victims of a ghastly frame-up, experts conclude that the verdicts and sentences passed upon them have stood the test of time.

When the switch was thrown on them in the death chamber at Sing-Sing Prison in New York on 19 June 1953, it was the end of one of the grimmest chapters of international espionage. Many thronged the streets in the hours before they were executed, some protesting their innocence, others merely asking for clemency. The problem with both Julius and Ethel Rosenberg, for those who believed them innocent, was that they looked so ordinary. But that, say the counter-intelligence chiefs who trapped them, was precisely what made them so good.

Outwardly, there was nothing to distinguish this married couple from their fellow citizens. Ethel, whose maiden name was Greenglass, had graduated from high school on the lower east side of Manhattan – a neigbourhood that embraced most of the races on earth. She left school at 16 and was employed in various clerical jobs and secretarial posts before becoming an active trade unionist.

Julius, the bespectacled electrical engineer who once underwent religious training in the hope of becoming a rabbi, sprang from similar roots. A graduate of the same high school as his future wife, he studied the Torah for a year before abandoning his religious leanings in favour of a degree in electrical engineering from the City College of New York. He knew Ethel at school as a friend, but when he met her later at a dance, their friendship blossomed into love. In 1939, while the storm clouds of war were gathering over Europe, he married her shortly after his twenty-first birthday.

The A-bomb explosion over Japan in 1945.

A SOCIALIST FAMILY MAN

After a year of odd jobs Julius became a junior engineer for the Army Signal Corps. In the spring of 1942 he and Ethel, after living in cramped conditions with his mother, rented a small apartment in a housing development on the·east side of Manhattan. Life was sweet for the Rosenbergs during the war years; he had a desk job which didn't require him to serve abroad, and there were few of the economic privations in America that tested British familes during the war. They had two sons, Michael and Robert, and the young Rosenbergs doted on them.

Julius, however was already a keeper of secrets. Years earlier he had joined the Communist Party, impressed by what he saw as the 'new order' shaping world events from Moscow. In 1945 he was expelled from the army when his covert membership of the organization was discovered by the FBI. America was yet to reach her peak of anti-communist hysteria under the McCarthy hearings, but to be 'red' was still an alien and utterly distasteful concept to the majority of her citizens. Unemployed and with a family to feed, Julius launched his own business with capital from Ethel's brothers, David and Bernard.

David Greenglass was an integral part of the conspiracy to sell US secrets to the USSR that Julius and Ethel Rosenberg had willingly joined several years previously. Greenglass worked during the war at the Los Alamos research centre, the top secret New Mexico site where Robert Oppenheimer and his scientists worked, in a desperate race to build the first atomic bomb before the Axis powers did. This remote site, formerly the home of a boys, school, was the centre for the greatest and most destructive scientific achievement of this or any age... and David Greenglass systematically stole its secrets for sale to the Russians.

Just like the British-born Soviet spies Burgess, Philby and Maclean, who were recruited as agents while at British universities, Greenglass saw the Soviet Union as the way of the future. The FBI later maintained that it was his sister and Julius who had recruited him to the cause. The Rosenbergs kept him sweet on the idea of world socialism with liberal handouts of money. With the family as his puppet masters, he agreed to use his work position to deliver the stolen blueprints for the bomb to their Kremlin bosses. When Greenglass eventually came to trial, he turned on his family to save his own neck. By pinning the blame exclusively on the Rosenbergs, claiming their own fanatical communist leanings were used to intimidate him, he saved himself.

It was the Rosenbergs who were the lynch-pin for the entire spying operation, which began to unravel in 1950 with the arrest of 39-year-old Harry Gold, a bachelor employed as a chemist at a Philadelphia hospital. He was named by the FBI and the US Attorney General as the accomplice of the disgraced nuclear boffin Klaus Fuchs, who was behind bars in England after pleading guilty to selling nuclear secrets to Moscow.

Julius Rosenberg is arrested by FBI
agents on charges of espionage.

REVELATIONS OF A BRITISH SPY

Fuchs, a brilliant physicist who had fled his native Germany when Hitler came to power, was part of the British mission that was granted access to the highest security levels surrounding the development of the bomb. He received a 14-year sentence for his treachery. He admitted that he had used Gold as the courier, although it is still unclear to this day whether Fuchs had had any contact with the Rosenbergs. He was indicted on wartime espionage charges that carried the death penalty, even though the war was over. Gold, who had been the contact in America for Fuchs was a wretched little man who sang like a canary once he was in custody. His confession that David Greenglass, the Los Alamos worker, had fed him atomic bomb secrets throughout the war years, exploded like the bomb itself across the front pages of the nation's newspapers.

The FBI built up a dossier detailing Greenglass's spying activities inside the Los Alamos complex. Greenglass had frequent access to top secret material on the 'lenses' for atomic bombs – the detonators that released the plutonium and uranium to create the single critical mass. On 17 July, under intense pressure from his captors, Greenglass sold out his brother-in-law. His sister's arrest was to follow shortly. Anti-communist hysteria was rising in America now and Americans were fighting once again, this time against the menace of communism in Korea.

The Department of Justice press release on the arrest of Rosenberg proclaimed: 'J. Edgar Hoover, the director of the FBI, said that Julius Rosenberg is a most important link in the Soviet espionage apparatus.

'Rosenberg, in early 1945, made available to Greenglass while he was on leave in New York City one half of an irregularly cut jelly-box top, the other half of which was given to Greenglass by Gold in Albuquerque, New Mexico, as a means of identifying Gold to Greenglass. Rosenberg aggressively sought ways and means to secretly conspire with the Soviet government to the detriment of his own country. Investigation to date also reveals that Rosenberg made himself available to Soviet espionage agents so he might "do something directly to help Russia".' This was all denied by the Rosenbergs who said they were trapped in a nightmare in which they had no part.

But the FBI had indeed assembled a massive body of evidence which they would later use against the couple at their trial. Another member of the spy ring to be arrested was Morton Sobell, a friend of the Rosenbergs who had studied electrical engineering with Julius. He was charged on a separate indictment of passing to them the details and plans of America's latest radar on its ships and submarines. This, too, would be used against them when they came to trial in March 1951.

A MISTAKEN IDEALISM

The full weight of the US government's case had shifted from Gold and the other arrested spies to the Rosenbergs. The FBI evidence depicted them as the architects of the spy ring who forged the contacts with the Soviet diplomats and agents. J. Edgar Hoover said that American intelligence predicted that Russia would not have the atomic bomb until the 1960s. Thanks to the secrets passed along by the Rosenbergs, they exploded their first device as early as 1949, rocketing them into the nuclear age and the Cold War. This, he said, was the end result of the American spies' 'misty-eyed idealism'.

Irving Saypol, the government prosecutor at the trial, left no-one in any doubt, when he rose to open the case, that he intended to press for the death penalty. He said: 'We will prove that the Rosenbergs devised and put into operation, with the aid of Soviet agents in this country, an elaborate scheme which allowed them to steal, through David Greenglass, this one weapon which might well hold the key to the survival of this nation and means the peace of the world, the atomic bomb. This love of Communism and the Soviet Union led them into a Soviet espionage ring.'

The fifteen-day trial was a sensation, the more so because of the spectacle of a brother betraying his own sister. There was a parade of witnesses who testified that the Rosenbergs had sold their souls for the beliefs of the hammer and sickle, not the stars and stripes. Max Elitcher, the first witness, testified that Julius Rosenberg had badgered him, asking him if his job in the Navy Department in Washington gave him access to secrets that he could pass on to the Soviets. Elizabeth Bentley, a Columbia University graduate, told how she was lured into the espionage web through a series of disastrous love affairs with Soviet agents. She testified that the bond between the Rosenbergs and Moscow was unusually strong.

Undoubtedly, it was the evidence of David Greenglass that sealed their fates. He testified that he worked in Los Alamos and had access to the greatest secrets, which he passed to his sister and brother-in-law. 'They preferred Russian socialism to our system of government,' he said. Greenglass said that he began passing on information, initially about the personnel at the closely guarded complex, then later on about the explosives used to trigger the detonator and the detonator mechanisms themselves. He detailed the jelly-box story that had been revealed by the Department of Justice press release at the time of the traitors' arrest. The words 'I come from Julius' displayed on the top of the

Sing-Sing prison where the traitors, Julius and Ethel Rosenberg, were executed.

box flashed by Gold, meant that the coast was clear and that the Rosenbergs required more information for their Russian bosses.

Greenglass passed on data and sketches and in one despatch, for which he received $200, he typed up 12 pages of notes about the mechanism of the bomb. He went on: 'Working in the Rosenbergs' living room Ethel did the typing and Julius, Ethel and my wife, Ruth, corrected the grammar. Julius told me he communicated with his Russian contacts by leaving microfilm in an alcove at a cinema. He said he had received an alcove table from the Russians as a reward – I saw this table at his apartment. It was used for microfilming.'

A BROTHER'S BETRAYAL

Greenglass said the spying operation ended with the arrest of Fuchs in 1950. He said that Julius visited him, Greenglass, and said: 'You remember the man who came to see you in Albuquerque? Well, Fuchs was one of his contacts. Doubtless this man will be arrested soon and this might lead to you.' He was referring to Gold and he was correct on both counts. Greenglass said he offered money for him to go away to Mexico and later came back with $4,000 for the purpose. However the plot was already unravelling because, by then, Greenglass was under surveillance.

Ruth Greenglass stepped into the witness box to corroborate everything her husband had said. She produced bank deposit receipts that showed large amounts of cash being placed in their account - sums far larger than her husband's salary at Los Alamos could have provided. She also recalled the last visit Julius made to their apartment, when he said they would have to flee before the arrests began. 'I was worried about my baby,' she said, 'and he at first said we should go to the Soviet Union. When I said that I could not travel with an infant he said: "My doctor says that if you take enough canned milk and boil the water, everything will be all right." He said that they were closing the net, that we could expect arrests soon. But we never intended to go.'

THE MEANING OF TREASON

Harry Gold, the US contact to the now-imprisoned Fuchs, also delivered damning testimony. He said that Anatoli Yakolev, the Soviet Union's vice-consul in New York City, was the paymaster and the money man who controlled him and Rosenberg. He said: 'Yakolev reported that the information I had given him had been sent immediately to the Soviet Union. He said that the information I had received from Greenglass was extremely excellent and very valuable.' Yakolev had left America rather rapidly on a ship bound for Europe in 1946 and was never quizzed about his role in the atom bomb spy ring.

Julius Rosenberg took the stand and answered every specific allegation of treachery with the three words: 'I did not.' He denied giving the Greenglasses any money other than some cash he owed David from the business that he helped finance. But he refused to say whether or not he was a member of the Communist Party – he was – although he admitted that he did have sympathy for the Soviet political system 'as it has done much to improve the lot of the underdog'.

Ethel, too, denied all allegations of espionage. She said she loved the brother who had branded her and her husband as traitors, but could offer no explanation why he had implicated them other than as a ploy to save himself. Observers at the time thought that she didn't help herself by refusing to explain why so often she had pleaded the Fifth Amendment – the right to remain silent – during the grand jury hearings which led to her trial.

Morton Sobell refused to take the stand at the trial of the traitors.

In his summing up the prosecutor was emphatic that the accused were spies. Saypol said: 'This is one of the most important cases ever submitted to a jury in this country. We know that these conspirators stole the most important scientific secrets ever known to mankind from this country and delivered them to the Soviet Union. David Greenglass's description of the atomic bomb was typed by Ethel Rosenberg, just as she had, on countless other occasions, sat at that typewriter and struck the keys, blow by blow, against her country in the interests of the Soviets.

'When Fuchs confessed, the Rosenbergs' position in the Soviet espionage hierachy in this country was jeopardized. The evidence of the guilt of the Rosenbergs is incontrovertible. No defendants ever stood before the bar of American justice less deserving than them and Sobell.' Their defence lawyers tried to pin the guilt on Greenglass, but were unable to dismiss the fact that Gold was involved with the Rosenbergs. They were all traitors.

On the morning of Tuesday, 29 March the jurors returned with guilty verdicts on Julius, Ethel and Sobell. Judge Irving Kaufman told the Rosenbergs: 'The thought that citizens of our country would lend themselves to the destruction of our country by the most destructive weapons known to man is so shocking that I can't find

'Old Sparky', the electric chair that despatched many felons in Sing-Sing, the prison in New York State.

words to describe this loathsome offence.' A week later, on 5 April 1951, when they appeared for sentencing, he told them: 'I consider your crime worse than murder. Plain, deliberate, contemplated murder is dwarfed in magnitude by comparison with the crime you have committed. I believe your conduct in putting the atom bomb in the hands of the Russians has already caused the resultant aggression in Korea with casualties exceeding fifty thousand.'

Hiroshima, Japan after the A-Bomb was dropped.

A CONTROVERSIAL VERDICT

'It is not in my power, Julius or Ethel Rosenberg, to forgive you. Only the Lord can find mercy for what you have done. You are hereby sentenced to the punishment of death, and it is ordered you shall be executed according to law.'

Morton Sobell got 30 years, of which he would serve 16. Later, Greenglass, who stole the secrets, got a remarkably light 15 years, as did his wife Ruth Greenglass, who collapsed in the dock as her sentence was handed down.

There was to be no reprieve for the Rosenbergs, despite 22 appeals and numerous stays of execution. Julius, 35, and Ethel, 37, died in the electric chair on the night of 19 June 1953.

Ever since then debate has raged about the possibility of their innocence, but top legal experts say their guilt is more than likely. Alexander Bickel, a Yale University law professor, said: 'It was a ghastly and shameful episode, but I believe they were guilty beyond a doubt.' And Roy Cohn, one of the prosecutors, added: 'I feel the guilt was overwhelming. Their apparent "ordinariness" made it possible for them to get away with it for so long.'

Only Cuba, satellite of the now-defunct Soviet Union for which they served, commemorated them on a set of postage stamps as 'assassinated heroes'.

'Save the Rosenbergs'. In Paris, certain groups decried the death sentence on the traitors.

CRIMES OF TERROR

TIMOTHY McVEIGH

THE OKLAHOMA BOMBER

It was 19 April 1995 – a perfect, sun-drenched spring morning in Oklahoma. A yellow Ryder Rental truck carefully made its way through the streets of downtown Oklahoma City. Just after 9 a.m., the truck pulled into a parking area outside the Alfred P. Murrah building and the driver stepped down from the truck's cab and casually walked away. A few minutes later, at 9.02, all hell broke loose as the truck's deadly 4,000-pound cargo blasted the government building with enough force to shatter one-third of the seven-storey structure.

Timothy McVeigh was born on 23 April 1968 in Pendleton, New York, and grew up in a rural community. He was the middle one of three children and the only boy.

His father worked at a nearby General Motors manufacturing plant and his mother worked for a travel agency. His parents, marriage was rather stormy and they separated for a third and final time in 1984.

Timothy's school classmates remember him as small, thin and quiet. He became involved in the normal school functions − football, athletics, extra-curricular activities − but usually dropped out shortly after joining them. He was shy, did not have a girlfriend, and in reality was something of a loner.

McVeigh graduated from high school in June 1986 and, in the autumn, started a two-year business college course. He attended for only a short time, during which he lived at home with his father, worked at a Burger King and drove dilapidated, old cars.

In 1987 he obtained a pistol permit from Niagara County and a job in Buffalo as a guard on an armoured car. A co-worker recalls that McVeigh owned numerous firearms and had a survivalist philosophy − a tendency to stockpile weapons and food in preparation for what he believed to be the imminent breakdown of society. In 1988 McVeigh and a friend bought 10 acres of rural land and used it as a shooting range.

JOINING THE ARMY

McVeigh enlisted in the army in Buffalo in May 1988, and went through basic training at Fort Benning, Georgia. After basic training, his unit was transferred to Fort Riley, Kansas, and became part of the army's 1st Infantry Division.

McVeigh had finally found his calling. The army was everything he wanted in life and more. When he joined, he was no leader, but an eager follower. There was discipline, a sense of order, and all the training a man could want in survival techniques. Most of all, there was an endless supply of weapons, and instruction on how to use and maintain them.

McVeigh became a gunner on a Bradley Fighting Vehicle. He was promoted to corporal, sergeant, then platoon leader. Fellow soldiers recalled that McVeigh was very interested in military hardware, kept his own personal collection of firearms and constantly cleaned and maintained them. Other soldiers went into town to look for entertainment or companionship but McVeigh stayed on base and cleaned his guns. During his time in the army, he also read and recommended to others *The Turner Diaries* – a racist, anti-Semitic novel about a soldier in an underground army. A former room-mate said that McVeigh would panic at the prospect of the government taking away people's guns, but that he was not a racist and was basically indifferent to racial matters.

While at Fort Riley, McVeigh re-enlisted in the army. He aspired to be a member of the Special Forces and in 1990 was sent on a three-week course, to assess his potential for joining that elite unit. He had barely begun to prepare himself physically for Special Forces training when, in January 1991, the 1st Infantry Division was sent to participate in the Gulf War. As a gunnery sergeant, McVeigh was in action during late February 1991. Pursuing his desire to join the Special Forces, he left the Gulf early and went to Fort Bragg, North Carolina, where he took a battery of IQ, personality and aptitude tests to qualify for Special Forces. However, his participation in the Gulf War had left him no time to prepare himself physically for the demands of Special Forces training. McVeigh was unable to endure a 90- minute march with a 45-pound pack and he withdrew from the programme after two days.

This disappointing experience left him facing years of active service due to his re-enlistment at Fort Riley. The army was downsizing, however, and after $3^1/_2$ years of service, McVeigh took the offer of an early discharge and left the military in the autumn of 1991.

OUT OF THE SERVICE

By January 1992, at the age of 24, McVeigh was back where he had started, living with his father in Pendleton, New York, driving an old car and working as a security guard.

In January 1993 McVeigh left Pendleton and began to travel, moving himself and his belongings about in a series of battered, old cars. He lived in cheap motels and caravan parks, but also stayed from time to time with two army buddies, Michael Fortier in Kingman, Arizona, and Terry Nichols in Decker, Michigan.

McVeigh travelled to Waco, Texas during the March–April 1993 stand-off between the Branch Davidians and federal agents, and was said to have been angry about what he saw. He sold firearms at a gun show in Arizona and was heard to remark on one weapon's ability to shoot down an ATF helicopter.

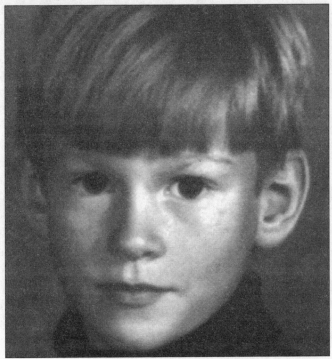

Timothy McVeigh as a child.

Although both Arizona and Michigan are host to militant, anti-tax, anti-government, survivalist and racist groups, there is no evidence that McVeigh ever belonged to any extremist groups. He did advertised to sell a weapon for sale in what is described as a virulently anti-Semitic publication. After renting a Ryder truck that was subsequently linked to the Oklahoma City bombing, McVeigh telephoned a religious community that preached white supremacy, but no-one there can recall recognising him or talking to him. His only known affiliations are as a registered Republican in his New York days, and as a member of the National Rifle Association while he was in the army.

An FBI agent comforts a weeping man whose loved one wass still trapped in the rubble of the bombed building.

CHANGES IN THE GUN LAW

On 13 September 1994, the gun shows that McVeigh attended had become sombre occasions. New laws had been passed to stop the manufacture of many types of weaponry, including a range of semi-automatic rifles and handguns. Gun traders and buyers alike were outraged to learn the government was controlling their 'right to bear arms'.

To McVeigh, it also meant his livelihood had become endangered. He had been buying weapons under his own name and charging a brokerage fee to other buyers – those who didn't want their names on government forms.

Paranoia rose on rumours that owners would be subject to surprise searches of their homes and businesses. McVeigh decided that action could no longer be postponed. From the Nichols home in Marion, Kansas, he wrote to Fortier. He insisted that the time had come for action, and he wanted Fortier to join him and Terry Nichols in their protest. Imitating *The Turner Diaries*, they planned to blow up a federal building. McVeigh cautioned Fortier against telling his wife Lori – but this was an instruction Fortier ignored. Furthermore, Fortier said he would never be part of the plan.

Undeterred, McVeigh and Nichols took advice from various bomb-making manuals. They followed the recipe and stockpiled their materials – bought under the alias 'Mike Havens' – in rented storage sheds. The recipe also called for other ingredients like blasting caps and liquid nitro-methane, which they stole – but that was not the only thing they stole.

To pay for their despicable enterprise, Nichols robbed gun collector Roger Moore at gunpoint. Moore claimed the thief had taken a variety of guns, gold, silver and jewels - about 60,000 dollars' worth. Nichols also stole Moore's van to transport the loot. When police made a list of visitors to the ranch, McVeigh's name was on it.

Earlier, McVeigh and Nichols travelled to the Fortiers' Kingman home and stashed the stolen explosives in a nearby storage shed McVeigh had rented. When Fortier saw the explosives, McVeigh explained his plan. He stayed with the Fortiers and while there he designed his bomb. He showed Lori – using soup cans – how the drums he planned on using could be arranged for maximum impact.

McVeigh wanted a rocket fuel called anhydrous hydrazine for his bomb. He phoned around the country to find some, but its expense made it impossible for him to obtain. So he settled on a satisfactory equivalent – nitro-methane. In the course of trying to locate volatile fuels, McVeigh had phoned from the Fortiers, knowing full well his calls could be traced to the Fortiers' telephone number – and the calling card he bought under the alias, Darel Bridges.

In mid-October 1994, McVeigh's plans were suddenly complicated when he received news that his grandfather had died. He referred home to Pendleton, New York. There, he helped sort out his grandfather's estate and further poisoned his younger sister against the government.

While McVeigh was in Pendleton, he was unable to reach Terry Nichols. The co-conspirator had gone to the Philippines to see his current wife and baby daughter, but before he left, he visited his son and first wife Lana Padilla. He left her a few items including a sealed package, telling her it was to be opened only in the event of him never returning. She opened it anyway. Included in its contents was a letter detailing the location of a plastic bag he'd hidden in Padilla's home. It contained a letter to McVeigh telling him he was now on his own – along with 20,000 dollars. There was also a combination to Nichols's storage locker. When she opened the shed, she found some of the spoils of the Moore robbery.

Sgt. Timothy James McVeigh

In mid-December 1994, McVeigh and the Fortiers met in McVeigh's room at the Mojave Motel in Kingman, Arizona. There, he asked Lori to giftwrap in Christmas paper boxes containing blasting caps. He then promised Fortier a cache of weapons from the Moore robbery if he would accompany McVeigh back to Kansas. On the way, McVeigh drove through Oklahoma City to show Fortier the building he intended to bomb and the route he would take to walk away from the building before the blast. They parted company.

The getaway car would be his 1977 yellow Marquis, since his other car had been damaged in an accident. The plan was for Nichols to follow the car in his truck and, after McVeigh had parked the car away from the bombsite, they would drive back to Kansas. The night before the bombing, they left the Marquis after McVeigh removed the licence plate and left a note had saying the car needed a battery. Then they drove away and Nichols dropped him off at his motel.

The next afternoon, McVeigh picked up the Ryder truck and parked it at the Dreamland Motel for the night. The following morning he drove it to the Herington storage unit. When Nichols finally arrived – late – they piled the bomb components in the truck and drove to Geary Lake, prepare the bomb. When they had finished, Nichols went home and McVeigh stayed with the lethal Ryder vehicle.

He parked in a gravel parking lot for the night and waited for dawn – and the drive to his target. He was dressed for the mission in his favourite T-shirt. On the front was a picture of Abraham Lincoln with the motto *sic semper tyrannis*, the words Booth shouted before he shot Lincoln. The translation: 'Thus ever to tyrants.'

On the back of the T-shirt was a tree with blood dripping from the branches. It read, 'The tree of liberty must be refreshed from time to time with the blood of patriots and tyrants.'

Like his role model in *The Turner Diaries*, he headed for a federal building where he was convinced ATF agents were working. There, the people of Oklahoma City would pay a terrible price for McVeigh's compulsive and irrational paranoia.

Around 9.02 a.m., just after parents had dropped their children off at day care at the Murrah federal building in downtown Oklahoma City, the unthinkable happened. A massive bomb inside the rental truck exploded, blowing half of the nine-storey building into oblivion.

A stunned nation watched as the bodies of men, women and children were pulled from the rubble for nearly two weeks. When the smoke cleared and the exhausted rescue workers packed up and left, 168 people, including 19 children, were dead, and hundreds more were wounded.

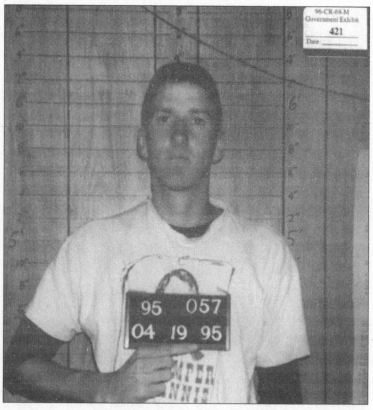

Prisoner number 95 057 04 19 95.

THE ARREST

McVeigh was finally arrested on the basis of a traffic violation and the charge of carrying a weapon. His yellow Mercury was left on the side of the highway and was not impounded.

Between 19 April 1995, and 21 April 1995, federal law enforcement officials traced a Vehicle Identification Number appearing upon the axle of the truck believed to have carried the bomb to a Ryder Rental truck dealership in Junction City, Kansas. The FBI prepared a composite drawing of 'unidentified subject #1' based upon descriptions provided by witnesses at the Ryder rental dealership. By showing the composite drawing to employees at various motels in Junction City, Kansas, the FBI determined that the drawing resembled a man named Timothy McVeigh who had been a guest at the Dreamland Motel in Junction City from 14 to 18 April 1995. On checking their records it then came to light that a man named Timothy McVeigh was in custody in the Noble County Jail in Perry, Oklahoma, facing state misdemeanour charges.

THE SENTENCE

It was a trial fraught with pitfalls and tough decisions for US District Judge Richard P. Matsch, who maintained strict control in his Denver courtroom. McVeigh was deemed responsible for the blast that killed 168 people – the worst terrorist attack ever on American soil until 11 September 2001.

Timothy McVeigh was found guilty of bombing the Oklahoma City federal building on 19 April 1995. During a separate phase of the trial, jurors condemned the 29-year-old Gulf War veteran to death by lethal injection.

Convicted Oklahoma City bomber Timothy McVeigh was, indeed, put to death by lethal injection at 7.14 a.m. on Monday, 11 June. He was the first federal prisoner to be executed in 38 years.

ILICH RAMIREZ SANCHEZ

SANCHEZ

CARLOS THE JACKAL

'Carlos' is one of the best known 'revolutionary terrorists' in the history of modern insurgent movements. He has reportedly worked for Mohamar Gaddafi of Libya, Saddam Hussein of Iraq, President Assad of Syria, Fidel Castro of Cuba, George Habash and the Popular Front for the Liberation of Palestine (PFLP), the Italian Red Brigade, Columbia's M-19 Movement, the Baader–Meinhof Gang and any number of other 'communist and socialist' employers.

Carlos was born in Caracas, Venezuela, on 12 October 1949. His mother, Elba Maria Sanchez, had planned to give him a Christian name in keeping with her strong Catholic beliefs. Jose Altagracia Ramifrez Navas, the boy's father, however, had other ideas. As a devout Marxist, he insisted that his first son should be named after his hero, Vladimir Ilich Ulyanov or Lenin as he was better known. Stubbornly ignoring his wife's protests, Jose registered his son as Ilich Ramifrez Sanchez.

Ironically, in his youth Jose had entered a Catholic seminary with the intention of becoming a priest. However, after completing only three years of study, he declared himself an atheist and returned home to the town of Michelena, in Tachira. Determined that Ilich would not waste his life pursuing Christian ideals, Jose taught his son the Marxist beliefs.

Carlos, a 1969 graduate of Moscow's Patrice Lamumba University, had been tied to 'communist revolutionary movements' since the age of 14, when he became a member of the Communist Party in Venezuela. His father, a wealthy Venezuelan Communist Party leader, was dedicated to Leninist/Marxist theory and practice. In his teens, Carlos was allegedly given guerrilla training in Cuba, and by the age of 20 had moved to Jordan and was being trained in the use of weapons and explosives by hard-core members of the PFLP commando. Soon after, he began what has turned out to be an infamous career as an international, mercenary terrorist.

THE POPULAR FRONT

In July 1970 Ilich travelled to the Middle East. His first stop was Beirut where he arrived unannounced at the office of Bassam Abu-Sharif, the unofficial 'recruiting officer' for the Popular Front. Abu-Sharif was impressed with the passion of Ilich's convictions and made arrangements for him to start his training. According to subsequent investigations, it was at that first meeting that Ilich was given the name that, in the years to come, would strike terror throughout the world. From that day forward, Ilich was known only as 'Carlos' .

Within weeks of the meeting, Carlos went to a Palestinian training camp in the hills north of Amman, Jordan to begin training in the handling of weapons and explosives. He longed for real action and, in the final week of his training, he got his wish. Israeli jets bombed an adjoining camp and killed a member of Yasser Arafat's personal guard. Keen to move on to 'more exciting' pursuits, Carlos contacted Abou Semir, a senior member of the Popular Front, and was sent to an advanced commando training camp.

BLACK SEPTEMBER

On 6 September 1970, the Popular Front, acting on the instructions of Dr Wadi Haddad, carried out one of the most memorable hijackings in history. They began with the simultaneous diversion to Jordan of a Swissair DC-8 and a TWA Boeing 707, which was followed six days later by the hijacking of a BOAC VC-10. The

Carlos a the age of sixteen.

aircraft were forced to land at Dawson Field, 30 miles from Amman, which was quickly renamed Revolutionary Airport. Meanwhile another Popular Front hijack team, which had failed to board an E1 A1 plane, managed to hijack a Pan Am Boeing 747 to Cairo and blow it up, while the media recorded the incident for a gasping world audience. The resulting conflict was dubbed 'Black September' and was to become Carlos's first taste of real warfare.

THE PLAYBOY

Carlos was appointed the Popular Front's representative in London. His task was to ingratiate himself into British society and draw up a list of 'high profile' targets who would either be murdered or kidnapped. He was sent to another training camp to learn the 'finer points' of terrorism and by February 1971, he was considered ready for his appointment. He travelled to London to be reunited with his family. With his mother's help, he quickly slipped back into the 'cocktail party set' and developed his playboy habits.

He attended the University of London to study economics and later took Russian language courses at Central London Polytechnic, all part of his carefully planned facade. His Popular Front contact in London was Mohamed Bouria, an Algerian who, as one of Haddad's most loyal followers, was responsible for European operations. In search of targets, Carlos read English newspapers, selecting any prominent citizens who were either Jewish or had Israeli sympathies. Once he had created his list, he went to great pains to learn as much about his targets as he could, including home addresses, telephone numbers, nicknames and as many personal details as he could glean. His list of names included famous film personalities, entertainers, politicians and prominent business figures.

By December 1971, he had compiled a detailed list containing hundreds of names. It was during this time that his early career as an undercover terrorist was almost terminated. Acting on a tip off, members of Scotland Yard's Special Branch raided the house in Walpole Street, Chelsea, where he lived with his mother, but after searching the house, found nothing of an incriminating nature. They were led to believe that Carlos was linked to a cache of illegal weapons that had been seized in a previous raid at the house of one of his friends. Incredibly, a fake Italian passport bearing a picture of Carlos was found in the raid but the police considered it unimportant. Apart from placing him under surveillance for several days after the raid, the police left him alone. The family later moved to a new apartment in Kensington.

During February 1972, while Carlos languished in London, one of Haddad's teams was hijacking a Lufthansa airliner to Aden. One of the 172 passengers taken hostage was Joseph Kennedy, son of the late Robert Kennedy. Following a short period of negotiations, Kennedy and the other hostages were released safely after the West German government paid a $5,000,000 ransom. The following May, Haddad sent three members of the Japanese Red Army to carry out a brutal attack at Tel Aviv's Lod airport. After arriving at the airport, the three men retrieved automatic weapons and grenades from their luggage and opened fire on the crowd. By the time the firing had stopped, 23 travellers were dead and another 76 were wounded.

MARIA TOBON

Maria Nydia Romero de Tobon was an attractive, 37-year-old Colombian divorcee who moved to London following her divorce to resume her university studies. She was not only attracted to Carlos's Latin American charm and impeccable manners, but also became enamoured of his passion for politics. Nydia, whose grandfather had founded the Colombian Liberal Party, was a revolutionary at heart and was won over by Carlos and the fervour he showed for his cause. Some months later, Carlos successfully recruited Nydia and enlisted her aid in securing a string of safe houses for visiting envoys.

At one point she posed as the wife of Antonio Dagues-Bouvier, the Ecuadorian guerrilla who had supposedly trained Carlos in Cuba, and she rented three apartments in central London. Her other duties included transporting documents and funds. Carlos would later tell investigators that he and Dagues-Bouvier had, at that time, carried out several 'missions' against selected targets. No record has ever been found of any such events having taken place. The general belief is that Carlos's time in London was largely one of inactivity, while in other parts of the world Haddad had selected others to play his deadly games.

TERRORIST ACTIVITIES

It is thought that by early 1972, Carlos was fighting and learning combat tactics in a guerrilla war against King Hussein in Jordan. It is also possible that 'The Jackal' had begun acting as an intelligence agent or informer for the KGB.

The Popular Front demanded the release of Fedayeen (members of the Palestinian movement) imprisoned in Germany, Switzland and Israel.

By 1973, however, his terrorist activities had begun in earnest. He publicly admitted to his 1973 assassination attempt on a British millionaire named Joseph Edward Sieff, who was a well-known Jewish businessman and owner of the Marks and Spencer stores in London. Within the next two years, he was involved in the siege of the French Embassy at The Hague, the killing of two French intelligence agents for which he was captured, and a 1976 kidnapping of OPEC oil ministers in Vienna, Austria. Later in 1976, he was involved in a skyjacking that led to the now famous Entebbe raid by Israeli commandos.

In the late seventies and early eighties, Carlos was blamed for any number of skyjackings, bombings and machine gun/grenade attacks on British, French and Israeli targets. He became a master of disguises and was known to have obtained any number of false identities, complete with passports and credit cards. Adding to his reputation as a 'terrorist mastermind' was the fact that, even if no real evidence could be produced to link him to an atrocity, it was often blamed on him, for reasons of convenience or ineptitude. Carlos was described as 'a ruthless terrorist who operates with cold-blooded, surgical precision', according to Ahmed Zaki Yamani. Acclaimed by some as a 'professional killer' with 'cool, deliberate actions', he was also described by others as a 'bumbling psychotic who shoots people in the face, and is extremely lucky'. However you look at it, Carlos seemed to revel in the limelight of his deadly performance.

In 1982 and 1983, he was suspected of several bombings in Paris, France, resulting in the deaths of at least 13 people and the wounding of 150 more. In the mid-1980s, it is believed that he may have also participated in the planning and execution of several operations against Israel, operating out of Syria and Lebanon. He is also reported to have consulted with Col. Muammar Qaddafi and even Saddam Hussein, during their conflicts with the United States.

REPORTS OF HIS DEATH

Nothing was heard of Carlos during the late 1980s and there were even reports of his death. Unconfirmed reports placed him in Mexico, Colombia, Damascus and Syria over several years. The end of the Cold War and the collapse of the USSR, may have placed him in a situation with few sponsors and little ideological motivation to continue his terror campaign.

The first floor flat at Phillimore Court, Kensington, which was occupied by Ilich Ramirez Sanchez during his period in London

He may have even been kicked out of Syria, as their relations with Israel warmed and they moved closer to a peace accord with one of their oldest enemies. 'The Jackal' may have found himself with few safe places to go.

Apparently, Sudan was one of them, or so he thought. Even they, however, were not willing to provide the beastly killer with a refuge. They arrested Carlos and turned him over to French authorities, who had previously notified the Sudanese of his presence in their country. In the end, even the Sudanese, who were thought to be moving closer to a 'fundamentalist-revolutionary- Moslem' government, decided to turn over the infamous 'Jackal', perhaps in the hope of gaining some eventual favour in world opinion.

CARLOS THE PRISONER

Joseph Edward Sieff, 68, was one of the most successful and influential Jewish businessmen in London, and was Carlos's first target.

On Friday, 12 December 1997, Carlos was led into a courtroom in the Palais de Justice and placed in the dock. Over the next eight days, he tried every tactic he could think of to counter the prosecution case against him. On 23 December 1997, after three hours and 48 minutes of deliberation, the jury returned with their verdict, guilty on all counts, the sentence – life imprisonment. Ironically, the death sentence that Carlos should have received for his crimes had been abolished years earlier by President François Mitterrand, the same man who had ordered his agents to find Carlos and kill him.

To this day Carlos is held in the maximum-security wing of La Santé Prison. He is allowed few visitors and spends his time reading, writing and watching television.

One thing is certain, the man who began life as Ilich Ramirez Sanchez and named himself Carlos the Jackal, is now known by a less flamboyant title. In La Santé he is known simply as 'Detainee 872686/X' and probably will be for the rest of his life.

Black September guerrillas give the 'V-sign' from a car, as it is driven away from the Saudi Arabian Embassy in Khartoum after handing over their two Arab diplomatic hostages and the bodies of the Belgian and two American diplomats they had shot.

KEY DATES IN THE LIFE OF CARLOS THE JACKAL

1949
Ilich Ramirez Sanchez born in Venezuela to wealthy communist lawyer, who gave his son Lenin's middle name.

1964
Joins Communist Students' Movement in Venezuela. Goes for guerrilla training in Cuba.

1968

Begins study at Patrice Lumumba University in Moscow, famous as training ground for future terrorists and KGB recruits.

1970

Joins the Popular Front for the Liberation of Palestine. Begins terrorist career.

1970-1982

Key attacks linked to Carlos include massacre of Israeli athletes at Munich Olympics, seizing OPEC oil ministers in Vienna, hijacking of Air France plane to Entebbe, half-a-dozen attacks on French targets.

1992

Convicted by a French court in absentia for 1975 killing of two French counter-intelligence agents and Lebanese citizen.

1994

Carlos arrested in Sudan. Transferred to France where he was jailed in solitary confinement in maximum-security prison.

1997

Carlos stands trial for the 1975 killing of the French counter-intelligence agents and the Lebanese citizen. French law requires re-trial upon repatriation.